THE FIELD MEN

Also by French MacLean

THE CRUEL HUNTERS: SS-SONDERKOMMANDO DIRLEWANGER

THE CAMP MEN: THE SS OFFICERS WHO RAN THE NAZI CONCENTRATION CAMP SYSTEM

THE FIELD MEN

The SS Officers Who Led the Einsatzkommandos - the Nazi Mobile Killing Units

French L. MacLean

Schiffer Military History
Atglen, PA

ACKNOWLEDGMENTS

The "usual suspects" once again took time out of their busy schedules to help bring this book to life. First, I would like to thank Niels Cordes and the staff at the National Archives who invariably provided timely assistance in finding a wide variety of microfilm needed for this project; many times they were able to recall documents they had seen in their reviewing process. Niels is, quite simply, the best archivist with whom I have ever worked.

Alex Rossino, Leslie Swift, Ron Kurpiers, and the research and photography assistants at the United States Holocaust Memorial Museum opened their extensive document and microfilm files as well as helped me navigate through their large library. Alex has specialized in many areas of the *Einsatzkommandos* in Poland, and his own writings are providing much-needed illumination on this complex subject.

A special word of thanks goes to Dr. Charles W. Sydnor, Jr., not only for writing his highly-regarded *Soldiers of Destruction* – a work that significantly influenced my own writing – but also for showing personal interest in this project. Dr. Sydnor graciously provided a copy of *Executive Instinct: Reinhard Heydrich and the Planning for the Final Solution*, a long summary chapter he has presented orally at the United States Holocaust Memorial Museum, and a contribution to the recent seminal work on the subject entitled *The Holocaust and History: The Known, the Unknown, the Disputed and the Reexamined*. I value Dr. Sydnor as a new friend. Charlie, thanks for all your help.

Another relatively new colleague is George Nipe who has encouraged my research and writing. George is an upcoming writer of note who has specialized in the Eastern Front. If his upcoming works are as masterful as his first, he will be famous one day.

On the other end, one of my oldest colleagues (from a perspective of association, not age!), Dr. Thomas Veve returned from duties in Europe to review and edit every page of the initial manuscript – in a way that contributed substantially to the flow of the book. Thanks, Tom. Thanks also to Andrew Mollo for the photographs.

Speaking of editors, Bob Biondi at Schiffer Publishing deserves a special word of thanks. During the editing of my previous work on the Holocaust – *The Camp Men* – I mentioned in passing that I was putting together a work on the *Einsatzkommandos*. Without seeing the manuscript, Bob developed a layout that enabled both books to be organized in a parallel, complimentary fashion.

To the understanding personnel at the photo archives at Koblenz, Germany – the *Bundesarchiv* – thank you for all your support over the years and also your understanding. In particular, I would like to acknowledge Herr Loosen and Frau Rochelmeyer.

A very special word of thanks goes to Mr. Simon Wiesenthal, resident of Vienna but citizen of the world. Mr. Wiesenthal challenged me in my research pursuit and his kind words of review for my first Holocaust-related work are worth far more to me than relative sales rankings.

Finally, I would also like to express my immense gratitude to my wife Olga. Almost every aspect of the *Einsatzkommando* is a dark, shocking, unpleasant one. Yet, she read and reread the work offering a critical eye to its construction and content. She made the final proclamation that it was ready to print – so here it is.

Finding appropriate photographs for this work proved to be a painstaking task as the SS security service did not "advertise" *Einsatzkommando* operations. But ultimately over 175 have been located through several sources and included in this book. The United States Holocaust Museum served as the most prolific source. All photographs herein from this organization are listed **USHMM.** Photographs obtained from the *Bundesarchiv* (Federal Archives) in Koblenz, Germany are annotated **BAK.** Sevral more illustartions came from the Berlin Document Center and are labeled **BDC.** Late arrivals, but much appreciated, came from the personal collection of Andrew Mollo in France.

To complete the layout, the editor and I have used images from the microfilmed SS officers' service records (Microfilm Publication A3343, *Records of SS Officers from the Berlin Document Center, Series SSO*) located at the United States National Archives at College Park, Maryland. The photographs produced from these images are labeled **NA.**

Book Design by Robert Biondi.
SD insignia courtesy of Matthew Reinert, Military History Shop.

Library of Congress Catalog Number: 99-60334.

Printed in China.
ISBN: 0-7643-0754-1

Published by Schiffer Publishing Ltd.
4880 Lower Valley Road
Atglen, PA 19310 USA
Phone: (610) 593-1777
FAX: (610) 593-2002
E-mail: Schifferbk@aol.com.
Visit our web site at: www.schifferbooks.com
Please write for a free catalog.
This book may be purchased from the publisher.
Please include $3.95 postage.
Try your bookstore first.

In Europe, Schiffer books are distributed by:
Bushwood Books
6 Marksbury Road
Kew Gardens
Surrey TW9 4JF
England
Phone: 44 (0)181 392-8585
FAX: 44 (0)181 392-9876
E-mail: Bushwd@aol.com.

Try your bookstore first.

CONTENTS

"A man is the lord over life and death when he gets an order to shoot 300 children – and he kills at least 150 himself."

Lothar Heimbach
A field man in *Einsatzgruppe* D

INTRODUCTION

Abroad people take us for bloodhounds, don't they? It is almost too hard for the individual, but we must be as hard as granite.[1]

- Reinhard Heydrich

Two thousand nine hundred forty-five men lined up in four motorized columns immediately behind the competent, confident German Army in the early hours of June 22, 1941 as it prepared to launch *Operation Barbarossa* – the German attack on the Soviet Union – an attack designed to win the war. The men sat tense, lost in their own thoughts during the dark night, on pulsating motorcycles, in open command cars that seemed chilly even on that first day of summer and in the back of cramped trucks – sitting between bulging bags of outgoing mail, near-full jerry cans sloshing with fuel, pristine belts of machine-gun ammunition, gunny sacks of the ever-present *kartoffeln* and well-worn copies of Goethe's *Faust*. Many were college graduates; quite a few were accomplished lawyers, musicians, writers, teachers – one was even a theologian, while still others upheld the secular law as senior police officials. Some were young and idealistic – others were older and more practical by nature.

Most of the men had spotless records, promising careers, proud parents, adoring wives, devoted children – and perhaps even a loyal *Hund*. Their stylish, field-gray uniforms, adorned with spotless black and silver insignia, were immaculately pressed, their tall, gleaming black-leather boots were carefully polished and their hands were finely manicured.

Their mission – for the glory of Greater Germany – was to butcher as many human beings as they could get those hands on – men, women and children who were at that very moment peacefully sleeping in their warm beds in dozens of large cities and scores of small hamlets from the Gulf of Finland to the Black Sea, and from the border with old Poland to the outskirts of Moscow.

The cultured men, the men of Bach and Beethoven, Grimm and Gutenberg – and now Hitler and Heydrich – were very efficient at what they did. Over the course of the next two years, by means of machine-guns, carbines, gas vans, explosives, rifle butts or ax handles, the field men would slaughter one million three hundred thousand people.

• • •

Today, we have forgotten the names of these men, assuming we knew them to begin with. We have forgotten the rattle of the machine-guns, the harsh guttural orders shouted at the trembling uncomprehending masses of people who were within minutes of their own deaths and who asked nothing more than to be left in peace. We have forgotten the system that produced these men; we think that the officers who led these mobile killing formations were somehow alien to our world – one-time misfits who could never again appear to darken our skies.

That then gets to the rationale for a work of this nature in the first place. I wrote this book because the crime was so immense, so unparalleled, that the SS officers who carried it out deserve to have a concise, centralized place in infamy. All the SS *Einsatzgruppe* and *Einsatzkommando* officers, not just the Nazi leaders like Adolf Hitler, Reinhard Heydrich and Heinrich Himmler, warrant recognition – not just the system, but the individuals. The purpose of this work is first and foremost to serve as a compendium of all *Schutzstaffel* (SS) officers who were assigned to the *Einsatzkommandos* during the years of the Third Reich, because no system can operate without individuals. There are some good starting points. Helmut Krausnick and Hans-Heinrich Wilhelm have produced perhaps the best in *Die Truppe des Weltanschauungskrieges: Die Einsatzgruppen der Sicherheitspolizei und des SD 1938-1942*. Another excellent source is *Nazi Mass Murder: A Documentary History of the Use of Poison Gas* edited by Eugen Kogon, Hermann Langbein and Adalbert Rückerl. There is also the excellent standby *The Destruction of the European Jews* by Raul Hilberg. Two recent books cover all facets of the *Einsatzgruppe* reports on their activities. The first is *The Einsatzgruppen Reports*, edited by Yitzhak Arad, Shmuel Krakowski and Shmuel Spector. The second is Ronald Headland's *Messages of Murder: A Study of the Reports of the Einsatzgruppen of the Security Police and the Security Service 1941-1943*. None, however, have made the attempt to cover all SS officers who were assigned to the *Einsatzkommandos*. In fact, it has proven quite difficult, even given the huge resources of the United States Holocaust Memorial Museum, to indeed find complete sources listing all SS personnel for even a single *Einsatzgruppe*. But the magnitude of the crimes demands we make an effort.

Who were these men? From what areas of Germany did they come? What was their rank structure? Were most married? What were their religious backgrounds? Had any served in World War I? What was their level of education? Were they awarded military decorations by the Nazi government for their activities? Were they members of the Nazi Party? Did many die later during the war in battle or did they survive? If they survived the war, were they prosecuted for their crimes?

So I have taken what is in existence – from the excellent research center at the United States Holocaust Memorial Museum – and then proceeded to the National Archives. There, I have reviewed a set of records known as Microfilm Publication A3343, *Records of SS Officers from the Berlin Document Center, Series SSO*. These rolls of microfilmed SS officers' service records consist of the personnel dossiers for more than 61,000 SS officers with the rank of second lieutenant and above in this large and complex organization. The date span of the records contained in the dossiers extends from 1932 to as late as March 1945 in some cases. There are nine-hundred and nine rolls in this set, parts of about a third detail the lives of every officer known to be assigned to the *Einsatzgruppen*. These records are truly an open book into the careers of these men and include marital status, religion, court-martial proceedings, promotions, recommendations for awards, transfers, assignment instructions, letters of reprimand, medical histories and family background.

In some instances there were no files to be found; I then turned to alternate sources such as the yearly *Dienstaltersliste der Schutzstaffel der N.S.D.A.P.* – the annual rank lists of the SS – for any information to piece together the puzzle. The search for *Einsatzkommando* officers proved much more difficult than that for concentration camp officers done in a previous work. Many SS officers appear to have been placed on temporary detail for operations in the east from their parent assignment in Germany. Additionally, the SS maintained a veil of secrecy over the *Einsatzkommando* operations, a veil that did not exist over most concentration camp service.[2] When an officer's personnel file had no direct connection to *Einsatzkommando* operations I was forced to examine secondary sources and other material to positively place an officer in the position. I feel certain the men in this book participated in *Einsatzkommando* operations; I am just as sure that many officers I chose to omit from the book due to a lack of evidence were in fact present in these formations. I just could not demonstrate their presence beyond a reasonable doubt.

First and foremost then, this work attempts to present information on every single SS officer who served at one time or another in one or more of the *Einsatzgruppe*. The reader will immediately note several names missing from the work to include Heinrich Himmler, Ernst Kaltenbrunner, and even Reinhard Heydrich – the man who conceived and supervised the *Einsatzgruppe*. But as they did not truly serve in the units, they do not appear here. Together with my previous work, *The Camp Men: The SS Officers Who Ran The Nazi Concentration Camp System*, this book provides a forum in which the officers who actually did the "dirty work" of the Holocaust are finally "present and accounted for."

I have divided the book into four sections. The first features a brief description of the *Einsatzgruppen*, their history, tactics, aims and organization, the SS officer rank system and the authorized SS officer positions in them in order to present a framework for later information.

The second, and by far the largest, section of the book contains biographical information on each of the 380 officers with a microfilm source roll to facilitate further research. Some of the personnel files contain only one summary sheet for an officer, while others feature up to eighty or ninety pages. In some lucky instances, there are officer efficiency reports describing service in one of the *Einsatzkommando*, but this is certainly the exception and not the rule. In fact, if one does not have an outside lead concerning *Einsatzkommando* service, it is quite possible to conclude an officer's file excludes *Einsatzkommando* service when such is not the case.

The third portion of the book examines over twenty significant facets of each officer's career by using a relational database. It will enable readers to see the "forest" rather than just the individual "trees." There are some interesting and hopefully controversial conclusions in this segment of the book.

The final segment, the photographic section of the book, with well over two hundred photographs, including a large portion previously unpublished, is the largest collection of photographs of SS *Einsatzkommando* officers ever to appear in one work. The images come from the extensive files of the United States Holocaust Memorial Museum, the Berlin Document Center, the United States National Archives and many other institutional collections.

Michael Geyer, in his chapter "German Strategy in the Age of Machine Warfare, 1914-1945," in Peter Peret's *Makers of Modern Strategy*, states that German National Socialism had twin goals, the enslavement of Eastern European populations and an Armageddon for its perceived mortal enemy, the Jewish minorities of occupied Europe.[3] If Geyer is correct, then the 3,050,000 German soldiers, sailors and airmen who were poised on June 22, 1941 to attack the Soviet Union were little more than a subordinate escort for the 2,945 men of the *Einsatzgruppen*, a tiny body of men in comparison, who were in reality the main effort for the entire Operation Barbarossa. If this is at least plausible, it is time the names and careers of the officers of these *Einsatzgruppen* receive the historical scrutiny they deserve.[4]

French MacLean
Falls Church, Virginia

Notes:

[1] Heinz Höhne, *The Order of the Death's Head*. Translated by Richard Barry. (New York: Coward-McCann, 1985), p.166.

[2] With the exception of the *Operation Reinhard* extermination centers of Treblinka, Sobibór and Belzec.

[3] Michael Geyer, "German Strategy in the Age of Machine Warfare, 1914-1945" in *Makers of Modern Strategy* ed. Peter Peret (Princeton, NJ: Princeton University Press, 1986), pp. 573-574.

[4] We do not know how many officers served in the *einsatzkommandos*, but I believe the 380 listed here are the lion's share of those who served on the eastern front, as well as a representative sample from many of the other *Einsatzkommandos*.

1

THE EINSATZKOMMANDOS

In short, the crimes of the Einsatzgruppen were not, fundamentally, military crimes at all. They were not committed in order to make military victory possible. On the contrary, military victory was sought in order to put the victors in a position where these crimes could be committed. These crimes were a war objective.[1]

- Brigadier General Telford Taylor, Prosecutor, at the Nürnberg Trials, 1946

HISTORY

The *Einsatzgruppen* were special SS, mobile formations charged with carrying out the mass murder of Jews, communist functionaries and others deemed by the Nazis as undesirable elements in occupied countries (primarily the Soviet Union), and of supervising various aspects of the Final Solution. The exact number of people killed by the *Einsatzgruppen* will never be known. Many historians believe the figure ranges from 850,000 to 1,300,000.

The *Einsatzgruppen* first operated in Austria and Czechoslovakia in 1938 as German troops moved into these two nations in relatively bloodless annexations and advances. Very little is known about these early formations – the unit participating in the Austrian operation was known as *Einsatzkommando Österreich*, while those in Czechoslovakia included *Einsatzgruppe Dresden*, *Einsatzgruppe Wien*, *Einsatzgruppe I Prag* and *Einsatzgruppe II Brünn*.[2] Each group in the invasion of Czechoslovakia consisted of Gestapo personnel, Czech-speaking interpreters, technical personnel, specialists organized in a total of six *Einsatzkommandos*.[3]

For the Polish campaign in 1939, Reinhard Heydrich, the chief of the Reich Security Service, formed six major *Einsatzgruppen der Sicherheitspolizei* (Sipo) – or *Einsatzgruppen* of security police – under the code name of *Operation Tannenberg*. Five of the groups were attached to the five advancing German armies while the other was designated for service in the Posen district. They were identified by Roman numerals (*Einsatzgruppe I - VI*). The groups' subordinate *Einsatzkommando* were each attached to an army corps. Additionally, Heydrich established an independent *Einsatzgruppe z.b.V. von Woyrsch*. The total strength of the *Einsatzgruppen* during the Polish campaign was approximately 2,700 men. The missions of the *Einsatzgruppen* in Poland included the arrest of the politically unreliable, confiscation of weapons, gathering of evidence deemed important for police intelligence activities, and actions against Jews, the Polish intelligentsia and members of the upper class.[4] During the Wehrmacht's administration of Poland, which continued from September 1 to October 25, 1939, some 531 towns and villages were burned and 16,376 persons were executed. The *Einsatzkommandos* and police auxiliaries are believed to have been responsible for forty percent of these incidents.[5]

The *Einsatzgruppen* that would ultimately participate in the campaign against Russia were formed in the spring of 1941 after Adolf Hitler issued an order that the Security Police and Security Service would assist the army in combating resistance behind the front. Shortly thereafter, Reinhard Heydrich met with the Quartermaster General of the Army, General Eduard Wagner, to reach an agreement concerning the activation, command and jurisdiction of the units of the Security Service which would operate in the rear operational areas of the field armies. They would carry out tasks specifically designated by Heydrich and Heinrich Himmler; their respective army commander would provide much logistical support. The Germans formed four *Einsatzgruppen*. *Einsatzgruppe A* was attached to Army Group

North, *Einsatzgruppe B* was attached to Army Group Center, *Einsatzgruppe C* was attached to Army Group South and *Einsatzgruppe D* was assigned to the German 11th Army.[6] In July 1941 Heydrich formed an additional, temporary group, *Einsatzgruppe z.b.V.*, which operated in eastern Poland behind *Einsatzgruppe B*.

CHAIN OF COMMAND

The *Einsatzgruppe* received their direct orders from the *Reichssicherheitshauptamt* (RSHA) or Reich Main Security Office in Berlin. Created on September 27, 1939, the RSHA joined the offices of the *Sicherheitspolizei* (Sipo) – the Security Police, and the *Sicherheitsdienst* (SD) – the Security Service, a political counter-espionage organization. The *Sicherheitspolizei* was itself composed of two organizations: the *Geheime Staatspolizei* (Gestapo) – the Secret State Police, and the *Kriminalpolizei* (Kripo) – the Criminal Police.[7] Reinhard Heydrich was the chief of the Sipo and was also the chief of the SD. Reinhard Heydrich was clearly a powerful man.

It is easy at first glance to attempt to understand the Sipo, Gestapo and Kripo as discrete entities. But in reality they were closely linked – some would say even fused – because the SD was a major part of each. The SD had the mission to penetrate key institutions of German society and guide these organizations along proper National Socialist (Nazi) lines toward the future Reich – and this included law enforcement agencies. With the creation of the RSHA, men within the Kripo and Sipo could be transferred to temporarily work in different branches or common missions. The line between a simple detective and rabid political operative became blurred.[8] Even so, many Kripo detectives thought their comrades in the Gestapo were politically tainted.[9]

Additionally, each *Einsatzgruppe* remained in direct contact with the senior SS leader for the area in which it operated. Heinrich Himmler created the positions of Higher SS and Police Leader (*Höhrere SS und Polizeiführer* [HSSPF]) by a decree in November 1937 for the purpose of promoting SS and police integration and to provide political direction in the various districts in Germany. In case of war, the HSSPF would take charge of all police forces within his area of responsibility. In occupied territories HSSPF forces would carry out assignments of a political nature, while remaining subordinate to army commanders in terms of supply, movement and other logistical considerations. On May 21, 1941, Himmler defined the position further:[10]

> The Higher SS and Police Leader is placed in charge of SS and police troops and also of the operational personnel in the Security Police in order to carry out the tasks allocated to him by me personally.

Many sarcastic Germans frequently referred to the Higher SS and Police Leaders as "Little Himmlers." Undoubtedly, the term was not used in the presence of these men, or in the presence of Himmler himself!

AIMS AND ORDERS

Adolf Hitler decided that the war in Russia would be not only a military war, but also a racial struggle for which the *Einsatzkommandos* would play a vital role. At the beginning of May 1941 recruits for the *Einsatzgruppen* gathered in the Elbe River town of Pretsch, northeast of Leipzig. Due to the limited billeting capacity of the Border Police School at which they would be trained, some of the men were accommodated in the towns of Düben and Bad Schmiedberg. In addition to receiving training on how to search and round up personnel, the men attended briefings about the aims and activities the *Einsatzgruppen* would be called upon to perform in the occupied territories. Two *Einsatzgruppen* commanders remembered what transpired:[11]

> During June, Heydrich, Chief of Security Police and the SD, and Streckenbach, head of Office I of the Reich Security Main Office [RSHA], lectured on the duties of the *Einsatzgruppen* and *Einsatzkommando*. At this time we were already being instructed about the tasks of exterminating the Jews. It was stated that Eastern Jewry was the intellectual reservoir of Bolshevism and, therefore, in the Führer's opinion, must be exterminated. This speech was given before a small select audience. Although I cannot remember the individuals present, I assume that many of the *Einsatzgruppe* and *Sonderkommando* chiefs were present.

Heydrich met with the senior *einsatgruppen* leaders in Berlin as well. Erwin Schulz, the former leader of *Einsatzkommando 5*, testified at the Nürnberg trials on the event.[12]

> Some time during the first ten days of June 1941, the chiefs of the *Einsatzgruppen* and the leaders of the *kommandos* were called to the RSHA in the Prinz Albrecht Palace to hear a speech by Heydrich in which he outlined the policy to be adopted, giving us some guidelines concerning the fulfillment of the tasks imposed upon the *Einsatzgruppen*.

Heydrich called a third meeting, which he was unable to attend, to take place a few days before the scheduled June 22nd attack date, for high level SS and police chiefs in the office of the Chief of the Order Police – the *Ordnungspolizei* (ORPO), the uniformed police forces in Germany, Kurt Daluege. It appears as though the participants discussed – among other things – the specifications of who was to be eliminated by the *Einsatzgruppen*. They included:[13]

> • Officials of the Commintern (together with Communist politicians in general);
> • Top- and medium-level officials and radical lower-level officials of the [Communist] Party. Central committee and district and sub-district committees;
> • People's Commissars;
> • Jews in [Communist] Party and State employment, and other radical elements (saboteurs, propagandists, snipers, assassins, etc.) insofar as they are, in any particular case, no longer required to supply information on political or economic matters which are of special importance for the further operations of the Security Police, or for the economic reconstruction of the Occupied Territories...

Otto Ohlendorf, former head of *Einsatzgruppe D*, put it more succinctly after the war:[14]

> The goal was to liberate the army's rear areas by killing Jews, Gypsies and Communist activists.

In mid-June, Reinhard Heydrich also spoke to the troops of the *Einsatzgruppen*. The 2,945 men paraded to the town of Düben where they were assembled in formation. Heydrich made a vigorous speech, although he spoke in vague generalities saying only that the task required "unparalleled hardness."[15]

ORGANIZATION AND EQUIPMENT

Each *Einsatzgruppe* was roughly a battalion in strength; *Einsatzgruppe A* had 990 men, *Einsatzgruppe B* fielded 655 troops, *Einsatzgruppe C* had a strength of 700 men and *Einsatzgruppe D*, the smallest of the groups, mustered 600 personnel. The officers generally came from the SD, SS, Kripo and Gestapo. Enlisted personnel were drawn from the *Waffen-SS*, Gestapo, ORPO and locally-recruited police. Some one thousand five-hundred *Waffen-SS* personnel served at some point during the war in an *Einsatzkommando*.[16] *Einsatzgruppen* were further divided into subordinate units called *Einsatzkommandos*.[17] These elements were roughly fifty to one hundred seventy-five men strong. Each *Einsatzkommando* could be further subdivided into still smaller units called *Teilkommandos* of ten to thirty men each.[18]

We have the greatest knowledge of *Einsatzgruppe A* concerning the organization and of the participants. The following table shows the makeup of *Einsatzgruppe A* (EG A), which consisted of a group staff, *Sonderkommando 1A* (SK 1A), *Sonderkommando 1B* (SK 1B), *Einsatzkommando 2* (EK 2) and *Einsatzkommando 3* (EK 3):[19]

Table 1
EINSATZGRUPPE A – ORGANIZATION

	EG A	Group HQ	SK 1A	SK 1B	EK 2	EK 3
Waffen-SS	340	216	25	26	41	32
Drivers	172	31	23	34	50	34
Administration	18	8	3	2	4	1
SD	35	6	8	3	8	10
Criminal Police	41	1	11	5	13	10
State Police	89	4	18	12	26	29
Auxiliary Police	87	52	0	20	0	15
Order Police	133	133	0	0	0	0
Female Auxiliaries	13	7	1	0	4	1
Translators	51	5	14	6	18	8
Teletypists	3	0	0	0	3	0
Radio Operators	8	1	2	1	3	1
	990	**464**	**105**	**110**	**170**	**141**

By knowing the personnel distribution within an *Einsatzgruppe*, we can make some general conclusions as to its equipment, an effort we must undertake as there appear to be no existing records describing how the units were outfitted. First, two assumptions are in order: everyone rode on vehicles; there were no foot mobile elements, or the *Einsatzgruppe* would not have been able to keep up with the German advance. Second, an *Einsatzgruppe* would have had no more vehicles than it had drivers assigned. Therefore in the case of *Einsatzgruppe A*, the total number of vehicles would have been no greater than 172. I believe the *Einsatzgruppe* would have had some "spare" drivers – therefore the total of vehicles would have been closer to 160. Of these I additionally am of the opinion that ten percent (16) were motorcycles (some of which probably had side cars) and probably another ten percent were staff cars, leaving some 128 as cargo and troop carrying trucks – most likely Opel "Blitz" 3-ton types. Looking at the manning levels, some 63 trucks would have been used to transport *Einsatzgruppe* soldiers; 50 others would have been remaining to haul required supplies (see below).

Each element, the group headquarters and each of the four *Einsatzkommandos*, would have possessed field radios and probably additional long range antenna kits. Radios and teletype machines (it appears that one *Einsatzkommando* had one of these) require electrical power, so each of the units would have had at least one field generating set, most commonly a large 507 pound, two cylinder variety. I do not believe the *Einsatzkommando* fielded bulldozers or any other large earth mover to facilitate digging execution pits, but each *Einsatzkommando* would have had at least forty D-handle shovels to accomplish this task. They would additionally have carried some other pioneer tools such as saws and carpentry kits. They would have some engineering measuring equipment, such as theodolites, to help in marking and recording the grave sites. Each group would have also had a large field range mounted on one of the trucks to provide food for the troops. All elements would have additionally carried their own ammunition, cold-weather heating stoves, medium-size tents, portable field desks and chairs, spare parts for vehicles, light sets, cooking and serving utensils, arms room supplies, a few days' worth of rations and water, gas and petroleum products for the vehicles, and sundry other items required for living in the field. At least one *Einsatzgruppe*, B, had access to a small observation aircraft which was probably used to scout future routes or target objectives, especially over swamps and wooded areas difficult to reconnoiter on foot.

The units had a wide variety of weapons including pistols for the officers – Walther P-38s, Lugers, Mauser Model 1910s and others as the personnel probably brought their own weapons from the various police and other agencies. Enlisted soldiers most likely carried Mauser Kar 98b rifles. Those soldiers who carried machine-pistols probably had Bergmann 9mm Model 35/Is or MP 38s. There were probably a few machine guns as well – most likely captured Czech guns, but also perhaps some MG 08/15s from World War I or a few Mauser MG 34s – although at 800-900 rounds per minute their rate of fire was much too high for the task at hand. The *Einsatzkommando* soldiers had some hand-grenades as well – for clearing small buildings whose inhabitants refused to come outside, but likely no larger weapons such as mortars. The mission of the *Einsatzkommando*, after all, was execution, not combat, and as such, small arms weapons would be the priority.

METHODS OF KILLING

The *Einsatzgruppen* generally accomplished their mission either by deceiving victims to report to a central location for the purposes of relocation and then killing them instead, or by conducting manhunts through a district. Although later, carbon monoxide gas vans were sometimes used, the preferred method of execution was by shooting.

To gain surprise, the *Einsatzgruppen* followed close behind the German Army spearheads to trap the Jews before the victims had an opportunity to ascertain their fate. To maximize efficiency of the small force, Heydrich directed the special units to the larger Russian cities where over ninety percent of Russian Jews were concentrated.[20] But the *Einsatzgruppen* did not move as consolidated units. The *Sonderkommandos* and *Einsatzkommandos* generally moved separate from the group staff and often further decentralized into *Vorkommandos* and *Teilkommandos*. The *Vorkommandos* served as advanced detachments while the *Teilkommandos* often moved with German Army divisions.

Sometimes the advancing *Einsatzkommando* would post bulletins in the towns and cities urging Jews to report to the city center for registration or some other type of administrative action. In other instances, the SD would attempt to convince senior Jewish leaders in the community to persuade remaining Jews to come out of hiding. In still other instances, the SD would do absolutely nothing for a few days. Lulled into a false sense of security, Jews in hiding would then return to their homes believing the worst to be over. It wasn't. The *Einsatzkommandos* did not have the mission to scare the Jews into cooperation or to resettle Jews to new locations, or to register them for potential deportations, or to send them to concentration camps. The *Einsatzkommandos* meant to murder them.

SHOOTING

Some *Einsatzkommando* seem to have preferred shooting their victims with pistols and rifles, while other units used machine-pistols and machine-guns. The following description by a German civilian testifying before the Nürnberg Military Tribunal (the Nürnberg Trials) is typical of an *Einsatzgruppe* shooting operation:[21]

> I walked around the mound and found myself confronted by a tremendous grave. People were closely wedged together and lying on top of each other so that their heads were visible. Nearly all had blood running over their shoulders from their heads. Some of the people shot were still moving. Some were lifting their arms and turning their heads to show that they were still alive. The pit was already two thirds full. I estimated that it contained about 1,000 people. I looked for the man who did the shooting. He was an SS man, who sat at the edge of the narrow end of the pit, his feet dangling into the pit. He had a tommy gun on his knees and was smoking a cigarette. The people, completely naked, went down some steps which were cut in the clay wall of the pit and clambered over the heads of the people lying there, to the place to which the SS man directed them. They lay down in front of the dead or injured people; some caressed those who were still alive and spoke to them in a low voice. Then I heard a series of shots. I looked into the pit and saw that the bodies were twitching or the heads lying already motionless on top of the bodies that lay before them. Blood was running from their necks. I was surprised that I was not ordered away, but saw that there were two or three postmen in uniform nearby. The next batch was approaching already. They went down into the pit, lined themselves up against the previous victims and were shot. When I walked around the mound, I noticed another truckload of people which had just arrived. This time it included sick and infirm persons. An old, very thin women with terribly thin legs was undressed by others who were already naked, while two people held her up. The woman appeared to be paralyzed. The naked people carried the woman around the mound.

When conducting executions by shooting, the Germans would frequently use existing ravines, sand pits and quarries in which to conduct the killings and bury the bodies there to save on labor. When these were not available, abandoned Russian anti-tank ditches served the same purpose. As a last resort – although *Einsatzgruppen* troops did not like to construct them – the Germans would dig huge burial ditches. While the victims were often forced to excavate these pits, such a technique always ran the risk that those about to die would realize their fate and attempt to escape or attack their tormentors. These killing sites were often no more than a few miles from Russian villages and towns, close enough that the local populace were probably able to hear the firing in many instances, although the sites were rarely observable to those not directly involved.[22] It would appear that the *Einsatzkommandos* normally did not transport their victims by truck to the shooting sites. Instead, the victims were forced to walk a last, lonely mile, lost in their own thoughts.

GAS VANS

Arthur Nebe, the commander of *Einsatzgruppe B*, was one of the first commanders to realize that the mass killings of men, women and children was causing a great degree of mental anguish for his troops. Nebe tried to use explosives to do the job, but these too proved unsatisfactory, as flying body parts seemed to be just as disconcerting as flying bullets.[23]

Nebe then came upon a technique of killing the victims by channeling the exhaust gas from a truck into a sealed chamber – the carbon monoxide worked its fatal process in about twenty minutes – outside the view of the *Einsatzgruppen* troops. Nebe reported his success to Berlin where Walter Rauff, the chief of RSHA technical affairs, was instructed to develop the concept more fully. Rauff hired the firm of Gaubschat, in Berlin, to install hermetically sealed vans on the chassis of large trucks. The SD workshop finished the modifications as recounted by a shop foreman after the war:[24]

> A flexible exhaust pipe was installed at the truck's exhaust, with a diameter of 58 to 60 millimeters (2.26 to 2.34 inches), and a hole of the same size was drilled in the van floor; a metal pipe was soldered into the hole from the outside to which the flexible exhaust pipe was fixed. When the various parts were connected, the truck engine was started and the exhaust fumes were channeled into the van, through the pipe leading from the exhaust to the hole in the van floor.

Gaubschat produced two types of van: a Diamond, which had a killing capacity of twenty-five to thirty people and a larger model, the Sauer, which could pack in fifty to sixty souls. The first vans did not arrive in Russia until October 1941. It appears as though *Einsatzgruppe A* was entrusted with two of the vehicles, while *Einsatzgruppe B* had four. Records indicate that *Einsatzkommando 7B*, *8* and *9* each had their own vehicle. The Germans with the *Einsatzkommando 8* gas van alone killed five to six thousand victims.[25]

Einsatzgruppe C was issued at least five gas vans and gave two to *Sonderkommando 4A*, two to *Einsatzkommando 6* and one to *Einsatzkommando 5*. A member of the group testified after the war as to the vehicle's efficiency:[26]

> Two gas vans were in service. I saw them myself. They drove into the prison yard, and the Jews – men, women, and children – had to get straight into the vans from their cells. I know what the interior of the vans looked like. It was covered with sheet metal and fitted with a wooden grid. The exhaust fumes were piped into the interior of the vans. I can still hear the hammering and the screaming of the Jews – "Dear Germans, let us out!" The Jews went through our cordon and into the van without hesitating. As soon as the doors were shut, the driver started the engine. He drove to a spot outside Poltava. I was there when the van arrived. As the doors were opened, dense smoke emerged, followed by a tangle of crumpled bodies. It was a frightful sight.

The driver for Paul Blobel, the commander of *Sonderkommando 4A*, provided gruesome details. He testified on what he saw at the unloading of one of the vans:[27]

> The use of the gas vans was the most horrible thing I have ever seen. I saw people being led into the vans and the doors closed. Then the van drove off. I had to drive Blobel to the place where the gas van was unloaded. The back doors of the van were opened, and the bodies that had not fallen out when the doors were opened were unloaded by Jews who were still alive. The bodies were covered with vomit and excrement. It was a terrible sight. Blobel looked, then he looked away, and we drove off. On such occasions Blobel always drank schnapps, sometimes even in the car.

Einsatzgruppe D was issued four of the vans. The unit used them at Simferopol', Jeissk, Cherkassy, Stravopol' and many other places. The vehicles were not perfect; the drive trains frequently broke on the rough roads and the exhaust tubing often leaked. The Russians nicknamed the vans the *dushegubky*, the "soul killers."[28] The Nazis may well have killed several hundred thousand victims in the vans. Dr. August Becker, a van technician, reported that 97,000 died in just three vans from December 1941 to June 1942.[29]

BURNING

Other methods were even more hideous. Former *SS-Hauptscharführer* Adolf Ruebe testified at Nürnberg after the war that there were SS executioners who invented novel ways to kill their victims.[30]

> On the occasion of an exhumation in Minsk, in November 1943, *SS-Obersturmführer* Heuser arrived with a Kommando of Latvians. They brought eight Jews, men and women, with them. The Latvians guarded the Jews while Harter [another SS man] and Heuser erected a funeral pyre with their own hands. The Jews were bound, put on the pile alive, drenched with gasoline and burned.

BLUDGEONING

Bludgeoning to death was a method not preferred by the commanders of the *Einsatzkommando* – it was inefficient, slow, and even more dehumanizing to the executioners than other methods of dispatch. But it did occur, none-the-less. Most recorded instances involved local police auxiliary units which were frequently subordinated to the *Einsatzkommando*. The following, provided by a German army colonel, is a description of one such incident:[31]

> ...when I inquired what was happening I was told that the 'Death-dealer of Kovno' was at work and that this was where collaborators and traitors were finally meted out their rightful punishment! When I stepped closer, however, I became witness to probably the most frightful event that I had seen during the course of two world wars. On the concrete forecourt of the petrol station a blond man of medium height, aged about twenty-five, stood leaning on a wooden club, resting. The club was as thick as his arm and came up to his chest. At his feet lay about fifteen to twenty dead or dying people. Water flowed continuously from a hose washing blood away into the drainage gully. Just a few steps behind this man some twenty men, guarded by armed civilians, stood waiting for their cruel execution in silent submission. In response to a cursory wave the next man stepped forward silently and was then beaten to death with the wooden club in the most bestial manner, each blow accompanied by enthusiastic shouts from the audience.

PRISONER OF WAR CAMPS

Members of the *Einsatzkommandos* also visited German Army transitional prisoner of war camps which held Soviet prisoners. The visiting SS men from the *Einsatzkommandos* would identify soldiers of Jewish religion and Communist commissars, remove these prisoners from the camps, and execute them not far from the camps.

Regardless of the usual success of their tactics, the *Einsatzkommandos* sometimes needed outside assistance. They frequently received it from the Army, the Order Police, auxiliary police and units of the *Waffen-SS*.

GERMAN ARMY ASSISTANCE

The *Einsatzgruppen* generally had a good working relationship with the German Army, freeing up army security forces for front-line action. Army commanders were often aware of the activities of these SS units. In a group of assembled army commanders at Orsha in December 1941, Colonel General Franz Halder, the Chief of Staff of the Army said:[32]

> These people [the *Einsatzgruppen*] are worth their weight in gold to us. They guarantee the security of our rear communications and so save us calling upon [army] troops for this purpose.

In addition to maintaining contact with the Higher SS and Police Leaders, each *Einsatzgruppe* would conduct close cooperation with German units. An *Einsatzgruppe* would maintain communications with an army – such as *Einsatzgruppe C* with the 6th Army. The *Einsatzkommando* would also work with an army staff; the *Teilkommando* would coordinate directly with a particular German army division.

This exchange of information happened at the highest levels between the SS and the Army. Copies of the *Einsatzgruppen* Operational Situation Reports – an extensive series of messages issued during the period from June 1941 to May 1943 – were distributed to Lieutenant Colonel Tippelskirch on the operational staff of the high command (*Oberkommando der Wehrmacht* [OKW]).[33]

The specific missions given to the *Einsatzgruppen* for the Russian campaign were agreed upon in advance by both the SS and the Army; they were as follows:[34]

> In the army's rear area, prior to the initiation of operations: listing of selected objects (material archives, card indexes of anti-German or anti-Government organizations, associations, groups, etc.) and selected important individuals (leading émigrés, saboteurs, terrorists, etc.). The Army commander is authorized to forbid the utilization of the special detachments in those areas where their employment may affect operations adversely.
>
> To discover and stamp out anti-German and anti-Government movements insofar as these are not part of the enemy's armed forces: provision of general information to the zone of communications commander regarding the political situation.
>
> Cooperation with field security officers of the Secret Field Police (GFP) will be governed by the 'Principles for Cooperation between the State Security Police and the Field Security Branch of the Reich War Ministry' on January 1, 1937.
>
> Cooperation between the special detachments and the military authorities in the Army's rear area: The special detachments (*Sonderkommandos*) of the *Sicherheitspolizei* (Sipo) will carry out their duties on their own responsibility. They will be controlled by the armies' movements in the following matters: movement, rations and accommodations.
>
> This does not affect the authority of the Chief of Sipo and SD in matters of discipline and jurisprudence. They will receive their technical instruction from the Chief of Sipo and SD but, when necessary, their activity will be restricted by orders from Army headquarters.
>
> A representative of the Chief of Sipo and SD will be placed in each army area to centralize the direction of these detachments. It will be his duty to inform the appropriate Army commander as soon as possible about the instructions he receives from the Chief of Sipo and SD. The military commander is authorized to give this representative such instructions as may be necessary to avoid interference with military operations. Such instructions will have precedence over all others.
>
> The *Sonderkommandos* are authorized, with reference to their tasks to take administrative measures affecting the civilian population on their own responsibility. In this connection, it is their duty to work in close cooperation with the field security service. Any measures which may affect operations must be agreed to by the commander of the army concerned.

Thus, the Army fed, provided some transportation and fuel, purveyed rations, distributed spare parts for vehicles, issued maps and supplied postal services, furnished ammunition, designated billeting areas and provided liaison with the *Einsatzgruppen*. The *Einsatzgruppen* notified the Army where they would be operating and provided general details as to the type of operation they would be conducting. The Army had the authority to veto an operation if they believed it would adversely affect their own activities.

That the army found the murders to be distasteful is certain. During the Polish campaign, Field Marshal Wilhelm List, the commander of the 14th Army, issued an order for everyone in his area – which included *Einsatzgruppe I*, to immediately stop all burning of synagogues and summary executions, and sought to court-martial members of the police who ignored his orders. In another incident, Field Marshal August von Mackensen slammed his fist on a table and demanded that *Einsatzgruppe z.b.V. von Woysch* be removed from his area immediately – it dutifully was.

But Wehrmacht resistance to the death tactics began to slacken by the Russian campaign. Field Marshal Gerd von Rundstedt, the commander of Army Group South – in whose area *Einsatzgruppe C* and *D* operated – issued an order forbidding his army troops to watch or photograph the executions. Field Marshal Fodor von Bock, the commander of Army Group Center, in October 1941 refused the entreaties of his staff officers to remove the *Einsatzkommandos* from the army group's rear area after the massacre of 7,620 Jews in Borisov – stating that it would be virtual civil war to employ force against a unit of the SS.[35] Walter Stahlecker the commander of *Einsatzgruppe A*, wrote to Reinhard Heydrich that he had found relations with Colonel General Erich Hoepner, the commander of Panzer Group 4, to be "close and almost cordial."[36] And Colonel General Ernst Busch, the commander of the 16th Army, a force supported by *Einsatzgruppe A*, when informed that men and women were being shot just outside his headquarters, reportedly told his adjutant to shut the curtains.[37]

Sometimes the army did more than just supply the *Einsatzgruppen* or "look the other way." Adolf Ott, commander of *Sonderkommando 7b*, stated at Nürnberg that on one occasion his unit temporarily buried the bodies of one hundred victims in the snow, which were later interred by the Army in a more permanent mass grave.[38] The massive massacre at Babi Yar, a suburb of Kiev, in September 1941 was conducted reportedly after extensive consultation with army Major General Kurt Eberhard[39], commander of Field Command 195.[40]

Army headquarters frequently approved awards and decorations to *Einsatzgruppen* personnel in their area. For example, on August 26, 1943, Colonel Paul Herrmann, the chief of staff for the 16th Army signed an order for an Infantry Assault Badge to Vice-corporal Leonid Waldowski (an auxiliary) of *Einsatzkommando 2* part of *Einsatzgruppe A*.[41] Lieutenant General Erich Friderici, the commander of all security forces for Army Group South, authorized the award of the Iron Cross 1st Class to *SS-Obersturmbannführer* Erich Ehrlinger on August 27, 1943.[42] There were many more such occurences.

Occasionally, the army "spine" stiffened. In May 1942, Lieutenant General Gotthard Heinrici, the commander of the 4th Army, persuaded his superior Field Marshal Günther von Kluge, the commander of Army Group Center, to keep the Security Police units out of the army group's immediate combat zone.[43]

GERMAN ORDER POLICE ASSISTANCE

The *Hauptamt Ordnungspolizei* – the Uniformed Police Main Office – was formed on June 17, 1936. It was responsible for all common police, fire coast guard and civil defense functions.[44] The most important subset of this office, the *Ordnungspolizei* (ORPO), the Order Police, was a large organization, growing from 131,000 officers and men in 1939 to some 310,000 personnel by 1943. Forty-two percent were reservists. The ORPO was composed of two entities, the Uniformed Police (*Schutzpolizei*) under which police battalions operated, and the Rural Police (*Gendarmerie*).[45] The men of the ORPO police battalions tended to be older individuals, some not fit for front-line regular military service. Additionally, they received less comprehensive training and equipment. None-the-less, the police battalions played a very key role in assisting the *Einsatzgruppen*.

Many ORPO police elements were directly attached to the *Einsatzkommandos*. *Einsatzgruppen B*, *C* and *D* had companies of Police Battalion 9 – a unit from Berlin; later they received men from Police Battalion 3 – also hailing from Berlin. The *Einsatzkommandos* frequently employed non-attached German police units to assist them in conducting large-scale actions. The following table shows some of this cooperation:[46]

Table 2
ORDER POLICE SUPPORT TO THE EINSATZGRUPPEN

Police Battalion	*Location of Action*	*Date of Action*	*Victims*
11	Slutsk	September 1941	1,000 +
13	Mlawa District	November - December 1942	12,000
	Plöhnen	1942	5,000
22	Riga	November - December 1941	25,000
	Slutsk	February 8 - 9, 1943	3,000

32	Lvov	September 1941	1,000 +
45	Berdichev	September 12, 1941	1,000
	Babi Yar	September 29 - 30, 1941	33,000
67	Szczebrzeszyn	September 1941	1,000
	Zamosc	1942	2,000
	Bilgoraj	1942	1,200
96	Rovno	November 7 - 8, 1941	21,000
101	Parcew	August 1942	5,000
	Miedzyrzec	August 25, 1942	10,000
133	Stanislawow	October 12, 1942	12,000
	Nadvornaya	October 16, 1941	2,000
	Delatyn	1941	2,000
251	Bialystok	August 16 - 20, 1943	25,000
255	Bialystok	August 16 - 20, 1943	25,000
256	Bialystok	August 16 - 20, 1943	25,000
303	Babi Yar	September 29 - 30, 1941	33,000
	Zhitomir	September 1941	18,000
306	Luninets	September 4, 1942	2,800
	Wysokie	September 9, 1942	1,400
	David Gorodok	September 10, 1942	1,100
	Stolin	September 11, 1942	6,500
	Janow Podlaski	September 25, 1942	2,500
	Pinsk	October - November 1942	16,200
307	Brest-Litovsk	July 1941	8,000
	Tarnow	June 1942	16,000
	Neu Sandau	August 1942	18,000
309	Bialystok	June 27, 1941	2,000
314	Dnepropetrovsk	November 1941	1,000 +
	Kharkov	January 1942	15,000
316	Bialystok	July 12 - 13, 1941	3,000
	Mogilev	November 1941	3,700
	Bobruisk	1942	2,000
320	Kaments-Podolski	August 27 - 28, 1941	23,600
	Rovno	November 7 - 8, 1941	21,000
	Kostopol	July 14, 1942	5,000
	Pinsk	October - November 1942	16,200
322	Bialystok	July 12 - 13, 1941	3,000
	Mogilev	October 19, 1941	3,700
	Minsk	November 1941	19,000
	Minsk	July 28 - 30, 1942	9,000

Assuming that each battalion fielded roughly five hundred policemen, we can see that from these major actions alone, the *Einsatzgruppen* received help from 10,000 members of the Order Police. And, assuming the above figures are correct concerning the victims, this assistance resulted in the death of over 462,000 people – roughly one-third of the estimated total for the *Einsatzgruppen* as a whole.

AUXILIARY POLICE ASSISTANCE

Local inhabitants, often organized into auxiliary forces, additionally provided valuable assistance to the *Einsatzkommandos*. Their motivations were many. Some hated the Communist rule, some wanted independence for their areas, others sought to ingratiate themselves with the conquering Germans and many simply hated Jews. The locals spoke the language, knew the terrain, and could convince neighbor to betray neighbor. In *Einsatzgruppe A*, the Germans organized Lithuanian anti-Soviet partisans into five police companies to assist them in the killing operations. In the Ukraine, local militias displayed great zeal in conducting many aspects of the hunt to include shooting women and children. While the exact figure may never be known, it is estimated that at least several thousand local auxiliaries assisted the *Einsatzgruppen* in some form.[47]

These local police, especially in Belorussia and the Ukraine, outnumbered the Germans in the *Einsatzkommandos*. Martin Dean, a member of the Metropolitan Police War Crimes Unit, New Scotland Yard, estimates that these police personnel probably accounted for some ten percent of all Jews killed in *Einsatzkommando* areas, but also states that the true numbers will never be known.[48]

While we do not have an accurate picture of the number of deaths inflicted by the auxiliary forces, it is safe to say that their use made the *Einsatzgruppe* much more efficient, if nothing else.

WAFFEN-SS ASSISTANCE

The *Waffen-SS* not only provided individual replacements to the *Einsatzkommandos*, they also assisted by deploying complete units to these operations. On August 21, 1941 the Operational Situation Report Number 59 reported that the 1st SS Brigade (motorized) carried out an action in which 300 male and 139 female Jews were executed. Operational Situation Report 86, dated September 17, 1941, again singled out the 1st SS Brigade. The brigade, commanded by *SS-Brigadeführer* Karl Demelhuber, directed the activities of SS Infantry Regiment 8 and SS Infantry Regiment 10.

At least one source states that the *Waffen-SS* Cavalry Brigade conducted *Einsatzkommando*-type operations in Russia. From July 29 through August 12, 1941 the brigade conducted operations in the Pripjet marshes area near Pinsk. *SS-Standartenführer* Hermann Fegelein, the brigade commander, reported that 14,178 looters, 1,001 partisans and 699 Red Army soldiers were executed. A reported eight thousand Jewish males were killed; the women and children were reportedly driven into the marshes. During the entire Pinsk operation at least eleven thousand Jews were executed.[49]

A third *Waffen-SS* unit, *SS-Sonderkommando Dirlewanger*, an anti-partisan unit led at that time by *SS-Sturmbannführer* Oskar Dirlewanger, has been documented as working extensively with *Einsatzkommando 8*.[50] Other *Waffen-SS* formations may have done so as well, although the documentation was not found in the preparation of this work.

Yehoshua Büchler, in his article *"Kommandostab Reichsführer-SS: Himmler's Personal Murder Brigades in 1941"*, estimates that the 1st SS Brigade, the 2nd SS Brigade, which oversaw the activities of SS Infantry Regiment 4 and SS Infantry Regiment 5, and the *Waffen-SS* Cavalry Brigade accounted for 100,000 victims during 1941 as they assisted the *Einsatzgruppen*.[51]

ERASING THE CRIMES

The Germans made attempts to keep much of the killing operations a secret. At the beginning of the summer of 1942, Gestapo chief Heinrich Müller appointed Paul Blobel, the outgoing commander of *Sonderkommando 4a* of *Einsatzgruppe C*, to head *Aktion 1005* – the operation to remove all traces of mass murder in the east. In July 1942, Blobel organized the nucleus of what would be called *Sonderkommando 1005*. During the fall of that year Blobel's men began to disinter corpses at various *Einsatzgruppen* killing sites for destruction by burning and conducted a similar undertaking at various concentration camps where the unit unearthed and burned hundreds of thousands of bodies.[52]

Blobel described the process of removing the traces of the *Einsatzgruppen* executions at his trial:[53]

> I myself witnessed the burning of corpses in a mass grave near Kiev during my visit in August [1943]. This grave was about 55 meters long, 3 meters wide, and 2 1/2 meters deep. When the cover had been lifted, the bodies were covered with fuel and set on fire. It took about two days for the grave to burn down. I myself saw that the grave became red-hot right down to the ground. Afterwards the grave was filled in, and thus all traces were as good as eliminated. Owing to the approach of the front, it was not possible to destroy the mass graves further to the south and the east, resulting from the executions of the *Einsatzgruppen*.

THE UNITS

While this book is primarily a discussion of the officers of the four *Einsatzgruppen* that served in Russia, many of these men got their start in previous campaigns, while some went on to serve in other *Einsatzkommandos* in other theaters. I have therefore included a brief summary on additional formations, even though information is unfortunately inadequate. The following is a summary of all known *Einsatzgruppen* and *Einsatzkommandos*[54]:

EINSATZKOMMANDO ÖSTERREICH

Formed: March 1938
Campaign: Annexation of Austria
Commanders: Dr. Franz Six
Parent Formation: RSHA
Army Area Assignment: N/A
Victims: Unknown
Disbanded: Unknown
Known Locations: Austria
Remarks: First *Einsatzgruppe* formed.

EINSATZGRUPPE DRESDEN

Formed: September 1938
Campaign: Annexation of the Sudetenland
Commanders: Heinz Jost
Parent Formation: RSHA
Army Area Assignment: N/A
Victims: Unknown
Disbanded: Unknown
Known Locations: Northern Czechoslovakia
Remarks: Controlled five *Einsatzkommandos*

EINSATZGRUPPE WIEN (VIENNA)

Formed: March 1938
Campaign: Annexation of Austria
Commanders: Walter Stahlecker
Parent Formation: RSHA
Army Area Assignment: N/A
Victims: Unknown
Disbanded: Unknown
Known Locations: Austria
Remarks: Controlled two *Einsatzkommandos*

EINSATZGRUPPE I PRAG (PRAGUE)

Formed: March 1939
Campaign: Annexation of remainder of Czechoslovakia
Commanders: Unknown
Parent Formation: RSHA
Army Area Assignment: N/A
Victims: Unknown
Disbanded: Unknown
Known Locations: Budweis, Prague, Kolin, Pardubitz
Remarks: Controlled the following four *Einsatzkommandos*: Budweis, Prague, Kolin and Pardubitz

EINSATZGRUPPE II BRÜNN

Formed: March 1938
Campaign: Annexation of Austria
Commanders: Walter Stahlecker
Parent Formation: RSHA
Army Area Assignment: N/A
Victims: Unknown
Disbanded: Unknown
Known Locations: Olmütz, Brünn, Zlin
Remarks: Controlled these three *Einsatzkommandos*: Olmütz, Brünn and Zlin.

EINSATZGRUPPE I

Formed: August 1939
Campaign: Poland 1939
Commanders: Bruno Streckenbach
Parent Formation: RSHA
Army Area Assignment: 14th Army (Colonel General List)
Victims: Unknown
Disbanded: November 20, 1939
Known Locations: Neutitschen, Bielsko, Rzeszow
Remarks: Fielded four *Einsatzkommandos* and one *Sonderkommando*, consisting of thirty men from the Munich Gestapo who wore civilian clothing throughout the operation. After November 1939, personnel from the *Einsatzgruppe* were assigned to the *Kommandeur der Sicherheitspolizei und des SD Krakau* (Commander of Security Police and the SD for Cracow).

EINSATZGRUPPE II

Formed: August 1939
Campaign: Poland 1939
Commanders: Dr. Emanuel Schäfer
Parent Formation: RSHA
Army Area Assignment: 10th Army (General of Artillery von Reichenau)
Victims: Unknown
Disbanded: November 20, 1939
Known Locations: Oppeln, Radomsko, Konskie
Remarks: Consisted of two *Einsatzkommandos*. After November 1939, personnel from the *Einsatzgruppe* were assigned to

the *Kommandeur der Sicherheitspolizei und des SD Lublin* (Commander of Security Police and the SD for Lublin).

EINSATZGRUPPE III

Formed: August 1939
Campaign: Poland 1939
Commanders: Dr. Ludwig Fischer
Parent Formation: RSHA
Army Area Assignment: 8th Army (General of Infantry Blaskowitz)
Victims: Unknown
Disbanded: November 20, 1939
Known Locations: Breslau, Gr. Wartenberg, Lodz
Remarks: Fielded two *Einsatzkommandos*. After November 1939, personnel from the *Einsatzgruppe* were assigned to the *Kommandeur der Sicherheitspolizei und des SD Radom* (Commander of Security Police and the SD for Radom).

EINSATZGRUPPE IV

Formed: August 1939
Campaign: Poland 1939
Commanders: Lothar Beutel
Parent Formation: RSHA
Army Area Assignment: 4th Army (General of Artillery von Kluge)
Victims: Unknown
Disbanded: November 20, 1939
Known Locations: Jastrow, Zambrow
Remarks: Fielded two *Einsatzkommandos*. After November 1939, personnel from the *Einsatzgruppe* were assigned to the *Kommandeur der Sicherheitspolizei und des SD Warschau* (Commander of Security Police and the SD for Warsaw).

EINSATZGRUPPE V

Formed: August 1939
Campaign: Poland 1939
Commanders: Ernst Damzog
Parent Formation: RSHA
Army Area Assignment: 3rd Army (General of Artillery von Küchler)
Victims: Unknown
Disbanded: November 20, 1939
Known Locations: Mohrungen, Wegrow
Remarks: Fielded three *Einsatzkommandos*.

EINSATZGRUPPE VI

Formed: August 1939
Campaign: Poland 1939
Commanders: Erich Naumann
Parent Formation: RSHA
Army Area Assignment: None; assigned to Posen district
Victims: Unknown
Disbanded: November 20, 1939
Known Locations: Posen
Remarks: Fielded two *Einsatzkommandos*.

EINSATZGRUPPE z.b.V. von WOYRSCH

Formed: August 1939
Campaign: Poland 1939
Commanders: Dr. Otto Rasch
Parent Formation: RSHA
Army Area Assignment: None; assigned to West Prussia district
Victims: Unknown
Disbanded: November 20, 1939
Known Locations: Danzig, Bromberg, Thorn
Remarks: Fielded two *Einsatzkommandos*.

EINSATZGRUPPE A

Formed: June 1941
Campaign: Operation Barbarossa (Invasion of Russia)
Commanders: Walter Stahlecker, Heinz Jost, Dr. Humbert Achamer-Pifrader, Friedrich Panzinger, Dr. Wilhelm Fuchs
Parent Formation: RSHA
Army Area Assignment: Army Group North
Victims: 363,337 +
Disbanded: October 1944
Known Locations: Gumbinnen, Tilsit, Kaunas, Siauliai, Riga, Pskov, Novoselye, Pesje, Kikerino, Krasnogvardeisk,
Remarks: Initially fielded four *Einsatzkommandos*.

EINSATZGRUPPE B

Formed: June 1941
Campaign: Operation Barbarossa (Invasion of Russia)
Commanders: Arthur Nebe, Erich Naumann, Horst Böhme, Dr. Erich Ehrlinger, Heinz Seetzen
Parent Formation: RSHA
Army Area Assignment: Army Group Center

Victims: 134,000 +
Disbanded: Summer 1944
Known Locations: Minsk, Smolensk
Remarks: Fielded six *Einsatzkommandos*.

EINSATZGRUPPE C

Formed: June 1941
Campaign: Operation Barbarossa (Invasion of Russia)
Commanders: Dr. Emil Otto Rasch, Dr. Max Thomas, Horst Böhme
Parent Formation: RSHA
Army Area Assignment: Army Group South
Victims: 118,341 +
Disbanded: March 1944
Known Locations: Kiev, Starobelsk, Poltava, Novograd-Volynski, Zhitomir, Novo-Ukrainka
Remarks: Fielded four *Einsatzkommandos*.

EINSATZGRUPPE D

Formed: June 1941
Campaign: Operation Barbarossa (Invasion of Russia)
Commanders: Otto Ohlendorf, Walter Bierkamp
Parent Formation: RSHA
Army Area Assignment: 11th Army
Victims: 91,728 +
Disbanded: July 1943
Known Locations: Piatra-Neamt, Ananyev, Nikolayev, Simferopol, Ovruch, Olschanka, Taganrog, Woroshilovsk
Remarks: Became *Kampfgruppe Bierkamp* in March 1943. Initially fielded five *Einsatzkommandos*.

EINSATZGRUPPE z.b.V.

Formed: July 1941
Campaign: Operation Barbarossa (Invasion of Russia)
Commanders: Dr. Eberhard Schöngarth
Parent Formation: BdS Cracow
Army Area Assignment: None; assigned to eastern Poland, western Belorussia
Victims: 10,000
Disbanded: Fall, 1941
Known Locations: Eastern Poland, Western Belorussia
Remarks: Fielded four *Einsatzkommandos*.

EINSATZGRUPPE E

Formed: Unknown
Campaign: Balkans
Commanders: Ludwig Teichmann, Günther Hermann, Dr. Wilhelm Fuchs
Parent Formation: RSHA
Army Area Assignment: 12th Army
Victims: Unknown
Disbanded: Unknown
Known Locations: Croatia

EINSATZGRUPPE G

Formed: Unknown
Campaign: Southeast Europe
Commanders: Dr. Josef Kreuzer
Parent Formation: RSHA
Victims: Unknown
Disbanded: Unknown
Known Locations: Unknown
Remarks: Fell under the jurisdiction of HSSPF Black Sea.

EINSATZGRUPPE SERBIEN (SERBIA)

Formed: May 1941
Campaign: Southeast Europe
Commanders: Wilhelm Fuchs, August Meyszner, Dr. Emanuel Schäfer
Parent Formation: RSHA
Army Area Assignment: Army Group E
Victims: Unknown
Disbanded: Unknown
Known Locations: Belgrade

EINSATZGRUPPE H

Formed: 1944
Campaign: Slovakia
Commanders: Dr. Josef Witiska
Parent Formation: RSHA
Army Area Assignment:
Victims: Unknown
Disbanded: Unknown
Known Locations: Unknown
Remarks: Helped suppress Slovakian Uprising in 1944

EINSATZGRUPPE NORWEGEN (NORWAY)

Formed: Unknown
Campaign: Norway
Commanders: Heinrich Fehlis
Parent Formation: RSHA
Army Area Assignment:
Victims: Unknown
Disbanded: Unknown
Known Locations: Oslo

EINSATZKOMMANDO 1/I

Formed: August 1939
Campaign: Poland 1939
Commanders: Dr. Ludwig Hahn
Parent Formation: Einsatzgruppe I
Army Area Assignment: 14th Army (Colonel General List)
Victims: Unknown
Disbanded: November 20, 1939
Known Locations: Neutitschen, Bielsko, Rzeszow
Remarks: After November 1939, personnel from the *Einsatzkommando* were assigned to the *Kommandeur der Sicherheitspolizei und des SD Krakau* (Commander of Security Police and the SD for Cracow).

EINSATZKOMMANDO 2/I

Formed: August 1939
Campaign: Poland 1939
Commanders: Müller
Parent Formation: Einsatzgruppe I
Army Area Assignment: 14th Army (Colonel General List)
Victims: Unknown
Disbanded: November 20, 1939
Known Locations: Neutitschen, Bielsko, Rzeszow
Remarks: After November 1939, personnel from the *Einsatzkommando* were assigned to the *Kommandeur der Sicherheitspolizei und des SD Krakau* (Commander of Security Police and the SD for Cracow).

EINSATZKOMMANDO 3/I

Formed: August 1939
Campaign: Poland 1939
Commanders: Dr. Alfred Hasselberg
Parent Formation: Einsatzgruppe I
Army Area Assignment: 14th Army (Colonel General List)
Victims: Unknown
Disbanded: November 20, 1939
Known Locations: Neutitschen, Bielsko, Rzeszow
Remarks: After November 1939, personnel from the *Einsatzkommando* were assigned to the *Kommandeur der Sicherheitspolizei und des SD Krakau* (Commander of Security Police and the SD for Cracow).

EINSATZKOMMANDO 4/I

Formed: August 1939
Campaign: Poland 1939
Commanders: Dr. Karl Brunner
Parent Formation: Einsatzgruppe I
Army Area Assignment: 14th Army (Colonel General List)
Victims: Unknown
Disbanded: November 20, 1939
Known Locations: Neutitschen, Bielsko, Rzeszow
Remarks: After November 1939, personnel from the *Einsatzkommando* were assigned to the *Kommandeur der Sicherheitspolizei und des SD Krakau* (Commander of Security Police and the SD for Cracow).

EINSATZKOMMANDO 1/II

Formed: August 1939
Campaign: Poland 1939
Commanders: Otto Sens
Parent Formation: Einsatzgruppe II
Army Area Assignment: 10th Army (General of Artillery von Reichenau)
Victims: Unknown
Disbanded: November 20, 1939
Known Locations: Oppeln, Radomsko, Konskie
Remarks: After November 1939, personnel from the *Einsatzgruppe* were assigned to the *Kommandeur der Sicherheitspolizei und des SD Lublin* (Commander of Security Police and the SD for Lublin).

EINSATZKOMMANDO 2/II

Formed: August 1939
Campaign: Poland 1939
Commanders: Karl-Heinz Rux
Parent Formation: Einsatzgruppe II
Army Area Assignment: 10th Army (General of Artillery von Reichenau)

Victims: Unknown
Disbanded: November 20, 1939
Known Locations: Oppeln, Radomsko, Konskie
Remarks: After November 1939, personnel from the *Einsatzgruppe* were assigned to the *Kommandeur der Sicherheitspolizei und des SD Lublin* (Commander of Security Police and the SD for Lublin).

EINSATZKOMMANDO 1/III

Formed: August 1939
Campaign: Poland 1939
Commanders: Dr. Wilhelm Scharpwinkel
Parent Formation: Einsatzgruppe III
Army Area Assignment: 8th Army (General of Infantry Blaskowitz)
Victims: Unknown
Disbanded: November 20, 1939
Known Locations: Breslau, Gr. Wartenberg, Lodz
Remarks: After November 1939, personnel from the *Einsatzkommando* were assigned to the *Kommandeur der Sicherheitspolizei und des SD Radom* (Commander of Security Police and the SD for Radom).

EINSATZKOMMANDO 2/III

Formed: August 1939
Campaign: Poland 1939
Commanders: Dr. Fritz Liphardt
Parent Formation: Einsatzgruppe III
Army Area Assignment: 8th Army (General of Infantry Blaskowitz)
Victims: Unknown
Disbanded: November 20, 1939
Known Locations: Breslau, Gr. Wartenberg, Lodz
Remarks: After November 1939, personnel from the *Einsatzkommando* were assigned to the *Kommandeur der Sicherheitspolizei und des SD Radom* (Commander of Security Police and the SD for Radom).

EINSATZKOMMANDO 1/IV

Formed: August 1939
Campaign: Poland 1939
Commanders: Dr. Helmut Bischoff
Parent Formation: Einsatzgruppe IV
Army Area Assignment: 4th Army (General of Artillery von Kluge)
Victims: Unknown
Disbanded: November 20, 1939
Known Locations: Jastrow, Zambrow
Remarks: After November 1939, personnel from the *Einsatzkommando* were assigned to the *Kommandeur der Sicherheitspolizei und des SD Warschau* (Commander of Security Police and the SD for Warsaw).

EINSATZKOMMANDO 2/IV

Formed: August 1939
Campaign: Poland 1939
Commanders: Dr. Walter Hammer
Parent Formation: Einsatzgruppe IV
Army Area Assignment: 4th Army (General of Artillery von Kluge)
Victims: Unknown
Disbanded: November 20, 1939
Known Locations: Jastrow, Zambrow
Remarks: After November 1939, personnel from the *Einsatzkommando* were assigned to the *Kommandeur der Sicherheitspolizei und des SD Warschau* (Commander of Security Police and the SD for Warsaw).

EINSATZKOMMANDO 1/V

Formed: August 1939
Campaign: Poland 1939
Commanders: Dr. Heinz Graefe
Parent Formation: Einsatzkommando V
Army Area Assignment: 3rd Army (General of Artillery von Küchler)
Victims: Unknown
Disbanded: November 20, 1939
Known Locations: Mohrungen, Wegrow
Remarks: After November 1939, *Einsatzkommando* personnel assigned to *Stapostelle Hohensalza* (State Police Hohensalza)

EINSATZKOMMANDO 2/V

Formed: August 1939
Campaign: Poland 1939
Commanders: Dr. Robert Schefe
Parent Formation: Einsatzkommando V
Army Area Assignment: 3rd Army (General of Artillery von Küchler)
Victims: Unknown

Disbanded: November 20, 1939
Known Locations: Mohrungen, Wegrow
Remarks: After November 1939, *Einsatzkommando* personnel appear to have returned to their original posts, staffs and units.

EINSATZKOMMANDO 3/V

Formed: August 1939
Campaign: Poland 1939
Commanders: Dr. Walter Albath
Parent Formation: Einsatzkommando V
Army Area Assignment: 3rd Army (General of Artillery von Küchler)
Victims: Unknown
Disbanded: November 20, 1939
Known Locations: Mohrungen, Wegrow
Remarks: After November 1939, *Einsatzkommando* personnel appear to have returned to their original posts, staffs and units.

EINSATZKOMMANDO 1/VI

Formed: August 1939
Campaign: Poland 1939
Commanders: Franz Sommer
Parent Formation: Einsatzgruppe VI
Army Area Assignment: None; assigned to Posen district
Victims: Unknown
Disbanded: November 20, 1939
Known Locations: Posen
Remarks: After November 1939, *Einsatzkommando* personnel assigned to *Stapostelle Lodz* (State Police Lodz).

EINSATZKOMMANDO 2/VI

Formed: August 1939
Campaign: Poland 1939
Commanders: Gerhard Flesch
Parent Formation: Einsatzgruppe VI
Army Area Assignment: None; assigned to Posen district
Victims: Unknown
Disbanded: November 20, 1939
Known Locations: Posen
Remarks: After November 1939, *Einsatzkommando* personnel assigned to *Stapostelle Posen* (State Police Posen).

EINSATZKOMMANDO 16

Formed: September 12, 1939
Campaign: Poland 1939
Commanders: Dr. Rudolf Tröger
Parent Formation: Einsatzgruppe z.b.V von Woysch
Army Area Assignment: None; assigned to West Prussia district
Victims: Unknown
Disbanded: November 20, 1939
Known Locations: Danzig, Bromberg, Thorn
Remarks: Strength was 100 Gestapo and KRIPO officials reinforced by police and SS personnel. After November 1939, *Einsatzkommando* personnel assigned to *Stapostellen Danzig, Bromberg* and *Graudenz* (State Police Danzig, Bromberg and Graudenz).

SONDERKOMMANDO 1a

Formed: June 1941
Campaign: Operation Barbarossa (Invasion of Russia)
Commanders: Dr. Martin Sandberger, Bernhard Baatz
Parent Formation: Einsatzgruppe A
Army Area Assignment: 18th Army
Victims: Unknown
Disbanded: October 1944
Known Locations: Gumbinnen, Liepaya, Yelgava, Mitau, Riga, Pskov, Fellin, Pärnu, Tallinn, Dorpat, Narva
Remarks: On December 3, 1941 its name was changed to *Kommandantur der Sicherheitspolizei und des Sicherheitsdienstes Estland* (Office of the Commander of the Security Police and Security Service Estonia)

SONDERKOMMANDO 1b

Formed: June 1941
Campaign: Operation Barbarossa (Invasion of Russia)
Commanders: Dr. Erich Ehrlinger, Dr. Eduard Strauch, Dr. Erich Isselhorst
Parent Formation: Einsatzgruppe A
Army Area Assignment: 16th Army
Victims: Unknown
Disbanded: October 1943
Known Locations: Kaunas, Minsk, Daugavpils, Zilupe, Ostrav, Rezekne, Staraya Russa, Tschudovo, Tosno, Wilejka
Remarks: On December 3, 1941 its name was changed to *Kommandantur der Sicherheitspolizei und des Sicherheits-*

dienstes Weiss-Ruthenien (Office of the Commander of the Security Police and Security Service in Belorussia)

EINSATZKOMMANDO 1b

Formed: Mid-1942
Campaign: Operation Barbarossa (Invasion of Russia)
Commanders: Dr. Hermann Hubig
Parent Formation: Einsatzgruppe A
Army Area Assignment: Army Group North
Victims: Unknown
Disbanded: November 1942
Known Locations: Loknja

EINSATZKOMMANDO 1c

Formed: August 1942
Campaign: Operation Barbarossa (Invasion of Russia)
Commanders: Kurt Graaf
Parent Formation: Einsatzgruppe A
Army Area Assignment: Army Group North
Victims: Unknown
Disbanded: November 1942
Known Locations: Krasnogwardeisk, Nataljewka

EINSATZKOMMANDO 2

Formed: June 1941
Campaign: Operation Barbarossa (Invasion of Russia)
Commanders: Rudolf Batz, Dr. Eduard Strauch, Dr. Rudolf Lange, Dr. Manfred Pechau, Reinhard Breder, Oswald Poche
Parent Formation: Einsatzgruppe A
Army Area Assignment: Army Group North
Victims: 34,193 +
Disbanded: 1944
Known Locations: Siauliai, Schaulen, Libau, Riga
Remarks: On December 3, 1941 its name was changed to *Kommandantur der Sicherheitspolizei und des Sicherheitsdienstes Lettland* (Office of the Commander of the Security Police and Security Service in Latvia)

EINSATZKOMMANDO 3

Formed: June 1941
Campaign: Operation Barbarossa (Invasion of Russia)
Commanders: Karl Jäger, Dr. Wilhelm Fuchs, Hans Jaochim Böhme
Parent Formation: Einsatzgruppe A
Army Area Assignment:
Victims: 137,346 +
Disbanded: January 1945
Known Locations: Kaunas
Remarks: On December 3, 1941 its name was changed to *Kommandantur der Sicherheitspolizei und des Sicherheitsdienstes Litauen* (Office of the Commander of the Security Police and Security Service Lithuania)

SONDERKOMMANDO 4a

Formed: June 1941
Campaign: Operation Barbarossa (Invasion of Russia)
Commanders: Paul Blobel, Dr. Erwin Weinmann, Eugen Steimle, Theodor Christensen
Parent Formation: Einsatzgruppe C
Army Area Assignment: Army Group South
Victims: 59,018
Disbanded: End of 1943
Known Locations: Lvov, Lutsk, Rovno, Zhitomir, Pereyaslav, Yagotin, Ivankov, Radomyshl, Lubny, Poltava, Kiev, Kursk, Kharkov

SONDERKOMMANDO 4b

Formed: June 1941
Campaign: Operation Barbarossa
Commanders: Günther Herrmann, Fritz Braune, Dr. Walter Haensch, August Meier, Friedrich Suhr, Waldemar Krause
Parent Formation: Einsatzgruppe C
Army Area Assignment: Army Group South
Victims: 6,329 +
Disbanded: January 1944
Known Locations: Lvov, Tarnopol, Kremenchug, Poltava, Slaviansk, Proskurov, Vinnitsa, Kramatorskaya, Gorlovka, Rostov

EINSATZKOMMANDO 5

Formed: June 1941
Campaign: Operation Barbarossa (Invasion of Russia)
Commanders: Erwin Schulz, August Meier
Parent Formation: Einsatzgruppe C
Army Area Assignment: Army Group South

Victims: 46,102 +
Disbanded: January 1942
Known Locations: Lvov, Skwira, Kiev

EINSATZKOMMANDO 6

Formed: June 1941
Campaign: Operation Barbarossa (Invasion of Russia)
Commanders: Dr. Erhard Kröger, Robert Mohr, Ernst Biberstein, Friedrich Suhr
Parent Formation: Einsatzgruppe C
Army Area Assignment: Army Group South
Victims: 5,577 +
Disbanded: November 1943
Known Locations: Lvov, Zlochev, Zhitomir, Proskurov, Vinniza, Dnjepropetrovsk, Krivoi Rog, Stalino, Rostov

SONDERKOMMANDO 7a

Formed: June 1941
Campaign: Operation Barbarossa (Invasion of Russia)
Commanders: Dr. Walter Blume, Eugen Steimle, Karl Matschke, Albert Rapp, Helmut Loos, Dr. Gerhard Bast
Parent Formation: Einsatzgruppe B
Army Area Assignment: 9th Army, 4th Panzer Army
Victims: 1,344 +
Disbanded: November 1944
Known Locations: Vilnius, Newel, Gorodok, Vitebsk, Welish, Rshev, Vyasma, Kalinin, Klinzy
Remarks: Vorkommando Moscow combined with *Sonderkommando 7A* as one unit in December 1943.

SONDERKOMMANDO 7b

Formed: June 1941
Campaign: Operation Barbarossa (Invasion of Russia)
Commanders: Gunther Rausch, Adolf Ott, Karl Rabe
Parent Formation: Einsatzgruppe B
Army Area Assignment: 4th Army, 2nd Army
Victims: 1,822 +
Disbanded: October 1944
Known Locations: Brest, Kobrin, Pruzhany, Slonim, Baranovici, Minsk, Orscha, Klinzy, Bryansk, Kursk, Tschernigov, Orel

EINSATZKOMMANDO 8

Formed: June 1941
Campaign: Operation Barbarossa (Invasion of Russia)
Commanders: Otto Bradfisch, Heinz Richter, Dr. Erich Isselhorst, Hans Schindhelm
Parent Formation: Einsatzgruppe B
Army Area Assignment: Army Group Center
Victims: 20,108 +
Disbanded: October 1943
Known Locations: Volkovisk, Baranovici, Bobruisk, Lahoysk, Mogilev, Minsk

EINSATZKOMMANDO 9

Formed: June 1941
Campaign: Operation Barbarossa (Invasion of Russia)
Commanders: Dr. Alfred Fischer, Oswald Schäfer, Wilhelm Wiebens, Dr. Friedrich Buchardt
Parent Formation: Einsatzgruppe B
Army Area Assignment:
Victims: 11,449 +
Disbanded: March 1944
Known Locations: Vilnius, Grodno, Lida, Bielsk-Podlaski, Nevel, Lepel, Surazh, Vyasma, Gshatsk, Mozhaisk, Vitebsk, Smolensk, Varena

SONDERKOMMANDO 10a

Formed: June 1941
Campaign: Operation Barbarossa (Invasion of Russia)
Commanders: Heinz Seetzen, Dr. Kurt Christmann
Parent Formation: Einsatzgruppe D
Army Area Assignment: 170th Infantry Division, XXXth Army Corps
Victims: Unknown
Disbanded: July 1943
Known Locations: Paleski, Iswary, Petshanka, Belzey, Sudak, Krasnodar, Taganrog

SONDERKOMMANDO 10b

Formed: June 1941
Campaign: Operation Barbarossa (Invasion of Russia)
Commanders: Alois Persterer, Eduard Jedamzik
Parent Formation: Einsatzgruppe D
Army Area Assignment: Army Group A, 11th Army

Victims: Unknown
Disbanded: May 1943
Known Locations: Chernowitz, Mogilev, Podolski, Skadowsk, Feodosia, Naltshik, Prochladny

EINSATZKOMMANDO 11

Formed: July 1942
Campaign: Operation Barbarossa (Invasion of Russia)
Commanders: Dr. Gerhard Bast
Parent Formation: Einsatzgruppe D
Army Area Assignment: Army Group A
Victims: Unknown
Disbanded: May 1943
Known Locations: Maykop, Belaja Glina, Kropotkin, Armawir, Tserkesk, Labinskaya, Chadyshenskaja
Remarks: Formed in July 1942 when *Einsatzkommando* 11a and 11b were combined.

EINSATZKOMMANDO 11a

Formed: June 1941
Campaign: Operation Barbarossa (Invasion of Russia)
Commanders: Paul Zapp
Parent Formation: Einsatzgruppe D
Army Area Assignment: Romanian Army, LIVth Army Corps
Victims: Unknown
Disbanded: July 1942
Known Locations: Nikolayev, Kherson, Kokkosy, Kishinew, Majatschka, Michailovka, Bachtschissari, Yalta

EINSATZKOMMANDO 11a

Formed: 1942
Campaign: Balkans
Commanders: Rudolf Korndorfer
Parent Formation: Einsatzgruppe E
Army Area Assignment: Army Group E
Victims: Unknown
Disbanded: Unknown
Known Locations: Croatia

EINSATZKOMMANDO 11b

Formed: June 1941
Campaign: Operation Barbarossa (Invasion of Russia)
Commanders: Bruno Müller, Dr. Werner Braune, Paul Schulz
Parent Formation: Einsatzgruppe D
Army Area Assignment: Army Group South
Victims: Unknown
Disbanded: July 1942
Known Locations: Odessa, Tighina

EINSATZKOMMANDO 12

Formed: June 1941
Campaign: Operation Barbarossa (Invasion of Russia)
Commanders: Gustav Nosske, Dr. Erich Müller, Günther Herrmann
Parent Formation: Einsatzgruppe D
Army Area Assignment. 6th Army
Victims: Unknown
Disbanded: March 1943
Known Locations: Nikolayev, Fedorovka, Stalino, Starobeschevko, Novoscherkask, Pjatigorsk

EINSATZKOMMANDO 13

Formed: 1944
Campaign: Slovakian Uprising
Commanders: Dr. Hans Jaskulsky
Parent Formation: Einsatzgruppe H
Army Area Assignment: N/A
Victims: Unknown
Disbanded: Late 1944
Known Locations: Slovakia

EINSATZKOMMANDO 14

Formed: Unknown
Campaign: Occupation of the Balkans
Commanders: Dr. Ernst Heuser
Parent Formation: Einsatzgruppe H
Army Area Assignment: Army Group E
Victims: Unknown
Disbanded: 1944
Known Locations: Unknown

EINSATZKOMMANDO 15

Formed: Unknown
Campaign: Occupation of the Balkans

Commanders: Wilhelm Wolter, Dr. Joachim Freitag
Parent Formation: Einsatzgruppe E
Army Area Assignment: Army Group E
Victims: Unknown
Disbanded: Unknown
Known Locations: Unknown

EINSATZKOMMANDO 16

Formed: Unknown
Campaign: Occupation of Balkans
Commanders: Unknown
Parent Formation: Einsatzgruppe E
Army Area Assignment: Croatia
Victims: Unknown

EINSATZKOMMANDO 29

Formed: Unknown
Campaign: Unknown
Commanders: Dr. Helmut Glaser
Parent Formation: Einsatzgruppe H
Army Area Assignment: Army Group E
Victims: Unknown

SONDERKOMMANDO ASTRACHAN

Formed: October 1942
Campaign: Operation Barbarossa (Invasion of Russia)
Commanders: Unknown
Parent Formation: Einsatzgruppe D
Army Area Assignment: Army Group A
Victims: Unknown
Disbanded: Late 1942
Known Locations: Elista

EINSATZKOMMANDO TILSIT

Formed: 1941
Campaign: Operation Barbarossa (Invasion of Russia)
Commanders: Hans-Joachim Böhme
Parent Formation: Einsatzgruppe A
Army Area Assignment: Army Group North
Victims: Unknown
Disbanded: Unknown
Known Locations: Tilsit

VORKOMMANDO MOSCOW

Formed: June 1941
Campaign: Operation Barbarossa (Invasion of Russia)
Commanders: Dr. Franz Six, Waldemar Klingenhöfer, Dr. Erich Körting, Wilhelm Bock, Rudolf Schmücker, Dr. Walter Blume, Wilhelm Eckhardt
Parent Formation: Einsatzgruppe B
Army Area Assignment: Army Group Center
Victims: Unknown
Disbanded: January 1942
Known Locations: Smolensk
Remarks: Also known as Sonderkommando 7C. Amalgamted into Sonderkommando 7A in December 1943.

EINSATZKOMMANDO LUXEMBOURG

Formed: Unknown
Campaign: occupation of Luxembourg
Commanders: Wilhelm Nölle, Erich Hartmann
Parent Formation: RSHA
Army Area Assignment: N/A
Victims: Unknown
Disbanded: 1945

SONDERKOMMANDO 1005

Formed: July 1942
Campaign: Conceal Nazi crimes at *Einsatzkommando* killing sites and at select extermination camps to include Chelmno, Belzec, Treblinka, Sobibór and Auschwitz
Commanders: Paul Blobel
Parent Formation: RSHA
Army Area Assignment: *Einsatzkommando* execution sites in Army Group North, Center and South
Victims: Several thousand; Jews and other prisoners did the heavy physical work of site destruction after which they were put to death.
Disbanded: October 1944
Remarks: *Sonderkommando* 1005 activities in the *Einsatzgruppen* areas got into full swing in the spring of 1943. In the Ukraine, Blobel organized two subordinate units, *Sonderkommando* 1005A and *Sonderkommando* 1005B. The units worked at Babi Yar and Dnepropetrovsk, as well as Berdichev, Uman and Nikolayev. At Minsk, Karl Harder, Blobel's deputy, organized an additional unit, *Sonderkommando* 1005-Mitte. This unit operated in Byelorussia. Other *Sonderkommando* 1005 units saw work in the Baltic states. Most of the German per-

sonnel in the *Sonderkommando* were assembled in Salzburg, Austria in October 1944 and reassigned – again under the command of Paul Blobel – to *Einsatzgruppe* Iltis to fight Yugoslav partisans in the area of Carinthia. *Einsatzgruppe* Iltis fielded two sub-units, *Einsatzkommando* 12 and *Einsatzkommando* 13.

Notes:

[1] International Military Tribunal Nürnberg. *Trials of the Criminals before the International Military Tribunal, Volume IV, United States of America vs. Otto Ohlendorf, et al., Case No.9.* (Washington, D.C.: U.S. Government Printing Office, 1949), p.382.

[2] One source lists the names of *Einsatzgruppe I Prag* as *Einsatzstäbe K* and that for *Einsatzgruppe II Brünn* as *Einsatzstäbe L.*

[3] Andrew Mollo, *Uniforms of the SS: Collected Edition, Volumes 1 to 6.* (London: Windrow & Greene, 1997), p.354.

[4] Yitzhak Arad, Shmuel Krakowski and Shmuel Spector, *The Einsatzgruppen Reports.* (New York: Holocaust Library, 1989), p.ii.

[5] Richard C. Lucas, *The Forgotten Holocaust: The Poles Under German Occupation 1939-1944.* (Lexington, Kentucky: The University Press of Kentucky, 1986), p. 3.

[6] International Military Tribunal Nürnberg. *Trials of War Criminals before the International Military Tribunal, Volume IV, United States of America vs. Otto Ohlendorf, et al.,Case No. 9.* (Washington, DC: U.S. Government Printing Office, 1949), pp. 36-37.

[7] Ronald Headland, *Messages of Murder: A Study of the Reports of the Einsatzgruppen of the Security Police and the Security Service, 1941-1943.* (London: Associated University Presses, 1992), pp. 17-22.

[8] George C. Browder, *Hitler's Enforcers: The Gestapo and the Security Service in the Nazi Revolution.* (New York: Oxford University Press, 1996), p. 233.

[9] Lecture by George C. Browder, U.S. Holocaust Memorial Museum, January 27, 1998.

[10] Headland, *Messages of Murder: A Study of the Reports of the Einsatzgruppen of the Security Police and the Security Service, 1941-1943.*, pp. 138-139.

[11] Arad, Krakowski and Spector, *The Einsatzgruppen Reports.*, pp. v-vii.

[12] Ibid., p. viii.

[13] Ibid., p. viii.

[14] Ibid., p. ix.

[15] Heinz Höhne, *The Order of the Death's Head.* (New York: Coward-McCann, INC., 1970), p. 358.

[16] George H. Stein, *The Waffen SS: Hitler's Elite Guard at War.* (Ithaca, NY: Cornell University Press, 1966), p. 264.

[17] Many of the *Waffen-SS* troops came from SS Infantry Regiment 14 (motorized), a unit formed in February 1941 but disbanded in June 1941.

[18] I believe the original intent was for the *Sonderkommandos* to continue to follow closely behind the German Army even after deep advances were made, while the *Einsatzkommandos* would drop off and be responsible for clearing geographic areas. In reality, the terms appear to have had little real difference; in fact, some reports misname the formations from time to time, substituting *Einsatzkommandos* for *Sonderkommandos.*

[19] Andrew Ezergailis, *The Holocaust in Latvia 1941-1944.* (Riga, Latvia: The Historical Institute of Latvia, 1996), pp.392-394.

[20] Höhne, *The Order of the Death's Head.*, p.358.

[21] International Military Tribunal Nürnberg, *Trials of War Criminals before the International Military Tribunal, Volume IV, United States of America vs. Otto Ohlendorf, et al.,Case No. 9.*, pp. 36-37.

[22] United States Holocaust Memorial Museum, Center for Advanced Holocaust Studies Presentation: *Collaboration in the Holocaust: Crimes of the Local Police in Belorussia and Ukraine, 1941-1944*, by Martin Dean, Senior Historian, Metropolitan Police War Crimes Unit, New Scotland Yard, London.

[23] Eugen Kogon, Herman Langbein and Adalbert Rückerl, *Nazi Mass Murder: A Documentary of the Use of Poison Gas.* (New Haven, CT: Yale University Press, 1993), p.52.

[24] Israel Gutman, editor in chief, *Encyclopedia of the Holocaust*, Volume 2. (New York: MacMillan Publishing Company, 1990), pp. 541-542.

[25] Eugen Kogon, Hermann Langbein, and Adalbert Rückerl, *Nazi Mass Murder. A Documentary of the Use of Poison Gas.* (New Haven, CN: Yale University Press, 1993), p.58

[26] Eugen Kogon, Hermann Langbein, and Adalbert Rückerl, *Nazi Mass Murder. A Documentary of the Use of Poison Gas.* (New Haven, CN: Yale University Press, 1993), pp. 59-61.

[27] Ibid., p. 61.

[28] Ibid., p. 60.

[29] Ernst Klee, Willi Dressen and Volker Riess, *The Good Old Days: The Holocaust as Seen by Its Perpetrators and Bystanders.* (New York: The Free Press, 1988), p.70.

[30] International Military Tribunal Nürnberg, *Trials of War Criminals before the International Military Tribunal, Volume IV, United States of America vs. Otto Ohlendorf, et al.,Case No. 9.*, p.448.

[31] Ernst Klee, Willi Dressen and Volker Riess, *The Good Old Days: The Holocaust as Seen by Its Perpetrators and Bystanders.* (New York: The Free Press, 1988), pp. 28-29.

[32] Höhne, *The Order of the Death's Head*, p.369.

[33] Headland, *Messages of Murder*, p.47.

[34] Arad, Krakowski and Spector, *The Einsatzgruppen Reports.*, pp. iv-v.

[35] Gerald Reitlinger, *The House Built on Sand: The Conflicts of German Policy in Russia.* (New York: The Viking Press, 1960), p. 85.

[36] Ibid., p. 96.

[37] Matthew Cooper, *The German Army 1933-1945.* (New York: Stein and Day, 1978), p. 548.

[38] International Military Tribunal Nürnberg, *Trials of War Criminals before the International Military Tribunal, Volume IV, United States of America vs. Otto Ohlendorf, et al., Case No. 9.* (Washington, DC: U.S. Government Printing Office, 1949), p. 43.

[39] Eberhard escaped post-war accountibility for Babi Yar; he died in Stuttgart in 1947.

[40] Reitlinger, *The House Built on Sand*, p. 111.

[41] Lothar Hartung, *Verleihungs-Urkunden des 3. Reiches*, (Fürstentum, Liechtenstein: Infora Research Est., 1982), p.71.

[42] Personalakt Erich Ehrlinger, Washington, D.C: National Archives Microfilm Publication A3343, Records of SS Officers from the Berlin Document Center, Roll SSO-177.

[43] Ibid., p. 235.

[44] Abraham J. Edelheit, and Hershel Edelheit, *History of the Holocaust.* (Boulder, CO: Westview Press, 1994), p. 420.

[45] Daniel Jonah Goldhagen, *Hitler's Willing Executioners.* (New York: Vintage Books, 1997), pp. 181-182.

[46] Ibid., pp. 271-273.

[47] United States Holocaust Memorial Museum. Center for Advanced Holocaust Studies Presentation: *Collaboration in the Holocaust: Crimes of the Local Police in Belorussia and Ukraine, 1941-1944*, by Martin Dean, Senior Historian, Metropolitan Police War Crimes Unit, New Scotland Yard, London.

[48] United States Holocaust Memorial Museum. Center for Advanced Holocaust Studies Presentation: *Collaboration in the Holocaust: Crimes of the Local Police in Belorussia and Ukraine, 1941-1944*, by Martin Dean, Senior Historian, Metropolitan Police War Crimes Unit, New Scotland Yard, London.

[49] Yehoshua Büchler, "*Kommandostab Reichsführer-SS: Himmler's Personal Murder Brigades in 1941*", *Holocaust and Genocide Studies*, Vol. 1, No. 1, (London: Pergamon, 1986), pp. 16-17.

[50] French MacLean, *The Cruel Hunters: SS-Sonderkommando Dirlewanger, Hitler's Most Notorious Anti-Partisan Unit.* (Atglen, PA: Schiffer Publishing, 1998).

[51] Yehoshua Büchler, *"Kommandostab Reichsführer-SS: Himmler's Personal Murder Brigades in 1941".*

[52] Shmuel Spector, "Aktion 1005", *Holocaust and Genocide Studies*, Vol.5 No.2. (Oxford, England: Pergamon Press, 1990), pp. 157-173.

[53] International Military Tribunal Nürnberg, *Trials of War Criminals before the International Military Tribunal, Volume IV, United States of America vs. Otto Ohlendorf, et al., Case No. 9.* (Washington, DC: U.S. Government Printing Office, 1949.), p. 479.

[54] The bulk of the information on the *Einsatzkommandos* came from Andrew Mollo's *Uniforms of the SS; Collected Edition, Volumes 1-6* (London: Windrow & Greene, 1997), pp. 354-359, and throughout Helmut Krausnick's and Hans-Heinrich Wilhelm's *Die Truppen des Weltanschauungs-Krieges: Die Einsatzgruppen der Sicherheitspolizei und des SD 1938-1942.*

2

THE SS OFFICERS

We get rid of these people [the Jews] the way a physician gets rid of bacteria.[1]

- Josef Goebbels, 1939

SS OFFICER RANKS

The SS initially established a rank system in August 1929 and modified the structure on four additional occasions.[2] The officer ranks, from lowest to highest, follow in their final form. These ranks belonged to the *Allgemeine-SS* – the general SS, the overall body of the SS, distinct from the *Waffen-SS*. Officers who also belonged to the *Waffen-SS* (the SS field troops) could have a separate rank in that organization. Therefore, a colonel in the *Allgemeine-SS*, who volunteered for front-line service in the *Waffen-SS*, might only be a captain in that organization. Not all *Allgemeine-SS* officers were in the *Waffen-SS*.[3]

SS-Untersturmführer – 2nd Lieutenant. The lowest commissioned officer rank in the SS, this position evolved in October 1934 from the original rank called *SS-Sturmführer*. An officer of this rank would command a platoon of approximately thirty men or hold a position of equal responsibility. By July 1935 there were 1,767 officers of this rank.[4] This figure increased to 6,650 by the end of 1938.[5]

SS-Obersturmführer – 1st Lieutenant. This rank was established in May 1933. An officer of this rank could serve as a platoon leader or, if necessary, a company commander in charge of seventy to one hundred twenty men. As of July 1935 there were 786 *SS-Obersturmführern*; the total increased to 3,449 by 1938.

SS-Hauptsturmführer – Captain. This rank evolved in October 1934 from the position of *SS-Sturmhauptführer*, which had been established in May 1933. This most senior of the company grade ranks would command a *Sturm*, or company, of between seventy and one hundred twenty men.[6] By July 1935 there were 495 officers in this rank. This number more than tripled to 1,855 in 1938.

SS-Sturmbannführer – Major. This was one of the original ranks from 1929 and was the junior field grade rank. He would command a *Sturmbann* (battalion) consisting of three *Sturm*. By July 1935 there were 474 *SS-Sturmbannführern*; by 1938 there were 892.

SS-Obersturmbannführer – Lieutenant Colonel. This rank was instituted in May 1933. An officer of this rank could command a battalion or hold an equivalent level of responsibility. By July 1935 there were 118 officers of this rank in the SS. This total increased to 382 by the end of 1938.

SS-Standartenführer – Colonel. This was one of the original 1929 ranks; this officer would command three or four *Sturmbanne* which made up a *Standarte* or regiment. By July 1935 there were 113 *SS-Standartenführern*; by the end of 1938 there were 307 officers of this rank.

SS-Oberführer – Senior Colonel. This was also one of the original ranks of 1929. This most senior field grade officer would command several *Standarten* which formed an *Untergruppe*. By July 1935 there were 60 officers of this rank. Three years later there were 215.

SS-Brigadeführer – Brigadier General ★. This lowest of the general officer ranks was formed in May 1933; this level officer would command several *Untergruppen* formed into a *Gruppe*. An officer of this rank in the *Waffen-SS* would be titled *SS-Brigadeführer und Generalmajor der Waffen-SS*.[7] By July 1935 there were 22 *SS-Brigadeführer*. At the end of 1938 there were 49.

SS-Gruppenführer – Major General ★★. This rank was one of the initial positions and its holder would command an *Oberabschnitt* or several *Gruppen*. In the *Waffen-SS* this rank was *SS-Gruppenführer und Generalleutnant der Waffen-SS*. By July 1935 there were 29 officers of this rank in the SS. This more than doubled to 51 by 1938.

SS-Obergruppenführer – Lieutenant General ★★★. These few individuals served as the corporate heads of the SS. An individual in the *Waffen-SS* would be titled *SS-Obergruppenführer und General der Waffen-SS*. By July 1935 there were 8 *SS-Obergruppenführer*; three years later there were 17 officers with this rank.

SS-Oberstgruppenführer – General ★★★★ – Colonel General in the German army system of ranks. This rank was introduced in the SS in 1942.

Reichsführer-SS – Field Marshal ★★★★★. Heinrich Himmler was the sole holder of this rank.

SS OFFICER POSITIONS

Officer positions within the mobile killing formations were very similar to positions in a battalion. Every *Einsatzgruppe*, *Einsatzkommando* and *Sonderkommando* had a commissioned officer as the commander. The commander of an *Einsatzgruppe* could generally be equated to a battalion commander, although the *Einsatzgruppe* commander was generally several ranks higher than his Waffen-SS battalion counterpart based on what Reinhard Heydrich undoubtedly perceived to be the sensitive and independent nature of the position. An *Einsatzkommando* or *Sonderkommando* commander had the resources similar to a Waffen-SS company commander – again, the ranks for these men were somewhat higher than those authorized for a *Waffen-SS* company. Some, but not all, *Teilkommandos* were commanded by an officer. A *Teilkommando* was similar in many respects to a platoon; although, again, a *Teilkommando* was a much more independently operating unit than even a *Waffen-SS* reconnaissance platoon. Some commanders had assistants, to help them in their daily tasks; these officers were known as either chiefs of staff or adjutants. The chief of staff or adjutant would assume temporary command if the unit commander were away on business or leave.

The *Einsatzgruppen* had additional officers who functioned as a battalion staff: administrative officers, signal officers, training officers, motor pool officers and supply officers. All these positions could be held by commissioned officers. Their functions were readily apparent. An administrative officer handled pay, reports, mail, personnel reports, etc. A signal officer commanded the radio and teletype operators; he would be the first to be blamed if required reports were not received in Berlin in a timely manner. The training officer handled mandatory tactical and indoctrination instruction. The motor pool officer had a big job keeping the relatively large numbers of motorcycles, command cars and trucks running. Mobility was crucial to the success of the *Einsatzkommando*, and the primitive roads, weather conditions and long lines of supply conspired to break both machines and mechanics. The supply officers worked hard as well, coordinating with the army and other SS units for rations, water, fuel, medical supplies, ammunition, spare parts and lodging. In some of the *Einsatzkommandos* these positions were manned by non-commissioned officers due to a shortage of officers.

Some additional SS officer positions are included in the compilation that follows because these officers were detailed temporarily to the operational zones of the *Einsatzkommandos* to issue mobile gas vans, conduct inspection tours, etc. These SS officers, however, were not directly assigned to the *Einsatzgruppen* or carried on the personnel rosters. They would visit the *Einsatzgruppen* for a few days and then return to Berlin.

OFFICER BIOGRAPHIES

The following pages detail the more important personal and career information of the SS officers who actually worked in an *Einsatzgruppe* or *Einsatzkommando*. To help standardize the information, and to assist in the evaluation of this data in Chapter 3, the following data-field explanations are provided:

Last Name – self-explanatory. This does not account for any officer who may have changed his last name after the war. One SS officer changed his name during the war and is so noted.

First Name – self-explanatory; includes any academic titles such as "Dr."

Date of Birth – self-explanatory. The final authority for this information came from the National Archives microfilm reels of the Berlin Document Center collection of SS officer personnel files.

Place of Birth – for officers born inside Germany, the town or city is listed. For those born outside of Germany, the country is included as well. A few of the very small towns could actually have been in Austria but were not so annotated in the file.

Highest SS Rank – denotes the highest rank an officer achieved in the *Allgemeine-SS*. The SS personnel files reliably kept this information through February/March 1945, so it is possible an officer could have received a further promotion after this date; there are no SS rank lists (*Dienstaltersliste*) for 1945. This category lists the highest rank achieved; if an officer was subsequently demoted due to a disciplinary infraction, that fact is annotated later in the record under ***Notes***.

SS Number – denotes the number each SS man received upon entering the organization. The lower the number, the earlier the individual entered the SS. There are a handful of instances where an officer did not have an SS number listed in his file; no two SS personnel had the same number.

Date Entered SS – self-explanatory.

NSDAP Number – denotes the number each new member received on joining the National Socialist Workers Party of Germany [*NSDAP*] (the Nazi Party). Again, the smaller the number, the earlier the individual joined. Many SS officers never joined the Nazi Party, as some felt party membership was superflous and unnecessary.

Date Entered NSDAP – self-explanatory.

Marital Status – found in the personnel records. If an officer had been divorced and then remarried, he is listed as "Married." Obviously, any change in marital status after the war is not reflected here.

Religion – found in the personnel records. A more detailed explanation of the categories is in Chapter 3.

Civilian Occupation – occupation of the officer before he joined the SS. In some instances, such as doctor or lawyer, the individual continued his trade in the SS/SD.

Education – level of schooling. When known, the institution of higher learning (e.g. University of Frankfurt) is listed.

World War I Service – information about an individual's service in the Great War. This includes decorations received, unit assigned, etc.

Einsatzkommando – lists all *Einsatzgruppen* or *Einsatzkommando* units in which the officer is known to have served.

Position – lists the specific position in which the officer served during his *Einsatzkommando* service. Unfortunately, this information is frequently not found in the officer's personnel file.

Einsatzkommando Service – period of service with the *Einsatzkommando*.

Other Assignments – lists other wartime assignments, both before and after *Einsatzkommando* service.

Post-War Sentence – describes known sentences and actual time served for those *Einsatzkommando* officers tried after the war. The Allies conducted several trials immediately after the war and some of the *Einsatzkommando* personnel were tried at this time. The Federal Republic of Germany held other war-related trials in the 1950s through the 1980s. Some *Einsatzkommando* officers were brought to justice in these proceedings. The absence of information in this category can indicate that an officer was not tried; it can also mean that he was, but that information on the length of sentence is sealed within the German court system, or that I simply could not find it.

Post-War Employment – self explanatory. If an individual did not survive the war, was executed after the war, or actually served a life imprisonment sentence, then this category is labeled N/A. Absence of any comment indicates the data is unknown.

Highest Decoration – this category lists the highest decoration received by each officer during the war. In Chapter 3 the various types and grades of each award will be discussed in full detail.

Notes – a catch-all category. The reader will find several instances of the notation "No mention of *Einsatzkommando* service in personnel file." In these instances I used secondary sources, to include law enforcement and judicial files to determine whether or not an individual served in an *Einsatzkommando*.

National Archives Microfilm Reel – gives the reel number from the set of records known as Microfilm Publication A3343, *Records of SS Officers from the Berlin Document Center, Se-*

ries SSO – Officer Personnel Records. These SS officers' service records consist of the personnel dossiers for more than 61,000 SS officers with the rank of second lieutenant and above. The date span of the records contained in the dossiers extends from 1932 to as late as March 1945 in some cases. In those instances where no personnel file exists on microfilm (either the file was destroyed in the war or for some reason was never microfilmed) I have referred to Microfilm Publication A3343, *Records of SS Officers from the Berlin Document Center, Series RS – SS Race and Settlement Office (RuSHA, Rasse-und Siedlungshauptamt)*. This office had the responsibility of safeguarding the racial purity of the SS – by serving as an oversight board for prospective marriages. The collection has 240,000 dossiers for individual SS personnel and their prospective spouses, who submitted detailed personal and family background information in order to receive permission to marry.

The overwhelming majority of information for each man comes from these microfilm reels. Post-war information can be found in the publication of the International Military Tribunal Nürmberg, "Trials of War Criminals Before the International Military Tribunal, Volume IV, United States of America vs. Otto Ohlendorf, et al., Case No.9." Additional sentencing information is included in Adelheid L. Rüter-Ehlermann's, *Justiz und NS-Verbrechen: Sammlung Deutscher Strafurteile wegen Nationalsozialistischer Tötungsverbrechen 1945-1966* (Amsterdam: University Amsterdam Press, 1968).

Notes:

[1] Viktor Reimann, *Goebbels*. Translated by Stephen Wendt. (Garden City, N.Y.: Doubleday & Company, 1976), p.102.

[2] All rank histories come from John Angolia, *Cloth Insignia of the SS*, (San Jose, CA: R. James Bender Publishing, 1983), p.21

[3] The SS Main Office (*SS-Hauptamt* or *SS-HA*) controlled the entire SS establishment to include the *Waffen-SS* and the *Allgemeine* or General SS. This office evolved in the mid-1930s and controlled such functions as personnel, administration, medical, physical training, education, communications and so forth. As the *SS-HA* controlled all branches of the SS, it grew in both complexity and size. In 1942 it was scaled back somewhat as more and more of the SS became centered around the *Waffen-SS*. The SS Main Operational Office (*SS-Führungshauptamt* or *SS-FHA*) was essentially the headquarters of the *Waffen-SS*. Created in August 1940, it was designed to control the organization of field units of the SS and to monitor the training and replacement units of the *Waffen-SS*. It additionally looked after training schools of the *Waffen-SS*. The *SS-FHA* had two subordinate branches, the *Kommandoamt Allgemeine-SS*, which dealt with the general SS, and the *Kommandoamt der Waffen-SS*. The *SS-FHA* was independent of the SS Main Office.

[4] All 1935 rank totals come from the *Dienstaltersliste der Schutzstaffel der N.S.D.A.P., Stand vom 1. Juli 1935* (Berlin: Personalkanzlei des Reichsführers-SS, 1935).

[5] All 1938 rank totals come from the *Dienstaltersliste der Schutzstaffel der N.S.D.A.P., Stand vom 1. December 1938*. (Berlin: Personalkanzlei des Reichsführers-SS, 1939).

[6] All SS unit descriptions come from Heinz Höhne, *The Order of the Death's Head*. Translated by Richard Barry. (New York: Coward-McCann, 1970), p. 58.

[7] In 1940 *Reichsführer-SS* Heinrich Himmler instituted combined titles through the equivalent Army general officer ranks in an effort to further assimilate the *Waffen-SS* with its Army comrades in arms, and give senior *Waffen-SS* officers some interservice credibility.

Achamer-Pifrader

First Name: Dr. Humbert
Date of Birth: 20 November 1900
Place of Birth: Teplitz-Schönau, Austria
Highest Rank: SS-Oberführer
SS Number: 275750
Date Entered SS: 3 September 1935
NSDAP Number: 614104
Date Entered NSDAP: 10 November 1931
Marital Status: Married
Religion: Agnostic
Civilian Occupation: Lawyer
Education: University
Foreign Language: French
World War I Service: Yes, 1st Tirolean Rifle Regiment
EINSATZKOMMANDO: **A**
Position: Commander
Einsatzkommando Service: 10 September 1942 – 4 September 1943
Other Assignment: SD Wiesbaden
SD Stettin
Highest Award: German Cross in Silver
Notes: Killed in bombing raid, 25 April 1945 in Linz
Received Iron Cross 2nd Class for *Einsatzkommando* service
National Archives File: A3343 SSO-002

Albath

First Name: Dr. Walter
Date of Birth: 7 December 1904
Place of Birth: Strasburg, Prussia
Highest Rank: SS-Standartenführer
SS Number: 260971
Date Entered SS: 1 June 1933
NSDAP Number: 1719177
Date Entered NSDAP: 1 April 1933
Marital Status: Married
Religion: Agnostic
Civilian Occupation: Lawyer
Education: University of Kiel, Göttingen
Foreign Language: No
World War I Service: No
EINSATZKOMMANDO: **3/V**
Position: Commander
Einsatzkommando Service: Polish Campaign
Other Assignment: SD Düsseldorf
Highest Award: War Service Cross 1st Class
Postwar Sentence: No judicial proceedings discovered
Notes: Short personnel file
National Archives File: A3343 SSO-004

Amelung

First Name: Waldemar
Date of Birth: 11 November 1914
Place of Birth: Kopjoni, Russia
Highest Rank: SS-Obersturmführer
SS Number: 357294
Date Entered SS: 1 February 1940
NSDAP Number: 8537705
Marital Status: Married
Religion: Agnostic
Civilian Occupation: Textile technician
Education: Grade School
Foreign Language: Latvian, Russian
World War I Service: No
EINSATZKOMMANDO: **A**
Commander: No
Position: Not listed
Einsatzkommando Service: Not listed
Other Assignment: RSHA, Office III B (SD, Ethnos)
Highest Award: Iron Cross 2nd Class
Postwar Sentence: No judicial proceedings discovered
Notes: Served in Latvian Army, 1933-1934; father killed in 1918
Eastern People's Medal, Infantry Assault Badge
National Archives File: A3343 SSO-012

Armbrecht

First Name: Helmuth
Date of Birth: 19 November 1908
Place of Birth: Goslar
Highest Rank: SS-Untersturmführer
SS Number: 353467
Date Entered SS: Not listed
NSDAP Number: 3117254
Date Entered NSDAP: 1 May 1933
Marital Status: Married
Religion: Agnostic
Civilian Occupation: Police
Education: Grade School
Foreign Language: No
World War I Service: No
EINSATZKOMMANDO: **D**
Position: Not listed
Einsatzkommando Service: May 1941 – 3 October 1942
Other Assignment: RSHA, Office IV D (Gestapo, Spheres of Influence)
Gestapo Hildesheim
Highest Award: War Service Cross 2nd Class
Postwar Sentence: No judicial proceedings discovered
Notes: In Police since 1928; wounded in action; Crimea Shield
National Archives File: A3343 SSO-017

Arnold

First Name: Johannes
Date of Birth: 25 September 1907
Place of Birth: Helbersdorf
Highest Rank: SS-Untersturmführer
SS Number: 267364
Date Entered SS: Not listed
NSDAP Number: 135311
Date Entered NSDAP: 1 June 1929
Marital Status: Single
Religion: Agnostic
Civilian Occupation: Businessman
Education: Grade School
Foreign Language: No
World War I Service: No
EINSATZKOMMANDO: **D**
Position: Not listed
Einsatzkommando Service: Not listed
Other Assignment: RSHA
Highest Award: War Service Cross 2nd Class
Postwar Sentence: No judicial proceedings discovered
Notes: Served in SA, 1929-1935; Crimea Shield
No mention of *Einsatzkommando* service in personnel file
National Archives File: A3343 SSO-018

Auerswald

First Name: Wilhelm
Date of Birth: 7 July 1907
Place of Birth: Eschwege
Highest Rank: SS-Untersturmführer
SS Number: 327404
Date Entered SS: 1 May 1939
NSDAP Number: 814348
Date Entered NSDAP: 1 December 1931
Marital Status: Married
Religion: Agnostic
Civilian Occupation: Police
Education: High School
Foreign Language: No
World War I Service: No
EINSATZKOMMANDO: **A**
Commander: No
Position: Administration section
Einsatzkommando Service: July 1941–1943
Other Assignment: SS Detachment Fulda-Werra
Highest Award: None listed
Postwar Sentence: No judicial proceedings discovered
Notes: Served in SA, 1931-1933
National Archives File: A3343 SSO-020

Auinger

First Name: Dr. Josef
Date of Birth: 1 December 1897
Place of Birth: Enzendorf, Austria
Highest Rank: SS-Obersturmbannführer
SS Number: 342812
Date Entered SS: 1 April 1934
NSDAP Number: 6149119
Date Entered NSDAP: 1 June 1933
Marital Status: Married
Religion: Catholic
Civilian Occupation: Police
Education: High School
Foreign Language: No
World War I Service: Yes, Prisoner of War in Russia
EINSATZKOMMANDO: **7b**
Position: Deputy Commander
Einsatzkommando Service: 1942
Other Assignment: SD Vienna
SD Budapest
Highest Award: None listed
Postwar Sentence: No judicial proceedings discovered
Notes: Short personnel file
National Archives File: A3343 SSO-021

Avril

First Name: Franz
Date of Birth: 27 October 1911
Place of Birth: Kaiserslautern
Highest Rank: SS-Untersturmführer
SS Number: 67687
Date Entered SS: 1 March 1930
NSDAP Number: 3070110
Date Entered NSDAP: 1 May 1933
Marital Status: Single
Religion: Agnostic
Civilian Occupation: Civil Servant
Education: High School
Foreign Language: No
World War I Service: No
EINSATZKOMMANDO: **IV, z.b.V.**
Position: z.b.V. – *Teilkommando* Bonifer
Einsatzkommando Service: IV, Polish Campaign; z.b.v., 3 July 1941 – 11 August 1941
Other Assignment: RSHA, Office III C (SD, Domestic, Culture)
SD Warsaw
Highest Award: War Service Cross 2nd Class
Postwar Sentence: No judicial proceedings discovered
Notes: No mention of *Einsatzkommando* z.b.V. service in file
National Archives File: A3343 SSO-022

Baatz

First Name: Bernhard
Date of Birth: 19 November 1910
Place of Birth: Doernitz
Highest Rank: SS-Obersturmbannführer
SS Number: 46414
Date Entered SS: 1 July 1932
NSDAP Number: 941790
Date Entered NSDAP: 1 March 1932
Marital Status: Married
Religion: Agnostic
Civilian Occupation: Lawyer Assistant
Education: High School
Foreign Language: No
World War I Service: No
EINSATZKOMMANDO: **1a**
Position: Commander
Einsatzkommando Service: 1 August 1943 – 15 October 1944
Other Assignment: RSHA, Office IV D (Gestapo, Spheres of Influence)
Security Police, Sudetenland
Highest Award: War Service Cross 1st Class
Postwar Sentence: No judicial proceedings discovered
Notes: Short personnel file
National Archives File: A3343 SSO-023

Backhaus

First Name: Gerhard-Alfred
Date of Birth: 14 June 1912
Place of Birth: Berlin
Highest Rank: SS-Hauptsturmführer
SS Number: 127570
Date Entered SS: 1 June 1933
NSDAP Number: 602665
Date Entered NSDAP: 1 August 1931
Marital Status: Married
Religion: Agnostic
Civilian Occupation: Police
Education: High School
Foreign Language: No
World War I Service: No
EINSATZKOMMANDO: **2**
Position: Pay inquiries officer
Einsatzkommando Service: Not listed
Other Assignment: SD Potsdam
RSHA, Office IV B4 (Gestapo, Evacuations and Jews)
Highest Award: War Service Cross 2nd Class
Postwar Sentence: No judicial proceedings discovered
Notes: Served 10 days house arrest in 1943
National Archives File: A3343 SSO-025

Barth

First Name: Dr. Horst
Date of Birth: 22 August 1890
Place of Birth: Stenn
Highest Rank: SS-Obersturmbannführer
SS Number: 381550
Date Entered SS: 6 December 1938
NSDAP Number: 4773187
Date Entered NSDAP: 1 May 1937
Marital Status: Single
Religion: Agnostic
Civilian Occupation: Lawyer
Education: University
Foreign Language: No
World War I Service: Yes, Iron Cross 2nd Class
EINSATZKOMMANDO: **2**
Position: Not listed
Einsatzkommando Service: 1941
Other Assignment: SD Zwickau
Criminal Police Cracow
Highest Award: War Service Cross 2nd Class
Notes: Suicide 1961 at beginning of judicial proceedings against him
National Archives File: A3343 SSO-035

Bast

First Name: Dr. Gerhard
Date of Birth: 12 January 1911
Place of Birth: Gottschen, Austria
Highest Rank: SS-Sturmbannführer
SS Number: 23064
Date Entered SS: Not listed
NSDAP Number: 612972
Date Entered NSDAP: 30 October 1931
Marital Status: Single
Religion: Agnostic
Civilian Occupation: Lawyer
Education: University of Graz
Foreign Language: No
World War I Service: No
EINSATZKOMMANDO: **11a, 7a, H**
Position: 11a – Commander; 7a – Commander
Einsatzkommando Service: 11a, November 1942 – December 1942; 7a, June 1944 – November 1944
Other Assignment: Police, Münster; Police Linz
Highest Award: War Service Cross 1st Class
Notes: Accidentally killed 12 year old in hunting accident. Murdered in 1947
National Archives File: A3343 SSO-038

Batz

First Name: Dr. Rudolf
Date of Birth: 10 November 1903
Place of Birth: Langensalza
Highest Rank: SS-Standartenführer
SS Number: 272458
Date Entered SS: 10 December 1935
NSDAP Number: 2955905
Date Entered NSDAP: 1 May 1933
Marital Status: Married
Religion: Agnostic
Civilian Occupation: Lawyer
Education: University of Göttingen, Munich
Foreign Language: No
World War I Service: No
EINSATZKOMMANDO: **2**
Position: Commander
Einsatzkommando Service: 1 June 1941– 4 November 1941
Other Assignment: Commander, SD Cracow
SD Den Haag
Highest Award: War Service Cross 1st Class
Postwar Sentence: No judicial proceedings discovered
Notes: Suicide 1961
National Archives File: A3343 SSO-038

Baumgarten

First Name: Wilhelm
Date of Birth: 22 December 1894
Place of Birth: Magdeburg
Highest Rank: SS-Hauptsturmführer
SS Number: 66997
Date Entered SS: 26 July 1933
NSDAP Number: 6979
Date Entered NSDAP: 4 June 1925
Marital Status: Married
Religion: Agnostic
Civilian Occupation: Businessman
Education: High School/Trade School
Foreign Language: No
World War I Service: Yes, 26th Infantry Regiment
EINSATZKOMMANDO: **B**
Position: Not listed
Einsatzkommando Service: Not listed
Other Assignment: SD Posen; SD Königsberg
Highest Award: War Service Cross 2nd Class
Postwar Sentence: No judicial proceedings discovered
Notes: Wounded WWI; served in SA 1931-33; Golden Party Badge
No mention of *Einsatzkommando* service in personnel file
National Archives File: A3343 SSO-044

Becker

First Name: Dr. August
Date of Birth: 17 August 1900
Place of Birth: Staufenberg
Highest Rank: SS-Obersturmführer
SS Number: 5325
Date Entered SS: 1 February 1931
NSDAP Number: 293346
Date Entered NSDAP: 1 September 1930
Marital Status: Married
Religion: None
Civilian Occupation: Chemist
Education: University of Giessen
Foreign Language: No
World War I Service: Yes, 25th Reserve Field Artillery Regiment
EINSATZKOMMANDO: **A, B, C, D**
Position: Gas van inspector from the RSHA
Einsatzkommando Service: 1941-1942
Other Assignment: RSHA, Office II D (SD, Technical Matters)
Highest Award: None listed
Postwar Sentence: No judicial proceedings discovered
Notes: Not actually assigned, but supervised gas van killings
Charged with assault in 1941
National Archives File: A3343 SSO-049

Bemmann

First Name: Horst
Date of Birth: 28 October 1912
Place of Birth: Chemnitz
Highest Rank: SS-Hauptsturmführer
SS Number: 348141
Date Entered SS: 1 December 1938
NSDAP Number: 4306478
Date Entered NSDAP: 1 May 1937
Marital Status: Married
Religion: Agnostic
Civilian Occupation: Police
Education: High School
Foreign Language: English, French
World War I Service: No
EINSATZKOMMANDO: **D**
Position: Criminal Police section
Einsatzkommando Service: Not listed
Other Assignment: RSHA; Criminal Police Linz
Highest Award: War Service Cross 1st Class
Postwar Sentence: No judicial proceedings discovered
Notes: Served in SA, 1933-1936; Anti-Partisan Badge
Short personnel file
National Archives File: A3343 SSO-055

Bergmann

First Name: Heinrich
Date of Birth: 21 November 1902
Place of Birth: Kassel
Highest Rank: SS-Hauptsturmführer
SS Number: 372279
Date Entered SS: 1 April 1939
NSDAP Number: 5698408
Date Entered NSDAP: 1 March 1937
Marital Status: Married
Religion: Agnostic
Civilian Occupation: Police
Education: Grade School
Foreign Language: English
World War I Service: Yes
EINSATZKOMMANDO: **A**
Position: Gestapo section; *teilkommando* leader
Einsatzkommando Service: 17 November 1941–1944
Other Assignment: RSHA, Office VI (SD, Foreign)
Highest Award: War Service Cross 1st Class
Postwar Sentence: No judicial proceedings discovered
Notes: Freikorps
House in Stuttgart destroyed in bombing raid
National Archives File: A3343 SSO-060

Besekow

First Name: Arno
Date of Birth: 3 January 1914
Place of Birth: Magdeburg
Highest Rank: SS-Hauptsturmführer
SS Number: 375209
Date Entered SS: 31 January 1938
NSDAP Number: 1631259
Date Entered NSDAP: 1 April 1933
Marital Status: Married
Religion: Agnostic
Civilian Occupation: Banker
Education: High School
Foreign Language: French, English
World War I Service: No
EINSATZKOMMANDO: **2**
Position: Gestapo section liaison with Latvians
Einsatzkommando Service: July 1941 – 2 October 1941
Other Assignment: Unknown
Highest Award: War Service Cross 1st Class
Postwar Sentence: No judicial proceedings discovered
Notes: War Service Cross 2nd Class while in *Einsatzkommando*
National Archives File: A3343 SSO-064

Beutel

First Name: Lothar
Date of Birth: 6 May 1902
Place of Birth: Leipzig
Highest Rank: SS-Brigadeführer
SS Number: 2422
Date Entered SS: 8 May 1930
NSDAP Number: 135238
Date Entered NSDAP: 1 June 1929
Marital Status: Divorced
Religion: Agnostic
Civilian Occupation: Pharmacist
Education: University
Foreign Language: No
World War I Service: No
EINSATZKOMMANDO: **IV**
Position: Commander
Einsatzkommando Service: Polish Campaign
Other Assignment: RSHA
Highest Award: None listed
Postwar Sentence: No judicial proceedings discovered
Notes: Thrown out of SS 23 October 1939
National Archives File: A3343 SSO-066

Biberstein

First Name: Ernst
Date of Birth: 15 February 1899
Place of Birth: Hilchenbach
Highest Rank: SS-Sturmbannführer
SS Number: 272692
Date Entered SS: 13 September 1936
NSDAP Number: 40718
Date Entered NSDAP: 19 July 1926
Marital Status: Married
Religion: Protestant
Civilian Occupation: Protestant pastor
Education: University of Kiel
Foreign Language: No
World War I Service: Yes, infantry private
EINSATZKOMMANDO: **6**
Position: Commander
Einsatzkommando Service: September 1942 – May 1943
Other Assignment: Economic office, Trieste
Highest Award: None listed
Postwar Sentence: 1948, Death commuted to Life, released
Notes: Golden Party Badge
Original surname of Szymanowski
National Archives File: A3343 SSO-066

Bierkamp

First Name: Dr. Walther
Date of Birth: 17 December 1901
Place of Birth: Hamburg
Highest Rank: SS-Brigadeführer
SS Number: 310172
Date Entered SS: 1 April 1939
NSDAP Number: 1408449
Date Entered NSDAP: 1 December 1932
Marital Status: Married
Religion: Agnostic
Civilian Occupation: Lawyer
Education: University
Foreign Language: No
World War I Service: Freikorps Bahrenfeld
EINSATZKOMMANDO: **D**
Position: Commander
Einsatzkommando Service: 30 June 1942 – 15 June 1943
Other Assignment: SD Cracow, Commander
HSSPF Southeast
Highest Award: War Service Cross 1st Class
Notes: SD Belgium and Northern France
Killed in action 16 April 1945 in Hamburg
National Archives File: A3343 SSO-068

Birkner

First Name: Wolfgang
Date of Birth: 27 October 1913
Place of Birth: Breslau
Highest Rank: SS-Hauptsturmführer
SS Number: 265793
Date Entered SS: 30 July 1934
NSDAP Number: 3601309
Date Entered NSDAP: 1 April 1935
Marital Status: Married
Religion: Agnostic
Civilian Occupation: Police
Education: University
Foreign Language: No
World War I Service: No
EINSATZKOMMANDO: *Einsatzkommando* in Poland, **z.b.V.**
Position: Not listed
Einsatzkommando Service: Polish Campaign; z.b.V., 1941
Other Assignment: RSHA; SD Schneidemuhl
Waffen-SS Service: LSSAH, 1934-1936
Highest Award: War Service Cross 2nd Class
Postwar Sentence: No judicial proceedings discovered
Notes: SD Warsaw; SD Halle
National Archives File: A3343 SSO-072

Bischoff

First Name: Helmut
Date of Birth: 1 March 1908
Place of Birth: Glogau
Highest Rank: SS-Obersturmbannführer
SS Number: 272403
Date Entered SS: Not listed
NSDAP Number: 203122
Date Entered NSDAP: 1 March 1930
Marital Status: Married
Religion: Agnostic
Civilian Occupation: Lawyer
Education: High School
Foreign Language: No
World War I Service: No
EINSATZKOMMANDO: **1/IV**
Position: Commander
Einsatzkommando Service: Polish Campaign
Other Assignment: SD Magdeburg
SD Posen
Highest Award: War Service Cross 1st Class
Postwar Sentence: No judicial proceedings discovered
Notes: Iron Cross 2nd Class
National Archives File: A3343 SSO-073

Bleckmann

First Name: Kurt
Date of Birth: 10 April 1902
Place of Birth: Barmen
Highest Rank: SS-Obersturmführer
SS Number: 391773
Date Entered SS: 15 February 1941
NSDAP Number: 5066984
Date Entered NSDAP: 1 May 1937
Marital Status: Married
Religion: Agnostic
Civilian Occupation: Dental Technician
Education: High School
Foreign Language: No
World War I Service: No
EINSATZKOMMANDO: **2**
Position: Not listed
Einsatzkommando Service: Not listed
Other Assignment: Unknown
Highest Award: None listed
Postwar Sentence: No judicial proceedings discovered
Notes: Served in German Army, 1936-1937
National Archives File: A3343 SSO-075

Bleymehl

First Name: Otto
Date of Birth: 23 April 1906
Place of Birth: Riegelsberg
Highest Rank: SS-Hauptsturmführer
SS Number: 278543
Date Entered SS: 15 January 1936
NSDAP Number: 6905631
Date Entered NSDAP: 1 June 1936
Marital Status: Married
Religion: Agnostic
Civilian Occupation: High School Teacher
Education: University of Kiel
Foreign Language: No
World War I Service: No
EINSATZKOMMANDO: **A**
Position: Criminal Police section
Einsatzkommando Service: 1941–1942
Other Assignment: RSHA, Office V (Kripo)
SD Leaders School
Highest Award: None listed
Postwar Sentence: No judicial proceedings discovered
Notes: Short personnel file
National Archives File: A3343 SSO-076

Blobel

First Name: Paul
Date of Birth: 13 August 1894
Place of Birth: Potsdam
Highest Rank: SS-Standartenführer
SS Number: 29100
Date Entered SS: 1 December 1931
NSDAP Number: 844662
Date Entered NSDAP: 1 December 1931
Marital Status: Married
Religion: Protestant
Civilian Occupation: Architect
Education: Vocational School
Foreign Language: No
World War I Service: Yes, Iron Cross 1st Class
EINSATZKOMMANDO: **4a, 1005**
Position: Commander
Einsatzkommando Service: 4a – June 1941 – January 1942;
1005 – July 1942 – July 1944
Other Assignment: Commander, SD Salzburg
SD Düsseldorf
Highest Award: Bar to Iron Cross 1st Class
Postwar Sentence: 1948, Death; executed 7 June 1951
Notes: Commander, *Einsatzgruppe Iltis*, 1944, fighting partisans
National Archives File: A3343 SSO-076

Blume

First Name: Dr. Walter
Date of Birth: 23 July 1906
Place of Birth: Dortmund
Highest Rank: SS-Standartenführer
SS Number: 267224
Date Entered SS: 11 April 1935
NSDAP Number: 3282505
Date Entered NSDAP: 1 May 1933
Marital Status: Married
Religion: Agnostic
Civilian Occupation: Lawyer
Education: University of Erlangen, Bonn, Jena, Münster
Foreign Language: No
World War I Service: No
EINSATZKOMMANDO: **7a**
Position: Commander
Einsatzkommando Service: June 1941–September 1941
Other Assignment: Commander, SD Greece; SD Düsseldorf
Highest Award: Iron Cross 1st Class
Postwar Sentence: 1948, Death commuted to Life, released
Notes: War Service Cross 1st Class
Iron Cross 2nd Class while in *Einsatzkommando*
National Archives File: A3343 SSO-078

Blunck

First Name: Adolf
Date of Birth: 19 August 1909
Place of Birth: Hamburg-Altona
Highest Rank: SS-Hauptsturmführer
SS Number: 36235
Date Entered SS: 5 October 1933
NSDAP Number: 156379
Date Entered NSDAP: 1 September 1929
Marital Status: Married
Religion: Agnostic
Civilian Occupation: Shipbuilding
Education: High School
Foreign Language: English
World War I Service: No
EINSATZKOMMANDO: **C, F**
Position: Not listed
Einsatzkommando Service: C, 1942–1944; F, 1944
Other Assignment: RSHA
SD Hungary
Highest Award: None listed
Postwar Sentence: No judicial proceedings discovered
Notes: Served in SA, 1929-1933
National Archives File: A3343 SSO-079

Bock

First Name: Wilhelm
Date of Birth: 11 September 1903
Place of Birth: Lübeck
Highest Rank: SS-Standartenführer
SS Number: 11348
Date Entered SS: 1 August 1935
NSDAP Number: 170613
Date Entered NSDAP: 1 November 1929
Marital Status: Married
Religion: Agnostic
Civilian Occupation: Police
Education: High School
Foreign Language: French, English
World War I Service: No
EINSATZKOMMANDO: **Vorkommando Moscow**
Position: Commander
Einsatzkommando Service: January 1942–June 1942
Other Assignment: SD Vienna
SSPF Winniza
Highest Award: War Service Cross 1st Class
Postwar Sentence: No judicial proceedings discovered
Notes: Short personnel file
National Archives File: A3343 SSO-080

Bock

First Name: Erich
Date of Birth: 10 April 1911
Place of Birth: Gleiwitz
Highest Rank: SS-Hauptsturmführer
SS Number: 119426
Date Entered SS: 1 March 1933
NSDAP Number: 1940762
Date Entered NSDAP: 1 May 1933
Marital Status: Married
Religion: Agnostic
Civilian Occupation: Student
Education: University of Berlin
Foreign Language: No
World War I Service: No
EINSATZKOMMANDO: **D**
Position: Not listed
Einsatzkommando Service: 1941
Other Assignment: RSHA
SD Breslau
Highest Award: War Service Cross 2nd Class
Postwar Sentence: No judicial proceedings discovered
Notes: Short personnel file
National Archives File: A3343 SSO-079

Böhm

First Name: Johannes
Date of Birth: 17 February 1912
Place of Birth: Dresden
Highest Rank: SS-Hauptsturmführer
SS Number: 133828
Date Entered SS: 14 March 1933
NSDAP Number: 1377591
Date Entered NSDAP: 1 November 1932
Marital Status: Married
Religion: Agnostic
Civilian Occupation: Police
Education: High School
Foreign Language: No
World War I Service: No
EINSATZKOMMANDO: **z.b.V.**
Position: *Teilkommando* Böhm, leader
Einsatzkommando Service: 3 July 1941–11 August 1941
Other Assignment: Unknown
Highest Award: None listed
Postwar Sentence: No judicial proceedings discovered
Notes: No mention of *Einsatzkommando* service in personnel file
National Archives File: A3343 SSO-082

Böhme

First Name: Hans-Joachim
Date of Birth: 10 January 1909
Place of Birth: Magdeburg
Highest Rank: SS-Sturmbannführer
SS Number: 151121
Date Entered SS: 1 November 1933
NSDAP Number: 2316680
Date Entered NSDAP: 1 May 1933
Marital Status: Single
Religion: Agnostic
Civilian Occupation: Lawyer
Education: University
EINSATZKOMMANDO: **3, Tilsit**
Position: Commander
Einsatzkommando Service: Tilsit, 1941-1942; 3, 11 May 1944 – 1 January 1945
Other Assignment: SD Kiel; SD Kauen
Waffen-SS Service: 4th SS Division "Polizei", 1945
Highest Award: None listed
Postwar Sentence: 1958, 15 years
Postwar Employment: Tax accountant
Notes: Black Wound Badge, 29 December 1943; RSHA
Died 31 May 1960
National Archives File: A3343 SSO-083

Böhme

First Name: Horst-Alwin
Date of Birth: 24 August 1902
Place of Birth: Colmnitz
Highest Rank: SS-Oberführer
SS Number: 2821
Date Entered SS: 1 February 1930
NSDAP Number: 236651
Date Entered NSDAP: 1 May 1930
Marital Status: Married
Religion: Agnostic
Civilian Occupation: Police
Education: Trade School
Foreign Language: English, French
World War I Service: No
EINSATZKOMMANDO: **B, C**
Position: B – Commander; C – Commander
Einsatzkommando Service: B, 12 March 1943 – 28 August 1943; C, 6 September 1943 – March 1944
Other Assignment: Commander, SD Königsberg; BdS Prague
Highest Award: War Service Cross 1st Class
Postwar Sentence: No judicial proceedings discovered
Notes : Proposed extermination of Lidice as retaliation for death of Reinhard Heydrich
National Archives File: A3343 SSO-083

Bolte

First Name: Dr. Heinrich
Date of Birth: 26 November 1908
Place of Birth: Winzlar
Highest Rank: SS-Sturmbannführer
SS Number: 107470
Date Entered SS: 9 March 1935
NSDAP Number: 252390
Date Entered NSDAP: 1 June 1930
Marital Status: Married
Religion: Agnostic
Civilian Occupation: Lawyer
Education: University of Göttingen, Munich
Foreign Language: No
World War I Service: No
EINSATZKOMMANDO: **D**
Position: Not listed
Einsatzkommando Service: Until 13 October 1942
Other Assignment: RSHA
SD Frankfurt/Main
Highest Award: War Service Cross 2nd Class
Postwar Sentence: No judicial proceedings discovered
Notes: SD Lodz
National Archives File: A3343 SSO-088

Bonifer

First Name: Adolf
Date of Birth: 23 November 1908
Place of Birth: Darmstadt
Highest Rank: SS-Sturmbannführer
SS Number: 107487
Date Entered SS: 10 March 1935
NSDAP Number: 1202335
Date Entered NSDAP: 1 August 1932
Marital Status: Married
Religion: Agnostic
Civilian Occupation: Architect
Education: University
Foreign Language: English, French
World War I Service: No
EINSATZKOMMANDO: **z.b.V.**
Position: *Teilkommando* Bonifer, leader
Einsatzkommando Service: 3 July 1941–11 August 1941
Other Assignment: HSSPF Paris; SD Dortmund
Highest Award: War Service Cross 2nd Class
Postwar Sentence: No judicial proceedings discovered
Notes: Served in SA, 1932-1935
No mention of *Einsatzkommando* service in personnel file
National Archives File: A3343 SSO-090

Borck

First Name: Waldemar
Date of Birth: 1 April 1897
Place of Birth: St. Petersburg, Russia
Highest Rank: SS-Hauptsturmführer
SS Number: 13089
Date Entered SS: 1 August 1931
NSDAP Number: 618520
Date Entered NSDAP: 1 September 1931
Marital Status: Married
Religion: Agnostic
Civilian Occupation: Businessman
Education: High School
Foreign Language: Russian
World War I Service: Yes, served in Russian Army
EINSATZKOMMANDO: **7a**
Position: Possibly interrogator
Einsatzkommando Service: 22 June 1941–undetermined
Other Assignment: RSHA; SD Danzig
Highest Award: War Service Cross 1st Class
Postwar Sentence: No judicial proceedings discovered
Notes: Baltic German; Iron Cross 2nd Class
Black Wound Badge, Eastern People's Medal; Anti-Partisan Badge
National Archives File: A3343 SSO-091

Bosse

First Name: Dr. Heinrich
Date of Birth: 10 August 1907
Place of Birth: Riga, Russia
Highest Rank: SS-Obersturmführer
SS Number: 357262
Date Entered SS: 1 February 1940
NSDAP Number: 8222713
Date Entered NSDAP: 1 August 1942
Marital Status: Married
Religion: Protestant
Civilian Occupation: Teacher
Education: University
Foreign Language: Latvian
World War I Service: No
EINSATZKOMMANDO: **A**
Position: Not listed, probably an interpreter
Einsatzkommando Service: 1941–June 1943
Other Assignment: Unknown
Highest Award: War Service Cross 1st Class
Postwar Sentence: No judicial proceedings discovered
Notes: Lived in Latvia until 1939
National Archives File: A3343 SSO-094

Botor

First Name: Paul-Anton
Date of Birth: 2 January 1907
Place of Birth: Unknown
Highest Rank: SS-Untersturmführer
SS Number: 52360
Date Entered SS: Not listed
NSDAP Number: Not a member
Marital Status: Unknown
Religion: Unknown
Civilian Occupation: Unknown
Education: Unknown
Foreign Language: No
World War I Service: No
EINSATZKOMMANDO: **2**
Position: Transportation section
Einsatzkommando Service: July 1941–May 1942
Other Assignment: Unknown
Highest Award: None listed
Killed in Action: No
Postwar Sentence: No judicial proceedings discovered
Notes: Short personnel file
National Archives File: A3343 SSO-095

Bradfisch

First Name: Dr. Otto
Date of Birth: 10 May 1903
Place of Birth: Zweibruecken
Highest Rank: SS-Obersturmbannführer
SS Number: 310180
Date Entered SS: 26 September 1938
NSDAP Number: 405869
Date Entered NSDAP: 1 January 1931
Marital Status: Married
Religion: Agnostic
Civilian Occupation: Lawyer
Education: University of Freiburg, Leipzig
Foreign Language: No
World War I Service: No
EINSATZKOMMANDO: **8**
Position: Commander
Einsatzkommando Service: June 1941–1 April 1942
Other Assignment: SD Neustadt
Commander, SD Lodz
Highest Award: War Service Cross 1st Class
Postwar Sentence: 1961, 13 years commuted to 6 years
Notes: Received Iron Cross 2nd Class in the *Einsatzkommando*
National Archives File: A3343 SSO-096

Brand

First Name: Paul
Date of Birth: 7 September 1911
Place of Birth: Fichtig
Highest Rank: SS-Obersturmführer
SS Number: 52830
Date Entered SS: 1 January 1932
NSDAP Number: 861838
Date Entered NSDAP: 1 December 1931
Marital Status: Married
Religion: Agnostic
Civilian Occupation: Salesman
Education: High School
Foreign Language: No
World War I Service: No
EINSATZKOMMANDO: **II**
Position: Not listed
Einsatzkommando Service: Polish Campaign
Other Assignment: RSHA; SD Lublin
Highest Award: War Service Cross 2nd Class
Postwar Sentence: No judicial proceedings discovered
Notes: Possibly in *Einsatzgruppe B*
Personnel file severely burned
National Archives File: A3343 SSO-098

Brauer

First Name:	Leo
Date of Birth:	3 July 1904
Place of Birth:	Minsk, Russia
Highest Rank:	SS-Obersturmführer
SS Number:	365187
Date Entered SS:	1 May 1940
NSDAP Number:	8606907
Date Entered NSDAP:	Not listed
Marital Status:	Married
Religion:	Protestant
Civilian Occupation:	Businessman
Education:	University of Cracow
Foreign Language:	Polish
World War I Service:	No
EINSATZKOMMANDO:	**B**
Position:	Interrogator
Einsatzkommando Service:	1941–1942
Other Assignment:	RSHA; SD Lodz
Highest Award:	War Service Cross 2nd Class
Postwar Sentence:	No judicial proceedings discovered
Notes:	Lived in Poland, 1918-1939 Served in Polish Army 1929-1930
National Archives File:	A3343 SSO-100

Braune

First Name:	Fritz
Date of Birth:	18 July 1910
Place of Birth:	Mehrstedt
Highest Rank:	SS-Obersturmbannführer
SS Number:	272564
Date Entered SS:	1 November 1935
NSDAP Number:	498084
Date Entered NSDAP:	1 December 1931
Marital Status:	Married
Religion:	Agnostic
Civilian Occupation:	Businessman
Education:	High School
Foreign Language:	No
World War I Service:	No
EINSATZKOMMANDO:	**4b**
Position:	Commander
Einsatzkommando Service:	1 October 1941–21 March 1942
Other Assignment:	RSHA, Office I A 4 (Personnel); SD Oslo
Highest Award:	War Service Cross 1st Class
Postwar Sentence:	1973, 9 years
Notes:	Probably served in an *Einsatzkommando* in Czechoslovakia in 1938; Served in SA, 1931-1936; SD District Southwest
National Archives File:	A3343 SSO-102

Braune

First Name:	Dr. Werner
Date of Birth:	11 April 1909
Place of Birth:	Mehrstedt
Highest Rank:	SS-Obersturmführer
SS Number:	107364
Date Entered SS:	18 November 1934
NSDAP Number:	581277
Date Entered NSDAP:	1 July 1931
Marital Status:	Married
Religion:	Agnostic
Civilian Occupation:	Lawyer
Education:	University of Jena, Bonn, Munich
Foreign Language:	No
World War I Service:	No
EINSATZKOMMANDO:	**11b**
Position:	Commander
Einsatzkommando Service:	October 1941–September 1942
Other Assignment:	SD Halle; SD Oslo
Highest Award:	None listed
Postwar Sentence:	1948, Death; executed 7 June 1951
Postwar Employment:	N/A
Notes:	Served in SA, 1931-1934; brother of Fritz Braune
National Archives File:	A3343 SSO-102

Breder

First Name:	Reinhard
Date of Birth:	2 February 1911
Place of Birth:	Steinhagen
Highest Rank:	SS-Sturmbannführer
SS Number:	116663
Date Entered SS:	Not listed
NSDAP Number:	5653771
Date Entered NSDAP:	1 May 1937
Marital Status:	Married
Religion:	Agnostic
Civilian Occupation:	Lawyer
Education:	University of Göttingen, Bamburg
Foreign Language:	English, French
World War I Service:	No
EINSATZKOMMANDO:	**2**
Position:	Commander
Einsatzkommando Service:	26 March 1942–July 1943
Other Assignment:	SD Düsseldorf SD Frankfurt/Main
Highest Award:	War Service Cross 1st Class
Postwar Sentence:	No judicial proceedings discovered
Notes:	Promoted to officer rank in 1939
National Archives File:	A3343 SSO-102

Breun

First Name: Hanns
Date of Birth: 20 October 1911
Place of Birth: Golgenhof
Highest Rank: SS-Obersturmführer
SS Number: 152193
Date Entered SS: 1 May 1935
NSDAP Number: 4583193
Date Entered NSDAP: 1 May 1937
Marital Status: Married
Religion: Agnostic
Civilian Occupation: Mechanic
Education: Trade School
Foreign Language: No
World War I Service: No
EINSATZKOMMANDO: **III, 4a**
Position: Not listed
Einsatzkommando Service: III, Polish Campaign; 4a, Unknown
Other Assignment: SD Kassel
Highest Award: War Service Cross 1st Class
Postwar Sentence: No judicial proceedings discovered
Notes: Promoted to officer rank in 1938
National Archives File: A3343 SSO-105

Bruennert

First Name: Reinhold-Max
Date of Birth: 26 April 1915
Place of Birth: Langenlohe
Highest Rank: SS-Untersturmführer
SS Number: 257788
Date Entered SS: 1 August 1934
NSDAP Number: 3601346
Date Entered NSDAP: 1 May 1935
Marital Status: Married
Religion: Agnostic
Civilian Occupation: Businessman
Education: High School
EINSATZKOMMANDO: **C,** *einsatzgruppe* in Poland
Position: Adjutant
Einsatzkommando Service: 1942–1943; Polish Campaign
Other Assignment: RSHA; SD Warsaw
Waffen-SS Service: 1st SS Division "Leibstandarte Adolf Hitler", 1940
Highest Award: War Service Cross 2nd Class
Postwar Sentence: 1961, 4 years
Postwar Employment: Construction firm
Notes: Served in SS propaganda company in 1st SS Division Lost a leg in a post-war accident
National Archives File: A3343 SSO-110

Brunner

First Name: Dr. Karl
Date of Birth: 26 July 1900
Place of Birth: Passau
Highest Rank: SS-Brigadeführer
SS Number: 107161
Date Entered SS: 15 June 1934
NSDAP Number: 1903386
Date Entered NSDAP: 1 May 1933
Marital Status: Married
Religion: Agnostic
Civilian Occupation: Lawyer
Education: University of Munich
Foreign Language: No
World War I Service: Yes, Iron Cross 2nd Class, 16th Bavarian Infantry (Hitler's Rgt.)
EINSATZKOMMANDO: **4/I**
Position: Commander
Einsatzkommando Service: Polish Campaign
Other Assignment: RSHA, Office I (Personnel); Gestapo Munich; SD Salzburg
Highest Award: Iron Cross 1st Class
Postwar Sentence: No judicial proceedings discovered
Notes: SSPF Bozen, Belluno Died 7 December 1980
National Archives File: A3343 SSO-112

Brunnschmid

First Name: Klaus
Date of Birth: 23 October 1913
Place of Birth: St. Johann, Austria
Highest Rank: SS-Obersturmführer
SS Number: 202967
Date Entered SS: 20 May 1932
NSDAP Number: 1451141
Date Entered NSDAP: 15 February 1933
Marital Status: Single
Religion: Agnostic
Civilian Occupation: Construction engineer
Education: University
Foreign Language: No
World War I Service: No
EINSATZKOMMANDO: **D**
Position: Not listed
Einsatzkommando Service: Not listed
Other Assignment: RSHA
Highest Award: None listed
Postwar Sentence: No judicial proceedings discovered
Notes: Served in Hitler Youth, 1929-1932
National Archives File: A3343 SSO-112

Buchardt

First Name: Dr. Friedrich
Date of Birth: 17 March 1909
Place of Birth: Riga, Russia
Highest Rank: SS-Obersturmbannführer
SS Number: 290961
Date Entered SS: 20 January 1938
NSDAP Number: 7675607
Date Entered NSDAP: 1 July 1940
Marital Status: Married
Religion: Agnostic
Civilian Occupation: Lawyer
Education: University
Foreign Language: Latvian, Russian
EINSATZKOMMANDO: **B, 9**
Position: Commander
Einsatzkommando Service: January 1943–March 1944
Other Assignment: SD Lodz; RSHA, Office III B (SD, Domestic, Ethnos)
Waffen-SS Service: XIIth SS Corps, 1944
Highest Award: Iron Cross 1st Class
Postwar Sentence: No judicial proceedings discovered
Notes: Infantry Assault Badge (while in 2nd SS Police Regiment)
Eastern People's Medal
National Archives File: A3343 SSO-113

Buschta

First Name: Franz
Date of Birth: 30 March 1905
Place of Birth: Graz, Austria
Highest Rank: SS-Untersturmführer
SS Number: 236855
Date Entered SS: 1 June 1932
NSDAP Number: 300715
Date Entered NSDAP: 1 October 1930
Marital Status: Married
Religion: Agnostic
Civilian Occupation: Bank teller
Education: Grade School
Foreign Language: No
World War I Service: No
EINSATZKOMMANDO: **D**
Position: Not listed
Einsatzkommando Service: Not listed
Other Assignment: RSHA, Office I (Personnel)
Highest Award: War Service Cross 2nd Class
Postwar Sentence: No judicial proceedings discovered
Notes: Served in Hitler Youth, 1922-1923; served in SA, 1923-1924
Golden Hitler Youth Badge
National Archives File: A3343 SSO-124

Callsen

First Name: Kuno
Date of Birth: 19 October 1911
Place of Birth: Wilster
Highest Rank: SS-Sturmbannführer
SS Number: 107362
Date Entered SS: 22 November 1934
NSDAP Number: 647505
Date Entered NSDAP: 1 October 1931
Marital Status: Married
Religion: Agnostic
Civilian Occupation: Newsman
Education: High School
Foreign Language: No
World War I Service: No
EINSATZKOMMANDO: **4a**
Position: *Teilkommando* leader
Einsatzkommando Service: 1942
Other Assignment: RSHA, Office I (Personnel);
RSHA, Office III (SD, Domestic)
Highest Award: Iron Cross 2nd Class
Postwar Sentence: 1968, 7 years
Notes: Iron Cross 2nd Class, 8 Dec 41
Commander, SD Lüneburg
National Archives File: A3343 SSO-125

Christensen

First Name: Theodor
Date of Birth: 7 May 1905
Place of Birth: Kiel
Highest Rank: SS-Sturmbannführer
SS Number: 36169
Date Entered SS: Not listed
NSDAP Number: 383020
Date Entered NSDAP: 1 December 1930
Marital Status: Married
Religion: Agnostic
Civilian Occupation: Banker
Education: Trade School
Foreign Language: No
World War I Service: No
EINSATZKOMMANDO: **4a, 12**
Position: 4a – Commander; 12 – Commander
Einsatzkommando Service: 4a – January 1943–1943; 12 – 1944
Other Assignment: SD Königsberg
RSHA, Office III (SD, Domestic)
Highest Award: Eastern Front Medal
Postwar Sentence: No judicial proceedings discovered
Notes: Also served in SD Paris
National Archives File: A3343 SSO-128

Christmann

First Name: Dr. Kurt
Date of Birth: 1 June 1907
Place of Birth: Munich
Highest Rank: SS-Obersturmbannführer
SS Number: 103057
Date Entered SS: Not listed
NSDAP Number: 3203599
Date Entered NSDAP: 1 May 1933
Marital Status: Married
Religion: Agnostic
Civilian Occupation: Accountant
Education: University of Munich
Foreign Language: No
EINSATZKOMMANDO: **10a**
Position: Commander
Einsatzkommando Service: 1 August 1942–July 1943
Other Assignment: Commander, SD Salzburg; RSHA
Highest Award: War Service Cross 1st Class
Postwar Sentence: 10 years
Postwar Employment: Furniture salesman
Notes: Iron Cross 2nd Class; Blood Order
Fled to Argentina; returned 1956
National Archives File: A3343 SSO-128

Daiber

First Name: Paul
Date of Birth: 17 June 1909
Place of Birth: Gosslershausen
Highest Rank: SS-Obersturmführer
SS Number: 267345
Date Entered SS: 30 January 1936
NSDAP Number: 577829
Date Entered NSDAP: 1 July 1931
Marital Status: Married
Religion: Agnostic
Civilian Occupation: Construction engineer
Education: Technical School Danzig
Foreign Language: English, French, Swedish
World War I Service: No
EINSATZKOMMANDO: **A**
Position: Signal officer
Einsatzkommando Service: Not listed
Other Assignment: HSSPF Spree, Signal Officer; RSHA
Highest Award: None listed
Postwar Sentence: No judicial proceedings discovered
Notes: Served in SA, 1931-1933
Served in Hitler Youth, 1933-1934
National Archives File: A3343 SSO-134

Damzog

First Name: Ernst
Date of Birth: 30 October 1882
Place of Birth: Strassburg
Highest Rank: SS-Brigadeführer
SS Number: 36157
Date Entered SS: 15 June 1933
NSDAP Number: 5081001
Date Entered NSDAP: 1 May 1937
Marital Status: Married
Religion: Agnostic
Civilian Occupation: Police
Education: Middle School
Foreign Language: No
World War I Service: Yes, Iron Cross 2nd Class, 6th Artillery Regiment
EINSATZKOMMANDO: **V**
Position: Commander
Einsatzkommando Service: Polish Campaign
Other Assignment: SD Posen
RSHA
Highest Award: War Service Cross 1st Class
Postwar Sentence: No judicial proceedings discovered
Notes: Bar to Iron Cross 2nd Class, 1940
National Archives File: A3343 SSO-135

Deumling

First Name: Dr. Joachim
Date of Birth: 25 January 1910
Place of Birth: Büngerhof
Highest Rank: SS-Obersturmbannführer
SS Number: 187708
Date Entered SS: Not listed
NSDAP Number: 1142286
Date Entered NSDAP: 1 May 1932
Marital Status: Married
Religion: Agnostic
Civilian Occupation: Lawyer
Education: University
Foreign Language: No
World War I Service: No
EINSATZKOMMANDO: **10b**
Position: Commander
Einsatzkommando Service: 1944, Croatia
Other Assignment: RSHA, Office IV D 2 (Gestapo, Spheres of Influence)
SD Oppeln
Highest Award: War Service Cross 1st Class
Postwar Sentence: No judicial proceedings discovered
Served in Army flak unit, 1935, 1937, 1938
National Archives File: A3343 SSO-145

Discar

First Name: Hans
Date of Birth: 26 July 1911
Place of Birth: Ransitsch
Highest Rank: SS-Hauptsturmführer
SS Number: 307412
Date Entered SS: Not listed
NSDAP Number: 874648
Date Entered NSDAP: 1 December 1931
Marital Status: Single
Religion: Agnostic
Civilian Occupation: Police
Education: Grade School
Foreign Language: No
World War I Service: No
EINSATZKOMMANDO: **D**
Position: Not listed
Einsatzkommando Service: Not listed
Other Assignment: RSHA
Highest Award: War Service Cross 2nd Class
Postwar Sentence: No judicial proceedings discovered
Notes: Served in SA, 1933-1934; served in Army's 30th Infantry Regiment, 1935
No mention of *Einsatzkommando* service in personnel file
National Archives File: A3343 SSO-154

Döring

First Name: Wilhelm
Date of Birth: 21 July 1917
Place of Birth: Hindenburg
Highest Rank: SS-Obersturmführer
SS Number: 375186
Date Entered SS: 1 May 1938
NSDAP Number: Not a member
Marital Status: Married
Religion: Catholic
Civilian Occupation: Police
Education: High School
Foreign Language: No
World War I Service: No
EINSATZKOMMANDO: **8**
Position: November 1941–April 1943
Other Assignment: Criminal Police Gleiwitz
Highest Award: None listed
Postwar Sentence: 1964, 4 years
Postwar Employment: Police, Sollingen, before 1964
Notes: Served in Hitler Youth 1933
No mention of *Einsatzkommando* service in personnel file
National Archives File: A3343 SSO-159

Domnick

First Name: Paul
Date of Birth: 21 December 1895
Place of Birth: Wartenburg
Highest Rank: SS-Obersturmführer
SS Number: 290837
Date Entered SS: Not listed
NSDAP Number: 2077744
Date Entered NSDAP: 1 May 1933
Marital Status: Married
Religion: Agnostic
Civilian Occupation: Police
Education: Grade School
Foreign Language: Polish
World War I Service: Yes, Iron Cross 2nd Class, 376th Infantry Regiment
EINSATZKOMMANDO: **C, H, EG** in Poland
Position: Not listed
Einsatzkommando Service: Polish Campaign; H – 1944
Other Assignment: Commander, Security Police Troppau
RSHA
Highest Award: War Service Cross 2nd Class
Postwar Sentence: No judicial proceedings discovered
Notes: Wounded in WWI; SD Lublin
National Archives File: A3343 SSO-160

Dressler

First Name: Hans-Eugen
Date of Birth: 19 January 1913
Place of Birth: Moscow, Russia
Highest Rank: SS-Hauptsturmführer
SS Number: 335605
Date Entered SS: Not listed
NSDAP Number: 7753638
Date Entered NSDAP: Not listed
Marital Status: Married
Religion: Agnostic
Civilian Occupation: Economist
Education: High School
Foreign Language: Danish, Latvian
World War I Service: No
EINSATZKOMMANDO: **A**
Position: Interrogator
Einsatzkommando Service: July 1941–November 1941
Other Assignment: RSHA
Highest Award: Iron Cross 2nd Class
Postwar Sentence: No judicial proceedings discovered
Notes: First wife died in childbirth
National Archives File: A3343 SSO-163

Drexel

First Name: Max
Date of Birth: 2 May 1914
Place of Birth: Böblingen
Highest Rank: SS-Hauptsturmführer
SS Number: 290148
Date Entered SS: Not listed
NSDAP Number: 5892002
Date Entered NSDAP: 1 May 1937
Marital Status: Married
Religion: Agnostic
Civilian Occupation: Unknown
Education: Grade School
Foreign Language: No
World War I Service: No
EINSATZKOMMANDO: **D**
Position: Not listed
Einsatzkommando Service: Not listed
Other Assignment: RSHA
Highest Award: None listed
Postwar Sentence: No judicial proceedings discovered
Notes: Served in Hitler Youth, 1933-1934; served in SA, 1934-1937 No mention of *Einsatzkommando* service in personnel file
National Archives File: A3343 SSO-163

Ebeling

First Name: Kurt
Date of Birth: 26 December 1908
Place of Birth: Pretzin
Highest Rank: SS-Obersturmführer
SS Number: 390577
Date Entered SS: 1 April 1939
NSDAP Number: 4604834
Date Entered NSDAP: 1 May 1937
Marital Status: Married
Religion: Agnostic
Civilian Occupation: Police
Education: High School
Foreign Language: No
World War I Service: No
EINSATZKOMMANDO: **B**
Position: Not listed
Einsatzkommando Service: Not listed
Other Assignment: RSHA; Police Hamburg; SD Lüneburg
Highest Award: None listed
Killed in Action: No
Postwar Sentence: No judicial proceedings discovered
Notes : Wife from Norway; in Police since 1934
National Archives File: A3343 SSO-167

Ebeling

First Name: Walter
Date of Birth: 11 March 1904
Place of Birth: Wolfenbüttel
Highest Rank: SS-Hauptsturmführer
SS Number: Not listed
Date Entered SS: Not listed
NSDAP Number: Not a member
Marital Status: Married
Religion: Agnostic
Civilian Occupation: Police
Education: Grade School
Foreign Language: No
World War I Service: No
EINSATZKOMMANDO: **C**
Position: Not listed
Einsatzkommando Service: 25 August 1942–15 January 1944
Other Assignment: RSHA
SD Berlin
Highest Award: Iron Cross 2nd Class
Postwar Sentence: No judicial proceedings discovered
Notes: SD Leipzig
National Archives File: A3343 SSO-167

Eck

First Name: Friedrich
Date of Birth: 7 January 1904
Place of Birth: Unknown
Highest Rank: SS-Untersturmführer
SS Number: 50068
Date Entered SS: Not listed
NSDAP Number: Not a member
Marital Status: Unknown
Religion: Unknown
Civilian Occupation: Unknown
Education: Unknown
Foreign Language: No
World War I Service: No
EINSATZKOMMANDO: **B**
Position: Propaganda section
Einsatzkommando Service: 1943
Other Assignment: Unknown
Waffen-SS Service: No
Highest Award: None listed
Postwar Sentence: No judicial proceedings discovered
Notes: Short personnel file
National Archives File: A3343 SSO-170

Ecke

First Name: Paul
Date of Birth: 17 December 1899
Place of Birth: Klementov, Russia
Highest Rank: SS-Obersturmführer
SS Number: 272588
Date Entered SS: 1 April 01,1936
NSDAP Number: 5304872
Date Entered NSDAP: 1 May 1937
Marital Status: Agnostic
Civilian Occupation: Police
Education: Grade School
Foreign Language: No
World War I Service: Yes, Iron Cross 1st Class, 376th Infantry Regiment
EINSATZKOMMANDO: einsatzgruppe in Czechoslovakia
Position: Not listed
Einsatzkommando Service: 1938
Other Assignment: SD Breslau; SD Linz
Highest Award: War Service Cross 2nd Class
Postwar Sentence: No judicial proceedings discovered
Notes: Served in SA, 1932
Wounded in action WWI
National Archives File: A3343 SSO-171

Eggers

First Name: Eggers
Date of Birth: 27 October 1908
Place of Birth: Hildesheim
Highest Rank: SS-Hauptsturmführer
SS Number: 8748
Date Entered SS: 1 April 1931
NSDAP Number: 468114
Date Entered NSDAP: 1 March 1931
Marital Status: Married
Religion: Agnostic
Civilian Occupation: Businessman
Education: High School
Foreign Language: No
EINSATZKOMMANDO: **1/VI, C**
Position: Not listed
Einsatzkommando Service: 1/VI, Polish Campaign; C, 1942
Other Assignment: RSHA; SD Kovel
Highest Award: War Service Cross 2nd Class
Postwar Sentence: N/A
Postwar Employment: N/A
Notes: Served in SA, 1931
Court martialed and executed for cowardice, 22 March 1944
National Archives File: A3343 SSO-174

Ehlers

First Name: Ernst
Date of Birth: 16 October 1909
Place of Birth: Spaarresshoop
Highest Rank: SS-Obersturmbannführer
SS Number: 307426
Date Entered SS: 1 May 1938
NSDAP Number: 95459
Date Entered NSDAP: 1 August 1928
Marital Status: Married
Religion: Agnostic
Civilian Occupation: Lawyer
Education: University
Foreign Language: No
World War I Service: No
EINSATZKOMMANDO: **B**
Position: Not listed
Einsatzkommando Service: June 1941–29 September 1941
Other Assignment: SD Brussels; SD Breslau
Highest Award: War Service Cross 1st Class
Postwar Sentence: No
Notes: Suicide, 4 October 1980
Golden Party Badge; served in SA 1928-1938
National Archives File: A3343 SSO-175

Ehlers

First Name: Erich
Date of Birth: 24 February 1912
Place of Birth: Kiel
Highest Rank: SS-Sturmbannführer
SS Number: 107014
Date Entered SS: 1 November 1933
NSDAP Number: 1114046
Date Entered NSDAP: 1 May 1932
Marital Status: Married
Religion: Agnostic
Civilian Occupation: Unknown
Education: High School
Foreign Language: No
EINSATZKOMMANDO: *einsatzgruppe* in Austria, Czechoslovakia, Poland
Position: Not listed
Einsatzkommando Service: Not listed
Other Assignment: RSHA, Office VII B 1a (Ideology)
RSHA, Office II/111 (Administration)
Highest Award: War Service Cross 2nd Class
Postwar Sentence: No judicial proceedings discovered
Notes: Expert on Free Masons
Einsatzkommando in Oslo; served in SA 1932-1933
National Archives File: A3343 SSO-175

Ehrlinger

First Name: Dr. Erich
Date of Birth: 14 October 1910
Place of Birth: Giengen
Highest Rank: SS-Oberführer
SS Number: 107493
Date Entered SS: 22 June 1935
NSDAP Number: 541195
Date Entered NSDAP: 1 June 1931
Marital Status: Married
Religion: Agnostic
Civilian Occupation: Lawyer
Education: University of Kiel, Berlin, Tübingen
Foreign Language: English
EINSATZKOMMANDO: **4a, 1b, B,** *einsatzgruppe* in Czechoslovakia
Position: B – Commander; 1b – Commander
Einsatzkommando Service: 4, Polish Campaign; 1b, May - December 1941; B –28 August 1943–1944
Other Assignment: Chief, Office I, RSHA (Personnel); BdS Minsk
Waffen-SS Service: 1st SS Division "Leibstandarte Adolf Hitler", 1940
Highest Award: Iron Cross 1st Class
Postwar Sentence: 1961, 12 years, released 1964
Postwar Employment: worked at a Volkswagen dealership
Notes: Infantry Assault Badge; SD Vienna; SD Prague
National Archives File: A3343 SSO-177

Eichler

First Name: Horst
Date of Birth: 19 July 1910
Place of Birth: Danzig
Highest Rank: SS-Hauptsturmführer
SS Number: 66309
Date Entered SS: 1 March 1933
NSDAP Number: 469670
Date Entered NSDAP: 1 February 1931
Marital Status: Single
Religion: Agnostic
Civilian Occupation: Police
Education: High School
Foreign Language: English
World War I Service: No
EINSATZKOMMANDO: **A**
Position: Adjutant
Einsatzkommando Service: July–October 1941
Other Assignment: Gestapo Bromberg RSHA, Office III (SD, Domestic)
Highest Award: Iron Cross 2nd Class
Postwar Sentence: No judicial proceedings discovered
Notes: Detective Officer
National Archives File: A3343 SSO-180

Engels

First Name: Erich
Date of Birth: 11 September 1908
Place of Birth: Eichenburg
Highest Rank: SS-Hauptsturmführer
SS Number: 290989
Date Entered SS: 2 July 1938
NSDAP Number: 201138
Date Entered NSDAP: 1 February 1930
Marital Status: Single
Religion: Agnostic
Civilian Occupation: Police
Education: High School
Foreign Language: No
World War I Service: No
EINSATZKOMMANDO: **z.b.V.**
Position: *Teilkommando* Engels, leader
Einsatzkommando Service: 3 July 1941–11 August 1941
Other Assignment: RSHA; State Police Kassel
Highest Award: None listed
Postwar Sentence: No judicial proceedings discovered
Notes: Served in SA, 1930-1938 No mention of *Einsatzkommando* service in personnel file
National Archives File: A3343 SSO-188

Feder

First Name: Johannes-Hugo
Date of Birth: 21 May 1911
Place of Birth: Liegnitz
Highest Rank: SS-Obersturmführer
SS Number: 392084
Date Entered SS: Not listed
NSDAP Number: 5004798
Date Entered NSDAP: 1 May 1937
Marital Status: Married
Religion: Unknown
Civilian Occupation: Police
Education: High School
Foreign Language: No
World War I Service: No
EINSATZKOMMANDO: **A, B**
Position: Not listed
Einsatzkommando Service: June 1941–September 1941; June 1942–December 1943
Other Assignment: Unknown
Highest Award: War Service Cross 2nd Class
Postwar Sentence: 1962, 4 years
Postwar Employment: Construction firm in Cologne
Notes: Awarded War Service Cross 2nd Class by commander of Army Group North
National Archives File: A3343 SSO-198

Fehlis

First Name: Dr. Heinrich
Date of Birth: 1 November 1906
Place of Birth: Wulften
Highest Rank: SS-Oberführer
SS Number: 272255
Date Entered SS: Not listed
NSDAP Number: 2862366
Date Entered NSDAP: 1 May 1933
Marital Status: Married
Religion: Agnostic
Civilian Occupation: Lawyer
Education: University
Foreign Language: English, French
EINSATZKOMMANDO: **1, Oslo**
Position: 1 – Commander; Oslo – Commander
Einsatzkommando Service: Norway, 1940
Other Assignment: RSHA; SD Stuttgart
Highest Award: War Service Cross 1st Class
Postwar Sentence: N/A
Postwar Employment: N/A
Notes: Served in SA, 1933-1935; *einsatzgruppe* in Austria
Suicide May 1945
National Archives File: A3343 SSO-198

Fendler

First Name: Lothar
Date of Birth: 13 August 1913
Place of Birth: Breslau
Highest Rank: SS-Sturmbannführer
SS Number: 272603
Date Entered SS: 15 April 1933
NSDAP Number: 5216392
Date Entered NSDAP: 1 May 1937
Marital Status: Married
Religion: Agnostic
Civilian Occupation: Dentist
Education: High School listed, but may have attended a university
Foreign Language: No
World War I Service: No
EINSATZKOMMANDO: **4b**
Position: Deputy Commander
Einsatzkommando Service: May 1941–2 October 1941; March 1942–July 1942
Other Assignment: RSHA, Office VI (SD, Foreign)
Highest Award: War Service Cross 1st Class
Postwar Sentence: 1948, 10 years, released
Notes: Expert on Spain and Portugal
National Archives File: A3343 SSO-201

Fest

First Name: Dr. Anton
Date of Birth: 29 December 1908
Place of Birth: Limburg
Highest Rank: SS-Obersturmbannführer
SS Number: 228521
Date Entered SS: 1 March 1934
NSDAP Number: 2758105
Date Entered NSDAP: 22 April 1933
Marital Status: Married
Religion: Agnostic
Civilian Occupation: Lawyer
Education: University
Foreign Language: No
World War I Service: No
EINSATZKOMMANDO: **10b**
Position: Commander
Einsatzkommando Service: Not listed
Other Assignment: RSHA
Highest Award: War Service Cross 1st Class
Postwar Sentence: No judicial proceedings discovered
Notes: Served in SA, 1933-1934
Police Attaché Copenhagen
National Archives File: A3343 SSO-203

Fiebig

First Name: Konrad
Date of Birth: 22 September 1909
Place of Birth: Breslau
Highest Rank: SS-Hauptsturmführer
SS Number: 404599
Date Entered SS: 1 August 1939
NSDAP Number: Not listed
Date Entered NSDAP: 1 May 1940
Marital Status: Married
Religion: Agnostic
Civilian Occupation: Police
Education: University
Foreign Language: No
World War I Service: No
EINSATZKOMMANDO: **9**
Position: *Teilkommando* leader
Einsatzkommando Service: 7 October 1941–undetermined
Other Assignment: Criminal Police Breslau
RSHA
Highest Award: War Service Cross 2nd Class
Postwar Sentence: Acquitted
Notes: Served in German Army 1934-1935
National Archives File: A3343 SSO-205

Filbert

First Name: Dr. Alfred
Date of Birth: 8 September 1905
Place of Birth: Darmstadt
Highest Rank: SS-Obersturmbannführer
SS Number: 44552
Date Entered SS: 23 August 1932
NSDAP Number: 1321414
Date Entered NSDAP: 1 September 1932
Marital Status: Married
Religion: Agnostic
Civilian Occupation: Lawyer
Education: University of Giessen, Heidelberg
Foreign Language: English, French
World War I Service: No
EINSATZKOMMANDO: **9**
Position: Commander
Einsatzkommando Service: June 1941–20 October 1941
Other Assignment: Chief, Office VI A, RSHA (SD, Foreign)
Highest Award: War Service Cross 1st Class
Postwar Sentence: 1962, Life
Postwar Employment: Furniture store employee
Notes: Post-war alias of Dr. Selbert
National Archives File: A3343 SSO-207

Finger

First Name: Karl
Date of Birth: 17 March 1910
Place of Birth: Wilhelmshaven
Highest Rank: SS-Hauptsturmführer
SS Number: 367305
Date Entered SS: 1 August 1939
NSDAP Number: 106349
Date Entered NSDAP: 1 December 1928
Marital Status: Married
Religion: Agnostic
Civilian Occupation: Police
Education: High School
Foreign Language: English
World War I Service: No
EINSATZKOMMANDO: **D**
Position: Not listed
Einsatzkommando Service: Not listed
Other Assignment: Police Wesermünde
Highest Award: Iron Cross 2nd Class
Postwar Sentence: No judicial proceedings discovered
Notes: Served in SA, 1928-1940
No mention of *Einsatzkommando* service in personnel file
National Archives File: A3343 SSO-207

Finnberg

First Name: Dr. Emil
Date of Birth: 27 June 1909
Place of Birth: Hamburg
Highest Rank: SS-Sturmbannführer
SS Number: 194365
Date Entered SS: 9 November 1933
NSDAP Number: 3027410
Date Entered NSDAP: 1 May 1933
Marital Status: Married
Religion: Unknown
Civilian Occupation: Lawyer
Education: University
Foreign Language: No
World War I Service: No
EINSATZKOMMANDO: **A**
Position: Adjutant
Einsatzkommando Service: June 1941–March 1942
Other Assignment: SD Düsseldorf; Gestapo Breslau
Highest Award: None listed
Killed in Action: No
Postwar Sentence: No judicial proceedings discovered
Notes: Short personnel file
National Archives File: A3343 SSO-207

Fischer

First Name: Dr. Herbert
Date of Birth: 30 December 1904
Place of Birth: Riesenburg
Highest Rank: SS-Sturmbannführer
SS Number: 267238
Date Entered SS: 8 June 1935
NSDAP Number: Not a member
Marital Status: Married
Religion: Agnostic
Civilian Occupation: Police
Education: University
Foreign Language: English, French
World War I Service: No
EINSATZKOMMANDO: **III, B**
Position: III – Commander
Einsatzkommando Service: III, Polish Campaign
Other Assignment: RSHA, Office IV E 3 (Gestapo, Counterintelligence, West)
Highest Award: Spanish Cross in Silver
Postwar Sentence: N/A
Postwar Employment: N/A
Notes: Served with German forces helping Franco in Spain, 1937
Reported dead 30 December 1945
National Archives File: A3343 SSO-209

Fischer

First Name: Leopold
Date of Birth: 10 October 1905
Place of Birth: St. Valentin, Austria
Highest Rank: SS-Untersturmführer
SS Number: 296854
Date Entered SS: 1 January 1933
NSDAP Number: 6376909
Date Entered NSDAP: 1 May 1938
Marital Status: Married
Religion: Agnostic
Civilian Occupation: Machinist
Education: Grade School
Foreign Language: No
World War I Service: No
EINSATZKOMMANDO: **2**
Position: Not listed
Einsatzkommando Service: Not listed
Other Assignment: RSHA
BdS Salzburg
Highest Award: War Service Cross 2nd Class
Postwar Sentence: No judicial proceedings discovered
Notes: Possible honorary SS member
National Archives File: A3343 SSO-209

Fischer

First Name: Konrad
Date of Birth: 13 August 1908
Place of Birth: Munich
Highest Rank: SS-Obersturmführer
SS Number: 107162
Date Entered SS: 14 February 1934
NSDAP Number: 4583124
Date Entered NSDAP: 1 May 1937
Marital Status: Married
Religion: Agnostic
Civilian Occupation: Businessman
Education: Grade School
Foreign Language: English
World War I Service: No
EINSATZKOMMANDO: **A**
Position: Not listed
Einsatzkommando Service: Not listed
Other Assignment: RSHA
SD Nürnberg
Highest Award: War Service Cross 2nd Class
Postwar Sentence: No judicial proceedings discovered
Notes: Served in Freikorps
National Archives File: A3343 SSO-209

Fischer-Schweder

First Name: Bernhard
Date of Birth: 12 January 1904
Place of Birth: Berlin-Spandau
Highest Rank: SS-Oberführer
SS Number: 401232
Date Entered SS: 15 August 1941
NSDAP Number: 17141
Date Entered NSDAP: 28 August 1925
Marital Status: Married
Religion: Agnostic
Civilian Occupation: Police
Education: Technical School
World War I Service: Freikorps
EINSATZKOMMANDO: **A, Tilsit**
Position: Attached *schutzpolizei* to *Einsatzgruppe*
Einsatzkommando Service: A – 1941, Tilsit – 1942
Other Assignment: Police Director Memel; SSPF Kharkov
Waffen-SS Service: 12th SS Division "Hitler Jugend", 1945
Highest Award: War Service Cross 2nd Class
Postwar Sentence: 1958, 10 years, released
Postwar Employment: Remington-Rand, Stuttgart
Notes: Golden Party Badge; died 28 November 1960;
Court martialed for public drunkeness in 1943
National Archives File: A3343 SSO-208

Fleischmann

First Name: Dr. Georg
Date of Birth: 14 July 1906
Place of Birth: Kolberg
Highest Rank: SS-Sturmbannführer
SS Number: 310191
Date Entered SS: 9 November 1938
NSDAP Number: 332884
Date Entered NSDAP: 1 October 1930
Marital Status: Married
Religion: Agnostic
Civilian Occupation: Lawyer
Education: University
Foreign Language: No
EINSATZKOMMANDO: **B**
Position: Not listed
Einsatzkommando Service: Not listed
Other Assignment: RSHA, Office I B 2 (SD Organization)
Highest Award: War Service Cross 2nd Class
Killed in Action: No
Postwar Sentence: No judicial proceedings discovered
Notes: Served in SA, 1930-1938
No mention of *Einsatzkommando* service in personnel file
National Archives File: A3343 SSO-212

Flesch

First Name: Gerhard
Date of Birth: 8 October 1909
Place of Birth: Posen
Highest Rank: SS-Obersturmbannführer
SS Number: 267300
Date Entered SS: 1 August 1933
NSDAP Number: 3018617
Date Entered NSDAP: 1 May 1933
Marital Status: Married
Religion: Agnostic
Civilian Occupation: Lawyer
Education: University
Foreign Language: No
World War I Service: Yes, Iron Cross 2nd Class, Wound Badge
EINSATZKOMMANDO: **2/VI**
Position: Commander
Einsatzkommando Service: Polish Campaign
Other Assignment: Gestapo Frankfurt/Oder; Commander, SD Drontheim
Highest Award: War Service Cross 1st Class
Postwar Sentence: No judicial proceedings discovered
Notes: Air raid caused wife to miscarry in 1942
Iron Cross 2nd Class for Polish Campaign
National Archives File: A3343 SSO-213

Foltis

First Name: Richard
Date of Birth: 22 November 1913
Place of Birth: Ratibor
Highest Rank: SS-Sturmbannführer
SS Number: 272683
Date Entered SS: 1 November 1935
NSDAP Number: 5216393
Date Entered NSDAP: 1 May 1937
Marital Status: Married
Religion: Agnostic
Civilian Occupation: Unknown
Education: High School
Foreign Language: No
World War I Service: No
EINSATZKOMMANDO: **7a**
Position: Not listed
Einsatzkommando Service: June 1941–October 1941; March–August 1942
Other Assignment: Gestapo Cologne
Highest Award: War Service Cross 2nd Class
Postwar Sentence: No judicial proceedings discovered
Notes: Served in Hitler Youth, 1932-1935
National Archives File: A3343 SSO-215

Freitag

First Name: Gerhard
Date of Birth: 18 March 1913
Place of Birth: Magdeburg
Highest Rank: SS-Hauptsturmführer
SS Number: 337662
Date Entered SS: 17 March 1939
NSDAP Number: 5540710
Date Entered NSDAP: 1 May 1937
Marital Status: Married
Religion: Agnostic
Civilian Occupation: Banker
Education: High School
Foreign Language: No
World War I Service: No
EINSATZKOMMANDO: **2**
Position: Personal staff
Einsatzkommando Service: 1941–September 1941
Other Assignment: Unknown
Highest Award: War Service Cross 2nd Class
Postwar Sentence: No judicial proceedings discovered
Notes: Served in SA, 1933-1934
Served in Army 1938
National Archives File: A3343 SSO-220

Freitag

First Name: Dr. Joachim
Date of Birth: 1 April 1911
Place of Birth: Stade
Highest Rank: SS-Sturmbannführer
SS Number: 164626
Date Entered SS: Not listed
NSDAP Number: 4111512
Date Entered NSDAP: 1 May 1937
Marital Status: Married
Religion: Agnostic
Civilian Occupation: Lawyer
Education: University
Foreign Language: English, French
World War I Service: No
EINSATZKOMMANDO: **15**
Position: Commander
Einsatzkommando Service: Not listed
Other Assignment: RSHA; Gestapo Schneidemühl
Highest Award: None listed
Postwar Sentence: No judicial proceedings discovered
Notes: *Einsatzkommando* Knin commander 1943
National Archives File: A3343 SSO-220

Friedrich

First Name: Franz
Date of Birth: 17 October 1905
Place of Birth: Aachen
Highest Rank: SS-Obersturmführer
SS Number: 74653
Date Entered SS: 15 March 1933
NSDAP Number: 2045998
Date Entered NSDAP: 1 May 1933
Marital Status: Married
Religion: Agnostic
Civilian Occupation: Police
Education: Unknown
Foreign Language: No
World War I Service: No
EINSATZKOMMANDO: **B**
Position: Not listed
Einsatzkommando Service: 1943
Other Assignment: RSHA; Police Aachen
Highest Award: Iron Cross 2nd Class
Postwar Sentence: No judicial proceedings discovered
Notes: Eastern People's Medal
No mention of *Einsatzkommando* service in personnel file
National Archives File: A3343 SSO-223

Frohwann

First Name: Dr. Erich
Date of Birth: 1 January 1902
Place of Birth: Gleiwitz
Highest Rank: SS-Hauptsturmführer
SS Number: 307428
Date Entered SS: 13 April 1937
NSDAP Number: 5708289
Date Entered NSDAP: 01-May-37
Marital Status: Married
Religion: Agnostic
Civilian Occupation: Lawyer
Education: University
Foreign Language: No
World War I Service: No
EINSATZKOMMANDO: **Tilsit**
Position: Not listed
Einsatzkommando Service: 1941
Other Assignment: Unknown
Highest Award: None listed
Postwar Sentence: No judicial proceedings discovered
Notes: Served in Freikorps
No mention of *Einsatzkommando* service in personnel file
National Archives File: A3343 SSO-227

Fuchs

First Name: Dr. Wilhelm
Date of Birth: 1 September 1898
Place of Birth: Mannheim
Highest Rank: SS-Oberführer
SS Number: 62760
Date Entered SS: 1 December 1932
NSDAP Number: 1038061
Date Entered NSDAP: 1 April 1932
Marital Status: Married
Religion: Agnostic
Civilian Occupation: Economist
Education: University of Leipzig
Foreign Language: No
World War I Service: Yes, Iron Cross 2nd Class
EINSATZKOMMANDO: **A, 3, E**
Position: A – Commander; 3 – Commander; E – Commander
Einsatzkommando Service: 3, 15 September 1943–6 May 1944; A, May 1944–October 1944; E, 1944
Other Assignment: SD Braunschweig, Inspector
Highest Award: War Service Cross 1st Class
Postwar Sentence: Executed
Postwar Employment: N/A
Notes: Bar to Iron Cross 2nd Class, 1940; executed in Yugoslavia
National Archives File: A3343 SSO-228

Fuchs

First Name: Günther
Date of Birth: 23 June 1911
Place of Birth: Breslau
Highest Rank: SS-Hauptsturmführer
SS Number: 459844
Date Entered SS: 25 May 1943
NSDAP Number: 1395892
Date Entered NSDAP: 1 December 1932
Marital Status: Married
Religion: Agnostic
Civilian Occupation: Police
Education: University
Foreign Language: No
World War I Service: No
EINSATZKOMMANDO: **1005**
Position: Not listed
Einsatzkommando Service: 1943
Other Assignment: RSHA, Gestapo Lodz
Waffen-SS Service: No
Highest Award: War Service Cross 2nd Class
Postwar Sentence: No judicial proceedings discovered
Notes: No mention of *Einsatzkommando* service in personnel file
National Archives File: A3343 SSO-228

Fuhrmann

First Name: Georg
Date of Birth: 21 April 1903
Place of Birth: Gross-Strelitz
Highest Rank: SS-Hauptsturmführer
SS Number: 1103
Date Entered SS: 1 January 1928
NSDAP Number: 2508
Date Entered NSDAP: 1 April 1923
Marital Status: Married
Religion: Agnostic
Civilian Occupation: Pharmacist
Education: Technical School
Foreign Language: No
World War I Service: No
EINSATZKOMMANDO: **A**
Position: Propaganda section
Einsatzkommando Service: 1942–1943
Other Assignment: RSHA
Highest Award: None listed
Postwar Sentence: No judicial proceedings discovered
Notes: Golden Party Badge; served in Freikorps
Served in SA, 1924-1927
National Archives File: A3343 SSO-230

Gabel

First Name: Hans
Date of Birth: 4 April 1909
Place of Birth: Magdeburg
Highest Rank: SS-Sturmbannführer
SS Number: 356891
Date Entered SS: 1 June 1940
NSDAP Number: 68669
Date Entered NSDAP: 11 October 1927
Marital Status: Married
Religion: Agnostic
Civilian Occupation: Businessman
Education: High School
Foreign Language: No
World War I Service: No
EINSATZKOMMANDO: **D**
Position: Attached police battalion officer
Einsatzkommando Service: 1941
Other Assignment: Schutzpolizei Berlin
Highest Award: War Service Cross 1st Class
Postwar Sentence: No judicial proceedings discovered
Notes: Golden Party Badge; Iron Cross 2nd Class; Crimea Shield
Served in SA, 1927-1935
National Archives File: A3343 SSO-001A

Gerke

First Name: Wilhelm
Date of Birth: 25 November 1906
Place of Birth: Ritze
Highest Rank: SS-Hauptsturmführer
SS Number: 358082
Date Entered SS: 13 April 13 1939
NSDAP Number: 2431086
Date Entered NSDAP: 1 May 1933
Marital Status: Married
Religion: Agnostic
Civilian Occupation: Police
Education: High School
Foreign Language: No
World War I Service: No
EINSATZKOMMANDO: **Tilsit**
Position: SD section
Einsatzkommando Service: 1941
Other Assignment: SD Tilsit
Highest Award: None listed
Postwar Sentence: 1957, 5 Years
Postwar Employment: Fled to Sweden
Notes: Served in Army 149th Volks Grenadier Division
National Archives File: A3343 SSO-009A

Girgensohn

First Name: Werner
Date of Birth: 27 Dec 1914
Place of Birth: Riga, Russia
Highest Rank: SS-Hauptsturmführer
SS Number: 357297
Date Entered SS: 1 June 1940
NSDAP Number: 8537664
Date Entered NSDAP: 1 September 1941
Marital Status: Unknown
Religion: Protestant
Civilian Occupation: Lawyer
Education: University
Foreign Language: Latvian
World War I Service: No
EINSATZKOMMANDO: **B**
Position: Not listed
Einsatzkommando Service: Not listed
Other Assignment: SD Posen
Highest Award: War Service Cross 2nd Class
Postwar Sentence: No judicial proceedings discovered
Notes: Served in Latvian Army, 1937-1938
National Archives File: A3343 SSO-014A

Glaser

First Name: Dr. Helmut
Date of Birth: 29 July 1910
Place of Birth: Gmünd, Austria
Highest Rank: SS-Sturmbannführer
SS Number: 301760
Date Entered SS: 10 October 1930
NSDAP Number: 444132
Date Entered NSDAP: 8 May 1931
Marital Status: Married
Religion: Agnostic
Civilian Occupation: Teacher
Education: University of Vienna
Foreign Language: French
World War I Service: No
EINSATZKOMMANDO: **4/I, 29**
Position: Commander
Einsatzkommando Service: 4/I, Polish Campaign; 29, 1944
Other Assignment: RSHA, Office III A (SD, Domestic, Legal Practice)
SD Klagenfurt; SD, Cracow
Highest Award: Iron Cross 1st Class
Postwar Sentence: No judicial proceedings discovered
Notes: Wound Badge
National Archives File: A3343 SSO-015A

Glende

First Name: Kurt
Date of Birth: 14 May 1898
Place of Birth: Stolp
Highest Rank: SS-Untersturmführer
SS Number: 353489
Date Entered SS: Not listed
NSDAP Number: 5785285
Date Entered NSDAP: 1 May 1937
Marital Status: Married
Religion: Agnostic
Civilian Occupation: Police
Education: Grade School
Foreign Language: No
World War I Service: Yes, German Navy
EINSATZKOMMANDO: **z.b.V.**
Position: *Teilkommando* Birkner
Einsatzkommando Service: 3 July 1941–11 August 1941
Other Assignment: RSHA; Police Lemberg
Highest Award: None listed
Postwar Sentence: No judicial proceedings discovered
Notes: In Police since 1919
No mention of *Einsatzkommando* service in personnel file
National Archives File: A3343 SSO-016A

Gluth

First Name: Max
Date of Birth: 26 April 1905
Place of Birth: Polenzhof
Highest Rank: SS-Untersturmführer
SS Number: 81391
Date Entered SS: 2 February 1932
NSDAP Number: 624090
Date Entered NSDAP: 1 August 1931
Marital Status: Married
Religion: Agnostic
Civilian Occupation: Businessman
Education: Grade School
Foreign Language: No
World War I Service: No
EINSATZKOMMANDO: **7a**
Position: Not listed
Einsatzkommando Service: Not listed
Other Assignment: Unknown
Highest Award: Iron Cross 2nd Class
Postwar Sentence: No judicial proceedings discovered
Notes: Iron Cross 2nd Class as army engineer in 1940
Served in SA, 1930-1932
National Archives File: A3343 SSO-017A

Gmeiner

First Name: Josef
Date of Birth: 22 December 1904
Place of Birth: Amberg
Highest Rank: SS-Obersturmbannführer
SS Number: 186633
Date Entered SS: 19 February 1934
NSDAP Number: 3656472
Date Entered NSDAP: 01-May-35
Marital Status: Married
Religion: Agnostic
Civilian Occupation: Lawyer
Education: University of Munich, Erlangen
Foreign Language: No
World War I Service: No
EINSATZKOMMANDO: **C**
Position: Not listed
Einsatzkommando Service: 15 June 1941–29 September 1941
Other Assignment: RSHA; Gestapo Karlsruhe
Highest Award: War Service Cross 1st Class
Postwar Sentence: No judicial proceedings discovered
Notes: SD, Strasbourg
Inspector Sipo and SD, Dresden
National Archives File: A3343 SSO-017A

Goerke

First Name: Heinz
Date of Birth: 4 April 1909
Place of Birth: Berlin
Highest Rank: SS-Obersturmführer
SS Number: 56976
Date Entered SS: 1 October 1932
NSDAP Number: 711630
Date Entered NSDAP: 1 November 1931
Marital Status: Married
Religion: Agnostic
Civilian Occupation: Businessman
Education: High School
Foreign Language: No
World War I Service: No
EINSATZKOMMANDO: **z.b.V.**
Position: *Teilkommando* Schoene
Einsatzkommando Service: 3 July 1941–11 August 1941
Other Assignment: RSHA; SD Warsaw
Highest Award: None listed
Postwar Sentence: N/A
Postwar Employment: N/A
Notes: Convicted December 1941 of race defilement; sentenced to death by SS – committed suicide shortly thereafter
National Archives File: A3343 SSO-019A

Gontard

First Name: Christoph
Date of Birth: 17 January 1908
Place of Birth: Dresden
Highest Rank: SS-Sturmbannführer
SS Number: 272233
Date Entered SS: Not listed
NSDAP Number: 713377
Date Entered NSDAP: 1 November 1931
Marital Status: Married
Religion: Agnostic
Civilian Occupation: Businessman
Education: University of Munich
Foreign Language: No
World War I Service: No
EINSATZKOMMANDO: **A**
Position: Not listed
Einsatzkommando Service: 1943
Other Assignment: SD Munich; SD Innsbruck
Highest Award: War Service Cross 1st Class
Postwar Sentence: No judicial proceedings discovered
Notes: Also served in SD, Weimar
Charged with adultery in 1942
National Archives File: A3343 SSO-023A

Graaf

First Name: Kurt
Date of Birth: 8 January 1909
Place of Birth: Kiel
Highest Rank: SS-Sturmbannführer
SS Number: 36179
Date Entered SS: 27 July 1932
NSDAP Number: 183351
Date Entered NSDAP: 1 January 1930
Marital Status: Married
Religion: Agnostic
Civilian Occupation: Businessman
Education: Trade School
Foreign Language: No
World War I Service: No
EINSATZKOMMANDO: **1c**
Position: Commander
Einsatzkommando Service: 1 August 1942–28 November 1942
Other Assignment: RSHA, Office I A 5b (Personnel) SD Schwerin
Highest Award: War Service Cross 2nd Class
Postwar Sentence: No judicial proceedings discovered
Notes: Reprimanded for drunken behavior
Served in SA, 1929-1932; served in Hitler Youth 1930
National Archives File: A3343 SSO-026A

Graalfs

First Name: Hans
Date of Birth: 11 November 1915
Place of Birth: Wieselstede
Highest Rank: SS-Hauptsturmführer
SS Number: 164791
Date Entered SS: 1 November 1933
NSDAP Number: 4198410
Date Entered NSDAP: 1 May 1937
Marital Status: Married
Religion: Agnostic
Civilian Occupation: Businessman
Education: University of Berlin
EINSATZKOMMANDO: **8**
Position: Waffen-SS platoon leader
Einsatzkommando Service: Undetermined to October 1941
Other Assignment: RSHA; SD Berlin
Waffen-SS Service: 502nd SS Heavy Tank Battalion
Highest Award: Iron Cross 1st Class
Postwar Sentence: 1964, 3 years
Postwar Employment: Knit-wear factory
Notes: Company commander in tank battalion
Wounded in action several times
National Archives File: A3343 SSO-026A

Gräfe

First Name: Dr. Heinz
Date of Birth: 15 July 1908
Place of Birth: Leipzig
Highest Rank: SS-Obersturmbannführer
SS Number: 107213
Date Entered SS: 21 December 1933
NSDAP Number: 3959575
Date Entered NSDAP: 1 May 1937
Marital Status: Married
Religion: Agnostic
Civilian Occupation: Lawyer
Education: University
Foreign Language: English, French
EINSATZKOMMANDO: **1/V**
Position: Commander
Einsatzkommando Service: Polish Campaign
Other Assignment: Chief, Office VI C, RSHA (SD, Foreign, Russo-Japanese Sphere); SD Gumbinnen
Highest Award: Iron Cross 2nd Class
Postwar Sentence: N/A
Postwar Employment: N/A
Notes: Leader of Operation Zeppelin (see chapter 3)
Died 25 January 1944 in a car wreck
National Archives File: A3343 SSO-026A

Graf

First Name: Matthias
Date of Birth: 8 May 1903
Place of Birth: Kottern
Highest Rank: SS-Untersturmführer
SS Number: 77431
Date Entered SS: Not listed
NSDAP Number: 3423504
Date Entered NSDAP: 1 May 1933
Marital Status: Married
Religion: Agnostic
Civilian Occupation: Businessman
Education: High School
Foreign Language: English, French, Italian, Portuguese
World War I Service: No
EINSATZKOMMANDO: **6**
Position: Not listed
Einsatzkommando Service: June 1941–October 1942
Other Assignment: RSHA
Highest Award: War Service Cross 2nd Class
Postwar Sentence: 1948, sentenced to time served
Notes: Lived in South America 1922-1928
No mention of *Einsatzkommando* service in personnel file
National Archives File: A3343 SSO-027A

Grauel

First Name: Erhard
Date of Birth: 8 June 1910
Place of Birth: Langensalza
Highest Rank: SS-Sturmbannführer
SS Number: 80793
Date Entered SS: 15 June 1933
NSDAP Number: 1682886
Date Entered NSDAP: 1 Aprril 1933
Marital Status: Married
Religion: Agnostic
Civilian Occupation: Student
Education: High School
Foreign Language: No
World War I Service: No
EINSATZKOMMANDO: **2**
Position: Security section leader
Einsatzkommando Service: July 1941–October 1941
Other Assignment: SD Würzburg; Gestapo Breslau
Highest Award: War Service Cross 2nd Class
Postwar Sentence: 1968
Notes: Also served in RSHA, Office I
Married one month before *Einsatzkommando* duty
National Archives File: A3343 SSO-029A

Greif

First Name: Herbert
Date of Birth: 8 April 1911
Place of Birth: Berlin
Highest Rank: SS-Obersturmführer
SS Number: 326476
Date Entered SS: 5 May 1939
NSDAP Number: 127479
Date Entered NSDAP: 1 May 1929
Marital Status: Married
Religion: Agnostic
Civilian Occupation: Baker
Education: Unknown
Foreign Language: No
World War I Service: No
EINSATZKOMMANDO: **2**
Position: Not listed
Einsatzkommando Service: Not listed
Other Assignment: RSHA
Highest Award: War Service Cross 2nd Class
Postwar Sentence: No judicial proceedings discovered
Notes: Served in SA, 1929-1936
National Archives File: A3343 SSO-030A

Greiffenberger

First Name: Wilhelm
Date of Birth: 26 February 1900
Place of Birth: St. Petersburg, Russia
Highest Rank: SS-Sturmbannführer
SS Number: 46738
Date Entered SS: 1 July 1932
NSDAP Number: 870363
Date Entered NSDAP: 1 January 1932
Marital Status: Married
Religion: Agnostic
Civilian Occupation: Businessman
Education: High School
Foreign Language: Russian
World War I Service: Yes, 13th Jaeger Battalion
EINSATZKOMMANDO: **9**
Position: Interrogator
Einsatzkommando Service: May 1941–November 1941
Other Assignment: RSHA, Office I A 4 (Personnel); SD Halle
Highest Award: War Service Cross 2nd Class
Postwar Sentence: 1962, 3 years
Postwar Employment: Accountant
Notes: SD Prague; wounded in British air raid on Berlin 1943
National Archives File: A3343 SSO-030A

Gröbel

First Name: Arno
Date of Birth: 16 March 1911
Place of Birth: Friedeburg
Highest Rank: SS-Hauptsturmführer
SS Number: 237757
Date Entered SS: 30 June 1934
NSDAP Number: 1399803
Date Entered NSDAP: 1 December 1932
Marital Status: Married
Religion: Agnostic
Civilian Occupation: Baker
Education: Grade School
Foreign Language: No
World War I Service: No
EINSATZKOMMANDO: **z.b.V.**
Position: *Teilkommando* Bonifer
Einsatzkommando Service: 3 July 1941–11 August 1941
Other Assignment: RSHA, Office VI F (SD, Foreign, West)
Highest Award: None listed
Postwar Sentence: No judicial proceedings discovered
Notes: Court martialed for drunkeness; took part in quelling 1944 Warsaw Uprising
Probably assigned to another *Einsatzkommando* in 1942
National Archives File: A3343 SSO-032A

Gröver

First Name: Theodor
Date of Birth: 5 December 1909
Place of Birth: Riesenback
Highest Rank: SS-Untersturmführer
SS Number: 280187
Date Entered SS: 18 June 1936
NSDAP Number: 4583133
Date Entered NSDAP: 1 May 1937
Marital Status: Married
Religion: Agnostic
Civilian Occupation: Police
Education: Grade School
Foreign Language: No
EINSATZKOMMANDO: **C, 6,** *Einsatzkommando* in Poland
Position: Not listed
Einsatzkommando Service: 13 September 1941–30 October 1941; Polish Campaign
Other Assignment: Gestapo Würzburg
Highest Award: None listed
Postwar Sentence: 1965, 5 years
Postwar Employment: Textile factory
Notes: Sentenced to 8 months house arrest by SS for alcohol abuse
Served in SA, 1933-1935;
Served in Hitler Youth 1935-36
National Archives File: A3343 SSO-033A

Grohmann

First Name: Dr. Herbert
Date of Birth: 13 September 1908
Place of Birth: Breslau
Highest Rank: SS-Sturmbannführer
SS Number: 51663
Date Entered SS: 18 January 1932
NSDAP Number: 544053
Date Entered NSDAP: 1 June 1931
Marital Status: Married
Religion: Agnostic
Civilian Occupation: Doctor
Education: University of Breslau
Foreign Language: No
World War I Service: No
EINSATZKOMMANDO: **B**
Position: Physician
Einsatzkommando Service: January 1943–1944
Other Assignment: RSHA; SD Lodz
Waffen-SS Service: 30th SS Division, 1944-1945
Highest Award: Iron Cross 2nd Class
Postwar Sentence: No judicial proceedings discovered
Notes: Served in SA, 1931-1932;
Eastern People's Medal
National Archives File: A3343 SSO-033A

Grünzfelder

First Name: Franz
Date of Birth: 27 November 1909
Place of Birth: Kahl
Highest Rank: SS-Untersturmführer
SS Number: 67831
Date Entered SS: Not listed
NSDAP Number: 3151407
Date Entered NSDAP: 1 May 1933
Marital Status: Married
Religion: Agnostic
Civilian Occupation: Student
Education: University of Würzburg
Foreign Language: No
EINSATZKOMMANDO: **A, 1b**
Position: Not listed
Einsatzkommando Service: Undetermined to 19 June 1942
Other Assignment: SD Koblenz
Waffen-SS Service: No
Highest Award: None listed
Postwar Sentence: N/A
Postwar Employment: N/A
Notes: Killed in action 19 June 1942 while in SK 1b
National Archives File: A3343 SSO-040A

Häfner

First Name: August
Date of Birth: 31 January 1912
Place of Birth: Mellingen, Switzerland
Highest Rank: SS-Obersturmführer
SS Number: 105693
Date Entered SS: 4 March 1933
NSDAP Number: 869199
Date Entered NSDAP: 1 January 1932
Marital Status: Married
Religion: Agnostic
Civilian Occupation: Cooper
Education: High School
Foreign Language: No
World War I Service: No
EINSATZKOMMANDO: **4a**
Position: *Teilkommando* leader
Einsatzkommando Service: June 1941 to undetermined
Other Assignment: RSHA
Highest Award: None listed
Postwar Sentence: 1973, 8 years
Notes: Served in Hitler Youth, 1932-1933
National Archives File: A3343 SSO-049A

Hänsch

First Name: Dr. Walter
Date of Birth: 3 March 1904
Place of Birth: Hirschfelde
Highest Rank: SS-Obersturmbannführer
SS Number: 272573
Date Entered SS: 1 August 1935
NSDAP Number: 537265
Date Entered NSDAP: 7 June 1931
Marital Status: Married
Religion: Agnostic
Civilian Occupation: Lawyer
Education: University of Leipzig
Foreign Language: No
World War I Service: No
EINSATZKOMMANDO: **4b**
Position: Commander
Einsatzkommando Service: March 1942–July 1942
Other Assignment: RSHA, Office I D (Personnel)
Waffen-SS Service: No
Highest Award: War Service Cross 2nd Class
Postwar Sentence: 1948, Death commuted to 15 years, released
Notes: Short personnel file
National Archives File: A3343 SSO-049A

Hänsel

First Name: Reinhold
Date of Birth: 24 June 1885
Place of Birth: Hirschfelde
Highest Rank: SS-Obersturmführer
SS Number: 107182
Date Entered SS: 1 October 1933
NSDAP Number: 658575
Date Entered NSDAP: 1 August 1931
Marital Status: Married
Religion: Agnostic
Civilian Occupation: Bartender
Education: Grade School
Foreign Language: Yes, unknown (illegible)
World War I Service: Yes, 64th Field Artillery Regiment
EINSATZKOMMANDO: **2**
Position: Translator
Einsatzkommando Service: July 1941–24 December 1941
Other Assignment: Gestapo Dresden
Waffen-SS Service: No
Highest Award: War Service Cross 2nd Class
Postwar Sentence: No judicial proceedings discovered
Notes: Short personnel file
National Archives File: A3343 SSO-049A

Hänsell

First Name: Egon
Date of Birth: 13 November 1910
Place of Birth: Doblen, Russia
Highest Rank: SS-Obersturmführer
SS Number: 361206
Date Entered SS: 1 June 1940
NSDAP Number: Not a member
Marital Status: Married
Religion: None
Civilian Occupation: Tanner
Education: Unknown
Foreign Language: Latvian
World War I Service: No
EINSATZKOMMANDO: **A**
Position: Not listed
Einsatzkommando Service: Not listed
Other Assignment: Unknown
Waffen-SS Service: No
Highest Award: War Service Cross 2nd Class
Postwar Sentence: No judicial proceedings discovered
Notes: Served in Latvian Army, 1932-1933
No mention of *Einsatzkommando* service in personnel file
National Archives File: A3343 SSO-049A

Hahn

First Name: Dr. Ludwig
Date of Birth: 23 January 1908
Place of Birth: Eitzen
Highest Rank: SS-Standartenführer
SS Number: 65823
Date Entered SS: 21 April 1933
NSDAP Number: 194463
Date Entered NSDAP: 1 February 1930
Marital Status: Agnostic
Civilian Occupation: Lawyer
Education: University of Jena, Göttingen
Foreign Language: English
World War I Service: No
EINSATZKOMMANDO: **1/I**
Position: Commander
Einsatzkommando Service: Polish Campaign
Other Assignment: Gestapo Weimar; Commander, SD Warsaw
Waffen-SS Service: No
Highest Award: Iron Cross 1st Class
Postwar Sentence: 1975, Life
Notes: Received Iron Cross 1st Class for Warsaw Uprising
National Archives File: A3343 SSO-053A

Hamann

First Name: Joachim
Date of Birth: 18 May 1913
Place of Birth: Kiel
Highest Rank: SS-Sturmbannführer
SS Number: 314267
Date Entered SS: 1 July 1938
NSDAP Number: 958322
Date Entered NSDAP: 1 February 1932
Marital Status: Married
Religion: Agnostic
Civilian Occupation: Pharmacist
Education: High School
Foreign Language: No
World War I Service: No
EINSATZKOMMANDO: **3, 4b**
Position: Not listed
Einsatzkommando Service: 22 June 1941–2 October 1941
Other Assignment: RSHA, Office IV (Gestapo)
Highest Award: War Service Cross 2nd Class
Postwar Sentence: N/A
Notes: Army paratrooper 1935-1938
Operation Zeppelin 1942; died 13 July 1945
National Archives File: A3343 SSO-056A

Hammer

First Name: Dr. Walter
Date of Birth: 30 June 1907
Place of Birth: Hagen
Highest Rank: SS-Obersturmbannführer
SS Number: 280155
Date Entered SS: 11 March 1937
NSDAP Number: 3196199
Date Entered NSDAP: 1 May 1933
Marital Status: Married
Religion: Agnostic
Civilian Occupation: Lawyer
Education: University
Foreign Language: No
World War I Service: No
EINSATZKOMMANDO: **2/IV**
Position: Commander
Einsatzkommando Service: Polish Campaign
Other Assignment: RSHA, Office VI E (SD, Foreign, Investigations); SD Prague
Waffen-SS Service: No
Highest Award: None listed
Postwar Sentence: No judicial proceedings discovered
Notes: Served in SA, 1933-1936
National Archives File: A3343 SSO-058A

Hampel

First Name:	Hugo
Date of Birth:	3 March 1912
Place of Birth:	Tomaschow, Poland
Highest Rank:	SS-Obersturmführer
SS Number:	392207
Date Entered SS:	Not listed
NSDAP Number:	Not a member
Marital Status:	Married
Religion:	Agnostic
Civilian Occupation:	Businessman
Education:	Grade School
Foreign Language:	Polish, Russian
World War I Service:	No
EINSATZKOMMANDO:	**VI**
Position:	Not listed
Einsatzkommando Service:	Polish Campaign
Other Assignment:	RSHA, Office I F (Personnel)
Waffen-SS Service:	No
Highest Award:	None listed
Postwar Sentence:	No judicial proceedings discovered
Notes:	Served in Polish Army 1933-1935 Reported to have served in *Einsatzgruppe D* as well
National Archives File:	A3343 SSO-059A

Hans

First Name:	Kurt
Date of Birth:	14 April 1911
Place of Birth:	Barmen
Highest Rank:	SS-Hauptsturmführer
SS Number:	335652
Date Entered SS:	Not listed
NSDAP Number:	1014830
Date Entered NSDAP:	1 March 1932
Marital Status:	Married
Religion:	Agnostic
Civilian Occupation:	Police
Education:	University
Foreign Language:	No
World War I Service:	No
EINSATZKOMMANDO:	**4a**
Position:	Criminal Police section
Einsatzkommando Service:	Not listed
Other Assignment:	Unknown
Waffen-SS Service:	No
Highest Award:	War Service Cross 2nd Class
Postwar Sentence:	No judicial proceedings discovered
Notes:	No mention of *Einsatzkommando* service in personnel file
National Archives File:	A3343 SSO-061A

Harder

First Name:	Karl-Arthur
Date of Birth:	19 September 1910
Place of Birth:	Frankfurt/Main
Highest Rank:	SS-Hauptsturmführer
SS Number:	4271
Date Entered SS:	Not listed
NSDAP Number:	173750
Date Entered NSDAP:	1 December 1929
Marital Status:	Married
Religion:	Agnostic
Civilian Occupation:	Businessman
Education:	Grade School
Foreign Language:	No
EINSATZKOMMANDO:	**1005, EG in Poland**
Position:	Not listed
Einsatzkommando Service:	1943-1944
Other Assignment:	Unknown
Highest Award:	None listed
Postwar Sentence:	1962, 3 years
Postwar Employment:	Krupp, Frankfurt/Main
Notes:	Served in SA, 1929-1930 No mention of *Sonderkommando 1005* service in personnel file
National Archives File:	A3343 SSO-063A

Hartl

First Name:	Albert
Date of Birth:	13 November 1904
Place of Birth:	Rossholzen
Highest Rank:	SS-Obersturmbannführer
SS Number:	107050
Date Entered SS:	25 April 1934
NSDAP Number:	3201046
Date Entered NSDAP:	1 May 1933
Marital Status:	Single
Religion:	Catholic
Civilian Occupation:	Catholic priest
Education:	University of Munich
Foreign Language:	French, Italian
EINSATZKOMMANDO:	**C**
Position:	Not listed
Einsatzkommando Service:	1941
Other Assignment:	RSHA, Office VI B (SD, Foreign, German-Italian Sphere) RSHA, Office IV (Gestapo)
Highest Award:	War Service Cross 2nd Class
Postwar Sentence:	No judicial proceedings discovered
Postwar Employment:	Writer
Notes:	Short personnel file
National Archives File:	A3343 SSO-066A

Hartmann

First Name: Erich
Date of Birth: 29 October 1897
Place of Birth: Schorndorf
Highest Rank: SS-Sturmbannführer
SS Number: 19761
Date Entered SS: 24 December 1932
NSDAP Number: 308471
Date Entered NSDAP: 1 September 1930
Marital Status: Married
Religion: Agnostic
Civilian Occupation: Unknown
Education: High School
Foreign Language: French, Italian
World War I Service: Yes, Iron Cross 2nd Class, 1st Foot Artillert Regiment
EINSATZKOMMANDO: **Luxembourg**
Position: Commander
Einsatzkommando Service: 1944
Waffen-SS Service: 2nd SS Infantry Brigade, 1941-1942
Highest Award: War Service Cross 2nd Class
Postwar Sentence: No judicial proceedings discovered
Notes: IIIrd SS Corps, 1943
No mention of *Einsatzkommando* service in personnel file
National Archives File: A3343 SSO-066A

Hasse

First Name: Hans
Date of Birth: 24 June 1905
Place of Birth: Barsinghausen
Highest Rank: SS-Obersturmführer
SS Number: 5731
Date Entered SS: 1 December 1930
NSDAP Number: 160489
Date Entered NSDAP: 1 November 1929
Marital Status: Married
Religion: Agnostic
Civilian Occupation: Government Counsel
Education: High School
Foreign Language: No
World War I Service: No
EINSATZKOMMANDO: **B, 8, C**
Position: Not listed
Einsatzkommando Service: B, C, 1941-1942; 8, 1944-1945
Other Assignment: Criminal Police Berlin; Gestapo Bremen
Waffen-SS Service: No
Highest Award: War Service Cross 1st Class
Postwar Sentence: 1969, 5 years
Notes: Eastern People's Medal
National Archives File: A3343 SSO-068A

Hasselberg

First Name: Dr. Alfred
Date of Birth: 30 August 1908
Place of Birth: Essen
Highest Rank: SS-Sturmbannführer
SS Number: 272286
Date Entered SS: Not listed
NSDAP Number: 2837238
Date Entered NSDAP: 1 May 1933
Marital Status: Married
Religion: Agnostic
Civilian Occupation: Lawyer
Education: University
Foreign Language: No
World War I Service: No
EINSATZKOMMANDO: **3/I**
Position: Commander
Einsatzkommando Service: Polish Campaign
Other Assignment: RSHA; Gestapo Lublin
Waffen-SS Service: No
Highest Award: None listed
Postwar Sentence: No judicial proceedings discovered
Notes: Reprimanded for multiple infractions by SS
National Archives File: A3343 SSO-068A

Haussmann

First Name: Emil
Date of Birth: 11 October 1910
Place of Birth: Ravensburg
Highest Rank: SS-Sturmbannführer
SS Number: 280307
Date Entered SS: 1 November 1936
NSDAP Number: 185729
Date Entered NSDAP: 1 January 1930
Marital Status: Married
Religion: Agnostic
Civilian Occupation: Teacher
Education: High School
Foreign Language: English, French
World War I Service: No
EINSATZKOMMANDO: **12**
Position: Not listed
Einsatzkommando Service: 21 June 1941–5 October 1941; 15 February 1942–15 July 1942
Other Assignment: RSHA
Highest Award: War Service Cross 2nd Class
Postwar Sentence: 1947, Indicted
Notes: Served in Hitler Youth, 1933-1936
Suicide, 31 July 1947
National Archives File: A3343 SSO-071A

Hayde

First Name: Ernst
Date of Birth: 19 January 1902
Place of Birth: Riga, Russia
Highest Rank: SS-Sturmbannführer
SS Number: 323705
Date Entered SS: 25 July 1938
NSDAP Number: 6186303
Date Entered NSDAP: 1 June 1933
Marital Status: Married
Religion: Agnostic
Civilian Occupation: Electroplate technician
Education: High School
Foreign Language: Russian, Latvian, English
EINSATZKOMMANDO: **D, Croatia**
Position: Not listed
Einsatzkommando Service: D, 1941-1942; Croatia, 1944
Other Assignment: SD Vienna
Waffen-SS Service: IIIrd SS Corps, 1943
Highest Award: War Service Cross 2nd Class
Postwar Sentence: No judicial proceedings discovered
Notes: Served in SA, 1933-1938
Lived in Russia, 1902-1918; lived in Latvia, 1918-1933
National Archives File: A3343 SSO-072A

Heier

First Name: Walter
Date of Birth: 7 May 1913
Place of Birth: Dortmund
Highest Rank: SS-Hauptsturmführer
SS Number: 349283
Date Entered SS: 1 October 1938
NSDAP Number: 2264430
Date Entered NSDAP: 1 May 1933
Marital Status: Married
Religion: Agnostic
Civilian Occupation: Police
Education: High School
Foreign Language: No
EINSATZKOMMANDO: **A**
Position: Personnel section
Einsatzkommando Service: July 1941–1944
Other Assignment: Gestapo Cologne
Waffen-SS Service: No
Highest Award: War Service Cross 2nd Class
Postwar Sentence: No judicial proceedings discovered
Notes: Served in SA, 1933-1938
No mention of *Einsatzkommando* service in personnel file
National Archives File: A3343 SSO-075A

Heimbach

First Name: Lothar
Date of Birth: 25 September 1908
Place of Birth: Hoffnungsthal
Highest Rank: SS-Hauptsturmführer
SS Number: 353607
Date Entered SS: Not listed
NSDAP Number: 5639833
Date Entered NSDAP: 1 May 1937
Marital Status: Married
Religion: Agnostic
Civilian Occupation: Police
Education: High School
Foreign Language: English, French
World War I Service: No
EINSATZKOMMANDO: Not listed
Einsatzkommando Service: Not listed
Other Assignment: BdS Northeast
Waffen-SS Service: 3rd SS Division "Totenkopf", 1945
Highest Award: War Service Cross 2nd Class
Postwar Sentence: No judicial proceedings discovered
Notes: Court martialed in 1944 for drunkeness and insubordination
National Archives File: A3343 SSO-077A

Heinritz

First Name: Dr. Martin
Date of Birth: 7 March 1907
Place of Birth: Schleiz
Highest Rank: SS-Sturmbannführer
SS Number: 326384
Date Entered SS: 5 May 1939
NSDAP Number: 450723
Date Entered NSDAP: 1 January 1931
Marital Status: Married
Religion: Agnostic
Civilian Occupation: Lawyer
Education: University
Foreign Language: No
World War I Service: No
EINSATZKOMMANDO: **D**
Position: Not listed
Einsatzkommando Service: November 1942 – September 1943
Other Assignment: RSHA, Office III D 2/1 (SD, Domestic, Economy)
Waffen-SS Service: No
Highest Award: Iron Cross 2nd Class
Notes: Served in SA, 1930-1931; Eastern People's Medal
Killed May 1, 1944 in a bombing raid on Berlin
National Archives File: A3343 SSO-079A

Heinz

First Name: Reinhold
Date of Birth: 4 February 1903
Place of Birth: Hohnsdorf/Limberg
Highest Rank: SS-Sturmbannführer
SS Number: 290635
Date Entered SS: 30 January 1938
NSDAP Number: 389515
Date Entered NSDAP: 1 December 1930
Marital Status: Married
Religion: Agnostic
Civilian Occupation: Businessman
Education: Grade School
Foreign Language: No
World War I Service: No
EINSATZKOMMANDO: **C**
Position: Not listed
Einsatzkommando Service: 1942
Other Assignment: RSHA, Office I A 4 (Law, Reichs Defense); SD Vienna
Highest Award: War Service Cross 1st Class
Postwar Sentence: No judicial proceedings discovered
Notes: Served in SA, 1931-1937
Fathered a child with a mistress in 1941
National Archives File: A3343 SSO-079A

Helfsgott

First Name: Walter
Date of Birth: 11 January 1911
Place of Birth: Barschdorf
Highest Rank: SS-Hauptsturmführer
SS Number: 327242
Date Entered SS: 16 December 1937
NSDAP Number: 4750512
Date Entered NSDAP: 1 May 1937
Marital Status: Married
Religion: Agnostic
Civilian Occupation: Police
Education: University
Foreign Language: No
EINSATZKOMMANDO: **C, 6, 1005**
Position: *Teilkommando* leader
Einsatzkommando Service: 13 August 1942–March 1943
Other Assignment: RSHA; Criminal Police Breslau
Highest Award: War Service Cross 2nd Class
Postwar Sentence: 1965, 4 years
Postwar Employment: Criminal Police Düsseldorf before 1964
Notes: Served in SA, 1933-1934
Served in *Einsatzgruppe Iltis*, 1944, fighting partisans
National Archives File: A3343 SSO-081A

Hellenbroich

First Name: Heinz
Date of Birth: 31 March 1906
Place of Birth: Düsseldorf
Highest Rank: SS-Sturmbannführer
SS Number: 396212
Date Entered SS: 16 September 1938
NSDAP Number: 1951324
Date Entered NSDAP: 1 May 1933
Marital Status: Married
Religion: Agnostic
Civilian Occupation: Government Counsel
Education: High School
Foreign Language: English, French
World War I Service: No
EINSATZKOMMANDO: **C**
Position: Not listed
Einsatzkommando Service: October 1941–February 1942
Other Assignment: Criminal Police Vienna; Gestapo Darmstadt
Waffen-SS Service: No
Highest Award: War Service Cross 2nd Class
Postwar Sentence: No judicial proceedings discovered
Notes: Joined Gestapo in 1934
National Archives File: A3343 SSO-081A

Hellwig

First Name: Otto
Date of Birth: 24 February 1898
Place of Birth: Nordhausen
Highest Rank: SS-Gruppenführer
SS Number: 272289
Date Entered SS: 1 July 1935
NSDAP Number: 2155531
Date Entered NSDAP: 30 April 1933
Marital Status: Married
Religion: Agnostic
Civilian Occupation: Police
Education: High School
Foreign Language: No
World War I Service: Yes, 2nd Pommeranian Ulan Regiment
EINSATZKOMMANDO: **von Woyrsch**
Position: *Einsatzkommando* leader
Einsatzkommando Service: Polish Campaign
Other Assignment: RSHA; Commander, SD/SP Leader's School
Highest Award: War Service Cross 1st Class
Postwar Sentence: No judicial proceedings discovered
Notes: Anti-Partisan Badge; SSPF Bialystok HSSPF Northeast
Died 20 August 1962
National Archives File: A3343 SSO-083A

Hengelhaupt

First Name: Dr. Erich
Date of Birth: 22 September 1911
Place of Birth: Magdeburg
Highest Rank: SS-Sturmbannführer
SS Number: 324972
Date Entered SS: 22 September 1938
NSDAP Number: 295880
Date Entered NSDAP: 1 August 1930
Marital Status: Married
Religion: Agnostic
Civilian Occupation: Student
Education: University
Foreign Language: No
World War I Service: No
EINSATZKOMMANDO: **A**
Position: Not listed
Einsatzkommando Service: Not listed
Other Assignment: RSHA, Office VI C (SD, Foreign, Russo-Japanese Sphere) RSHA, Office II D 1 (Technical Matters)
Highest Award: War Service Cross 1st Class
Postwar Sentence: No judicial proceedings discovered
Notes: No mention of *Einsatzkommando* service in personnel file
National Archives File: A3343 SSO-084A

Hennicke

First Name: Karl
Date of Birth: 21 January 1910
Place of Birth: Erfurt
Highest Rank: SS-Obersturmbannführer
SS Number: 3276
Date Entered SS: 1 December 1929
NSDAP Number: 119609
Date Entered NSDAP: 1 February 1929
Marital Status: Married
Religion: Agnostic
Civilian Occupation: Businessman
Education: High School
Foreign Language: No
World War I Service: No
EINSATZKOMMANDO: **C**
Position: Not listed
Einsatzkommando Service: Not listed
Other Assignment: Commander, SD Cologne; SD Karlsruhe
Highest Award: War Service Cross 1st Class
Postwar Sentence: No judicial proceedings discovered
Notes: Iron Cross 2nd Class 1941
No mention of *Einsatzkommando* service in personnel file
National Archives File: A3343 SSO-086A

Herrmann

First Name: Günther
Date of Birth: 15 September 1908
Place of Birth: Minden
Highest Rank: SS-Standartenführer
SS Number: 267283
Date Entered SS: 25 June 1935
NSDAP Number: 2475252
Date Entered NSDAP: 1 May 1933
Marital Status: Married
Religion: Agnostic
Civilian Occupation: Lawyer
Education: University of Kiel, Göttingen, Münster
Foreign Language: No
World War I Service: No
EINSATZKOMMANDO: **4b, 12, E**
Position: 4b – Commander; 12 – Commander; E–Commander
Einsatzkommando Service: 4b, – September 1941; 12, October 1942–March 1943 E, 1943–1945
Other Assignment: Gestapo Brünn; SD Fulda-Werra
Waffen-SS Service: No
Highest Award: War Service Cross 1st Class
Postwar Sentence: 1973, 7 years
Notes: Served in SA, 1933-1935
National Archives File: A3343 SSO-092A

Hersmann

First Name: Werner
Date of Birth: 11 September 1904
Place of Birth: Duisburg
Highest Rank: SS-Sturmbannführer
SS Number: 9416
Date Entered SS: 1 April 1931
NSDAP Number: 298562
Date Entered NSDAP: 1 September 1930
Marital Status: Married
Religion: Agnostic
Civilian Occupation: Engineer
Education: High School
Foreign Language: English, French
World War I Service: No
EINSATZKOMMANDO: **11a, Tilsit**
Position: Commander
Einsatzkommando Service: December 1942–May 1943
Other Assignment: SD Weimar; SD Königsberg
Waffen-SS Service: 36th SS Division "Dirlewanger", 1944 38th SS Division "Niebelungen", 1945
Highest Award: War Service Cross 2nd Class
Postwar Sentence: 1957, 13 Years
National Archives File: A3343 SSO-092A

Heuchert

First Name: Georg
Date of Birth: 24 February 1910
Place of Birth: Kolmea, Galicia
Highest Rank: SS-Obersturmführer
SS Number: 413310
Date Entered SS: 1 January 1941
NSDAP Number: Not a member
Marital Status: Married
Religion: Agnostic
Civilian Occupation: Lawyer
Education: University of Lemberg
Foreign Language: Polish, Russian, Ukrainian
World War I Service: No
EINSATZKOMMANDO: **D**
Position: Not listed; probably an interrogator
Einsatzkommando Service: June 1941–November 1942
Other Assignment: RSHA, Office VII B 6 (Marxism-Bolshevism)
Waffen-SS Service: No
Highest Award: War Service Cross 2nd Class
Postwar Sentence: No judicial proceedings discovered
Notes: Served in Polish Army 1930-1931
National Archives File: A3343 SSO-094A

Heuser

First Name: Georg-Albert
Date of Birth: 27 February 1913
Place of Birth: Berlin
Highest Rank: SS-Hauptsturmführer
SS Number: Not listed
Date Entered SS: Not listed
NSDAP Number: Not a member
Marital Status: Married
Religion: Unknown
Civilian Occupation: Police
Education: University of Berlin, Königsberg, Prague
Foreign Language: Unknown
World War I Service: No
EINSATZKOMMANDO: **A, 1b, 14**
Position: 14 – Commander
Einsatzkommando Service: A, September 1941–August 1944; 14, August 1944–undetermined
Other Assignment: RSHA; Criminal Police Berlin
Waffen-SS Service: Unknown
Highest Award: None listed
Postwar Sentence: 1962, 15 years commuted to 5 years
Postwar Employment: Lawyer
Notes: Short personnel file
National Archives File: No File

Hinze

First Name: Willi
Date of Birth: 24 March 1907
Place of Birth: Eickendorf
Highest Rank: SS-Hauptsturmführer
SS Number: 17476
Date Entered SS: 1 May 1931
NSDAP Number: 472276
Date Entered NSDAP: 1 January 1931
Marital Status: Married
Religion: Agnostic
Civilian Occupation: Lawyer
Education: University
Foreign Language: French
World War I Service: No
EINSATZKOMMANDO: **A**
Position: Not listed
Einsatzkommando Service: Not listed
Other Assignment: RSHA; SD Riga; SD Stettin
Waffen-SS Service: No
Highest Award: None listed
Postwar Sentence: No judicial proceedings discovered
Notes: Gestapo Kösslin
National Archives File: A3343 SSO-100A

Hödle

First Name: Emil
Date of Birth: 2 April 1908
Place of Birth: Villingen/Black Forest
Highest Rank: SS-Untersturmführer
SS Number: 308030
Date Entered SS: Not listed
NSDAP Number: 4144539
Date Entered NSDAP: 1 May 1937
Marital Status: Married
Religion: Agnostic
Civilian Occupation: Police
Education: High School
Foreign Language: French
World War I Service: No
EINSATZKOMMANDO: **Elsass**
Position: Not listed
Einsatzkommando Service: 1940
Other Assignment: RSHA; SD Stuttgart
Waffen-SS Service: No
Highest Award: None listed
Postwar Employment: N/A
Notes: Killed in a hand grenade training accident
National Archives File: A3343 SSO-102A

Höfler

First Name: Albert
Date of Birth: 16 November 1906
Place of Birth: Frankfurt/Main
Highest Rank: SS-Hauptsturmführer
SS Number: 92258
Date Entered SS: 20 February 1933
NSDAP Number: 2532286
Date Entered NSDAP: 1 May 1933
Marital Status: Single
Religion: Agnostic
Civilian Occupation: Businessman
Education: University
Foreign Language: Spanish
World War I Service: No
EINSATZKOMMANDO: **A**
Position: Not listed
Einsatzkommando Service: Not listed
Other Assignment: RSHA, Office III A 4 (SD, Domestic, Legal Practice)
Highest Award: Iron Cross 2nd Class
Postwar Sentence: No judicial proceedings discovered
Notes: Infantry Assault Badge
Wounded; right arm amputated 1944
National Archives File: A3343 SSO-102A

Höhmann

First Name: Gottlieb
Date of Birth: 7 January 1907
Place of Birth: Remscheid
Highest Rank: SS-Hauptsturmführer
SS Number: 353228
Date Entered SS: Not listed
NSDAP Number: 360034
Date Entered NSDAP: 23 October 1930
Marital Status: Married
Religion: Agnostic
Civilian Occupation: Detective Officer
Education: University
Foreign Language: No
World War I Service: No
EINSATZKOMMANDO: **C**
Position: Not listed
Einsatzkommando Service: Not listed
Other Assignment: Criminal Police Münster; Gestapo Düsseldorf
Waffen-SS Service: No
Highest Award: None listed
Postwar Sentence: No judicial proceedings discovered
Notes: Served in SA, 1930-1934
National Archives File: A3343 SSO-103A

Hofmann

First Name: Dr. Walter
Date of Birth: 26 September 1905
Place of Birth: Frankfurt/Main
Highest Rank: SS-Sturmbannführer
SS Number: 92210
Date Entered SS: 15 April 1933
NSDAP Number: 1821949
Date Entered NSDAP: 1 April 1933
Marital Status: Married
Religion: Protestant
Civilian Occupation: Lawyer
Education: University of Frankfurt/Main, Berlin
Foreign Language: No
World War I Service: No
EINSATZKOMMANDO: **C**
Position: Chief of Staff
Einsatzkommando Service: 1941–1942
Other Assignment: RSHA
Waffen-SS Service: No
Highest Award: None listed
Postwar Sentence: No judicial proceedings discovered
Notes: No mention of *Einsatzkommando* service in personnel file
National Archives File: A3343 SSO-112A

Holste

First Name: Eduard
Date of Birth: 14 February 1904
Place of Birth: Braunschweig
Highest Rank: SS-Obersturmbannführer
SS Number: 86068
Date Entered SS: 10 July 1933
NSDAP Number: 3552385
Date Entered NSDAP: 1 May 1933
Marital Status: Married
Religion: Agnostic
Civilian Occupation: Lawyer
Education: University of Göttingen
Foreign Language: No
World War I Service: No
EINSATZKOMMANDO: **II, B**
Position: II, Liaison officer to 10th Army
Einsatzkommando Service: II, Polish Campaign; B, 29 September 1941–6 March 1943
Other Assignment: RSHA
Waffen-SS Service: No
Highest Award: War Service Cross 1st Class
Postwar Sentence: No judicial proceedings discovered
Notes: House was destroyed in a 22 November 1943 air raid on Berlin
National Archives File: A3343 SSO-114A

Hoyer

First Name: Hans
Date of Birth: 25 November 1910
Place of Birth: Freiberg
Highest Rank: SS-Untersturmführer
SS Number: 19917
Date Entered SS: 2 October 1931
NSDAP Number: 714826
Date Entered NSDAP: 1 November 1931
Marital Status: Married
Religion: Agnostic
Civilian Occupation: Machinist
Education: Grade School
Foreign Language: No
World War I Service: No
EINSATZKOMMANDO: **D**
Position: Not listed
Einsatzkommando Service: 19 May 1941–15 July 1942
Other Assignment: RSHA; Police Plauen
Waffen-SS Service: No
Highest Award: War Service Cross 2nd Class
Postwar Sentence: No judicial proceedings discovered
Notes: Short personnel file
National Archives File: A3343 SSO-117A

Hubig

First Name: Dr. Hermann
Date of Birth: 12 March 1912
Place of Birth: Völkingen
Highest Rank: SS-Sturmbannführer
SS Number: 290303
Date Entered SS: 1 October 1936
NSDAP Number: 2709693
Date Entered NSDAP: 1 April 1933
Marital Status: Divorced
Religion: Agnostic
Civilian Occupation: Lawyer
Education: University
Foreign Language: No
EINSATZKOMMANDO: **A, 1b**
Position: 1b – Commander
Einsatzkommando Service: A, 15 September 1941–5 December 1941; 1b, 1942–October 1942
Other Assignment: RSHA, Office VI B (SD, Foreign, German-Italian Sphere); SD Prague
Highest Award: Iron Cross 1st Class
Postwar Sentence: No judicial proceedings discovered
Notes: Operation Zeppelin; Infantry Assault Badge
Used the alias of Helmut Haller after WWII
National Archives File: A3343 SSO-119A

Huck

First Name: Heinrich
Date of Birth: 7 October 1905
Place of Birth: Veltheim
Highest Rank: SS-Hauptsturmführer
SS Number: 291000
Date Entered SS: Not listed
NSDAP Number: Not a member
Marital Status: Married
Religion: Agnostic
Civilian Occupation: Detective Officer
Education: Technical School
Foreign Language: English
World War I Service: No
EINSATZKOMMANDO: **D**
Position: Not listed
Einsatzkommando Service: Not listed
Other Assignment: Criminal Police Munich; Gestapo Hannover
Waffen-SS Service: No
Highest Award: None listed
Killed in Action: No
Postwar Sentence: No judicial proceedings discovered
Notes: Punished for mishandling a prisoner in 1942
National Archives File: A3343 SSO-119A

Hüsch

First Name: Willi
Date of Birth: 8 April 1910
Place of Birth: Leverkusen
Highest Rank: SS-Untersturmführer
SS Number: 39600
Date Entered SS: Not listed
NSDAP Number: Not a member
Marital Status: Married
Religion: Unknown
Civilian Occupation: Unknown
Education: Unknown
Foreign Language: No
World War I Service: No
EINSATZKOMMANDO: **C**
Position: Not listed
Einsatzkommando Service: Undetermined to 26 December 1942
Other Assignment: Unknown
Waffen-SS Service: Unknown
Highest Award: Iron Cross 1st Class
Notes: Wounded several times; killed in action fighting partisans, 26 December 1942
Extremely short personnel file
National Archives File: A3343 SSO-120A

Hüttig

First Name: Ludwig
Date of Birth: 29 May 1912
Place of Birth: Titschendorf
Highest Rank: SS-Hauptsturmführer
SS Number: 353433
Date Entered SS: 1 May 1940
NSDAP Number: 2905310
Date Entered NSDAP: 1 May 1933
Marital Status: Married
Religion: Agnostic
Civilian Occupation: Police
Education: University of Jena, Tübingen
Foreign Language: No
EINSATZKOMMANDO: **1b**
Position: Not listed
Einsatzkommando Service: June 1941–November 1941
Other Assignment: RSHA; Gestapo Erfurt
Highest Award: Iron Cross 2nd Class
Postwar Sentence: 1961, Acquitted
Postwar Employment: Chemical factory
Notes: Served in SA, 1933-1936
No mention of *Einsatzkommando* service in personnel file
National Archives File: A3343 SSO-121A

Hummel

First Name: Wilhelm
Date of Birth: 14 September 1902
Place of Birth: Kitzingen
Highest Rank: SS-Untersturmführer
SS Number: 353538
Date Entered SS: Not listed
NSDAP Number: 1014094
Date Entered NSDAP: 1 March 1932
Marital Status: Married
Religion: Agnostic
Civilian Occupation: Businessman
Education: Trade School
Foreign Language: No
World War I Service: No
EINSATZKOMMANDO: **D**
Position: Not listed
Einsatzkommando Service: 17 May 1941–10 May 1942
Other Assignment: RSHA; SD Nürnberg
Highest Award: None listed
Postwar Sentence: No judicial proceedings discovered
Notes: Served in SA, 1932-1934
Crimea Shield
National Archives File: A3343 SSO-121A

Huppenkothen

First Name: Walter
Date of Birth: 31 December 1907
Place of Birth: Haan
Highest Rank: SS-Standartenführer
SS Number: 126785
Date Entered SS: 1 April 1933
NSDAP Number: 1950150
Date Entered NSDAP: 1 May 1933
Marital Status: Married
Religion: Agnostic
Civilian Occupation: Lawyer
Education: University
Foreign Language: English, French
EINSATZKOMMANDO: **I**
Position: Chief of Staff
Einsatzkommando Service: Polish Campaign
Other Assignment: Chief, Office IV E, RSHA, (Gestapo, Counterintelligence)
SD Lüneburg
Highest Award: War Service Cross 1st Class
Postwar Sentence: 1951, 6 years
Notes: Deputy for Border Police in the RSHA
Served as a judge in trial against Admiral Canaris
National Archives File: A3343 SSO-122A

Ilges

First Name: Wolfgang
Date of Birth: 22 August 1909
Place of Birth: Cologne
Highest Rank: SS-Sturmbannführer
SS Number: 107304
Date Entered SS: 30 July 1934
NSDAP Number: 4583156
Date Entered NSDAP: 1 May 1937
Marital Status: Married
Religion: Agnostic
Civilian Occupation: Lawyer
Education: University of Cologne
Foreign Language: No
EINSATZKOMMANDO: **Tilsit**
Position: Not listed
Einsatzkommando Service: Not listed
Other Assignment: RSHA, Office III A 3 (SD, Domestic, Legal Practice)
SD Düsseldorf
Highest Award: War Service Cross 2nd Class
Postwar Sentence: 1957, 4 years
Postwar Employment: Life insurance agency
Notes: No mention of *Einsatzkommando* service in personnel file
National Archives File: A3343 SSO-125A

Isselhorst

First Name: Dr. Erich
Date of Birth: 5 February 1906
Place of Birth: St. Apold
Highest Rank: SS-Standartenführer
SS Number: 267313
Date Entered SS: 15 November 1934
NSDAP Number: 1269847
Date Entered NSDAP: 1 August 1932
Marital Status: Married
Religion: Agnostic
Civilian Occupation: Lawyer
Education: University of Cologne, Munich
Foreign Language: No
World War I Service: No
EINSATZKOMMANDO: **8, 1b, 1a**
Position: 8 – Commander; 1b – Commander; 1 – Commander
Einsatzkommando Service: 8, September 1942–November 1942 1b, 30 June 1943 – October 1943
Other Assignment: SD Strassbourg; SD Stuttgart
Highest Award: Iron Cross 2nd Class
Postwar Sentence: Executed 23 February 1948
Notes: Executed by French for activities with SD Strasbourg
National Archives File: A3343 SSO-127A

Jäger

First Name: Karl
Date of Birth: 20 September 1888
Place of Birth: Schaffhausen, Switzerland
Highest Rank: SS-Standartenführer
SS Number: 62823
Date Entered SS: 9 April 1933
NSDAP Number: 359269
Date Entered NSDAP: 1 November 1930
Marital Status: Married
Religion: Agnostic
Civilian Occupation: Businessman
Education: Trade School
World War I Service: Yes, Iron Cross 1st Class
EINSATZKOMMANDO: **3**
Position: Commander
Einsatzkommando Service: June 1941–1943
Other Assignment: RSHA; SD Münster
Highest Award: War Service Cross 1st Class
Postwar Sentence: Proceedings terminated by suicide in 1959
Postwar Employment: Farmer, Heidelberg
Notes: Son died on the eastern front in 1942
Suicide, 22 June 1959
National Archives File: A3343 SSO-129A

Jahr

First Name: Dr. Ernst
Date of Birth: 12 June 1909
Place of Birth: Cramon
Highest Rank: SS-Sturmbannführer
SS Number: 86155
Date Entered SS: 30 June 1933
NSDAP Number: 196793
Date Entered NSDAP: 2 June 1930
Marital Status: Single
Religion: Agnostic
Civilian Occupation: Lawyer
Education: University of Rostock, Graz, Berlin, Göttingen
Foreign Language: No
EINSATZKOMMANDO: **Tilsit**
Position: Not listed
Einsatzkommando Service: June 1941–December 1941
Other Assignment: RSHA, Office IV A (Gestapo, Enemies)
RSHA, Office IV C 3 (Card Files)
Highest Award: War Service Cross 2nd Class
Postwar Sentence: 1957, 3 Years
Notes: Entered NSDAP while living in Austria; SD Königsberg
Served in Army 18th Infantry Regiment in 1936 and 1937
National Archives File: A3343 SSO-131A

Janssen

First Name: Adolf
Date of Birth: 20 May 1916
Place of Birth: Hoehr.-Grenzhausen
Highest Rank: SS-Hauptsturmführer
SS Number: 392501
Date Entered SS: 18 February 1938
NSDAP Number: 3501019
Date Entered NSDAP: 1 May 1934
Marital Status: Married
Religion: Agnostic
Civilian Occupation: Police
Education: High School
Foreign Language: No
World War I Service: No
EINSATZKOMMANDO: **4a**
Position: *Teilkommando* leader
Einsatzkommando Service: 1941
Other Assignment: Gestapo Frankfurt/Main
Highest Award: Iron Cross 2nd Class
Postwar Sentence: 1968, 11 years
Notes: Served in Hitler Youth, 1929-1935
No mention of *Einsatzkommando* service in personnel file
National Archives File: A3343 SSO-134A

Jaskulsky

First Name: Dr. Hans
Date of Birth: 14 September 1912
Place of Birth: Samotschin (Posen)
Highest Rank: SS-Sturmbannführer
SS Number: 276308
Date Entered SS: 1 December 1935
NSDAP Number: 2636039
Date Entered NSDAP: 1 May 1933
Marital Status: Married
Religion: Agnostic
Civilian Occupation: Lawyer
Education: University of Heidelberg, Graz
Foreign Language: English, French
World War I Service: No
EINSATZKOMMANDO: **13, H**
Position: Commander
Einsatzkommando Service: H, 1944
Other Assignment: RSHA; SD Graz
Highest Award: War Service Cross 1st Class
Postwar Sentence: No judicial proceedings discovered
Notes: Served in Hitler Youth, 1928-1931; served in SA 1933-1935
SD Bayreuth; won Iron Cross 2nd Class in *Einsatzgruppe H*
National Archives File: A3343 SSO-135A

Jedamzik

First Name: Eduard
Date of Birth: 17 June 1901
Place of Birth: Alt-Ukta
Highest Rank: SS-Sturmbannführer
SS Number: 130610
Date Entered SS: Not listed
NSDAP Number: 1333091
Date Entered NSDAP: Not listed
Marital Status: Married
Religion: Agnostic
Civilian Occupation: Lawyer
Education: Unknown
Foreign Language: No
World War I Service: Yes, 38th Field Artillery Regiment
EINSATZKOMMANDO: **10b**
Position: Commander
Einsatzkommando Service: February 1943–May 1943
Other Assignment: RSHA Office III (SD, Domestic); Gestapo Plauen; Gestapo Koblenz; Gestapo Chemnitz
Waffen-SS Service: No
Highest Award: War Service Cross 2nd Class
Postwar Sentence: No judicial proceedings discovered
Notes: Died 1966
National Archives File: A3343 SSO-135A

Jonas

First Name: Karl
Date of Birth: 3 August 1909
Place of Birth: Gimine, Austria
Highest Rank: SS-Obersturmführer
SS Number: 352386
Date Entered SS: Not listed
NSDAP Number: 6307691
Date Entered NSDAP: 1 April 1937
Marital Status: Married
Religion: Agnostic
Civilian Occupation: Police
Education: High School
Foreign Language: Italian
World War I Service: No
EINSATZKOMMANDO: **D**
Position: attached element from Police Battalion 9
Einsatzkommando Service: Not listed
Other Assignment: Unknown
Waffen-SS Service: No
Highest Award: War Service Cross 2nd Class
Postwar Sentence: No judicial proceedings discovered
Notes: Served in SA, 1937-1938
National Archives File: A3343 SSO-141A

Jost

First Name: Dr. Heinz
Date of Birth: 9 July 1904
Place of Birth: Holzhausen
Highest Rank: SS-Brigadeführer
SS Number: 36243
Date Entered SS: 25 July 1934
NSDAP Number: 75946
Date Entered NSDAP: 1 February 1928
Marital Status: Widowed
Religion: Agnostic
Civilian Occupation: Lawyer
Education: University of Munich, Giessen
Foreign Language: No
EINSATZKOMMANDO: **A**
Position: Commander
Einsatzkommando Service: 29 March 1942 – 2 September 1942
Other Assignment: Chief, Office VI, RSHA (SD, Foreign)
Chief, Office III, RSHA, (SD, Domestic)
Highest Award: Golden Party Badge
Postwar Sentence: 1948, Death, released 1951
Notes: Sick throughout the war
Died 12 November 1964
National Archives File: A3343 SSO-141A

Jürges

First Name: Albert
Date of Birth: 12 October 1910
Place of Birth: Haverlah
Highest Rank: SS-Obersturmführer
SS Number: 68246
Date Entered SS: 28 February 1933
NSDAP Number: 1513512
Date Entered NSDAP: 1 March 1933
Marital Status: Married
Religion: Agnostic
Civilian Occupation: Machinist
Education: Grade School
Foreign Language: No
World War I Service: No
EINSATZKOMMANDO: **D**
Position: Not listed
Einsatzkommando Service: Not listed
Other Assignment: RSHA; SD Hamburg
Highest Award: Iron Cross 2nd Class
Postwar Sentence: No judicial proceedings discovered
Notes: Served in SA, 1932; Eastern People's Medal
No mention of *Einsatzkommando* service in personnel file
National Archives File: A3343 SSO-142A

Junker

First Name: Kurt
Date of Birth: 15 June 1902
Place of Birth: Cologne
Highest Rank: SS-Hauptsturmführer
SS Number: 49398
Date Entered SS: 1 May 1932
NSDAP Number: 781640
Date Entered NSDAP: 1 January 1932
Marital Status: Married
Religion: Agnostic
Civilian Occupation: Businessman
Education: High School
Foreign Language: No
World War I Service: Yes, 8th Currasier Regiment
EINSATZKOMMANDO: **A**
Position: Not listed
Einsatzkommando Service: 1942
Other Assignment: Unknown
Waffen-SS Service: SS Regiment "Der Führer", 1940
Highest Award: Iron Cross 2nd Class
Postwar Sentence: No judicial proceedings discovered
Notes: Commander 13th White Russian Security Battalion
National Archives File: A3343 SSO-145A

Kah

First Name: Dr. Ernst
Date of Birth: 20 June 1899
Place of Birth: Baden-Baden
Highest Rank: SS-Obersturmbannführer
SS Number: 290543
Date Entered SS: 1 August 1937
NSDAP Number: 1298873
Date Entered NSDAP: 1 September 1932
Marital Status: Married
Religion: Agnostic
Civilian Occupation: Lawyer
Education: University of Heidelberg, Tübingen, Freiburg
Foreign Language: No
World War I Service: Yes, 170th Infantry Regiment, Iron Cross 2nd Class
EINSATZKOMMANDO: **IV**
Position: Unknown
Einsatzkommando Service: Polish Campaign
Other Assignment: RSHA, IdS Munich, SD Warsaw
Waffen-SS Service: No
Highest Award: None listed
National Archives File: A3343 SSO-147A

Kallbach

First Name: Friedrich
Date of Birth: 19 July 1911
Place of Birth: Sommerfeld
Highest Rank: SS-Sturmbannführer
SS Number: 272324
Date Entered SS: 26 June 1935
NSDAP Number: 280184
Date Entered NSDAP: 1 August 1930
Marital Status: Married
Religion: Agnostic
Civilian Occupation: Lawyer
Education: University of Berlin
Foreign Language: No
World War I Service: No
EINSATZKOMMANDO: **C**
Position: Not listed
Einsatzkommando Service: 1 May 1942–1943
Other Assignment: RSHA; SD Oppeln, SD Kattowitz, SD Nürnberg
Waffen-SS Service: No
Highest Award: War Service Cross 1st Class
Postwar Sentence: Proceedings started but defendant died
Notes: Died 1966
National Archives File: A3343 SSO-149A

Kerschl

First Name: Josef
Date of Birth: 14 February 1902
Place of Birth: Donauwörth
Highest Rank: SS-Untersturmführer
SS Number: 354325
Date Entered SS: Not listed
NSDAP Number: Not a member
Marital Status: Married
Religion: Catholic
Civilian Occupation: Police
Education: Grade School
Foreign Language: No
World War I Service: No
EINSATZKOMMANDO: **7a**
Position: Not listed
Einsatzkommando Service: Not listed
Other Assignment: Gestapo Neustadt
Waffen-SS Service: No
Highest Award: None listed
Killed in Action: No
Postwar Sentence: No judicial proceedings discovered
Notes: In police since 1922
National Archives File: A3343 SSO-165A

Kirste

First Name: Arnold
Date of Birth: 4 August 1901
Place of Birth: Jarotschin
Highest Rank: SS-Sturmbannführer
SS Number: 52191
Date Entered SS: Not listed
NSDAP Number: Not a member
Marital Status: Unknown
Religion: Unknown
Civilian Occupation: Police
Education: Unknown
Foreign Language: Unknown
World War I Service: Unknown
EINSATZKOMMANDO: **2**
Position: Gestapo section leader
Einsatzkommando Service: July 1941–1944
Other Assignment: Police Breslau
Waffen-SS Service: No
Highest Award: War Service Cross 2nd Class
Killed in Action: No
Postwar Sentence: No judicial proceedings discovered
Notes: Awarded War Service Cross 2nd Class by commander Army Group North
National Archives File: A3343 SSO-172A

Klemmer

First Name: Werner
Date of Birth: 18 July 1912
Place of Birth: Altenwald/Saarbrücken
Highest Rank: 426597
Date Entered SS: 1 July 1942
NSDAP Number: 2697381
Date Entered NSDAP: 1 June 1933
Marital Status: Married
Religion: Agnostic
Civilian Occupation: Police
Education: High School
Foreign Language: No
EINSATZKOMMANDO: **C**
Position: Not listed
Einsatzkommando Service: December 1942–1944
Other Assignment: RSHA, Office V (Kripo); SD Cologne
Highest Award: War Service Cross 2nd Class
Postwar Sentence: 1961, Acquitted
Postwar Employment: State Police, Saarbrücken
Notes: Served in Hitler Youth, 1935
Served in Army during Polish Campaign
National Archives File: A3343 SSO-179A

Klingelhöfer

First Name: Waldemar
Date of Birth: 4 April 1900
Place of Birth: Moscow, Russia
Highest Rank: SS-Sturmbannführer
SS Number: 52744
Date Entered SS: 1 February 1933
NSDAP Number: 258951
Date Entered NSDAP: 1 June 1930
Marital Status: Married
Religion: Agnostic
Civilian Occupation: Opera singer
Education: High School
Foreign Language: Russian
World War I Service: Yes, 11th Pionier Battalion
EINSATZKOMMANDO: **Vorkommando Moscow, B**
Position: Vorkommando Moscow – Commander; B – staff
Einsatzkommando Service: Vorkommando Moscow, 22 June 1941–October 1941 B, December 1941–December 1943
Other Assignment: RSHA, Office VI (SD, Foreign); SD Fulda-Werra
Highest Award: War Service Cross 1st Class
Postwar Sentence: 1948, Death commuted to Life, released
Notes: Operation Zeppelin
SD Kassel
National Archives File: A3343 SSO-180A

Knop

First Name:	Fritz
Date of Birth:	18 February 1897
Place of Birth:	Neuklenz
Highest Rank:	SS-Untersturmführer
SS Number:	385164
Date Entered SS:	25 October 1938
NSDAP Number:	8014533
Date Entered NSDAP:	1 April 1941
Marital Status:	Married
Religion:	Agnostic
Civilian Occupation:	Police
Education:	Grade School
Foreign Language:	No
World War I Service:	Yes, Infantry, Prisoner of War of the British
EINSATZKOMMANDO:	**C**
Position:	Not listed
Einsatzkommando Service:	Not listed
Other Assignment:	RSHA; Criminal Police Berlin
Highest Award:	None listed
Postwar Sentence:	1961, 3 years
Notes:	Served in Police since 1921 No mention of *Einsatzkommando* service in personnel file
National Archives File:	A3343 SSO-187A

Kockerols

First Name:	Friedrich
Date of Birth:	27 June 1904
Place of Birth:	Ichendorf
Highest Rank:	SS-Untersturmführer
SS Number:	280239
Date Entered SS:	Not listed
NSDAP Number:	738328
Date Entered NSDAP:	1 December 1931
Marital Status:	Married
Religion:	Agnostic
Civilian Occupation:	Police
Education:	High School
Foreign Language:	No
World War I Service:	No
EINSATZKOMMANDO:	**B**
Position:	Not listed
Einsatzkommando Service:	1942
Other Assignment:	RSHA; Gestapo Hohensalza
Waffen-SS Service:	No
Highest Award:	None listed
Postwar Sentence:	No judicial proceedings discovered
Notes:	Court martialed in 1942 and sentenced to 2 years imprisonment
National Archives File:	A3343 SSO-190A

Körting

First Name:	Dr. Erich
Date of Birth:	22 January 1902
Place of Birth:	Teerten/Dessau
Highest Rank:	SS-Obersturmbannführer
SS Number:	3395
Date Entered SS:	1 May 1929
NSDAP Number:	126764
Date Entered NSDAP:	1 May 1929
Marital Status:	Married
Religion:	Agnostic
Civilian Occupation:	Businessman
Education:	University
Foreign Language:	No
World War I Service:	No
EINSATZKOMMANDO:	**Vorkommando Moscow**
Position:	Commander
Einsatzkommando Service:	September 1941 – December 1941
Other Assignment:	SD Dessau
Highest Award:	War Service Cross 1st Class
Postwar Sentence:	No judicial proceedings discovered
Notes:	Propaganda bureau Magdeburg, 1932 Spent 4 months in jail in 1920s for Nazi activities
National Archives File:	A3343 SSC-194A

Korndörfer

First Name:	Rudolf
Date of Birth:	20 June 1906
Place of Birth:	Reichenbach
Highest Rank:	SS-Sturmbannführer
SS Number:	107409
Date Entered SS:	1 February 01,1934
NSDAP Number:	1918161
Date Entered NSDAP:	1 May 1933
Marital Status:	Single
Religion:	Unknown
Civilian Occupation:	Lawyer
Education:	University
Foreign Language:	No
World War I Service:	No
EINSATZKOMMANDO:	**11a, Agram** (Zagreb)
Position:	Commander
Einsatzkommando Service:	1944-1945
Other Assignment:	RSHA; SD Metz
Waffen-SS Service:	No
Highest Award:	War Service Cross 1st Class
Postwar Sentence:	No judicial proceedings discovered
Notes:	*Einsatzkommando I/II* Metz 1941
National Archives File:	A3343 SSO-202A

Kortkampf

First Name: Gerhard
Date of Birth: 26 August 1912
Place of Birth: Emden
Highest Rank: SS-Sturmbannführer
SS Number: 77067
Date Entered SS: 1 March 1933
NSDAP Number: 572902
Date Entered NSDAP: 1 May 1931
Marital Status: Married
Religion: Agnostic
Civilian Occupation: Bookseller
Education: High School
Foreign Language: English
World War I Service: No
EINSATZKOMMANDO: **A**
Position: Not listed
Einsatzkommando Service: 21 June 1941–5 October 1941; 15 February 1942–15 July 1942
Other Assignment: RSHA, Office III B 2 (SD, Domestic); SD Stettin
Waffen-SS Service: No
Highest Award: Iron Cross 2nd Class
Postwar Sentence: No judicial proceedings discovered
Notes: Served in SA, 193; KdS Reval
National Archives File: A3343 SSO-203A

Koskull

First Name: Andreas von
Date of Birth: 13 December 1906
Place of Birth: Talsen, Russia
Highest Rank: SS-Sturmbannführer
SS Number: 357284
Date Entered SS: 1 June 1940
NSDAP Number: 8434512
Date Entered NSDAP: 1 August 1941
Marital Status: Married
Religion: Protestant
Civilian Occupation: Farmer
Education: High School
Foreign Language: French, Russian, Latvian
World War I Service: No
EINSATZKOMMANDO: **C, 6**
Position: Not listed, prbabbly interrogator
Einsatzkommando Service: June 1941-June 1942
Other Assignment: SS Hauptamt, Office D
Waffen-SS Service: IInd SS Flak Detachment
Highest Award: Iron Cross 2nd Class
Postwar Sentence: No judicial proceedings discovered
Notes: Served in Latvian Army before the war
National Archives File: A3343 SSO-203A

Krahner

First Name: Max
Date of Birth: 8 March 1904
Place of Birth: Neustadt
Highest Rank: SS-Hauptsturmführer
SS Number: 9777
Date Entered SS: Not listed (c. 1930-1931)
NSDAP Number: 472617
Date Entered NSDAP: 1 January 1931
Marital Status: Widowed
Religion: Agnostic
Civilian Occupation: Businessman
Education: High School
Foreign Language: No
World War I Service: No
EINSATZKOMMANDO: **1005**
Position: Not listed
Einsatzkommando Service: Not listed
Other Assignment: RSHA; SS District Elbe
Highest Award: War Service Cross 2nd Class
Postwar Sentence: No judicial proceedings discovered
Notes: Served in *Einsatzgruppe Iltis*, 1944, fighting partisans
No mention of *Einsatzkommando* service in personnel file
National Archives File: A3343 SSO-206A

Kraus

First Name: Otto
Date of Birth: 22 February 1906
Place of Birth: Riga, Russia
Highest Rank: SS-Sturmbannführer
SS Number: 357285
Date Entered SS: 1 June 1940
NSDAP Number: Not a member
Marital Status: Widowed
Religion: Protestant
Civilian Occupation: Architect
Education: High School
Foreign Language: Russian, Latvian
World War I Service: No
EINSATZKOMMANDO: **A, 2**
Position: A – Translator; 2 – Security section leader
Einsatzkommando Service: 1941–November 1942
Other Assignment: SS District Warthe
Waffen-SS Service: No
Highest Award: War Service Cross 1st Class
Postwar Sentence: No judicial proceedings discovered
Notes: Served in Latvian Army, 1933-1934 Operation Zeppelin
Iron Cross 2nd Class for *einatzkommando*
Eastern People's Medal
National Archives File: A3343 SSO-208A

Kraus

First Name: Hans
Date of Birth: 6 January 1904
Place of Birth: Riga, Russia
Highest Rank: SS-Sturmbannführer
SS Number: 357289
Date Entered SS: 1 June 1940
NSDAP Number: Not a member
Marital Status: Married
Religion: Protestant
Civilian Occupation: Tester
Education: University
Foreign Language: Russian, Latvian
World War I Service: No
EINSATZKOMMANDO: **3, 1b**
Position: Intelligence Officer
Einsatzkommando Service: June 1941–August 1942
Other Assignment: RSHA; SD Cracow
Highest Award: Iron Cross 1st Class
Postwar Sentence: 1961, Acquitted
Postwar Employment: German Baltic Association
Notes: Served in Latvian Army, 1931-1932; wounded in action 1 August 1942
Infantry Assault Badge; praised in efficiency reports
National Archives File: A3343 SSO-208A

Krause

First Name: Waldemar
Date of Birth: 15 July 1908
Place of Birth: Strasburg
Highest Rank: SS-Sturmbannführer
SS Number: 346964
Date Entered SS: 10 September 1939
NSDAP Number: 2953348
Date Entered NSDAP: 1 May 1933
Marital Status: Married
Religion: Agnostic
Civilian Occupation: Police
Education: High School
Foreign Language: English, French
World War I Service: No
EINSATZKOMMANDO: **4b**
Position: Commander
Einsatzkommando Service: August 1943–January 1944
Other Assignment: RSHA; Police, Saarbrücken
Highest Award: Iron Cross 2nd Class
Postwar Sentence: No judicial proceedings discovered
Notes: Criminal Police Berlin
Served in SA, 1933-1939
National Archives File: A3343 SSO-209A

Kreuzer

First Name: Dr. Josef
Date of Birth: 8 April 1907
Place of Birth: Heringhausen
Highest Rank: SS-Standartenführer
SS Number: 163103
Date Entered SS: 26 June 1933
NSDAP Number: 646335
Date Entered NSDAP: 1 October 1931
Marital Status: Married
Religion: Agnostic
Civilian Occupation: Lawyer
Education: University
Foreign Language: No
World War I Service: No
EINSATZKOMMANDO: **G**
Position: Commander
Einsatzkommando Service: 1944
Other Assignment: RSHA; Gestapo Cologne; Police Hamburg
Waffen-SS Service: No
Highest Award: Iron Cross 1st Class
Postwar Sentence: No judicial proceedings discovered
Notes: Gestapo Düsseldorf
National Archives File: A3343 SSO-214A

Kreuzmann

First Name: Werner
Date of Birth: 4 June 1909
Place of Birth: Königsberg
Highest Rank: SS-Hauptsturmführer
SS Number: 290988
Date Entered SS: Not listed
NSDAP Number: 1 May 1937
Marital Status: Married
Religion: Agnostic
Civilian Occupation: Lawyer
Education: University of Königsberg
Foreign Language: No
EINSATZKOMMANDO: **Tilsit**
Position: SD section
Einsatzkommando Service: 1941–1944
Other Assignment: RSHA; Gestapo Insterburg
Highest Award: War Service Cross 1st Class
Postwar Sentence: 1957, 5 Years
Postwar Employment: Construction engineer, Hamburg
Notes: Wounded in action against partisans; lost right ring finger
No mention of *Einsatzkommando* service in personnel file
National Archives File: A3343 SSO-214A

Krieger

First Name: Dr. Hans
Date of Birth: 22 February 1910
Place of Birth: Berlin
Highest Rank: SS-Sturmbannführer
SS Number: 307404
Date Entered SS: 2 July 1938
NSDAP Number: 8423491
Date Entered NSDAP: 30 January 1942
Marital Status: Married
Religion: Agnostic
Civilian Occupation: Police
Education: University
Foreign Language: No
World War I Service: No
EINSATZKOMMANDO: **C**
Position: Not listed
Einsatzkommando Service: 31 May 1941–5 October 1941, 4 March 1942–5 August 1942
Other Assignment: RSHA
Waffen-SS Service: No
Highest Award: War Service Cross 1st Class
Postwar Sentence: No judicial proceedings discovered
Notes: Both children died at a young age
National Archives File: A3343 SSO-214A

Kröger

First Name: Dr. Erhard
Date of Birth: 24 March 1905
Place of Birth: Riga, Russia
Highest Rank: SS-Standartenführer
SS Number: 357243
Date Entered SS: 23 October 1938
NSDAP Number: 7675747
Date Entered NSDAP: 1 August 1940
Marital Status: Married
Religion: Agnostic
Civilian Occupation: Lawyer
Education: University of Tübingen, Königsberg
Foreign Language: Russian, Latvian
World War I Service: No
EINSATZKOMMANDO: **6**
Position: Commander
Einsatzkommando Service: June–November 1941
Other Assignment: RSHA; SS Hauptamt
Waffen-SS Service: 9th SS Division "Hohenstaufen", 1943
Highest Award: Iron Cross 2nd Class
Postwar Sentence: 1969, 3 years
Notes: Iron Cross 2nd Class for *Einsatzkommando* service
National Archives File: A3343 SSO-215A

Kröger

First Name: Dr. Peter
Date of Birth: 24 January 1912
Place of Birth: Riga, Russia
Highest Rank: SS-Hauptsturmführer
SS Number: 347189
Date Entered SS: Not listed
NSDAP Number: Not a member
Marital Status: Married
Religion: Protestant
Civilian Occupation: Doctor
Education: University
Foreign Language: Latvian
World War I Service: No
EINSATZKOMMANDO: **C**
Position: Not listed
Einsatzkommando Service: Not listed
Other Assignment: SS Main Medical Department
Waffen-SS Service: 9th SS Division "Hohenstaufen", 1943-1944
Highest Award: War Service Cross 2nd Class
Postwar Sentence: No judicial proceedings discovered
Notes: Served in SD from 1941-1943 No mention of *Einsatzkommando* service in personnel file
National Archives File: A3343 SSO-215A

Krumbach

First Name: Alfred
Date of Birth: 12 April 1911
Place of Birth: Berlin
Highest Rank: SS-Hauptsturmführer
SS Number: 280142
Date Entered SS: 25 August 1936
NSDAP Number: 567909
Date Entered NSDAP: 1 July 1931
Marital Status: Married
Religion: Agnostic
Civilian Occupation: Police
Education: Technical School
Foreign Language: No
World War I Service: No
EINSATZKOMMANDO: **Tilsit**
Position: Not listed
Einsatzkommando Service: 1941–1944
Other Assignment: RSHA, Office IV A (Gestapo, Enemies)
Highest Award: None listed
Postwar Sentence: 1957, 3 Years
Postwar Employment: Credit affairs bureau, Hannover
Notes: Seriously injured in a car wreck in 1942
National Archives File: A3343 SSO-221A

Kubiak

First Name: Erich
Date of Birth: 19 February 1904
Place of Birth: Gelsenkirchen
Highest Rank: SS-Hauptsturmführer
SS Number: 375094
Date Entered SS: Not listed
NSDAP Number: 797574
Date Entered NSDAP: 1 May 1937
Marital Status: Married
Religion: Agnostic
Civilian Occupation: Detective Officer
Education: High School
Foreign Language: No
World War I Service: No
EINSATZKOMMANDO: **D, 11b**
Position: Not listed
Einsatzkommando Service: 25 October 1941–1 July 1943
Other Assignment: Criminal Police Recklinghausen; SD Cracow
Waffen-SS Service: No
Highest Award: Iron Cross 2nd Class
Postwar Sentence: No judicial proceedings discovered
Notes: Eastern People's Medal, Crimea Shield
National Archives File: A3343 SSO-222A

Kügler

First Name: Wolfgang
Date of Birth: 3 December 1909
Place of Birth: Breslau
Highest Rank: SS-Untersturmführer
SS Number: 290270
Date Entered SS: 30 January 1938
NSDAP Number: 352559
Date Entered NSDAP: 1 November 1930
Marital Status: Married
Religion: Agnostic
Civilian Occupation: Detective Officer
Education: High School
Foreign Language: Italian, French, English
World War I Service: No
EINSATZKOMMANDO: **2**
Position: *Teilkommando* leader
Einsatzkommando Service: 1941–1943
Other Assignment: SD Liegnitz; Gestapo Breslau
Highest Award: War Service Cross 2nd Class
Postwar Sentence: No judicial proceedings discovered
Notes: Thrown out of SS in 1943 and spent 1 1/2 years in prison
National Archives File: A3343 SSO-224A

Kulas

First Name: Siegfried
Date of Birth: 13 October 1914
Place of Birth: Berlin-Treptow
Highest Rank: SS-Hauptsturmführer
SS Number: 344707
Date Entered SS: 10 March 1939
NSDAP Number: 3255473
Date Entered NSDAP: 1 May 1933
Marital Status: Married
Religion: Agnostic
Civilian Occupation: Police
Education: High School
Foreign Language: No
EINSATZKOMMANDO: **1b**
Position: Not listed
Einsatzkommando Service: Not listed
Other Assignment: RSHA
Waffen-SS Service: No
Highest Award: None listed
Postwar Sentence: 1961, Acquitted
Notes: Served in Hitler Youth, 1930-1936; served in Army 5th Panzer Regiment 1935
Wounded in action
National Archives File: A3343 SSO-229A

Kunberger

First Name: Paul
Date of Birth: 22 April 1913
Place of Birth: Kornwestheim
Highest Rank: SS-Untersturmführer
SS Number: 47429
Date Entered SS: 1 October 1932
NSDAP Number: 807839
Date Entered NSDAP: 1 December 1931
Marital Status: Married
Religion: Agnostic
Civilian Occupation: Police
Education: Unknown
Foreign Language: No
EINSATZKOMMANDO: **B**
Position: Not listed
Einsatzkommando Service: Not listed
Other Assignment: RSHA
Waffen-SS Service: No
Highest Award: Iron Cross 1st Class
Postwar Sentence: No judicial proceedings discovered
Notes: Served in SA, 1931-1932; Anti-Partisan Badge, Infantry Assault Badge
Served in *Einsatzkommando* as an enlisted man
National Archives File: A3343 SSO-230A

Landgraf

First Name: Dr. Alexander
Date of Birth: 20 May 1906
Place of Birth: Lorsch
Highest Rank: SS-Obersturmbannführer
SS Number: 280440
Date Entered SS: 30 April 1936
NSDAP Number: 75943
Date Entered NSDAP: 4 February 1928
Marital Status: Single
Religion: Agnostic
Civilian Occupation: Lawyer
Education: University of Heidelberg, Giessen
Foreign Language: English, French
EINSATZKOMMANDO: **A**
Position: Administrative advisor
Einsatzkommando Service: 25 January 1942–September 1942
Other Assignment: RSHA; Gestapo Münster
Waffen-SS Service: No
Highest Award: War Service Cross 1st Class
Postwar Sentence: No judicial proceedings discovered
Notes: Golden Party Badge
Died 1961
National Archives File: A3343 SSO-238A

Lange

First Name: Herbert
Date of Birth: 29 September 1909
Place of Birth: Menzlin
Highest Rank: SS-Sturmbannführer
SS Number: 93501
Date Entered SS: 1 March 1933
NSDAP Number: 1159583
Date Entered NSDAP: 1 May 1932
Marital Status: Married
Religion: Protestant
Civilian Occupation: Lawyer
Education: University
Foreign Language: No
World War I Service: No
EINSATZKOMMANDO: **2**
Position: Commander
Einsatzkommando Service: 3 December 1941–March 1943
Other Assignment: RSHA; SD Aachen
Waffen-SS Service: No
Highest Award: War Service Cross 1st Class
Notes: Probably served in *Einsatzkommando* in Poland
Kommandant Chelmno; killed in action 20 April 1945
National Archives File: A3343 SSO-240A

Lange

First Name: Dr. Rudolf
Date of Birth: 18 April 1910
Place of Birth: Weisswasser
Highest Rank: SS-Standartenführer
SS Number: 290308
Date Entered SS: 30 September 1937
NSDAP Number: 4922869
Date Entered NSDAP: 1 May 1937
Marital Status: Married
Religion: Agnostic
Civilian Occupation: Lawyer
Education: University
Foreign Language: English, French
World War I Service: No
EINSATZKOMMANDO: **A, 2**
Position: A – Gestapo section leader; 2 – Commander
Einsatzkommando Service: A, July 1941 – 3 December 1941; 2, 3 December 1941–1944
Other Assignment: Commander, SD Riga; Commander, SD Posen
Highest Award: German Cross in Gold
Postwar Sentence: N/A
Notes: Served in SA, 1933-1936
Killed in action, Posen February 1945
National Archives File: A3343 SSO-241A

Legath

First Name: Hanns-Elmar
Date of Birth: 14 March 1908
Place of Birth: Markt Schwaben
Highest Rank: SS-Hauptsturmführer
SS Number: 280487
Date Entered SS: 1 November 1934
NSDAP Number: Not a member
Marital Status: Married
Religion: Agnostic
Civilian Occupation: Police
Education: University
Foreign Language: No
World War I Service: No
EINSATZKOMMANDO: **1005**
Position: Not listed
Einsatzkommando Service: 1944
Other Assignment: RSHA
Waffen-SS Service: No
Highest Award: War Service Cross 1st Class
Killed in Action: No
Postwar Sentence: No judicial proceedings discovered
Notes: Served in SA, 1933-1935
National Archives File: A3343 SSO-249A

Lepek

First Name: Gerhard
Date of Birth: 12 May 1910
Place of Birth: Mariendorf
Highest Rank: SS-Hauptsturmführer
SS Number: 50853
Date Entered SS: 25 July 1932
NSDAP Number: 855827
Date Entered NSDAP: 1 January 1932
Marital Status: Married
Religion: Agnostic
Civilian Occupation: Detective Officer
Education: University
Foreign Language: English, French
World War I Service: No
EINSATZKOMMANDO: **D**
Position: Not listed
Einsatzkommando Service: Not listed
Other Assignment: RSHA, Office II A 5 (Confiscations); Criminal Police Karlsbad
Waffen-SS Service: No
Highest Award: None listed
Postwar Sentence: No judicial proceedings discovered
Notes: Short personnel file
National Archives File: A3343 SSO-256A

Leskow

First Name: Reinhold
Date of Birth: 5 January 1907
Place of Birth: Forbach
Highest Rank: SS-Hauptsturmführer
SS Number: 307995
Date Entered SS: 1 September 1936
NSDAP Number: 1414038
Date Entered NSDAP: 1 December 1932
Marital Status: Single
Religion: Agnostic
Civilian Occupation: Police
Education: High School
Foreign Language: English, French
World War I Service: No
EINSATZKOMMANDO: **C**
Position: Not listed
Einsatzkommando Service: 1941–1942
Other Assignment: Gestapo Lodz; SD Warsaw; SD Rovno
Waffen-SS Service: No
Highest Award: None listed
Postwar Sentence: No judicial proceedings discovered
Notes: Reprimanded in 1942 for adultery
National Archives File: A3343 SSO-257A

Lindner

First Name: Alfred
Date of Birth: 22 May 1904
Place of Birth: Königsee/Thüringen
Highest Rank: SS-Obersturmführer
SS Number: 47521
Date Entered SS: 20 May 1935
NSDAP Number: 1449463
Date Entered NSDAP: 1 October 1932
Marital Status: Married
Religion: Protestant
Civilian Occupation: Police
Education: Grade School
Foreign Language: No
EINSATZKOMMANDO: **D, Croatia**
Position: Not listed
Einsatzkommando Service: D, 1941; Croatia, 1943
Other Assignment: SD Kassel; Police Weimar
Waffen-SS Service: No
Highest Award: War Service Cross 1st Class
Postwar Sentence: No judicial proceedings discovered
Notes: In Police since 1923
Two of three children died in infancy
National Archives File: A3343 SSO-263A

Liphardt

First Name: Dr. Fritz
Date of Birth: 3 May 1905
Place of Birth: Stettin
Highest Rank: SS-Obersturmbannführer
SS Number: 280121
Date Entered SS: 15 November 1936
NSDAP Number: 2653601
Date Entered NSDAP: 1 May 1933
Marital Status: Married
Religion: Agnostic
Civilian Occupation: Lawyer
Education: University of Jena, Leipzig, Berlin
Foreign Language: No
EINSATZKOMMANDO: **2/III**
Position: Commander
Einsatzkommando Service: Polish Campaign
Other Assignment: Gestapo Stettin; Gestapo Radom
Waffen-SS Service: No
Highest Award: War Service Cross 1st Class
Postwar Sentence: No judicial proceedings discovered
Notes: Served in SA, 1933-1936
Gestapo Frankfurt/Oder
National Archives File: A3343 SSO-268A

Loleit

First Name: Egon
Date of Birth: 2 December 1910
Place of Birth: Moscow, Russia
Highest Rank: SS-Obersturmführer
SS Number: 357298
Date Entered SS: 1 June 1940
NSDAP Number: Not a member
Marital Status: Married
Religion: Agnostic
Civilian Occupation: Businessman
Education: High School
Foreign Language: Latvian, Russian
EINSATZKOMMANDO: **C**
Position: Not listed
Einsatzkommando Service: June 1941–1943
Other Assignment: RSHA
Waffen-SS Service: 29th SS Division, 1944-1945
Highest Award: Iron Cross 2nd Class
Killed in Action: No
Postwar Sentence: No judicial proceedings discovered
Notes: Served in Latvian Army, 1932-1933
Eastern People's Medal
National Archives File: A3343 SSO-275A

Looss

First Name: Helmut
Date of Birth: 31 May 1910
Place of Birth: Eisenach
Highest Rank: SS-Obersturmbannführer
SS Number: 84617
Date Entered SS: 30 June 1933
NSDAP Number: 4863389
Date Entered NSDAP: 1 May 1937
Marital Status: Married
Religion: Agnostic
Civilian Occupation: Student
Education: University of Berlin, Göttingen, Königsberg
Foreign Language: English
EINSATZKOMMANDO: **7a**
Position: Commander
Einsatzkommando Service: June 1943–June 1944
Other Assignment: RSHA, Office VI E (SD, Foreign, Investigations)
RSHA, Office II (Organization and Law)
Waffen-SS Service: 16th SS Division "Reichsführer-SS", 1944-1945
Highest Award: Iron Cross 1st Class
Notes: Probably served in an *Einsatzkommando* in France 1940
Served as 16th SS Division Intelligence Officer
National Archives File: A3343 SSO-276A

Lopass

First Name: Hans-Werner
Date of Birth: 23 March 1896
Place of Birth: Demmin
Highest Rank: SS-Sturmbannführer
SS Number: 20072
Date Entered SS: 1 August 1931
NSDAP Number: 193091
Date Entered NSDAP: 1 February 1930
Marital Status: Married
Religion: Agnostic
Civilian Occupation: Farmer
Education: Grade School
Foreign Language: No
World War I Service: Yes, Iron Cross 2nd Class
EINSATZKOMMANDO: **D**
Position: Not listed
Einsatzkommando Service: Not listed
Other Assignment: RSHA, Office I A 5 (Personnel - Judiciary)
Waffen-SS Service: No
Highest Award: War Service Cross 2nd Class
Postwar Sentence: No judicial proceedings discovered
Notes: Worked in SS personnal office
National Archives File: A3343 SSO-276A

Lumm

First Name: Hermann
Date of Birth: 2 March 1912
Place of Birth: Bremen
Highest Rank: SS-Sturmbannführer
SS Number: 272349
Date Entered SS: 1 May 1933
NSDAP Number: 4183394
Date Entered NSDAP: 1 May 1937
Marital Status: Married
Religion: Agnostic
Civilian Occupation: Police
Education: Trade School
Foreign Language: English, French, Danish, Norwegen
EINSATZKOMMANDO: **5**
Position: Not listed
Einsatzkommando Service: 22 June 1941–5 October 1941
Other Assignment: RSHA, Office VI (SD, Foreign); SD Bremerhaven
Waffen-SS Service: No
Highest Award: War Service Cross 1st Class
Postwar Sentence: No judicial proceedings discovered
Notes: Operation Zeppelin
SD Oslo
National Archives File: A3343 SSO-284A

Mariunas

First Name: Alexander
Date of Birth: 3 June 1903
Place of Birth: Dewynaney, Russia
Highest Rank: SS-Untersturmführer
SS Number: 52237
Date Entered SS: Not listed
NSDAP Number: Not a member
Marital Status: Married
Religion: Unknown
Civilian Occupation: Pilot
Education: Unknown
Foreign Language: Unknown
World War I Service: No
EINSATZKOMMANDO: **B**
Position: Reconnaissance pilot
Einsatzkommando Service: 1942–1943
Other Assignment: Unknown
Waffen-SS Service: No
Highest Award: Iron Cross 2nd Class
Killed in Action: No
Postwar Sentence: No judicial proceedings discovered
Notes: Possible honorary SS member
National Archives File: A3343 SSO-297A

Matschke

First Name: Kurt
Date of Birth: 4 May 1908
Place of Birth: Domsel
Highest Rank: SS-Hauptsturmführer
SS Number: 45856
Date Entered SS: 25 July 1932
NSDAP Number: 1239097
Date Entered NSDAP: 1 August 1932
Marital Status: Married
Religion: Catholic
Civilian Occupation: Detective Officer
Education: University
Foreign Language: No
EINSATZKOMMANDO: **7a**
Position: Not listed
Einsatzkommando Service: Not listed
Other Assignment: Criminal Police Saarbrücken; Gestapo Cologne
Waffen-SS Service: No
Highest Award: War Service Cross 2nd Class
Postwar Sentence: No judicial proceedings discovered
Notes: Served in the Army 1937
No mention of *Einsatzkommando* service in personnel file
National Archives File: A3343 SSO-300A

Matysiak

First Name: Hanns
Date of Birth: 13 May 1909
Place of Birth: Riegersdorf
Highest Rank: SS-Hauptsturmführer
SS Number: 5828
Date Entered SS: 1 January 1931
NSDAP Number: 412983
Date Entered NSDAP: 1 December 1930
Marital Status: Married
Religion: Agnostic
Civilian Occupation: Businessman
Education: High School
Foreign Language: No
EINSATZKOMMANDO: **A**
Position: Not listed
Einsatzkommando Service: 1942
Other Assignment: RSHA
Waffen-SS Service: No
Highest Award: None listed
Postwar Sentence: No judicial proceedings discovered
Notes: Operation Zeppelin; Infantry Assault Badge; served in SA, 1930-1931
No mention of *Einsatzkommando* service in personnel file
National Archives File: A3343 SSO-300A

Maywald

First Name: Gerhard
Date of Birth: 16 April 1913
Place of Birth: Karlsruhe
Highest Rank: SS-Obersturmführer
SS Number: 404663
Date Entered SS: Not listed
NSDAP Number: 4665155
Date Entered NSDAP: 1 May 1937
Marital Status: Married
Religion: Agnostic
Civilian Occupation: Police
Education: High School
Foreign Language: No
World War I Service: No
EINSATZKOMMANDO: **A**
Position: Training officer
Einsatzkommando Service: July 1941–May 1942
Other Assignment: Criminal Police Kiel
Waffen-SS Service: No
Highest Award: None listed
Postwar Sentence: 1960
Notes: Served in Army 30th Infantry Division, 1939
National Archives File: A3343 SSO-304A

Meier

First Name: August
Date of Birth: 8 October 1900
Place of Birth: Mainz
Highest Rank: SS-Obersturmbannführer
SS Number: 73073
Date Entered SS: 15 September 1933
NSDAP Number: 2019775
Date Entered NSDAP: 1 May 1933
Marital Status: Married
Religion: Agnostic
Civilian Occupation: Businessman
Education: Trade School
Foreign Language: No
World War I Service: Yes, 27th Field Artillery Regiment
EINSATZKOMMANDO: **5, 4b**
Position: 4b – Commander; 5 – Commander
Einsatzkommando Service: 5, September 1941 – January 1942, 4b, July 1942-November 1942
Other Assignment: RSHA; SD Limoges
Highest Award: War Service Cross 1st Class
Postwar Sentence: No judicial proceedings discovered
Notes: Served in an *Einsatzkommando 2* in Limoges, 1944
SD Breslau; SD Wiesbaden; suicide
National Archives File: A3343 SSO-305A

Meixner

First Name: Dr. Johann-Georg
Date of Birth: 5 November 1906
Place of Birth: Reichertshofen
Highest Rank: SS-Obersturmbannführer
SS Number: 3429
Date Entered SS: 1 October 1930
NSDAP Number: 707707
Date Entered NSDAP: 1 October 1930
Marital Status: Married
Religion: Catholic
Civilian Occupation: Physician
Education: University
Foreign Language: No
EINSATZKOMMANDO: **A**
Position: Medical officer
Einsatzkommando Service: February 1942–1944
Other Assignment: Camp doctor, Dachau 1933-1934; RSHA
Waffen-SS Service: No
Highest Award: None listed
Postwar Sentence: No judicial proceedings discovered
Notes: Short personnel file
National Archives File: A3343 SSO-307A

Merbach

First Name: Fritz
Date of Birth: 27 April 1912
Place of Birth: Gotha-Siebleben
Highest Rank: SS-Obersturmführer
SS Number: 42604
Date Entered SS: 1 December 1931
NSDAP Number: 860449
Date Entered NSDAP: 1 December 1931
Marital Status: Married
Religion: Agnostic
Civilian Occupation: Auto mechanic
Education: Grade School
Foreign Language: No
EINSATZKOMMANDO: **1b**
Position: Not listed
Einsatzkommando Service: October 1941–March 1943
Other Assignment: RSHA
Waffen-SS Service: No
Highest Award: None listed
Postwar Sentence: 1963, 7 years
Postwar Employment: Tire factory; Volkswagen dealership
Notes: No mention of *Einsatzkommando* service in personnel file
National Archives File: A3343 SSO-309A

Meyszner

First Name: August von
Date of Birth: 3 August 1886
Place of Birth: Graz, Austria
Highest Rank: SS-Gruppenführer
SS Number: 263406
Date Entered SS: 20 February 1935
NSDAP Number: 6119650
Date Entered NSDAP: 1 May 1938
Marital Status: Married
Religion: Agnostic
Civilian Occupation: Police
Education: High School
Foreign Language: No
World War I Service: Yes, mountain company in Austrian Army
EINSATZKOMMANDO: **Serbia**
Position: Commander
Einsatzkommando Service: 1942–1944
Other Assignment: HSSPF Serbia; HSSPF Montenegro
Highest Award: Iron Cross 1st Class
Postwar Sentence: 1946, Death
Notes: Executed in Yugoslavia 24 January 1947
Wounded in action WWI
National Archives File: A3343 SSO-315A

Migge

First Name: Kurt
Date of Birth: 15 February 1908
Place of Birth: Berlin-Tegel
Highest Rank: SS-Obersturmführer
SS Number: 353303
Date Entered SS: Unknown
NSDAP Number: 168444
Date Entered NSDAP: 1 November 1929
Marital Status: Married
Religion: Unknown
Civilian Occupation: Police
Education: Grade School
Foreign Language: No
World War I Service: No
EINSATZKOMMANDO: **A, 2**
Position: Not listed
Einsatzkommando Service: February 1942–June 1942
Other Assignment: KdS Riga
Waffen-SS Service: No
Highest Award: Unknown
Postwar Sentence: 1951, Life
Notes: Mother died when he was 10
National Archives File: A3343 SSO-318A

Möhlmeyer

First Name: Georg
Date of Birth: 23 December 1911
Place of Birth: Rüstringen
Highest Rank: SS-Obersturmführer
SS Number: 43254
Date Entered SS: 22 November 1932
NSDAP Number: 1052588
Date Entered NSDAP: 1 March 1932
Marital Status: Married
Religion: Agnostic
Civilian Occupation: Tailor
Education: Grade School
Foreign Language: No
World War I Service: No
EINSATZKOMMANDO: **D**
Position: Not listed
Einsatzkommando Service: 1942
Other Assignment: RSHA, Office I A 5b (Personnel)
Waffen-SS Service: No
Highest Award: Iron Cross 2nd Class
Postwar Sentence: No judicial proceedings discovered
Notes: No mention of *Einsatzkommando* service in personnel file
National Archives File: A3343 SSO-321A

Mohr

First Name: Robert
Date of Birth: 24 December 1909
Place of Birth: Frankfurt/Main
Highest Rank: SS-Obersturmbannführer
SS Number: 180205
Date Entered SS: 1 March 1933
NSDAP Number: 2257332
Date Entered NSDAP: 1 May 1933
Marital Status: Married
Religion: Agnostic
Civilian Occupation: Lawyer
Education: University of Giessen
Foreign Language: No
World War I Service: No
EINSATZKOMMANDO: **6**
Position: Commander
Einsatzkommando Service: November 1941 – September 1942
Other Assignment: Gestapo Darmstadt; Gestapo Magdeburg
Waffen-SS Service: No
Highest Award: War Service Cross 1st Class
Postwar Sentence: 1965, 8 years
Notes: Praised by superiors in personnel file
National Archives File: A3343 SSO-323A

Moors

First Name: Hans
Date of Birth: 4 October 1916
Place of Birth: Kaldenkirchen
Highest Rank: SS-Untersturmführer
SS Number: 452181
Date Entered SS: Not listed
NSDAP Number: Not a member
Marital Status: Married
Religion: Agnostic
Civilian Occupation: Barber
Education: Grade School
Foreign Language: Dutch
World War I Service: No
EINSATZKOMMANDO: **7a**
Position: Not listed
Einsatzkommando Service: Not listed
Other Assignment: Gestapo Düsseldorf
Waffen-SS Service: No
Highest Award: None listed
Killed in Action: No
Postwar Sentence: No judicial proceedings discovered
Notes: No mention of *Einsatzkommando* service in personnel file
National Archives File: A3343 SSO-324A

Mosig

First Name: Walter
Date of Birth: 24 May 1907
Place of Birth: Giessen
Highest Rank: SS-Sturmbannführer
SS Number: 46671
Date Entered SS: 1 July 1932
NSDAP Number: 11670
Date Entered NSDAP: 29 July 1925
Marital Status: Married
Religion: Agnostic
Civilian Occupation: Government Counsel
Education: High School
Foreign Language: Spanish, French
EINSATZKOMMANDO: **A**
Position: Not listed
Einsatzkommando Service: Not listed
Other Assignment: RSHA, Office VI (SD, Foreign); Criminal Police Breslau
Waffen-SS Service: No
Highest Award: War Service Cross 2nd Class
Postwar Sentence: No judicial proceedings discovered
Notes: Golden Party Badge; Spanish Cross in Silver
No mention of *Einsatzkommando* service in personnel file
National Archives File: A3343 SSO-325A

Mühlthaler

First Name: Lorenz
Date of Birth: 13 September 1897
Place of Birth: Taglaching
Highest Rank: SS-Untersturmführer
SS Number: 396235
Date Entered SS: 29 March 1941
NSDAP Number: 1853368
Date Entered NSDAP: 1 May 1933
Marital Status: Married
Religion: Agnostic
Civilian Occupation: Police
Education: Grade School
Foreign Language: No
World War I Service: Yes
EINSATZKOMMANDO: **B**
Position: Not listed
Einsatzkommando Service: 12 April 1942–1944
Other Assignment: Police Saarbrücken
Highest Award: Iron Cross 2nd Class
Postwar Sentence: No judicial proceedings discovered
Notes: Eastern People's Medal; wounded in action in 1942
In Police since 1920
National Archives File: A3343 SSO-326A

Müller

First Name: Dr. Erich
Date of Birth: 30 August 1902
Place of Birth: Münster
Highest Rank: SS-Standartenführer
SS Number: 105979
Date Entered SS: 30 April 1936
NSDAP Number: 1240093
Date Entered NSDAP: 1 July 1932
Marital Status: Married
Religion: Agnostic
Civilian Occupation: Lawyer
Education: University
Foreign Language: No
World War I Service: No
EINSATZKOMMANDO: **12**
Position: Commander
Einsatzkommando Service: February 1942–October 1942
Other Assignment: RSHA, Office III (SD, Domestic); Propaganda Ministry
Highest Award: War Service Cross 1st Class
Postwar Sentence: No judicial proceedings discovered
Notes: Gestapo Berlin; wound badge
Reportedly fled to Argentina after the war
National Archives File: A3343 SSO-328A

Müller

First Name: Bruno
Date of Birth: 13 September 1905
Place of Birth: Strassburg
Highest Rank: SS-Obersturmbannführer
SS Number: 23884
Date Entered SS: 1 December 1931
NSDAP Number: 885088
Date Entered NSDAP: 1 December 1931
Marital Status: Married
Religion: Agnostic
Civilian Occupation: Lawyer
Education: University
Foreign Language: French
EINSATZKOMMANDO: **11b, G**
Position: Commander
Einsatzkommando Service: July 1941–October 1941
Other Assignment: RSHA, Office IV (Gestapo); Gestapo Stettin
Waffen-SS Service: No
Highest Award: Iron Cross 2nd Class
Postwar Sentence: No judicial proceedings discovered
Notes: Gestapo Wilhelmshaven
Died 1960
National Archives File: A3343 SSO-327A

Müller

First Name:	Erich
Date of Birth:	16 December 1905
Place of Birth:	Berlin
Highest Rank:	SS-Untersturmführer
SS Number:	396219
Date Entered SS:	23 May 1938
NSDAP Number:	5886001
Date Entered NSDAP:	1 May 1937
Marital Status:	Married
Religion:	Agnostic
Civilian Occupation:	Police
Education:	High School
Foreign Language:	No
World War I Service:	No
EINSATZKOMMANDO:	**B**
Position:	Not listed
Einsatzkommando Service:	20 June 1941–11 April 1942
Other Assignment:	RSHA, Office I D (Personnel)
Waffen-SS Service:	No
Highest Award:	War Service Cross 2nd Class
Postwar Sentence:	No judicial proceedings discovered
Notes:	Short personnel file
National Archives File:	A3343 SSO-328A

Müller

First Name:	Gerhard
Date of Birth:	1 August 1910
Place of Birth:	Greifenhagen
Highest Rank:	SS-Obersturmführer
SS Number:	48796
Date Entered SS:	1 March 1932
NSDAP Number:	1162585
Date Entered NSDAP:	1 May 1932
Marital Status:	Married
Religion:	Agnostic
Civilian Occupation:	Police
Education:	University
Foreign Language:	No
EINSATZKOMMANDO:	**B**
Position:	Not listed
Einsatzkommando Service:	Not listed
Other Assignment:	RSHA; Police Stettin
Waffen-SS Service:	No
Highest Award:	Iron Cross 2nd Class
Postwar Sentence:	No judicial proceedings discovered
Notes:	Eastern People's Medal; studied to be a dentist No mention of *Einsatzkommando* service in personnel file
National Archives File:	A3343 SSO-330A

Müller

First Name:	Karl
Date of Birth:	28 March 1898
Place of Birth:	Tempelburg
Highest Rank:	SS-Untersturmführer
SS Number:	290540
Date Entered SS:	25 November 1938
NSDAP Number:	1645325
Date Entered NSDAP:	1 April 1933
Marital Status:	Married
Religion:	Protestant
Civilian Occupation:	Draftsman
Education:	Unknown
Foreign Language:	No
World War I Service:	Yes, 76th Infantry Regiment
EINSATZKOMMANDO:	**B**
Position:	Not listed
Einsatzkommando Service:	Not listed
Other Assignment:	RSHA; Gestapo Stettin
Waffen-SS Service:	Iron Cross 2nd Class
Postwar Sentence:	No judicial proceedings discovered
Notes:	Short personnel file
National Archives File:	A3343 SSO-334A

Nakaten

First Name:	Franz
Date of Birth:	6 April 1908
Place of Birth:	Düsseldorf
Highest Rank:	SS-Hauptsturmführer
SS Number:	385408
Date Entered SS:	Not listed
NSDAP Number:	2178477
Date Entered NSDAP:	1 May 1933
Marital Status:	Married
Religion:	Agnostic
Civilian Occupation:	Police
Education:	High School
Foreign Language:	English
World War I Service:	No
EINSATZKOMMANDO:	**2**
Position:	Criminal Police section
Einsatzkommando Service:	September 1941–August 1942
Other Assignment:	Criminal Police Linz
Waffen-SS Service:	No
Highest Award:	None listed
Postwar Sentence:	No judicial proceedings discovered
Notes:	Short personnel file
National Archives File:	A3343 SSO-343A

Naumann

First Name: Erich
Date of Birth: 29 April 1905
Place of Birth: Meissen
Highest Rank: SS-Brigadeführer
SS Number: 107496
Date Entered SS: 1 July 1935
NSDAP Number: 170257
Date Entered NSDAP: 1 November 1929
Marital Status: Married
Religion: Agnostic
Civilian Occupation: Merchant
Education: High School
Foreign Language: No
World War I Service: No
EINSATZKOMMANDO: **B**
Position: Commander
Einsatzkommando Service: November 1941–March 1943
Other Assignment: SD Nürnberg; SD Den Haag
Highest Award: Iron Cross 1st Class
Postwar Sentence: 1948, Death; executed 7 June 1951
Notes: Served in border protection force, 1931-1933
Served in SA, 1930-1935, Inspector SD Berlin
National Archives File: A3343 SSO-344A

Nebe

First Name: Arthur
Date of Birth: 13 November 1894
Place of Birth: Berlin
Highest Rank: SS-Gruppenführer
SS Number: 280152
Date Entered SS: 2 December 1936
NSDAP Number: 574307
Date Entered NSDAP: 1 July 1931
Marital Status: Married
Religion: Protestant
Civilian Occupation: Police
Education: High School
Foreign Language: No
World War I Service: Yes, Iron Cross 1st Class, 17th Pionier Battalion
EINSATZKOMMANDO: **B**
Position: Commander
Einsatzkommando Service: June 1941–November 1941
Other Assignment: Chief, Office V, RSHA (Kripo)
Waffen-SS Service: No
Highest Award: None listed
Notes: Wounded twice by poison gas in WWI. Head of Kripo. Implicated in 20 July plot; killed by SS, 2 March 1945
National Archives File: A3343 SSO-345A

Nölle

First Name: Wilhelm
Date of Birth: 26 January 1904
Place of Birth: Brächen
Highest Rank: SS-Obersturmbannführer
SS Number: 134702
Date Entered SS: 19 March 1933
NSDAP Number: 2323554
Date Entered NSDAP: 1 May 1933
Marital Status: Single
Religion: Agnostic
Civilian Occupation: Lawyer
Education: High School listed (probably university)
Foreign Language: No
World War I Service: No
EINSATZKOMMANDO: **Luxembourg**
Position: Commander
Einsatzkommando Service: 1944
Other Assignment: Gestapo Brünn; SD Trier
Commander, SD Marseille
Highest Award: None listed
Postwar Sentence: No judicial proceedings discovered
Notes: Served 6 months confinement by SS
National Archives File: A3343 SSO-352A

Nosske

First Name: Gustav
Date of Birth: 29 December 1902
Place of Birth: Halle
Highest Rank: SS-Obersturmbannführer
SS Number: 290213
Date Entered SS: Not listed
NSDAP Number: 2784256
Date Entered NSDAP: 30 April 1933
Marital Status: Married
Religion: Protestant
Civilian Occupation: Lawyer
Education: University
Foreign Language: No
World War I Service: No
EINSATZKOMMANDO: **12**
Position: Commander
Einsatzkommando Service: 19 June 1941–February 1942
Other Assignment: Gestapo Aachen; SD Düsseldorf
Waffen-SS Service: No
Highest Award: None listed
Postwar Sentence: 1948, Life commuted to 10 years
Notes: Gestapo Frankfurt/Oder
National Archives File: A3343 SSO-353A

Nyhögen

First Name: Gerhard
Date of Birth: 2 June 1914
Place of Birth: Bentheim
Highest Rank: SS-Obersturmführer
SS Number: 367418
Date Entered SS: 20 April 1940
NSDAP Number: 2847060
Date Entered NSDAP: 1 April 1933
Marital Status: Single
Religion: Agnostic
Civilian Occupation: Student
Education: High School
Foreign Language: No
EINSATZKOMMANDO: **A**
Position: Adjutant
Einsatzkommando Service: March 1942–September 1942
Other Assignment: RSHA, Office VI (SD, Foreign)
Waffen-SS Service: No
Highest Award: War Service Cross 2nd Class
Postwar Sentence: No judicial proceedings discovered
Notes: Served in SA, 1933-1934
Served in Army, 1935-1938 (6th Artillery Regiment)
National Archives File: A3343 SSO-354A

Oebsger-Roeder

First Name: Rudolf
Date of Birth: 9 March 1912
Place of Birth: Leipzig
Highest Rank: SS-Obersturmführer
SS Number: 267293
Date Entered SS: Not listed
NSDAP Number: 475061
Date Entered NSDAP: 1 March 1931
Marital Status: Married
Religion: Agnostic
Civilian Occupation: Professor
Education: University of Leipzig
Foreign Language: No
EINSATZKOMMANDO: **16, A**
Position: Commander
Einsatzkommando Service: Polish Campaign; 1942
Other Assignment: RSHA, Office VI B4 (SD, Foreign, German-Italian Sphere)
Waffen-SS Service: No
Highest Award: War Service Cross 1st Class
Postwar Sentence: No judicial proceedings discovered
Notes: Served in SA, 1931-1935
Operation Zeppelin; Infantry Assault Badge, Eastern People's Medal
National Archives File: A3343 SSO-355A

Ohlendorf

First Name: Otto
Date of Birth: 4 February 1907
Place of Birth: Hoheneggelsen
Highest Rank: SS-Gruppenführer
SS Number: 880
Date Entered SS: 28 May 1925
NSDAP Number: 6531
Date Entered NSDAP: 28 May 1925
Marital Status: Married
Religion: Protestant
Civilian Occupation: Lawyer
Education: University of Göttingen
Foreign Language: No
EINSATZKOMMANDO: **D**
Position: Commander
Einsatzkommando Service: June 1941 to June 1942
Other Assignment: Chief, Office III, RSHA (SD, Domestic)
Economic Ministry
Highest Award: War Service Cross 1st Class
Postwar Sentence: 1948, Death; executed 7 June 1951
Notes: War Service Cross 2nd Class while in *Einsatzkommando*
Golden Party Badge
National Archives File: A3343 SSO-356A

Oswald

First Name: Jakob
Date of Birth: 1 March 1900
Place of Birth: Marburg
Highest Rank: SS-Obersturmführer
SS Number: 80421
Date Entered SS: Not listed
NSDAP Number: 301593
Date Entered NSDAP: 1 November 1930
Marital Status: Married
Religion: Agnostic
Civilian Occupation: Electrician
Education: Grade School
Foreign Language: No
World War I Service: Yes, 21st Reserve Division
EINSATZKOMMANDO: **B**
Position: Not listed
Einsatzkommando Service: 1942–1943
Other Assignment: RSHA; SD Königsberg
Highest Award: War Service Cross 1st Class
Postwar Sentence: No judicial proceedings discovered
Notes: Served in SA, 1927-1930
Blood Order #3722; Eastern People's Medal
National Archives File: A3343 SSO-360A

Ott

First Name:	Adolf
Date of Birth:	29 December 1904
Place of Birth:	Waidhaus
Highest Rank:	SS-Obersturmbannführer
SS Number:	13294
Date Entered SS:	Not listed
NSDAP Number:	2433
Date Entered NSDAP:	1 Sep 1931
Marital Status:	Married
Religion:	Agnostic
Civilian Occupation:	Laborer
Education:	High School
Foreign Language:	No
World War I Service:	No
EINSATZKOMMANDO:	**7b**
Position:	Commander
Einsatzkommando Service:	15 February 1942 – January 1943
Other Assignment:	RSHA; SD Königsberg; SD Saarbrücken
Waffen-SS Service:	No
Highest Award:	War Service Cross 2nd Class
Postwar Sentence:	1948, Death commuted to Life, released
Notes:	SD Munich
National Archives File:	A3343 SSO-360A

Panzinger

First Name:	Dr. Friedrich
Date of Birth:	1 February 1903
Place of Birth:	Munich
Highest Rank:	SS-Oberführer
SS Number:	322118
Date Entered SS:	20 April 1939
NSDAP Number:	5017341
Date Entered NSDAP:	1 May 1937
Marital Status:	Married
Religion:	Agnostic
Civilian Occupation:	Lawyer
Education:	University
Foreign Language:	No
World War I Service:	No
EINSATZKOMMANDO:	**A**
Position:	Commander
Einsatzkommando Service:	5 September 1943–May 1944
Other Assignment:	Chief, Office IV A, RSHA (Gestapo, Enemies) SD Berlin; SD Ostland
Highest Award:	German Cross in Silver
Postwar Sentence:	No judicial proceedings discovered
Notes:	Served in SA, 1933-1938
National Archives File:	A3343 SSO-364A

Paust

First Name:	Karl-Heinz
Date of Birth:	11 November 1907
Place of Birth:	Leipzig
Highest Rank:	SS-Hauptsturmführer
SS Number:	272204
Date Entered SS:	6 November 1936
NSDAP Number:	601522
Date Entered NSDAP:	1 August 1938
Marital Status:	Single
Religion:	Agnostic
Civilian Occupation:	Businessman
Education:	High School
Foreign Language:	No
World War I Service:	No
EINSATZKOMMANDO:	**C**
Position:	Not listed
Einsatzkommando Service:	Not listed
Other Assignment:	RSHA, Office II (Organization and Law)
Highest Award:	Iron Cross 2nd Class
Postwar Sentence:	No judicial proceedings discovered
Notes:	Served in SA, 1931-1937 No mention of *Einsatzkommando* service in personnel file
National Archives File:	A3343 SSO-376A

Pechau

First Name:	Dr. Manfred
Date of Birth:	23 December 1909
Place of Birth:	Halle
Highest Rank:	SS-Sturmbannführer
SS Number:	367111
Date Entered SS:	Not listed
NSDAP Number:	1159621
Date Entered NSDAP:	1 May 1932
Marital Status:	Married
Religion:	Agnostic
Civilian Occupation:	Teacher
Education:	University of Berlin
Foreign Language:	No
EINSATZKOMMANDO:	**1b**
Position:	Commander
Einsatzkommando Service:	October 1942
Other Assignment:	RSHA, Office I B 3 (Personnel); SD Berlin
Waffen-SS Service:	No
Highest Award:	War Service Cross 2nd Class
Postwar Sentence:	No judicial proceedings discovered
Notes:	Served in SA, 1931-1939 Suicide, 1950
National Archives File:	A3343 SSO-368A

Persterer

First Name: Alois
Date of Birth: 29 September 1909
Place of Birth: Saalfelden, Austria
Highest Rank: SS-Obersturmbannführer
SS Number: 309697
Date Entered SS: Not listed
NSDAP Number: 897521
Date Entered NSDAP: 1 March 1930
Marital Status: Married
Religion: Protestant
Civilian Occupation: Auto mechanic
Education: Grade School
Foreign Language: No
EINSATZKOMMANDO: **10b**
Position: Commander
Einsatzkommando Service: May 1941–February 1943
Other Assignment: RSHA; SD Salzburg
Waffen-SS Service: No
Highest Award: Iron Cross 1st Class
Postwar Sentence: N/A
Notes: Blood Order; Wound Badge; Infantry Assault Badge Served in Austrian Army 1928-1933; killed 1945
National Archives File: A3343 SSO-369A

Pinnow

First Name: Erwin
Date of Birth: 10 May 1913
Place of Birth: Illowo
Highest Rank: SS-Untersturmführer
SS Number: 158831
Date Entered SS: 1 October 1933
NSDAP Number: 5637062
Date Entered NSDAP: 1 May 1937
Marital Status: Married
Religion: Agnostic
Civilian Occupation: Businessman
Education: High School
Foreign Language: No
World War I Service: No
EINSATZKOMMANDO: **III, z.b.V.**
Position: *Teilkommando* Boehm in *Einsatzgruppe* z.b.V.
Einsatzkommando Service: III, Polish Campaign; z.b.V., 3 July 1941–11 August 1941
Other Assignment: RSHA; SD Radom; KdS Warsaw
Waffen-SS Service: No
Highest Award: War Service Cross 2nd Class
Killed in Action: No
Postwar Sentence: No judicial proceedings discovered
National Archives File: A3343 SSO-380A

Plath

First Name: Karl-Julius
Date of Birth: 11 April 1910
Place of Birth: Unknown
Highest Rank: SS-Sturmbannführer
SS Number: 107030
Date Entered SS: Not listed
NSDAP Number: 644623
Date Entered NSDAP: 1 October 1931
Marital Status: Married
Religion: Unknown
Civilian Occupation: Unknown
Education: Unknown
Foreign Language: No
World War I Service: No
EINSATZKOMMANDO: **C**
Position: Not listed
Einsatzkommando Service: Undetermined to 29 July 1943
Other Assignment: RSHA, Office VI B 4 (SD, Foreign, German-Italian Spheres)
Waffen-SS Service: No
Highest Award: None listed
Notes: Killed in action 29 July 1943 Very incomplete personnel file
National Archives File: A3343 SSO-383A

Poche

First Name: Oswald
Date of Birth: 28 January 1908
Place of Birth: Brandenburg
Highest Rank: SS-Obersturmbannführer
SS Number: 267316
Date Entered SS: Not listed
NSDAP Number: 378342
Date Entered NSDAP: 1 December 1930
Marital Status: Married
Religion: Agnostic
Civilian Occupation: Assessor
Education: University of Jena
Foreign Language: No
EINSATZKOMMANDO: **2**
Position: Commander
Einsatzkommando Service: 30 July 1943–2 March 1944
Other Assignment: SD Tromso; Gestapo Frankfurt/Main
Waffen-SS Service: No
Highest Award: War Service Cross 2nd Class
Postwar Sentence: No judicial proceedings discovered
Notes: Served in SA, 1933-1935; RSHA, Office III Wounded in action; died 1962
National Archives File: A3343 SSO-384A

Podlich

First Name:	Oskar
Date of Birth:	1 July 1908
Place of Birth:	Striegau
Highest Rank:	SS-Obersturmbannführer
SS Number:	61984
Date Entered SS:	12 December 1932
NSDAP Number:	1500445
Date Entered NSDAP:	1 March 1933
Marital Status:	Divorced
Religion:	Agnostic
Civilian Occupation:	Businessman
Education:	High School
Foreign Language:	No
EINSATZKOMMANDO:	**1 (Norway)**
Position:	Not listed
Einsatzkommando Service:	April 1940–16 June 1941
Other Assignment:	SD Kattowitz; SD Metz
Waffen-SS Service:	No
Highest Award:	War Service Cross 2nd Class
Postwar Sentence:	No judicial proceedings discovered
Notes:	Divorced in 1944 Served 10 days arrest by SS
National Archives File:	A3343 SSO-385A

Pohl

First Name:	Kurt
Date of Birth:	16 November 1906
Place of Birth:	Posen
Highest Rank:	SS-Obersturmbannführer
SS Number:	107434
Date Entered SS:	1 September 1934
NSDAP Number:	1936714
Date Entered NSDAP:	1 May 1932
Marital Status:	Married
Religion:	Agnostic
Civilian Occupation:	Lawyer
Education:	University of Breslau, Marburg
Foreign Language:	French
EINSATZKOMMANDO:	**A**
Position:	*Teilkommando* leader
Einsatzkommando Service:	September 1941–1 July 1942
Other Assignment:	SD Strasburg; SD Frankfurt/Main
Waffen-SS Service:	No
Highest Award:	War Service Cross 1st Class
Postwar Sentence:	No judicial proceedings discovered
Notes:	Served in SA, 1933-1934 Served in Hitler Youth, 1934
National Archives File:	A3343 SSO-387A

Potzelt

First Name:	Walter
Date of Birth:	16 July 1903
Place of Birth:	Chemnitz
Highest Rank:	SS-Standartenführer
SS Number:	3838
Date Entered SS:	22 November 1930
NSDAP Number:	266433
Date Entered NSDAP:	1 June 1930
Marital Status:	Married
Religion:	Agnostic
Civilian Occupation:	Banker
Education:	High School
Foreign Language:	No
World War I Service:	No
EINSATZKOMMANDO:	**A**
Position:	Personal staff
Einsatzkommando Service:	20 April 1942–1 July 1942
Other Assignment:	RSHA; SD Fulda-Werra
Waffen-SS Service:	1st SS Division "Leibstandarte Adolf Hitler", 1941 and 1943
Highest Award:	Iron Cross 2nd Class
Killed in Action:	No
Postwar Sentence:	No judicial proceedings discovered
National Archives File:	A3343 SSO-390A

Prast

First Name:	Otto-Ernst
Date of Birth:	26 July 1913
Place of Birth:	Potsdam
Highest Rank:	SS-Sturmbannführer
SS Number:	267258
Date Entered SS:	1 March 1935
NSDAP Number:	414048
Date Entered NSDAP:	1 December 1930
Marital Status:	Married
Religion:	Agnostic
Civilian Occupation:	Photography business
Education:	High School
Foreign Language:	No
EINSATZKOMMANDO:	**10a**
Position:	Not listed
Einsatzkommando Service:	21 June 1941–5 October 1941 13 February 1942–15 July 1942
Other Assignment:	Gestapo Dresden
Waffen-SS Service:	No
Highest Award:	None listed
Postwar Sentence:	No judicial proceedings discovered
Notes:	Served in SA, 1930-1935 Possibly served in *Einsatzkommando* in Poland, 1939
National Archives File:	A3343 SSO-391A

Querner

First Name: Rudolf
Date of Birth: 10 June 1893
Place of Birth: Lehndorf
Highest Rank: SS-Obergruppenführer
SS Number: 308240
Date Entered SS: 22 May 1938
NSDAP Number: 2385386
Date Entered NSDAP: 1 May 1933
Marital Status: Married
Religion: Agnostic
Civilian Occupation: Police
Education: High School
Foreign Language: French
World War I Service: Yes, Iron Cross 2nd Class, POW
EINSATZKOMMANDO: *Einsatzkommando* in Czechoslovakia
Position: Commander
Einsatzkommando Service: 1939
Other Assignment: HSSPF Nordsee; HSSPF Donau
Waffen-SS Service: No
Highest Award: War Service Cross 1st Class
Killed in Action: No
Notes: Suicide 27 May 1945 in Magdeburg
National Archives File: A3343 SSO-398A

Rabe

First Name: Karl
Date of Birth: 11 June 1905
Place of Birth: Mühlhausen
Highest Rank: SS-Obersturmbannführer
SS Number: 54628
Date Entered SS: 1 June 1932
NSDAP Number: 259544
Date Entered NSDAP: 1 June 1930
Marital Status: Married
Religion: Agnostic
Civilian Occupation: Businessman
Education: High School
Foreign Language: No
World War I Service: Freikorps Ehrhard Brigade
EINSATZKOMMANDO: **7b**
Position: Commander
Einsatzkommando Service: January 1943–October 1944
Other Assignment: RSHA, Office I (Personnel); SD Cracow
Waffen-SS Service: No
Highest Award: None listed
Postwar Sentence: No judicial proceedings discovered
Notes: Served in SA, 1931-1932
National Archives File: A3343 SSO-001B

Radetzky

First Name: Waldemar von
Date of Birth: 8 May 1910
Place of Birth: Moscow, Russia
Highest Rank: SS-Sturmbannführer
SS Number: 351254
Date Entered SS: 13 December 1939
NSDAP Number: 8047747
Date Entered NSDAP: 1 December 1940
Marital Status: Engaged
Religion: Agnostic
Civilian Occupation: Businessman
Education: Trade School
Foreign Language: Latvian
EINSATZKOMMANDO: **A, 4a**
Position: Translator; *Teilkommando* leader
Einsatzkommando Service: 19 May 1941–1942
Other Assignment: SS District Warthe
Waffen-SS Service: No
Highest Award: Iron Cross 2nd Class
Postwar Sentence: 1948, 20 years, released 1951
Notes: Grew up in Riga; wounded in action 20 September 1943
Wound Badge; Infantry Assault Badge
Eastern People's Medal
National Archives File: A3343 SSO-002B

Radif

First Name: Franz
Date of Birth: 28 September 1908
Place of Birth: Klagenfurt, Austria
Highest Rank: SS-Obersturmführer
SS Number: 2675
Date Entered SS: 1 April 1930
NSDAP Number: 51198
Date Entered NSDAP: 17 September 1926
Marital Status: Married
Religion: Agnostic
Civilian Occupation: Police
Education: Not listed
Foreign Language: No
EINSATZKOMMANDO: **1005**
Position: Not listed
Einsatzkommando Service: 1943-1944
Other Assignment: Gestapo Brünn
Waffen-SS Service: No
Highest Award: None listed
Postwar Sentence: No judicial proceedings discovered
Notes: Golden Party Badge
Thrown out of SS in 1944
National Archives File: A3343 SSO-002B

Rapp

First Name: Albert
Date of Birth: 16 November 1908
Place of Birth: Schorndorf
Highest Rank: SS-Obersturmbannführer
SS Number: 280341
Date Entered SS: 1 June 1936
NSDAP Number: 774433
Date Entered NSDAP: 1 December 1931
Marital Status: Married
Religion: Agnostic
Civilian Occupation: Lawyer
Education: University of Munich, Tübingen
Foreign Language: French, English
EINSATZKOMMANDO: **7a**
Position: Commander
Einsatzkommando Service: February 1942 – 28 January 1943
Other Assignment: Chief, Office VI C, RSHA (SD, Foreign,Russo-Japanese Sphere)
SD Braunschweig
Highest Award: War Service Cross 1st Class
Postwar Sentence: 1965, Life
Notes: Iron Cross 2nd Class, Wound Badge
Served in SA, 1932-1936
National Archives File: A3343 SSO-007B

Rasch

First Name: Dr. Otto
Date of Birth: 7 December 1891
Place of Birth: Friedrichsruh
Highest Rank: SS-Brigadeführer
SS Number: 107100
Date Entered SS: 10 March 1933
NSDAP Number: 620976
Date Entered NSDAP: 1 October 1931
Marital Status: Widowed
Religion: Agnostic
Civilian Occupation: Lawyer
Education: University
Foreign Language: French, English, Italian
World War I Service: Yes, Iron Cross 2nd Class, Navy
EINSATZKOMMANDO: **Prague, von Woyrsch, C**
Position: Commander
Einsatzkommando Service: Prague: 1939 von Woyrsch: Polish Campaign C: June 1941–October 1941
Other Assignment: RSHA; Inspector, SD Königsberg
Highest Award: Iron Cross 2nd Class
Notes: Widowed 1944
Died 1 November 1948
National Archives File: A3343 SSO-007B

Raschdorf

First Name: Hans-Joachim
Date of Birth: 2 December 1916
Place of Birth: Berlin-Steglitz
Highest Rank: SS-Obersturmführer
SS Number: 392181
Date Entered SS: Not listed
NSDAP Number: 7053519
Date Entered NSDAP: 1 May 1939
Marital Status: Married
Religion: Protestant
Civilian Occupation: Police
Education: University
Foreign Language: No
EINSATZKOMMANDO: **B**
Position: Criminal Police section
Einsatzkommando Service: May 1944
Other Assignment: RSHA; Criminal Police Kiel
Waffen-SS Service: No
Highest Award: None listed
Postwar Sentence: No judicial proceedings discovered
Notes: Served in Hitler Youth, 1931-1933; served in SA, 1933-1936
Served in German Navy, 1937-1940
National Archives File: A3343 SSO-007B

Rausch

First Name: Günther
Date of Birth: 19 May 1909
Place of Birth: Sondershausen
Highest Rank: SS-Obersturmbannführer
SS Number: 17852
Date Entered SS: 15 October 1931
NSDAP Number: 224360
Date Entered NSDAP: 1 April 1930
Marital Status: Married
Religion: Agnostic
Civilian Occupation: Economist
Education: University of Berlin, Jena
Foreign Language: No
EINSATZKOMMANDO: **7b**
Position: Commander
Einsatzkommando Service: June 1941–January 1942
Other Assignment: RSHA, Office II (Organization and Law); SD Stuttgart
Waffen-SS Service: No
Highest Award: War Service Cross 1st Class
Postwar Sentence: No judicial proceedings discovered
Notes: Iron Cross 2nd Class; SD Lille
Died 1964
National Archives File: A3343 SSO-011B

Reese

First Name: Rudolf
Date of Birth: 15 May 1909
Place of Birth: Steinbusch
Highest Rank: SS-Obersturmführer
SS Number: 19199
Date Entered SS: 1 October 1931
NSDAP Number: 224191
Date Entered NSDAP: 1 March 1930
Marital Status: Married
Religion: Agnostic
Civilian Occupation: Police
Education: Grade School
Foreign Language: No
EINSATZKOMMANDO: **A**
Position: Administration
Einsatzkommando Service: 1941–June 1942
Other Assignment: Police Frankfurt/Oder
Waffen-SS Service: No
Highest Award: None listed
Postwar Sentence: No judicial proceedings discovered
Notes: Served in SA, 1930-1931
Went through complicated divorce
National Archives File: A3343 SSO-014B

Reichert

First Name: Fritz
Date of Birth: 4 December 1912
Place of Birth: Neuenbürg/Württemburg
Highest Rank: SS-Sturmbannführer
SS Number: 342012
Date Entered SS: 1 September 1939
NSDAP Number: 717286
Date Entered NSDAP: 1 November 1931
Marital Status: Married
Religion: Protestant
Civilian Occupation: Notary Public
Education: High School
Foreign Language: No
EINSATZKOMMANDO: **A**
Position: Not listed
Einsatzkommando Service: 21 June 1941–5 October 1941
15 December 1941 – 15 July 1942
Other Assignment: RSHA, Office VI (SD, Foreign)
Waffen-SS Service: No
Highest Award: Iron Cross 2nd Class
Postwar Sentence: No judicial proceedings discovered
Notes: Served in Hitler Youth, 1931-1938
Served in SA, 1933-1934
National Archives File: A3343 SSO-017B

Reipert

First Name: Albert
Date of Birth: 7 June 1907
Place of Birth: Gravenstein
Highest Rank: SS-Sturmbannführer
SS Number: 210901
Date Entered SS: 20 June 1933
NSDAP Number: 4175329
Date Entered NSDAP: 1 May 1937
Marital Status: Married
Religion: Agnostic
Civilian Occupation: Lawyer
Education: University
Foreign Language: No
World War I Service: No
EINSATZKOMMANDO: **A**
Position: Not listed
Einsatzkommando Service: April 1942–23 May 1944
Other Assignment: RSHA, Office II A 2 (Legislation); BdS Ostland
Waffen-SS Service: No
Highest Award: None listed
Postwar Sentence: No judicial proceedings discovered
Notes: Short personnel file
National Archives File: A3343 SSO-021B

Remmers

First Name: Hans Hermann
Date of Birth: 13 July 1906
Place of Birth: Wilhelmshaven
Highest Rank: SS-Obersturmbannführer
SS Number: 40876
Date Entered SS: Not listed
NSDAP Number: 982009
Date Entered NSDAP: 1 February 1932
Marital Status: Married
Religion: Agnostic
Civilian Occupation: Businessman
Education: Trade School
Foreign Language: No
EINSATZKOMMANDO: **1b**
Position: *Teilkommando* leader
Einsatzkommando Service: November 1941–February 1942
Other Assignment: SD Munich
Waffen-SS Service: No
Highest Award: War Service Cross 2nd Class
Postwar Sentence: 1961, 8 years commuted to 5 years
Postwar Employment: Department store Munich
Notes: Proficient in Morse Code
National Archives File: A3343 SSO-023B

Reschke

First Name: Erich
Date of Birth: 25 March 1896
Place of Birth: Zbiczno
Highest Rank: SS-Obersturmführer
SS Number: 353244
Date Entered SS: Not listed
NSDAP Number: 1645347
Date Entered NSDAP: Not listed
Marital Status: Married
Religion: Protestant
Civilian Occupation: Roof layer
Education: Grade School
Foreign Language: No
World War I Service: Yes, Wound Badge
EINSATZKOMMANDO: **z.b.V.**
Position: z.b.V. staff
Einsatzkommando Service: 3 July 1941–11 August 1941
Other Assignment: RSHA; SD Schneidemühl
Highest Award: None listed
Postwar Sentence: No judicial proceedings discovered
Notes: Joined Police before the war
No mention of *Einsatzkommando* service in personnel file
National Archives File: A3343 SSO-024B

Richter

First Name: Heinz
Date of Birth: 13 February 1903
Place of Birth: Güben
Highest Rank: SS-Obersturmbannführer
SS Number: 280049
Date Entered SS: 1 October 1936
NSDAP Number: 48512
Date Entered NSDAP: 6 December 1926
Marital Status: Married
Religion: Agnostic
Civilian Occupation: Lawyer
Education: University of Jena
Foreign Language: No
World War I Service: No
EINSATZKOMMANDO: **8**
Position: Commander
Einsatzkommando Service: 1 April 1942–September 1942
Other Assignment: SD Paris; Gestapo Vienna
Highest Award: War Service Cross 2nd Class
Postwar Sentence: 1969, 7 years
Notes: Found unsuitable for *Einsatzkommando* in 1942
Served in SA, 1933-1936
National Archives File: A3343 SSO-027B

Röder

First Name: Dr. Rudolf
Date of Birth: 30 October 1902
Place of Birth: Munich
Highest Rank: SS-Hauptsturmführer
SS Number: 60390
Date Entered SS: 30 June 1932
NSDAP Number: 1200757
Date Entered NSDAP: 1 August 1932
Marital Status: Married
Religion: Agnostic
Civilian Occupation: Businessman
Education: University
Foreign Language: No
World War I Service: No
EINSATZKOMMANDO: **Bydgoszcz**
Position: Commander
Einsatzkommando Service: Polish Campaign
Other Assignment: None
Waffen-SS Service: No
Highest Award: None listed
Postwar Sentence: No judicial proceedings discovered
Notes: Cashiered from the SS and sent to Buchenwald as a prisoner!
National Archives File: A3343 SSO-039B

Rohlfing

First Name: Hermann
Date of Birth: 27 August 1900
Place of Birth: Minden
Highest Rank: SS-Untersturmführer
SS Number: 280129
Date Entered SS: Not listed
NSDAP Number: 5632257
Date Entered NSDAP: 1 May 1937
Marital Status: Married
Religion: Agnostic
Civilian Occupation: Police
Education: Grade School
Foreign Language: No
World War I Service: Yes
EINSATZKOMMANDO: **1005**
Position: Not listed
Einsatzkommando Service: 1943-1944
Other Assignment: RSHA; SD Lublin
Highest Award: War Service Cross 2nd Class
Postwar Sentence: No judicial proceedings discovered
Notes: No mention of *Einsatzkommando* service in personnel file
Died 1 February 1961
National Archives File: A3343 SSO-044B

Rohrich

First Name: Hans
Date of Birth: 29 June 1900
Place of Birth: Berlin
Highest Rank: SS-Obersturmführer
SS Number: 430286
Date Entered SS: Not listed
NSDAP Number: 8734918
Date Entered NSDAP: 1 January 1942
Marital Status: Married
Religion: Agnostic
Civilian Occupation: Police
Education: Grade School
Foreign Language: No
World War I Service: Yes
EINSATZKOMMANDO: **C**
Position: Not listed
Einsatzkommando Service: 2 March 1942 to undetermined
Other Assignment: RSHA, Office II B (Passports)
RSHA, Office III A (Legal Practice)
Postwar Sentence: No judicial proceedings discovered
Notes: Freikorps, "Iron Division"; served in Police since 1923
RSHA, Office II C 4 (Budget)
National Archives File: A3343 SSO-039B

Rühl

First Name: Felix
Date of Birth: 12 August 1910
Place of Birth: Neheim
Highest Rank: SS-Hauptsturmführer
SS Number: 51305
Date Entered SS: 1 October 1932
NSDAP Number: 408461
Date Entered NSDAP: 1 December 1930
Marital Status: Single
Religion: Agnostic
Civilian Occupation: Clerk
Education: Grade School
Foreign Language: No
EINSATZKOMMANDO: **10b**
Position: Not listed
Einsatzkommando Service: May 1941–1 October 1941
Other Assignment: Gestapo Augsburg
Waffen-SS Service: No
Highest Award: War Service Cross 2nd Class
Postwar Sentence: 1948, 10 years, released 1949
Notes: Lived in England 1929-1930
Served in SA, 1930-1932
National Archives File: A3343 SSO-053B

Ruhrberg

First Name: Karl
Date of Birth: 22 May 1914
Place of Birth: Munich
Highest Rank: SS-Obersturmführer
SS Number: 386719
Date Entered SS: 10 January 1937
NSDAP Number: 5898126
Date Entered NSDAP: Married
Religion: Agnostic
Civilian Occupation: Police
Education: University of Bonn, Frankfurt/Main, Berlin
Foreign Language: French, English
EINSATZKOMMANDO: **8**
Position: Not listed
Einsatzkommando Service: May 1941–October 1941
Other Assignment: SD Königsberg; SD Nürnberg
Waffen-SS Service: No
Highest Award: None listed
Postwar Sentence: Acquitted
Notes: Criminal Police since 1935
Served in Army 6th and 15th Cavalry Regiments 1934-1938
National Archives File: A3343 SSO-055B

Rux

First Name: Karl-Heinz
Date of Birth: 3 September 1907
Place of Birth: Bromberg
Highest Rank: SS-Obersturmbannführer
SS Number: 231696
Date Entered SS: 20 April 1938
NSDAP Number: 1444292
Date Entered NSDAP: 1 February 1933
Marital Status: Married
Religion: Agnostic
Civilian Occupation: Administrator
Education: University
Foreign Language: No
World War I Service: No
EINSATZKOMMANDO: **2/II**
Position: Commander
Einsatzkommando Service: Polish Campaign
Other Assignment: SD Bromberg; SD Veldes
Waffen-SS Service: No
Highest Award: War Service Cross 1st Class
Postwar Sentence: No judicial proceedings discovered
Notes: SD Salzburg
National Archives File: A3343 SSO-057B

Sakuth

First Name: Edwin
Date of Birth: 3 June 1909
Place of Birth: Tilsit
Highest Rank: SS-Hauptsturmführer
SS Number: 314055
Date Entered SS: Not listed
NSDAP Number: 725083
Date Entered NSDAP: 1 November 1931
Marital Status: Married
Religion: Protestant
Civilian Occupation: Businessman
Education: Grade School listed (probably high school)
Foreign Language: English
EINSATZKOMMANDO: **Tilsit**
Position: SD section
Einsatzkommando Service: June 1941–December 1941
Other Assignment: RSHA, Office VI (SD, Foreign); SD Königsberg
Waffen-SS Service: No
Highest Award: None listed
Postwar Sentence: 1957, 3 Years
Notes: Spent 1929-1930 in Canada; served in SA 1931
Operation Zeppelin
No mention of *Einsatzkommando* service in personnel file
National Archives File: A3343 SSO-059B

Sandberger

First Name: Dr. Martin
Date of Birth: 17 August 1911
Place of Birth: Berlin-Charlottenburg
Highest Rank: SS-Obersturmbannführer
SS Number: 272495
Date Entered SS: 11 May 1935
NSDAP Number: 774980
Date Entered NSDAP: 1 December 1931
Marital Status: Married
Religion: Agnostic
Civilian Occupation: Lawyer
Education: University of Freiburg, Munich, Cologne, Tübingen
Foreign Language: No
EINSATZKOMMANDO: **1a**
Position: Commander
Einsatzkommando Service: June 1941–1943
Other Assignment: Chief, Office VI B, RSHA (SD, Foreign, German-Italian Sphere)
SD Stuttgart; BdS Italy
Waffen-SS Service: No
Highest Award: War Service Cross 1st Class
Postwar Sentence: 1948, Death commuted to Life, released 1953
Notes: Iron Cross 2nd Class
National Archives File: A3343 SSO-060B

Schäfer

First Name: Dr. Emanuel
Date of Birth: 20 April 1900
Place of Birth: Hultschin
Highest Rank: SS-Oberführer
SS Number: 280018
Date Entered SS: 26 September 1936
NSDAP Number: 4659879
Date Entered NSDAP: 1 May 1937
Marital Status: Married
Religion: Protestant
Civilian Occupation: Police
Education: University of Breslau
Foreign Language: No
World War I Service: Yes, 3rd Guards Field Artillery Regiment
EINSATZKOMMANDO: **II, Serbia**
Position: II – Commander; Serbia – Commander
Einsatzkommando Service: Polish Campaign; Serbia, 6 January 1942 to undetermined
Other Assignment: SD Trieste; Personal staff, RFSS
Highest Award: Iron Cross 1st Class
Postwar Sentence: 1953, 6 years
Notes: Served in Freikorps von Eycken
Served in SA, 1933-1936
National Archives File: A3343 SSO-066B

Schäfer

First Name: Dr. Oswald
Date of Birth: 14 June 1908
Place of Birth: Braunschweig
Highest Rank: SS-Obersturmbannführer
SS Number: 272488
Date Entered SS: 1 January 1936
NSDAP Number: 1772081
Date Entered NSDAP: 1 April 1933
Marital Status: Married
Religion: Agnostic
Civilian Occupation: Lawyer
Education: University of Berlin
Foreign Language: English, French
EINSATZKOMMANDO: **9**
Position: Commander
Einsatzkommando Service: October 1941–February 1942
Other Assignment: RSHA; Gestapo Munich
Waffen-SS Service: No
Highest Award: War Service Cross 1st Class
Postwar Sentence: 1966, acquitted
Notes: Served in SA, 1933-1936
No mention of *Einsatzkommando* service in personnel file
National Archives File: A3343 SSO-067B

Schallock

First Name: Walter
Date of Birth: 8 May 1903
Place of Birth: Stettin
Highest Rank: SS-Untersturmführer
SS Number: 5738
Date Entered SS: 1 October 1930
NSDAP Number: 315477
Date Entered NSDAP: 1 October 1930
Marital Status: Married
Religion: Agnostic
Civilian Occupation: Police
Education: Grade School
Foreign Language: No
World War I Service: No
EINSATZKOMMANDO: **1005**
Position: Not listed
Einsatzkommando Service: 1944
Other Assignment: Police Stettin
Waffen-SS Service: No
Highest Award: None listed
Postwar Sentence: No judicial proceedings discovered
Notes: Served in SA, 1930
National Archives File: A3343 SSO-069B

Schallwig

First Name: Dr. Friedrich
Date of Birth: 22 October 1902
Place of Birth: Unknown
Highest Rank: SS-Hauptsturmführer
SS Number: 51954
Date Entered SS: Not listed
NSDAP Number: Not a member
Marital Status: Unknown
Religion: Unknown
Civilian Occupation: Unknown
Education: Unknown
Foreign Language: No
World War I Service: No
EINSATZKOMMANDO: **A**
Position: Not listed
Einsatzkommando Service: July 1941–March 1944
Other Assignment: Unknown
Waffen-SS Service: No
Highest Award: None listed
Killed in Action: No
Postwar Sentence: No judicial proceedings discovered
Notes: Possible honorary SS member
National Archives File: A3343 SSO-069B

Scharpwinkel

First Name: Dr. Wilhelm
Date of Birth: 4 December 1904
Place of Birth: Wanne-Eickel
Highest Rank: SS-Obersturmbannführer
SS Number: 290803
Date Entered SS: Not listed
NSDAP Number: 1053578
Date Entered NSDAP: 1 April 1932
Marital Status: Married
Religion: Agnostic
Civilian Occupation: Lawyer
Education: University of Münster, Munich, Erlangen
Foreign Language: No
EINSATZKOMMANDO: **1/III**
Position: Commander
Einsatzkommando Service: Polish Campaign
Other Assignment: RSHA; Police Breslau; Police Liegnitz
Waffen-SS Service: No
Highest Award: War Service Cross 1st Class
Killed in Action: No
Postwar Sentence: No judicial proceedings discovered
Notes: Served in SA, 1933-1934
National Archives File: A3343 SSO-071B

Schefe

First Name: Dr. Robert
Date of Birth: 23 August 1909
Place of Birth: Schwerin
Highest Rank: SS-Obersturmbannführer
SS Number: 267268
Date Entered SS: Not listed
NSDAP Number: 1027861
Date Entered NSDAP: 1 April 1932
Marital Status: Married
Religion: Agnostic
Civilian Occupation: Lawyer
Education: University
Foreign Language: No
EINSATZKOMMANDO: **2/V**
Position: Commander
Einsatzkommando Service: Polish Campaign
Other Assignment: RSHA, Office V A (Kripo, Policy); SD Allenstein
Waffen-SS Service: No
Highest Award: Iron Cross 2nd Class
Killed in Action: No
Postwar Sentence: No judicial proceedings discovered
Notes: Received Iron Cross 2nd Class for *Einsatzkommando* duty
National Archives File: A3343 SSO-072B

Scherwitz

First Name: Fritz
Date of Birth: 21 August 1903
Place of Birth: Unknown
Highest Rank: SS-Untersturmführer
SS Number: 51561
Date Entered SS: Not listed
NSDAP Number: Not a member
Marital Status: Unknown
Religion: Unknown
Civilian Occupation: Unknown
Education: Unknown
Foreign Language: No
World War I Service: No
EINSATZKOMMANDO: **A**
Position: Not listed
Einsatzkommando Service: October 1941–October 1944
Other Assignment: Unknown
Highest Award: None listed
Killed in Action: No
Postwar Sentence: No judicial proceedings discovered
Notes: Possible honorary SS member
Post-war alias Elias Sirewitz
National Archives File: A3343 SSO-075B

Scheuring

First Name: Adam
Date of Birth: 13 March 1899
Place of Birth: Veitshöchheim
Highest Rank: SS-Obersturmführer
SS Number: 108826
Date Entered SS: 1 June 1933
NSDAP Number: 1648248
Date Entered NSDAP: 1 April 1933
Marital Status: Married
Religion: Agnostic
Civilian Occupation: Orthopedic equipment
Education: Grade School
Foreign Language: No
World War I Service: Yes
EINSATZKOMMANDO: **D**
Position: Not listed
Einsatzkommando Service: 1942
Other Assignment: RSHA
Highest Award: Iron Cross 2nd Class
Postwar Sentence: No judicial proceedings discovered
Notes: Crimea Shield; wounded in action 1942
No mention of *Einsatzkommando* service in personnel file
National Archives File: A3343 SSO-076B

Schieffer

First Name: Wilhelm
Date of Birth: 18 April 1911
Place of Birth: Lautzkirchen
Highest Rank: SS-Obersturmführer
SS Number: 120471
Date Entered SS: 14 May 1933
NSDAP Number: 2694833
Date Entered NSDAP: 1 August 1933
Marital Status: Married
Religion: Agnostic
Civilian Occupation: Lawyer
Education: University
Foreign Language: No
World War I Service: No
EINSATZKOMMANDO: **7b**
Position: Not listed
Einsatzkommando Service: 22 May 1942–30 August 1943
Other Assignment: SD Saarbrücken
Waffen-SS Service: No
Highest Award: None listed
Postwar Sentence: No judicial proceedings discovered
Notes: Very small personnel file
National Archives File: A3343 SSO-077B

Schiemann

First Name: Waldemar
Date of Birth: 2 May 1903
Place of Birth: St. Petersburg, Russia
Highest Rank: SS-Obersturmführer
SS Number: 36535
Date Entered SS: 1 February 1932
NSDAP Number: 601701
Date Entered NSDAP: 1 August 1931
Marital Status: Married
Religion: Agnostic
Civilian Occupation: Lathe operator
Education: Grade School
Foreign Language: Russian
World War I Service: No
EINSATZKOMMANDO: **A**
Position: Motor pool supervisor
Einsatzkommando Service: 1941–1944
Other Assignment: RSHA, Office II D 3a (Technical Matters)
Waffen-SS Service: No
Highest Award: None listed
Postwar Sentence: No judicial proceedings discovered
Notes: Served in SA, 1931
National Archives File: A3343 SSO-077B

Schilling

First Name: Dr. Heinrich
Date of Birth: 24 October 1906
Place of Birth: Nürnberg
Highest Rank: SS-Sturmbannführer
SS Number: 104104
Date Entered SS: 1 May 1933
NSDAP Number: 2614246
Date Entered NSDAP: 1 May 1933
Marital Status: Single
Religion: Agnostic
Civilian Occupation: Lawyer
Education: University of Erlangen
Foreign Language: French
World War I Service: Freikorps Oberland
EINSATZKOMMANDO: **B**
Position: Not listed
Einsatzkommando Service: August 1942 to undetermined
Other Assignment: RSHA; Gestapo Vienna
Waffen-SS Service: No
Highest Award: Iron Cross 2nd Class
Postwar Sentence: No judicial proceedings discovered
Notes: Eastern People's Medal
National Archives File: A3343 SSO-077B

Schimmerohn

First Name: Dr. Heinz
Date of Birth: 22 January 1911
Place of Birth: Chemnitz
Highest Rank: SS-Obersturmbannführer
SS Number: 107115
Date Entered SS: 15 October 1933
NSDAP Number: 266440
Date Entered NSDAP: 1 June 1930
Marital Status: Married
Religion: Agnostic
Civilian Occupation: Lawyer
Education: University
Foreign Language: English, French
EINSATZKOMMANDO: **C**
Position: Not listed
Einsatzkommando Service: 31 May 1942–1 April 1943
Other Assignment: RSHA; SD Halle; SD Stettin
Waffen-SS Service: No
Highest Award: War Service Cross 1st Class
Killed in Action: No
Postwar Sentence: No judicial proceedings discovered
Notes: Served in Hitler Youth, 1929-1931; served in SA, 1932-1933
National Archives File: A3343 SSO-078B

Schindhelm

First Name: Hans-Gerhard
Date of Birth: 5 July 1908
Place of Birth: Dresden
Highest Rank: SS-Obersturmbannführer
SS Number: 353427
Date Entered SS: 27 June 1938
NSDAP Number: 2452706
Date Entered NSDAP: 1 May 1933
Marital Status: Married
Religion: Agnostic
Civilian Occupation: Lawyer
Education: University of Dresden, Leipzig
Foreign Language: No
EINSATZKOMMANDO: **8**
Position: Commander
Einsatzkommando Service: 13 November 1942 – October 1943
Other Assignment: Gestapo Cracow; SD Leipzig
Waffen-SS Service: No
Highest Award: War Service Cross 1st Class
Killed in Action: No
Postwar Sentence: No judicial proceedings discovered
Notes: Short personnel file
National Archives File: A3343 SSO-078B

Schindowski

First Name: Dr. Hans
Date of Birth: 11 July 1904
Place of Birth: Königsberg
Highest Rank: SS-Sturmbannführer
SS Number: 51388
Date Entered SS: Not listed
NSDAP Number: Not a member
Marital Status: Unknown
Religion: Unknown
Civilian Occupation: Unknown
Education: Unknown
Foreign Language: No
World War I Service: No
EINSATZKOMMANDO: **A**
Position: Not listed
Einsatzkommando Service: 1941–1942
Other Assignment: Unknown
Waffen-SS Service: No
Highest Award: None listed
Killed in Action: No
Postwar Sentence: No judicial proceedings discovered
Notes: Short personnel file
National Archives File: A3343 SSO-078B

Schlätel

First Name: Werner
Date of Birth: 21 January 1913
Place of Birth: Bad Segeberg
Highest Rank: SS-Sturmbannführer
SS Number: 11871
Date Entered SS: 1 June 1931
NSDAP Number: 193592
Date Entered NSDAP: Not listed
Marital Status: Married
Religion: Agnostic
Civilian Occupation: Pharmacist
Education: High School
Foreign Language: No
EINSATZKOMMANDO: *Einsatzkommando* in Czechoslovakia
Position: Not listed
Einsatzkommando Service: 1938
Other Assignment: Unknown
Waffen-SS Service: 4th SS Division "Polizei", 1942-1944
Highest Award: Iron Cross 2nd Class
Postwar Sentence: No judicial proceedings discovered
Notes: Served in Hitler Youth, 1929-1930; served in SA, 1930-1931
Infantry Assault Badge; wounded in action 1942
National Archives File: A3343 SSO-079B

Schlegel

First Name: Rudolf
Date of Birth: 11 June 1913
Place of Birth: Chemnitz
Highest Rank: SS-Hauptsturmführer
SS Number: 353537
Date Entered SS: 5 May 1937
NSDAP Number: 4949731
Date Entered NSDAP: 1 May 1937
Marital Status: Married
Religion: Agnostic
Civilian Occupation: Teacher
Education: University
Foreign Language: No
EINSATZKOMMANDO: **B**
Position: *Teilkommando* leader
Einsatzkommando Service: June 1941–1943
Other Assignment: RSHA
Highest Award: War Service Cross 1st Class
Postwar Sentence: 1962, 8 years commuted to 3 years
Postwar Employment: Daimler-Benz, Stuttgart
Notes: Served in SA, 1933-1935; Iron Cross 2nd Class
Eastern Peoples Medal
No mention of *Einsatzkommando* service in personnel file
National Archives File: A3343 SSO-080B

Schlierbach

First Name: Dr. Hellmut
Date of Birth: 17 June 1913
Place of Birth: Offenbach
Highest Rank: SS-Sturmbannführer
SS Number: 107970
Date Entered SS: 15 June 1933
NSDAP Number: 5628167
Date Entered NSDAP: 1 May 1937
Marital Status: Married
Religion: Agnostic
Civilian Occupation: Lawyer
Education: University of Frankfurt/Main, Berlin
Foreign Language: No
EINSATZKOMMANDO: **C, 4a**
Position: Liaison Officer to 6th Army
Einsatzkommando Service: 1941–1942
Other Assignment: RSHA, Office IV (Gestapo); SD Strassbourg
RSHA, Office I D 2 (Personnel)
Waffen-SS Service: No
Highest Award: None listed
Postwar Sentence: No judicial proceedings discovered
Notes: In SS *Totenkopfverbände* for two months in 1938
National Archives File: A3343 SSO-081B

Schlupper

First Name: Hans
Date of Birth: 17 October 1908
Place of Birth: Reickenbach
Highest Rank: SS-Obersturmführer
SS Number: 4287
Date Entered SS: Not listed
NSDAP Number: 227850
Date Entered NSDAP: 1 April 1930
Marital Status: Married
Religion: Lutheran
Civilian Occupation: Businessman
Education: Unknown
Foreign Language: No
EINSATZKOMMANDO: **D**
Position: Not listed
Einsatzkommando Service: 1941-1942
Other Assignment: RSHA; Gestapo Plauen
Waffen-SS Service: No
Highest Award: War Service Cross 1st Class
Postwar Sentence: No judicial proceedings discovered
Notes: Served in Hitler Youth, 1928-1930; served in SA, 1930
Iron Cross 2nd Class, Crimea Shield
National Archives File: A3343 SSO-082B

Schmiel

First Name: Erwin
Date of Birth: 17 November 1913
Place of Birth: Berlin-Neukölln
Highest Rank: SS-Hauptsturmführer
SS Number: 257784
Date Entered SS: 1 December 1932
NSDAP Number: 3044832
Date Entered NSDAP: 1 May 1933
Marital Status: Married
Religion: Agnostic
Civilian Occupation: Businessman
Education: Unknown
Foreign Language: No
EINSATZKOMMANDO: **2**
Position: Not listed
Einsatzkommando Service: 1941
Other Assignment: RSHA
Waffen-SS Service: SS Infantry Regiment "Leibstandarte Adolf Hitler", 1933-1937
Highest Award: None listed
Killed in Action: No
Postwar Sentence: No judicial proceedings discovered
Notes: No mention of *Einsatzkommando* service in personnel file
National Archives File: A3343 SSO-088B

Schmitz

First Name: Heinrich
Date of Birth: 15 February 1907
Place of Birth: Höchst
Highest Rank: SS-Hauptsturmführer
SS Number: 392038
Date Entered SS: 1 November 1936
NSDAP Number: 8034478
Date Entered NSDAP: 1 April 1940
Marital Status: Married
Religion: Agnostic
Civilian Occupation: Detective Officer
Education: University
Foreign Language: No
EINSATZKOMMANDO: **A**
Position: Not listed
Einsatzkommando Service: Not listed
Other Assignment: Criminal Police Trier; KdS Königsberg
Waffen-SS Service: No
Highest Award: War Service Cross 2nd Class
Postwar Sentence: No judicial proceedings discovered
Notes: Served two months in Flak Regiment 32 in 1938
No mention of *Einsatzkommando* service in personnel file
National Archives File: A3343 SSO-089B

Schmücker

First Name: Rudi
Date of Birth: 22 May 1915
Place of Birth: Nassau
Highest Rank: SS-Hauptsturmführer
SS Number: 385407
Date Entered SS: 11 November 1939
NSDAP Number: 7128077
Date Entered NSDAP: 1 September 1939
Marital Status: Single
Religion: Catholic
Civilian Occupation: Detective Officer
Education: High School
Foreign Language: French
EINSATZKOMMANDO: **Vorkommando Moscow**
Einsatzkommando Service: June 1942–October 1942
Other Assignment: Commander, Security Police Posen
Waffen-SS Service: No
Highest Award: War Service Cross 2nd Class
Killed in Action: No
Postwar Sentence: No judicial proceedings discovered
Notes: Served in Hitler Youth, 1933-1938
Served in Luftwaffe, 1936-1938
National Archives File: A3343 SSO-090B

Schneider

First Name: Gerhard-Oskar
Date of Birth: 13 October 1913
Place of Birth: Magdeburg
Highest Rank: SS-Hauptsturmführer
SS Number: 117980
Date Entered SS: 4 May 1933
NSDAP Number: 7552651
Date Entered NSDAP: 1 March 1940
Marital Status: Married
Religion: Agnostic
Civilian Occupation: Police
Education: High School
Foreign Language: No
EINSATZKOMMANDO: **9**
Position: Police section
Einsatzkommando Service: June 1941–August 1941
Other Assignment: RSHA
Waffen-SS Service: No
Highest Award: Iron Cross 2nd Class
Postwar Sentence: 1962, 10 years
Notes: Served in Army 9th Infantry Regiment 1934-1935
No mention of *Einsatzkommando* service in personnel file
National Archives File: A3343 SSO-092B

Schneider

First Name:	Hans
Date of Birth:	28 November 1908
Place of Birth:	Riga, Russia
Highest Rank:	SS-Sturmbannführer
SS Number:	357299
Date Entered SS:	1 June 1940
NSDAP Number:	8048041
Date Entered NSDAP:	1 December 1940
Marital Status:	Married
Religion:	Protestant
Civilian Occupation:	Lawyer
Education:	University of Riga
Foreign Language:	Russian, Latvian
EINSATZKOMMANDO:	**B**
Position:	August 1942 to undetermined
Other Assignment:	RSHA, Office IV E 3 (Gestapo, Treason); SD Prague
Waffen-SS Service:	No
Highest Award:	Iron Cross 2nd Class
Postwar Sentence:	No judicial proceedings discovered
Notes:	Police Königsberg; served in Latvian Army, 1931-1932 Eastern People's Medal
National Archives File:	A3343 SSO-092B

Schnopfhagen

First Name:	Dr. Otto
Date of Birth:	17 November 1909
Place of Birth:	Linz, Austria
Highest Rank:	SS-Obersturmführer
SS Number:	279561
Date Entered SS:	1 January 1936
NSDAP Number:	1618076
Date Entered NSDAP:	15 May 1933
Marital Status:	Single
Religion:	Unknown
Civilian Occupation:	Doctor
Education:	University
Foreign Language:	No
EINSATZKOMMANDO:	**D**
Position:	Physician
Einsatzkommando Service:	1941–1942
Other Assignment:	SS Medical Department; SS District Physician Vienna
Waffen-SS Service:	No
Highest Award:	None listed
Killed in Action:	No
Postwar Sentence:	No judicial proceedings discovered
Notes:	No mention of *Einsatzkommando* service in personnel file
National Archives File:	A3343 SSO-094B

Schöne

First Name:	Edmund
Date of Birth:	15 October 1905
Place of Birth:	Unknown
Highest Rank:	SS-Hauptsturmführer
SS Number:	290994
Date Entered SS:	Not listed
NSDAP Number:	2593567
Date Entered NSDAP:	1 May 1933
Marital Status:	Unknown
Religion:	Unknown
Civilian Occupation:	Unknown
Education:	Unknown
Foreign Language:	Unknown
EINSATZKOMMANDO:	**I**
Position:	Not listed
Einsatzkommando Service:	Polish Campaign
Other Assignment:	RSHA
Waffen-SS Service:	Unknown
Highest Award:	Unknown
Killed in Action:	No
Postwar Sentence:	No judicial proceedings discovered
Notes:	Short personnel file
National Archives File:	No File

Schönemann

First Name:	Werner
Date of Birth:	27 November 1911
Place of Birth:	Berlin
Highest Rank:	SS-Hauptsturmführer
SS Number:	290678
Date Entered SS:	1 October 1936
NSDAP Number:	7599367
Date Entered NSDAP:	Not listed
Marital Status:	Single
Religion:	Agnostic
Civilian Occupation:	Police
Education:	University of Berlin
Foreign Language:	No
EINSATZKOMMANDO:	**8**
Position:	*Teilkommando* leader
Einsatzkommando Service:	1941
Other Assignment:	RSHA
Highest Award:	Iron Cross 2nd Class
Postwar Sentence:	1964, 6 years commuted to 3 years
Postwar Employment:	Motor factory
Notes:	Served in SA, 1934-1935; wounded in action No mention of *Einsatzkommando* service in personnel file
National Archives File:	A3343 SSO-096B

Schöngarth

First Name: Dr. Eberhard
Date of Birth: 22 April 1903
Place of Birth: Leipzig
Highest Rank: SS-Brigadeführer
SS Number: 67174
Date Entered SS: 1 March 1933
NSDAP Number: 2848857
Date Entered NSDAP: 1 May 1933
Marital Status: Married
Religion: Agnostic
Civilian Occupation: Lawyer
Education: University of Leipzig
World War I Service: Freikorps
EINSATZKOMMANDO: **z.b.V.**
Position: Commander
Einsatzkommando Service: 3 July 1941–11 August 1941
Other Assignment: RSHA; Gestapo Dortmund; SD, Cracow; SD Dresden
Waffen-SS Service: 4th SS Division "Polizei", 1943-1944
Highest Award: War Service Cross 1st Class
Postwar Sentence: 1946, Death; executed 15 May 1946 by the British at Hameln
Notes: Gestapo Bielefeld; Commander SD, den Haag
Served in SA, 1922-1924
National Archives File: A3343 SSO-096B

Schönpflug

First Name: Egon
Date of Birth: 5 December 1913
Place of Birth: Innsbruck, Austria
Highest Rank: SS-Hauptsturmführer
SS Number: 372267
Date Entered SS: 1 March 1938
NSDAP Number: 6199420
Date Entered NSDAP: 13 May 1938
Marital Status: Married
Religion: Agnostic
Civilian Occupation: Lawyer
Education: University
Foreign Language: French
EINSATZKOMMANDO: **8**
Position: Not listed
Einsatzkommando Service: Not listed
Other Assignment: RSHA; Criminal Police Kattowitz
Waffen-SS Service: No
Highest Award: War Service Cross 2nd Class
Postwar Sentence: 1961, 9 years
Notes: Served in SA, 1933-1938
No mention of *Einsatzkommando* service in personnel file
National Archives File: A3343 SSO-097B

Schramm

First Name: Walter
Date of Birth: 15 July 1909
Place of Birth: Saarbrücken
Highest Rank: SS-Obersturmführer
SS Number: 72584
Date Entered SS: 15 March 1933
NSDAP Number: 2317636
Date Entered NSDAP: 1 May 1933
Marital Status: Married
Religion: Agnostic
Civilian Occupation: Agricultural official
Education: High School
Foreign Language: No
EINSATZKOMMANDO: **B**
Position: Not listed
Einsatzkommando Service: 1942
Other Assignment: RSHA, Office II A 3 (Indemnification)
RSHA, Office II C 4 (Budget)
Highest Award: None listed
Postwar Sentence: No judicial proceedings discovered
Notes: SD Brussels; SD Breslau
Gestapo Kattowitz
National Archives File: A3343 SSO-100B

Schröder

First Name: Rudolf
Date of Birth: 7 November 1903
Place of Birth: Dresden
Highest Rank: SS-Obersturmbannführer
SS Number: 272288
Date Entered SS: 15 November 1934
NSDAP Number: 825801
Date Entered NSDAP: 1 December 1931
Marital Status: Married
Religion: Agnostic
Civilian Occupation: Lawyer
Education: University of Leipzig, Tübingen
Foreign Language: English, French
EINSATZKOMMANDO: **B**
Position: Not listed
Einsatzkommando Service: June 1941–November 1941
Other Assignment: RSHA; Police Stuttgart
Waffen-SS Service: No
Highest Award: War Service Cross 2nd Class
Postwar Sentence: No judicial proceedings discovered
Notes: Served in SA, 1931-1934
SD Reichenberg
National Archives File: A3343 SSO-102B

Schroer

First Name: Dr. Wilhelm
Date of Birth: 24 July 1911
Place of Birth: Hochhalen
Highest Rank: SS-Obersturmführer
SS Number: 418257
Date Entered SS: 26 February 1942
NSDAP Number: 1225702
Date Entered NSDAP: 1 August 1932
Marital Status: Married
Religion: Protestant
Civilian Occupation: Lawyer
Education: University
Foreign Language: No
EINSATZKOMMANDO: **D**
Position: Propaganda officer
Einsatzkommando Service: 1942
Other Assignment: Unknown
Waffen-SS Service: No
Highest Award: War Service Cross 2nd Class
Postwar Sentence: No judicial proceedings discovered
Notes: Crimea Shield
Operation Zeppelin
National Archives File: A3343 SSO-103B

Schuback

First Name: Kurt
Date of Birth: 12 July 1913
Place of Birth: Hamburg
Highest Rank: SS-Sturmbannführer
SS Number: 314137
Date Entered SS: 16 January 1939
NSDAP Number: 5647235
Date Entered NSDAP: 1 May 1937
Marital Status: Married
Religion: Agnostic
Civilian Occupation: Unknown
Education: University of Innsbruck, Rostock
Foreign Language: No
EINSATZKOMMANDO: *Einsatzkommando* in Poland, **A**
Position: Not listed
Einsatzkommando Service: Polish Campaign; A, 1941–1942
Other Assignment: RSHA, Office VI C (SD, Foreign, Russo-Japanese Sphere)
SD Königsberg
Highest Award: War Service Cross 1st Class
Postwar Sentence: No judicial proceedings discovered
Notes: Served in SA, 1933-1934
Served in Hitler Youth, 1934-1939
National Archives File: A3343 SSO-103B

Schubert

First Name: Heinz-Hermann
Date of Birth: 27 August 1914
Place of Birth: Berlin
Highest Rank: SS-Obersturmführer
SS Number: 107326
Date Entered SS: 10 October 1934
NSDAP Number: 3474350
Date Entered NSDAP: 1 May 1934
Marital Status: Married
Religion: Agnostic
Civilian Occupation: Law clerk
Education: Trade School
Foreign Language: No
EINSATZKOMMANDO: **D**
Position: Adjutant
Einsatzkommando Service: October 1941–June 1942
Other Assignment: RSHA, Office I A 4 (Personnel); SD Augsburg
Waffen-SS Service: No
Highest Award: None listed
Postwar Sentence: 1948, Death commuted to 10 years, released 1952
Notes: Served in Hitler Youth, 1932-1934
Golden Hitler Youth Badge
National Archives File: A3343 SSO-104B

Schulte

First Name: Christian
Date of Birth: 30 July 1912
Place of Birth: Kiel
Highest Rank: SS-Obersturmführer
SS Number: 107202
Date Entered SS: 1 October 1934
NSDAP Number: 753374
Date Entered NSDAP: 1 December 1931
Marital Status: Married
Religion: Agnostic
Civilian Occupation: Engineer
Education: Trade School
Foreign Language: No
EINSATZKOMMANDO: **C**
Position: Adjutant
Einsatzkommando Service: Not listed
Other Assignment: Unknown
Waffen-SS Service: No
Highest Award: None listed
Postwar Sentence: 4 1/2 years
Notes: Served in SA, 1933-1934
No mention of *Einsatzkommando* service in personnel file
National Archives File: A3343 SSO-110B

Schulz

First Name: Paul
Date of Birth: 22 September 1910
Place of Birth: Berlin
Highest Rank: SS-Untersturmführer
SS Number: 337668
Date Entered SS: Not listed
NSDAP Number: Not a member
Marital Status: Married
Religion: Protestant
Civilian Occupation: Police
Education: Grade School
Foreign Language: No
World War I Service: No
EINSATZKOMMANDO: *Einsatzkommando* in Poland
Position: Not listed
Einsatzkommando Service: Polish Campaign
Other Assignment: RSHA, Office IV A 2 (Gestapo, Sabotage); SD Oslo
Waffen-SS Service: No
Highest Award: War Service Cross 2nd Class
Postwar Sentence: No judicial proceedings discovered
Notes: Probably in *Einsatzkommando* in Czechoslovakia 1938
SD Den Haag
National Archives File: A3343 SSO-114B

Schulz

First Name: Erwin
Date of Birth: 27 November 1900
Place of Birth: Berlin
Highest Rank: SS-Brigadeführer
SS Number: 107484
Date Entered SS: 20 April 1935
NSDAP Number: 2902238
Date Entered NSDAP: 1 May 1933
Marital Status: Married
Religion: Agnostic
Civilian Occupation: Police
Education: University of Berlin (2 semesters)
Foreign Language: No
World War I Service: Yes
EINSATZKOMMANDO: **5**
Position: Commander
Einsatzkommando Service: May 1941–September 1941
Highest Award: War Service Cross 1st Class
Postwar Sentence: 1948, 20 years commuted to 15 years, released
Notes: Died 11 November 1981
HSSPF Alpenland, Inspector of SD and SIPO Schools
National Archives File: A3343 SSO-112B

Schulz

First Name: Bruno
Date of Birth: 19 April 1903
Place of Birth: Braunsberg
Highest Rank: SS-Untersturmführer
SS Number: 367661
Date Entered SS: 8 December 1936
NSDAP Number: 4754191
Date Entered NSDAP: 1 May 1937
Marital Status: Married
Religion: None
Civilian Occupation: Police
Education: Grade School
Foreign Language: No
EINSATZKOMMANDO: **A**
Position: SD section
Einsatzkommando Service: June 1941–June 1944
Other Assignment: SD Copenhagen; SD Tilsit
Waffen-SS Service: No
Highest Award: None listed
Postwar Sentence: 1961, 3 years
Postwar Employment: Tax accountant
Notes: No mention of *Einsatzkommando* service in personnel file
National Archives File: A3343 SSO-112B

Schulz

First Name: Wilhelm
Date of Birth: 14 October 1909
Place of Birth: Recklinghausen
Highest Rank: SS-Hauptsturmführer
SS Number: 51465
Date Entered SS: Not listed
NSDAP Number: Not a member
Date Entered NSDAP: 1 May 1931
Marital Status: Married
Religion: None
Civilian Occupation: Police
Education: High School
Foreign Language: No
EINSATZKOMMANDO: **8**
Position: *Teilkommando* leader
Einsatzkommando Service: June 1941–September 1943
Other Assignment: Unknown
Waffen-SS Service: No
Highest Award: None listed
Postwar Sentence: 1961, 7 years commuted to 6 years
Postwar Employment: Wall paper factory
Notes: No mention of *Einsatzkommando* service in personnel file
National Archives File: A3343 SSO-115B

Schumacher

First Name: Hans-Karl
Date of Birth: 12 June 1907
Place of Birth: Barmen
Highest Rank: SS-Sturmbannführer
SS Number: 306629
Date Entered SS: 1 January 1939
NSDAP Number: 2880022
Date Entered NSDAP: 1 May 1933
Marital Status: Married
Religion: Agnostic
Civilian Occupation: Police
Education: University of Würzburg, Bonn, Erlangen
Foreign Language: No
EINSATZKOMMANDO: **C**
Position: SD section
Einsatzkommando Service: 25 October 1941–August 1942
Other Assignment: RSHA, Office V (Kripo); RSHA, Office I D (Personnel)
Highest Award: War Service Cross 2nd Class
Postwar Sentence: 1961, 4 years
Postwar Employment: Construction company
Notes: Kripo Vienna, Kripo Breslau, Kripo Düsseldorf
Wounded in air raid 1943
National Archives File: A3343 SSO-118B

Schwietering

First Name: Rudolf
Date of Birth: 1 January 1912
Place of Birth: Gelsenkirchen
Highest Rank: SS-Hauptsturmführer
SS Number: 56111
Date Entered SS: 28 January 1933
NSDAP Number: 1322520
Date Entered NSDAP: 1 April 1931
Marital Status: Married
Religion: Agnostic
Civilian Occupation: Student
Education: University of Königsberg
Foreign Language: No
EINSATZKOMMANDO: **2**
Position: Not listed
Einsatzkommando Service: Not listed
Other Assignment: RSHA, Office I A V b (Personnel); SD Dortmund
Waffen-SS Service: No
Highest Award: Iron Cross 2nd Class
Postwar Sentence: No judicial proceedings discovered
Notes: Served in Hitler Youth, 1930-1932; served in SA, 1930-1933
Eastern People's Medal; SD Münster
National Archives File: A3343 SSO-127B

Seefeld

First Name: Gert von
Date of Birth: 6 June 1908
Place of Birth: Degahlen, Russia
Highest Rank: SS-Untersturmführer
SS Number: 430408
Date Entered SS: Not listed
NSDAP Number: 8434586
Date Entered NSDAP: 1 August 1941
Marital Status: Married
Religion: Agnostic
Civilian Occupation: Shipping
Education: High School
Foreign Language: English, Latvian
EINSATZKOMMANDO: **A**
Position: Not listed
Einsatzkommando Service: June 1941–1943
Other Assignment: Ethnic German Liaison Office (VOMI); SD Reval
Waffen-SS Service: No
Highest Award: Iron Cross 2nd Class
Killed in Action: No
Postwar Sentence: No judicial proceedings discovered
Notes: Traveled throughout the Baltic before the war
National Archives File: A3343 SSO-128B

Seekel

First Name: Dr. Friedrich
Date of Birth: 20 May 1910
Place of Birth: Berlin
Highest Rank: SS-Sturmbannführer
SS Number: 386689
Date Entered SS: Not listed
NSDAP Number: Not a member
Marital Status: Married
Religion: Agnostic
Civilian Occupation: Teacher
Education: University
Foreign Language: No
EINSATZKOMMANDO: **8, 1005**
Position: 8 – Commander
Einsatzkommando Service: 1942–1944
Other Assignment: RSHA, Office I B 3 (Personnel)
Waffen-SS Service: No
Highest Award: Iron Cross 1st Class
Killed in Action: No
Postwar Sentence: No judicial proceedings discovered
Notes: Served in SA, 1933-1935
No mention of *Einsatzkommando* service in personnel file
National Archives File: A3343 SSO-129B

Seetzen

First Name: Heinz
Date of Birth: 22 June 1906
Place of Birth: Rüstringen
Highest Rank: SS-Standartenführer
SS Number: 267231
Date Entered SS: 1 February 1935
NSDAP Number: 2732725
Date Entered NSDAP: 1 May 1933
Marital Status: Married
Religion: Protestant
Civilian Occupation: Lawyer
Education: University of Marburg, Kiel
Foreign Language: No
EINSATZKOMMANDO: **10a, B**
Position: B – Commander; 10a – Commander
Einsatzkommando Service: 10a, –July 1942; B, 28 April 1944–August 1944
Other Assignment: Security Police, Kassel; Gestapo Hamburg
Waffen-SS Service: No
Highest Award: War Service Cross 1st Class
Postwar Sentence: N/A
Notes: SD Breslau; reprimanded for looting while in *Einsatzkommando*
Suicide, 28 September 1945
National Archives File: A3343 SSO-129B

Seibert

First Name: Willy
Date of Birth: 17 June 1908
Place of Birth: Hannover
Highest Rank: SS-Standartenführer
SS Number: 272375
Date Entered SS: 1 November 1935
NSDAP Number: 1886112
Date Entered NSDAP: 1 May 1933
Marital Status: Married
Religion: Agnostic
Civilian Occupation: Economist
Education: University of Göttingen
Foreign Language: No
EINSATZKOMMANDO: **D**
Position: Executive officer
Einsatzkommando Service: 15 May 1941–15 August 1942
Other Assignment: Chief, Office III D, RSHA (SD, Domestic, Economy)
RSHA, Office III C (SD, Domestic, Culture)
Highest Award: Iron Cross 2nd Class
Postwar Sentence: 1948, Death commuted to 15 years, released
Notes: Reserve lieutenant in German Army
National Archives File: A3343 SSO-130B

Sens

First Name: Otto
Date of Birth: 14 April 1898
Place of Birth: Dessau
Highest Rank: SS-Standartenführer
SS Number: 23662
Date Entered SS: 30 November 1931
NSDAP Number: 278102
Date Entered NSDAP: 1 August 1930
Marital Status: Married
Religion: Agnostic
Civilian Occupation: Construction firm
Education: High School
Foreign Language: No
World War I Service: Yes, Navy; Cruiser "Moltke"
EINSATZKOMMANDO: **1/II**
Position: Commander, 1/II
Einsatzkommando Service: Polish Campaign
Other Assignment: RSHA; Gestapo Stettin
Waffen-SS Service: No
Highest Award: War Service Cross 1st Class
Postwar Sentence: No judicial proceedings discovered
Notes: Served in Freikorps, IIIrd Marine Brigade
National Archives File: A3343 SSO-133B

Simon

First Name: Gustav
Date of Birth: 15 November 1900
Place of Birth: Elsterberg
Highest Rank: SS-Obersturmführer
SS Number: 455763
Date Entered SS: Not listed
NSDAP Number: 8168
Date Entered NSDAP: 19 June 1925
Marital Status: Married
Religion: Agnostic
Civilian Occupation: Police
Education: Grade School
Foreign Language: No
World War I Service: No
EINSATZKOMMANDO: **A**
Position: Not listed
Einsatzkommando Service: Not listed
Other Assignment: RSHA, Office IV A 1 (Communism)
Highest Award: War Service Cross 2nd Class
Postwar Sentence: No judicial proceedings discovered
Notes: Served in SA, 1925-1941; Golden Party Badge
No mention of *Einsatzkommando* service in personnel file
National Archives File: A3343 SSO-138B

Six

First Name: Dr. Franz (Alfred)
Date of Birth: 12 August 1909
Place of Birth: Mannheim
Highest Rank: SS-Brigadeführer
SS Number: 107480
Date Entered SS: 20 April 1935
NSDAP Number: 245670
Date Entered NSDAP: 1 March 1930
Marital Status: Married
Religion: Agnostic
Civilian Occupation: University Professor
Education: University of Heidelberg
Foreign Language: No
EINSATZKOMMANDO: **Vorkommando Moscow**
Position: Commander
Einsatzkommando Service: 20 June 1941–20 August 1941
Other Assignment: Chief, Office VII, RSHA (Ideology)
Waffen-SS Service: 2nd SS Division "Das Reich", 1941
Highest Award: War Service Cross 1st Class
Postwar Sentence: 1948, 20 years commuted to 10 years, released 1952
Postwar Employment: Advertising consultant
Notes: Well traveled before the war
National Archives File: A3343 SSO-139B

Söding

First Name: Bernard
Date of Birth: 10 January 1908
Place of Birth: Heiniegen
Highest Rank: SS-Obersturmführer
SS Number: 369771
Date Entered SS: 30 September 1940
NSDAP Number: 3219500
Date Entered NSDAP: 1 May 1939
Marital Status: Married
Religion: Agnostic
Civilian Occupation: Businessman
Education: Grade School
Foreign Language: No
EINSATZKOMMANDO: **D**
Position: Not listed
Einsatzkommando Service: 1942
Other Assignment: Police Munich
Waffen-SS Service: No
Highest Award: War Service Cross 2nd Class
Postwar Sentence: No judicial proceedings discovered
Notes: Wounded in action
No mention of *Einsatzkommando* service in personnel file
National Archives File: A3343 SSO-141B

Sohns

First Name: Hans-Fritz
Date of Birth: 15 September 1907
Place of Birth: Illingen
Highest Rank: SS-Sturmbannführer
SS Number: 107396
Date Entered SS: 1 January 1935
NSDAP Number: 10820
Date Entered NSDAP: 1 July 1925
Marital Status: Married
Religion: Agnostic
Civilian Occupation: Lawyer
Education: University
Foreign Language: English
EINSATZKOMMANDO: **C, 1005**
Position: Not listed
Einsatzkommando Service: 1944
Other Assignment: RSHA, Office III A (SD, Domestic, Legal Practice)
Office of Reichskommisar Ostland
Highest Award: War Service Cross 2nd Class
Postwar Sentence: No judicial proceedings discovered
Notes: Served in SA, 1922-1934; served in Army 19th Infantry Regiment in 1923
Golden Party Badge; Blood Order #1125
National Archives File: A3343 SSO-141B

Sommer

First Name: Franz
Date of Birth: 30 November 1897
Place of Birth: Düsseldorf
Highest Rank: SS-Obersturmbannführer
SS Number: 272578
Date Entered SS: 4 March 1936
NSDAP Number: 2266842
Date Entered NSDAP: 1 May 1933
Marital Status: Married
Religion: Agnostic
Civilian Occupation: Police
Education: High School
Foreign Language: No
World War I Service: Yes, Iron Cross 2nd Class, Black Wound Badge
EINSATZKOMMANDO: **1/VI**
Position: Commander
Einsatzkommando Service: Polish Campaign
Other Assignment: RSHA; Criminal Police Cologne; SD Düsseldorf
Waffen-SS Service: No
Highest Award: Bar to Iron Cross 2nd Class
Postwar Sentence: No judicial proceedings discovered
Notes: 39th Infantry Regiment WWI
National Archives File: A3343 SSO-142B

Spiekermann

First Name: Wilhelm
Date of Birth: 21 September 1912
Place of Birth: Oldenburg
Highest Rank: SS-Hauptsturmführer
SS Number: 86668
Date Entered SS: 28 April 1933
NSDAP Number: 7753659
Date Entered NSDAP: 1 May 1937
Marital Status: Divorced
Religion: Agnostic
Civilian Occupation: Butcher
Education: High School
Foreign Language: No
EINSATZKOMMANDO: **10a**
Position: Not listed
Einsatzkommando Service: 1941
Other Assignment: Unknown
Waffen-SS Service: No
Highest Award: None listed
Killed in Action: No
Postwar Sentence: No judicial proceedings discovered
Notes: Divorced in 1943
National Archives File: A3343 SSO-146B

Spiess

First Name: Horst
Date of Birth: 10 October 1910
Place of Birth: Berlin
Highest Rank: SS-Untersturmführer
SS Number: 248001
Date Entered SS: 1 November 1933
NSDAP Number: 4360924
Date Entered NSDAP: 1 May 1937
Marital Status: Married
Religion: Agnostic
Civilian Occupation: Businessman
Education: Grade School
Foreign Language: No
EINSATZKOMMANDO: **B**
Position: Not listed
Einsatzkommando Service: Not listed
Other Assignment: RSHA, Office II D 3b (Technical Matters)
Waffen-SS Service: No
Highest Award: None listed
Killed in Action: No
Postwar Sentence: No judicial proceedings discovered
Notes: No mention of *Einsatzkommando* service in personnel file
National Archives File: A3343 SSO-146B

Stahlecker

First Name: Dr. Franz Walter
Date of Birth: 10 October 1900
Place of Birth: Sternenfels
Highest Rank: SS-Brigadeführer
SS Number: 73041
Date Entered SS: 1 May 1932
NSDAP Number: 1069130
Date Entered NSDAP: 1 May 1932
Marital Status: Married
Religion: Unknown
Civilian Occupation: Lawyer
Education: University of Tübingen
Foreign Language: Unknown
World War I Service: Freikorps
EINSATZKOMMANDO: **A**
Position: Commander
Einsatzkommando Service: 22 June 1941 – 23 March 1942
Other Assignment: Chief, Office VI A, RSHA, (SD, Foreign); BdS Prague
Waffen-SS Service: No
Highest Award: Wound Badge
Notes: Died of wounds 23 March 1942 (on hospital train)
Funeral held at Hradcany Castle in Prague
National Archives File: A3340 MFOK W008

Stark

First Name: Franz
Date of Birth: 7 October 1901
Place of Birth: St. Louis, USA
Highest Rank: SS-Hauptsturmführer
SS Number: 36220
Date Entered SS: Not listed
NSDAP Number: 127445
Date Entered NSDAP: 7 May 1929
Marital Status: Married
Religion: Unknown
Civilian Occupation: Mechanic
Education: Grade School
Foreign Language: No
World War I Service: Yes
EINSATZKOMMANDO: **A**
Position: Not listed
Einsatzkommando Service: November 1941–May 1942
Other Assignment: SD Augsburg
Highest Award: War Service Cross 2nd Class
Postwar Sentence: 1962, 8 years
Notes: Blood Order
Illegimate child of German mother in St. Louis; returned to Germany as a child
National Archives File: A3343 SSO-150B

Stehr

First Name: Edmund
Date of Birth: 6 September 1905
Place of Birth: Unknown
Highest Rank: SS-Obersturmführer
SS Number: 52077
Date Entered SS: Not listed
NSDAP Number: Not a member
Marital Status: Unknown
Religion: Unknown
Civilian Occupation: Police
Education: Unknown
Foreign Language: No
World War I Service: No
EINSATZKOMMANDO: **z.b.V.**
Position: *Teilkommando* Bonifer
Einsatzkommando Service: 3 July 1941–11 August 1941
Other Assignment: Unknown
Waffen-SS Service: No
Highest Award: None listed
Postwar Sentence: No judicial proceedings discovered
Notes: Possible honorary SS member
No mention of *Einsatzkommando* service in personnel file
National Archives File: A3343 SSO-151B

Steimle

First Name: Eugen
Date of Birth: 8 December 1909
Place of Birth: Neubulach
Highest Rank: SS-Standartenführer
SS Number: 272575
Date Entered SS: Not listed
NSDAP Number: 1075555
Date Entered NSDAP: 1 May 1932
Marital Status: Married
Religion: Agnostic
Civilian Occupation: Teacher
Education: University of Tübingen
Foreign Language: French
EINSATZKOMMANDO: **7a, 4a**
Position: 7a – Commander; 4a – Commander
Einsatzkommando Service: 7a, 7 September–15 January 1942
Other Assignment: Chief, Office VI B, RSHA (SD, Foreign,German-Italian Sphere)
Personal staff, RFSS
Highest Award: War Service Cross 1st Class
Postwar Sentence: 1948, Death, released
Notes: SD Württemburg
Served in SA, 1932-1936
National Archives File: A3343 SSO-151B

Stock

First Name: Walther
Date of Birth: 26 July 1904
Place of Birth: Höchst
Highest Rank: SS-Hauptsturmführer
SS Number: 9553
Date Entered SS: Not listed
NSDAP Number: 650827
Date Entered NSDAP: Not listed
Marital Status: Married
Religion: Agnostic
Civilian Occupation: Detective Officer
Education: High School
Foreign Language: No
World War I Service: No
EINSATZKOMMANDO: **B**
Position: Not listed
Einsatzkommando Service: Not listed
Other Assignment: SD Copenhagen
Waffen-SS Service: No
Highest Award: War Service Cross 2nd Class
Postwar Sentence: No judicial proceedings discovered
Notes: No mention of *Einsatzkommando* service in personnel file
National Archives File: A3343 SSO-162B

Störtz

First Name: Friedrich
Date of Birth: 30 May 1912
Place of Birth: Kaiserslautern
Highest Rank: SS-Sturmbannführer
SS Number: 283241
Date Entered SS: 1 March 1937
NSDAP Number: 1031500
Date Entered NSDAP: 1 April 1932
Marital Status: Married
Religion: Agnostic
Civilian Occupation: Businessman
Education: High School
Foreign Language: Greek, Latvian, English
EINSATZKOMMANDO: **1a**
Position: Attached from SS Infantry Regiment 14
Einsatzkommando Service: 1941–1942
Other Assignment: Unknown
Waffen-SS Service: 20th SS Division
Highest Award: Iron Cross 1st Class
Postwar Sentence: No judicial proceedings discovered
Notes: Served in special battalion of RFSS; served in Hitler Youth, 1932-1935
Infantry Assault Badge
National Archives File: A3343 SSO-163B

Straub

First Name: Franz
Date of Birth: 25 February 1889
Place of Birth: Bergrothenfels
Highest Rank: SS-Sturmbannführer
SS Number: 342170
Date Entered SS: 1 December 1938
NSDAP Number: 2651455
Date Entered NSDAP: 1 May 1935
Marital Status: Married
Religion: Catholic
Civilian Occupation: Police
Education: Technical School
Foreign Language: No
World War I Service: No
EINSATZKOMMANDO: **Vienna**
Position: Not listed
Einsatzkommando Service: 1938
Other Assignment: Gestapo Brussels; Gestapo Munich
Waffen-SS Service: No
Highest Award: None listed
Postwar Sentence: No judicial proceedings discovered
Notes: Reported to have served in another *Einsatzkommando* in 1942
National Archives File: A3343 SSO-164B

Strauch

First Name: Dr. Eduard
Date of Birth: 17 August 1906
Place of Birth: Essen
Highest Rank: SS-Obersturmbannführer
SS Number: 19312
Date Entered SS: 1 December 1931
NSDAP Number: 623392
Date Entered NSDAP: 1 October 1931
Marital Status: Married
Religion: Agnostic
Civilian Occupation: Lawyer
Education: University of Erlangen, Münster
Foreign Language: English, French
World War I Service: No
EINSATZKOMMANDO: **1b, 2**
Position: 2 – Commander; 1b – Commander
Einsatzkommando Service: 2, 4 November 1941 – 2 December 1941, 1b, 3 December 1941–June 1943
Other Assignment: SD Belgium; SD Dortmund; KdS Wallonia
Waffen-SS Service: IIIrd SS Corps, 1944
Highest Award: Iron Cross 1st Class
Postwar Sentence: 1948, Death, released due to insanity
Notes: Infantry Assault Badge; died 9 September 1955
National Archives File: A3343 SSO-165B

Streckenbach

First Name: Bruno
Date of Birth: 7 February 1902
Place of Birth: Hamburg
Highest Rank: SS-Gruppenführer
SS Number: 14713
Date Entered SS: 31 August 1931
NSDAP Number: 489972
Date Entered NSDAP: 1 December 1930
Marital Status: Married
Religion: Agnostic
Civilian Occupation: Merchant
Education: High School
Foreign Language: English, French
EINSATZKOMMANDO: **I**
Position: Commander
Einsatzkommando Service: Polish Campaign
Other Assignment: RSHA, Office I (Personnel)
Waffen-SS Service: 8th SS Division "Florian Geyer", 1943-1944 19th SS Division, 1944-1945
Highest Award: Knight's Cross with Oak Leaves
Postwar Sentence: 1973, case dismissed due to ill health of defendant
Notes: Freikorps; awarded Golden Party Badge in 1939; prisoner of war in Russia until 1955; died 28 October 1977 in Hamburg
National Archives File: A3343 SSO-165B

Strohschneider

First Name: Dr. Walter
Date of Birth: 6 October 1908
Place of Birth: Drahowitz, Austria
Highest Rank: SS-Obersturmführer
SS Number: 328862
Date Entered SS: 1 November 1938
NSDAP Number: 6459693
Date Entered NSDAP: 1 November 1938
Marital Status: Married
Religion: Agnostic
Civilian Occupation: Lawyer
Education: University
Foreign Language: Czech
World War I Service: No
EINSATZKOMMANDO: **D**
Position: Not listed
Einsatzkommando Service: 1942
Other Assignment: RSHA; Criminal Police Berlin
Highest Award: War Service Cross 2nd Class
Postwar Sentence: No judicial proceedings discovered
Notes: Served in Czech Army 1935-1937 No mention of *Einsatzkommando* service in personnel file
National Archives File: A3343 SSO-167B

Strube

First Name: Ludwig
Date of Birth: 26 July 1900
Place of Birth: Trendelburg
Highest Rank: SS-Sturmbannführer
SS Number: 314411
Date Entered SS: 1 June 1936
NSDAP Number: 2927821
Date Entered NSDAP: 1 May 1933
Marital Status: Married
Religion: Agnostic
Civilian Occupation: Bureaucrat
Education: Technical School
Foreign Language: No
World War I Service: Yes, 22nd Field Artillery Regiment
EINSATZKOMMANDO: **B**
Position: Administration section
Einsatzkommando Service: 1 February 1942 – 1 September 1942
Other Assignment: SD Vienna; SD Saarbrücken; SD Metz; Police Stuttgart
Waffen-SS Service: No
Highest Award: War Service Cross 1st Class
Killed in Action: No
Postwar Sentence: No judicial proceedings discovered
National Archives File: A3343 SSO-167B

Stueber

First Name: Josef
Date of Birth: 19 August 1906
Place of Birth: Hervest-Dorstein
Highest Rank: SS-Obersturmbannführer
SS Number: 256813
Date Entered SS: 1 February 1934
NSDAP Number: 5354465
Date Entered NSDAP: 1 May 1937
Marital Status: Married
Religion: Agnostic
Civilian Occupation: Lawyer
Education: University of Münster, Berlin
Foreign Language: French
World War I Service: No
EINSATZKOMMANDO: **A**
Position: Gestapo section leader
Einsatzkommando Service: 1 January 1942–15 August 1942
Other Assignment: Gestapo Graz; Gestapo Oppeln; Gestapo Hannover
Waffen-SS Service: No
Highest Award: War Service Cross 2nd Class
Postwar Sentence: No judicial proceedings discovered
Notes: SD Saarbrücken
National Archives File: A3343 SSO-168B

Suhr

First Name: Friedrich
Date of Birth: 6 May 1907
Place of Birth: Lüneburg
Highest Rank: SS-Obersturmbannführer
SS Number: 65824
Date Entered SS: 1 February 1933
NSDAP Number: 2623241
Date Entered NSDAP: 1 May 1933
Marital Status: Married
Religion: Agnostic
Civilian Occupation: Lawyer
Education: University of Freiburg, Göttingen
Foreign Language: English, French
World War I Service: No
EINSATZKOMMANDO: **4b, 6**
Position: 4b – Commander; 6 – Commander
Einsatzkommando Service: 4b, November 1942 – August 1943
6, August 1943 – November 1943
Other Assignment: RSHA; SD Toulouse, France 1944
Highest Award: Knight's Cross
Notes: German Cross in Gold, Infantry Assault Badge,
Close Combat Badge
SSPF Ober-Elsass; died 31 May 1946
National Archives File: A3343 SSO-170B

Suthoff

First Name: Karl
Date of Birth: 14 March 1911
Place of Birth: Northeim
Highest Rank: SS-Hauptsturmführer
SS Number: 12973
Date Entered SS: Not listed
NSDAP Number: 4255
Date Entered NSDAP: 11 May 1925
Marital Status: Single
Religion: Agnostic
Civilian Occupation: Teacher
Education: University
Foreign Language: No
World War I Service: No
EINSATZKOMMANDO: **C, 4b**
Position: Not listed
Einsatzkommando Service: Not listed
Other Assignment: Unknown
Highest Award: None listed
Postwar Sentence: No judicial proceedings discovered
Notes: Served in SA, 1925-1930
Served in Army, 1939-1940
National Archives File: A3343 SSO-170B

Tabbert

First Name: Günter
Date of Birth: 21 August 1916
Place of Birth: Berlin
Highest Rank: SS-Hauptsturmführer
SS Number: 463360
Date Entered SS: 12 July 1943
NSDAP Number: Not a member
Marital Status: Married
Religion: Unknown
Civilian Occupation: Detective Officer
Education: University
Foreign Language: English
World War I Service: No
EINSATZKOMMANDO: **2**
Position: Not listed (attached police)
Einsatzkommando Service: September 1941 – 10 December 1941
Other Assignment: SD Berlin
Waffen-SS Service: No
Highest Award: None listed
Killed in Action: No
Postwar Sentence: No judicial proceedings discovered
Notes: Served in German Navy, 1937-1940
National Archives File: A3343 SSO-171B

Teichmann

First Name: Ludwig
Date of Birth: 14 May 1909
Place of Birth: Uelzen
Highest Rank: SS-Obersturmbannführer
SS Number: 1789
Date Entered SS: 1 June 1929
NSDAP Number: 134523
Date Entered NSDAP: Not listed
Marital Status: Married
Religion: Agnostic
Civilian Occupation: Unknown
Education: University of Berlin, Munich, Göttingen
Foreign Language: No
EINSATZKOMMANDO: **E, H**
Position: Commander
Einsatzkommando Service: 1944
Other Assignment: RSHA; RuS HA
Waffen-SS Service: No
Highest Award: War Service Cross 1st Class
Postwar Sentence: No judicial proceedings discovered
Notes: Iron Cross 2nd Class
Personal Staff RFSS
National Archives File: A3343 SSO-174B

Tempfer

First Name: Alfred
Date of Birth: 5 January 1921
Place of Birth: Penzberg
Highest Rank: SS-Obersturmführer
SS Number: Not listed
Date Entered SS: 1 November 1938
NSDAP Number: Not a member
Marital Status: Single
Religion: Agnostic
Civilian Occupation: Unknown
Education: High School
Foreign Language: No
World War I Service: No
EINSATZKOMMANDO: **7a**
Position: 2nd Company, 14th SS Regiment
Einsatzkommando Service: 1941
Other Assignment: N/A
Waffen-SS Service: 18th SS Division "Horst Wessel"
Highest Award: None listed
Killed in Action: Yes
Notes: Served in Hitler Youth, 1932-1938
1st SS Infantry Brigade; killed in action 22 September 1944
National Archives File: A3343 SSO-175B

Teuffel

First Name: Herbert
Date of Birth: 23 August 1905
Place of Birth: Danzig-Brösen
Highest Rank: SS-Hauptsturmführer
SS Number: 18531
Date Entered SS: 7 December 1931
NSDAP Number: 577405
Date Entered NSDAP: 1 July 1931
Marital Status: Married
Religion: Agnostic
Civilian Occupation: Police
Education: High School
Foreign Language: No
World War I Service: No
EINSATZKOMMANDO: **2**
Position: Not listed
Einsatzkommando Service: Not listed
Other Assignment: Police Danzig
Waffen-SS Service: No
Highest Award: War Service Cross 2nd Class
Postwar Sentence: No judicial proceedings discovered
Notes: Served three days arrest during the war for drunkeness
National Archives File: A3343 SSO-176B

Thiemann

First Name: Jobst
Date of Birth: 12 June 1911
Place of Birth: Gutersloh
Highest Rank: SS-Sturmbannführer
SS Number: 372272
Date Entered SS: 27 June 1939
NSDAP Number: 1642158
Date Entered NSDAP: 1 April 1933
Marital Status: Married
Religion: Agnostic
Civilian Occupation: Lawyer
Education: University
Foreign Language: No
World War I Service: No
EINSATZKOMMANDO: **4b**
Position: Not listed
Einsatzkommando Service: 4 November 1941 – 7 September 1942
Other Assignment: RSHA, Office IV D 2 (Gestapo, Spheres of Influence)
Waffen-SS Service: No
Highest Award: War Service Cross 2nd Class
Postwar Sentence: No judicial proceedings discovered
Notes: Served in SA, 1933
National Archives File: A3343 SSO-178B

Thomas

First Name: Dr. Max
Date of Birth: 4 August 1891
Place of Birth: Düsseldorf
Highest Rank: SS-Gruppenführer
SS Number: 141341
Date Entered SS: 1 July 1933
NSDAP Number: 1848453
Date Entered NSDAP: 1 May 1933
Marital Status: Married
Religion: Agnostic
Civilian Occupation: Doctor
Education: University of Göttingen, Freiburg
Foreign Language: No
World War I Service: Yes, Iron Cross 1st Class, 7th Field Artillery Regiment
EINSATZKOMMANDO: C
Position: Commander
Einsatzkommando Service: October 1941–28 August 1943
Other Assignment: RSHA
HSSPF Black Sea
Waffen-SS Service: No
Highest Award: Iron Cross 1st Class
Notes: Wounded in action 7 July 1942; Anti-Partisan Badge
Suicide 1945
National Archives File: A3343 SSO-180B

Tolle

First Name: Nikolaus
Date of Birth: 17 December 1899
Place of Birth: Vladivostok, Russia
Highest Rank: SS-Hauptsturmführer
SS Number: 275920
Date Entered SS: 15 March 1934
NSDAP Number: 1082535
Date Entered NSDAP: 10 June 1932
Marital Status: Married
Religion: Agnostic
Civilian Occupation: Businessman
Education: High School
Foreign Language: English, Russian
World War I Service: No
EINSATZKOMMANDO: **1b**
Position: Not listed
Einsatzkommando Service: Not listed
Other Assignment: RSHA
Highest Award: None listed
Postwar Sentence: No judicial proceedings discovered
Notes: Lived in Russia 1899-1910; China 1910-1919
Took part in Kapp Putsch
National Archives File: A3343 SSO-186B

Tormann

First Name: Franz
Date of Birth: 14 November 1910
Place of Birth: Olkenbach
Highest Rank: SS-Hauptsturmführer
SS Number: 290924
Date Entered SS: 5 October 1937
NSDAP Number: 4698015
Date Entered NSDAP: 1 May 1937
Marital Status: Divorced
Religion: Agnostic
Civilian Occupation: Police
Education: University
Foreign Language: No
EINSATZKOMMANDO: **7a**
Position: Not listed
Einsatzkommando Service: Not listed
Other Assignment: RSHA; Gestapo Lodz
Waffen-SS Service: No
Highest Award: War Service Cross 2nd Class
Postwar Sentence: No judicial proceedings discovered
Notes: Served in SA, 1933-1937; served in Army's 58th Infantry Regiment, 1935
No mention of *Einsatzkommando* service in personnel file
National Archives File: A3343 SSO-187B

Traut

First Name: Karl
Date of Birth: 29 January 1906
Place of Birth: Schillingstadt
Highest Rank: SS-Obersturmbannführer
SS Number: 290554
Date Entered SS: 1 July 1935
NSDAP Number: 400262
Date Entered NSDAP: 1 January 1931
Marital Status: Married
Religion: Agnostic
Civilian Occupation: Bureaucrat
Education: Trade School
Foreign Language: No
World War I Service: No
EINSATZKOMMANDO: **3**
Position: Commander
Einsatzkommando Service: November 1942–May 1943
Other Assignment: RSHA; SD Salzburg; SD Hohensalza
Waffen-SS Service: No
Highest Award: War Service Cross 2nd Class
Postwar Sentence: No judicial proceedings discovered
Notes: Served in SA, 1928-1938
National Archives File: A3343 SSO-188B

Trautwein

First Name: Walter
Date of Birth: 21 November 1910
Place of Birth: Mannheim
Highest Rank: SS-Obersturmführer
SS Number: 107112
Date Entered SS: Not listed
NSDAP Number: 210651
Date Entered NSDAP: 1 March 1930
Marital Status: Married
Religion: Agnostic
Civilian Occupation: Mechanic
Education: Unknown
Foreign Language: No
EINSATZKOMMANDO: **B**
Position: Criminal Police section
Einsatzkommando Service: Not listed
Other Assignment: RSHA; Police Trier
Waffen-SS Service: No
Highest Award: None listed
Postwar Sentence: No judicial proceedings discovered
Notes: Served in SA, 1929-1934
Wounded in action
National Archives File: A3343 SSO-189B

Trodler

First Name: Herbert
Date of Birth: 20 December 1915
Place of Birth: Witten
Highest Rank: SS-Obersturmführer
SS Number: 277767
Date Entered SS: 1 September 1935
NSDAP Number: 3394426
Date Entered NSDAP: 1 May 1933
Marital Status: Married
Religion: Agnostic
Civilian Occupation: Police
Education: University
Foreign Language: English, French
EINSATZKOMMANDO: **2**
Position: Criminal commissioner
Einsatzkommando Service: Not listed
Other Assignment: Gestapo Dortmund
Waffen-SS Service: No
Highest Award: None listed
Postwar Sentence: No judicial proceedings discovered
Notes: Served in Hitler Youth, 1932-1935; served in German Army, 1936-1938
No mention of *Einsatzkommando* service in personnel file
National Archives File: A3343 SSO-190B

Tröger

First Name: Dr. Rudolf
Date of Birth: 23 April 1905
Place of Birth: Leipzig
Highest Rank: SS-Obersturmbannführer
SS Number: 261192
Date Entered SS: 1 May 1933
NSDAP Number: 2434089
Date Entered NSDAP: 1 May 1933
Marital Status: Married
Religion: Protestant
Civilian Occupation: Lawyer
Education: University
Foreign Language: English, French, Spanish
EINSATZKOMMANDO: **16**
Position: Commander
Einsatzkommando Service: Polish Campaign
Other Assignment: RSHA; SD Chemnitz
Waffen-SS Service: No
Highest Award: None listed
Postwar Sentence: N/A
Postwar Employment: N/A
Notes: Killed in action with 60th Infantry Division in France, 18 June 1940
National Archives File: A3343 SSO-190B

Trühe

First Name: Heinz
Date of Birth: 4 December 1908
Place of Birth: Berlin-Schöneberg
Highest Rank: SS-Hauptsturmführer
SS Number: 219493
Date Entered SS: 1 November 1933
NSDAP Number: 4157302
Date Entered NSDAP: 1 May 1937
Marital Status: Married
Religion: Agnostic
Civilian Occupation: Police
Education: University
Foreign Language: No
EINSATZKOMMANDO: **A**
Position: Personnel/Administration leader
Einsatzkommando Service: July 1941–January 1944
Other Assignment: RSHA
Waffen-SS Service: No
Highest Award: War Service Cross 2nd Class
Killed in Action: No
Postwar Sentence: No judicial proceedings discovered
Notes: Awarded War Service Cross 2nd Class by commander Army Group North
National Archives File: A3343 SSO-191B

Trummler

First Name: Dr. Hans
Date of Birth: 24 October 1900
Place of Birth: Fredrichsroda
Highest Rank: SS-Oberführer
SS Number: 254581
Date Entered SS: 1 January 1934
NSDAP Number: 73599
Date Entered NSDAP: 1 January 1928
Marital Status: Married
Religion: Agnostic
Civilian Occupation: Banker
Education: University of Leipzig
World War I Service: Yes, 104th Infantry Regiment
EINSATZKOMMANDO: **von Woyrsch**
Position: Not listed
Einsatzkommando Service: Polish Campaign
Other Assignment: RSHA, Office I B 3 (Personnel) HSSPF Rheinland-Westphalia
Highest Award: Iron Cross 2nd Class
Postwar Sentence: No judicial proceedings discovered
Notes: Golden Party Badge Served in SA, 1928-1934; Police School Fürstenberg
National Archives File: A3343 SSO-191B

Tschierschky

First Name: Karl
Date of Birth: 15 March 1906
Place of Birth: Friedenshütte
Highest Rank: SS-Standartenführer
SS Number: 19984
Date Entered SS: 1 January 1931
NSDAP Number: 918746
Date Entered NSDAP: 1 February 1932
Marital Status: Married
Religion: Agnostic
Civilian Occupation: Businessman
Education: Trade School
Foreign Language: No
EINSATZKOMMANDO: **A, 1a**
Position: A – Security section, 1 – Commander
Einsatzkommando Service: July 1941–31 October 1942
Other Assignment: Chief, Office VI C, RSHA (SD, Foreign,Russo-Japanese Sphere); SD Dresden
Highest Award: Iron Cross 1st Class
Postwar Sentence: No judicial proceedings discovered
Notes: Infantry Assault Badge; Died 1974
National Archives File: A3343 SSO-192B

Tunnat

First Name: Heinrich
Date of Birth: 2 January 1913
Place of Birth: Trier
Highest Rank: SS-Hauptsturmführer
SS Number: 294005
Date Entered SS: 1 May 1934
NSDAP Number: 5219699
Date Entered NSDAP: 1 May 1937
Marital Status: Married
Religion: Agnostic
Civilian Occupation: Police
Education: University
Foreign Language: Greek, English, Spanish
EINSATZKOMMANDO: **9**
Position: Police section
Einsatzkommando Service: June 1941–September 1941
Other Assignment: RSHA, Office VI C (SD, Foreign, Russo-Japanese Sphere)
Highest Award: Iron Cross 2nd Class
Postwar Sentence: 1962, 3 years
Postwar Employment: Faculty, University of Göttingen
Notes: Operation Zeppelin; served in Army 17th Infantry Regiment, 1937; Eastern People's Medal; Criminal Police Hannover
National Archives File: A3343 SSO-193B

Unglaube

First Name: Heinz
Date of Birth: 10 May 1910
Place of Birth: Jauer
Highest Rank: SS-Hauptsturmführer
SS Number: 290926
Date Entered SS: 1 September 1937
NSDAP Number: 531447
Date Entered NSDAP: 1 May 1931
Marital Status: Married
Religion: Agnostic
Civilian Occupation: Banker
Education: University
Foreign Language: No
EINSATZKOMMANDO: **C**
Position: Not listed
Einsatzkommando Service: 1942
Other Assignment: RSHA; SD Tilsit
Waffen-SS Service: No
Highest Award: None listed
Postwar Sentence: No judicial proceedings discovered
Notes: Served in SA, 1932-1934; served in Hitler Youth, 1933-1934
Operation Zeppelin
National Archives File: A3343 SSO-199B

Virnekaes

First Name: Alfred
Date of Birth: 13 March 1904
Place of Birth: Alt-Warthau
Highest Rank: SS-Untersturmführer
SS Number: 248570
Date Entered SS: 15 June 1933
NSDAP Number: 4836926
Date Entered NSDAP: 1 May 1937
Marital Status: Married
Religion: Agnostic
Civilian Occupation: Truck driver
Education: Grade School
Foreign Language: No
EINSATZKOMMANDO: **D**
Position: Not listed
Einsatzkommando Service: 1941–1942
Other Assignment: RSHA; SD Oppeln
Waffen-SS Service: No
Highest Award: War Service Cross 2nd Class
Postwar Sentence: No judicial proceedings discovered
Notes: Crimea Shield; SD Lodz
No mention of *Einsatzkommando* service in personnel file
National Archives File: A3343 SSO-206B

Wassermann

First Name: Wilhelm
Date of Birth: 26 February 1912
Place of Birth: Hamburg
Highest Rank: SS-Obersturmführer
SS Number: 290570
Date Entered SS: 30 January 1938
NSDAP Number: 1345373
Date Entered NSDAP: 1 October 1932
Marital Status: Married
Religion: Agnostic
Civilian Occupation: Unknown
Education: University of Hamburg
Foreign Language: English, French
World War I Service: No
EINSATZKOMMANDO: **A**
Position: Not listed
Einsatzkommando Service: Not listed
Other Assignment: RSHA; SD Ostland
Highest Award: War Service Cross 2nd Class
Postwar Sentence: No judicial proceedings discovered
Notes: Served in SA, 1932-1938; SD Linz
No mention of *Einsatzkommando* service in personnel file
National Archives File: A3343 SSO-221B

Weibrecht

First Name: Hans
Date of Birth: 23 September 1911
Place of Birth: Fürth
Highest Rank: SS-Sturmbannführer
SS Number: 55080
Date Entered SS: 15 April 1933
NSDAP Number: 1003285
Date Entered NSDAP: 1 March 1932
Marital Status: Married
Religion: Agnostic
Civilian Occupation: Businessman
Education: High School
Foreign Language: No
World War I Service: No
EINSATZKOMMANDO: **B, 10a**
Position: Not listed
Einsatzkommando Service: B, 1942; 10a, 6 August 1942–1943
Other Assignment: RSHA; SD Posen
Highest Award: Iron Cross 1st Class
Postwar Sentence: No judicial proceedings discovered
Notes: Served at Dachau concentration camp, 1933
Infantry Assault Badge, Eastern People's Medal, Anti-Partisan Badge
National Archives File: A3343 SSO-226B

Weigel

First Name: Dr. Willi
Date of Birth: 23 May 1908
Place of Birth: Hatzfeld
Highest Rank: SS-Hauptsturmführer
SS Number: 206879
Date Entered SS: Not listed
NSDAP Number: 271683
Date Entered NSDAP: 1 August 1930
Marital Status: Married
Religion: Agnostic
Civilian Occupation: Doctor
Education: University
Foreign Language: No
World War I Service: No
EINSATZKOMMANDO: **A**
Position: Not listed
Einsatzkommando Service: Not listed
Other Assignment: Unknown
Highest Award: War Service Cross 1st Class
Postwar Sentence: No judicial proceedings discovered
Notes: Served in SA, 1930-1932
No mention of *Einsatzkommando* service in personnel file
National Archives File: A3343 SSO-228B

Weinmann

First Name: Dr. Erwin
Date of Birth: 6 July 1909
Place of Birth: Frommenhausen
Highest Rank: SS-Oberführer
SS Number: 280196
Date Entered SS: 30 January 1937
NSDAP Number: 774436
Date Entered NSDAP: 1 December 1931
Marital Status: Married
Religion: Agnostic
Civilian Occupation: Doctor
Education: University of Tübingen
Foreign Language: No
World War I Service: No
EINSATZKOMMANDO: **4a**
Position: Commander
Einsatzkommando Service: 13 January 1942–July 1942
Other Assignment: Chief, Office IV D, RSHA (Gestapo, Spheres of Influence)
BdS Prague; SD Stuttgart
Waffen-SS Service: No
Highest Award: War Service Cross 1st Class
Notes: Died December 1949
National Archives File: A3343 SSO-229B

Weis

First Name: Friedrich
Date of Birth: 15 August 1905
Place of Birth: Frankfurt/Main
Highest Rank: SS-Hauptsturmführer
SS Number: 367196
Date Entered SS: 13 September 1938
NSDAP Number: 126777
Date Entered NSDAP: 1 May 1929
Marital Status: Widowed
Religion: Agnostic
Civilian Occupation: Electrician
Education: High School
Foreign Language: No
EINSATZKOMMANDO: **D**
Position: Not listed
Einsatzkommando Service: 25 September 1941 – 9 April 1942
Other Assignment: RSHA
Highest Award: War Service Cross 2nd Class
Postwar Sentence: 1951, Life
Postwar Employment: Houseporter
Notes: Lived in Ochsenfurth until apprehended in 1950
Golden Party Badge; thrown out of SS; readmitted
National Archives File: A3343 SSO-230B

Weiss-Bollandt

First Name: Anton
Date of Birth: 17 June 1909
Place of Birth: Munich
Highest Rank: SS-Sturmbannführer
SS Number: 2641
Date Entered SS: 1 April 1930
NSDAP Number: 247643
Date Entered NSDAP: 1 June 1930
Marital Status: Single
Religion: Agnostic
Civilian Occupation: Lawyer
Education: University of Munich
Foreign Language: English, French
World War I Service: No
EINSATZKOMMANDO: **C, D**
Position: Not listed
Einsatzkommando Service: 1942
Other Assignment: RSHA
Waffen-SS Service: No
Highest Award: None listed
Postwar Sentence: No judicial proceedings discovered
Notes: Served at Simferopol; Gestapo
National Archives File: A3343 SSO-230B

Weisser

First Name: Max
Date of Birth: 24 October 1911
Place of Birth: Wölkenstein
Highest Rank: SS-Obersturmführer
SS Number: 280305
Date Entered SS: 15 August 1936
NSDAP Number: 768383
Date Entered NSDAP: 1 December 1931
Marital Status: Married
Religion: Agnostic
Civilian Occupation: Textiles
Education: Trade School
Foreign Language: No
World War I Service: No
EINSATZKOMMANDO: **7a**
Position: Not listed
Einsatzkommando Service: Not listed
Other Assignment: SD Fünfkirchen; SD Posen
Waffen-SS Service: No
Highest Award: War Service Cross 2nd Class
Postwar Sentence: No judicial proceedings discovered
Notes: No mention of *Einsatzkommando* service in personnel file
National Archives File: A3343 SSO-232B

Welsch

First Name: Johann
Date of Birth: 14 June 1912
Place of Birth: Dudweiler-Jägersfreude
Highest Rank: SS-Obersturmführer
SS Number: 407021
Date Entered SS: 21 June 1939
NSDAP Number: 2696546
Date Entered NSDAP: 1 February 1933
Marital Status: Married
Religion: Unknown
Civilian Occupation: Police
Education: High School
Foreign Language: No
World War I Service: No
EINSATZKOMMANDO: **D**
Position: Criminal Police section
Einsatzkommando Service: 1942
Other Assignment: RSHA; Criminal Police Berlin
Highest Award: War Service Cross 2nd Class
Postwar Sentence: No judicial proceedings discovered
Notes: Served in SA, 1935-1936
Crimea Shield
National Archives File: A3343 SSO-235B

Wenskaht

First Name: Helmut
Date of Birth: 30 August 1905
Place of Birth: Berlin-Oberschöneweide
Highest Rank: SS-Obersturmführer
SS Number: 3993
Date Entered SS: Not listed
NSDAP Number: 88759
Date Entered NSDAP: 1 May 1928
Marital Status: Married
Religion: Protestant
Civilian Occupation: Businessman
Education: High School
Foreign Language: No
World War I Service: No
EINSATZKOMMANDO: **z.b.V.**
Position: *Teilkommando* Bonifer
Einsatzkommando Service: 3 July 1941–11 August 1941
Other Assignment: RSHA
Highest Award: War Service Cross 2nd Class
Postwar Sentence: No judicial proceedings discovered
Notes: Served in SA, 1928-1930;
Golden Party Badge
No mention of *Einsatzkommando* service in personnel file
National Archives File: A3343 SSO-236B

Wenzel

First Name: Willy
Date of Birth: 1 March 1904
Place of Birth: Leipzig
Highest Rank: SS-Untersturmführer
SS Number: 367131
Date Entered SS: 28 November 1938
NSDAP Number: 3217756
Date Entered NSDAP: 1 May 1933
Marital Status: Married
Religion: Agnostic
Civilian Occupation: Locksmith
Education: Grade School
Foreign Language: No
World War I Service: No
EINSATZKOMMANDO: **B**
Position: Not listed
Einsatzkommando Service: 1 April 1943–1 July 1944
Other Assignment: RSHA
Highest Award: War Service Cross 2nd Class
Postwar Sentence: No judicial proceedings discovered
Notes: Served in *Einsatzkommando* as an enlisted man
Eastern People's Medal
National Archives File: A3343 SSO-236B

Wenzel

First Name: Franz
Date of Birth: 6 May 1896
Place of Birth: Unknown
Highest Rank: SS-Hauptsturmführer
SS Number: 51935
Date Entered SS: Not listed
NSDAP Number: Not a member
Marital Status: Unknown
Religion: Unknown
Civilian Occupation: Police
Education: Unknown
Foreign Language: No
World War I Service: Unknown
EINSATZKOMMANDO: **z.b.V.**
Position: z.b.V. staff
Einsatzkommando Service: 3 July 1941–11 August 1941
Other Assignment: Police Stettin
Waffen-SS Service: No
Highest Award: None listed
Postwar Sentence: No judicial proceedings discovered
Notes: Possible honorary SS member
No mention of *Einsatzkommando* service in personnel file
National Archives File: A3343 SSO-236B

Wessel

First Name: Robert
Date of Birth: 22 March 1904
Place of Birth: Remscheid
Highest Rank: SS-Sturmbannführer
SS Number: 39585
Date Entered SS: 1 May 1932
NSDAP Number: 724345
Date Entered NSDAP: 1 November 1931
Marital Status: Married
Religion: Agnostic
Civilian Occupation: Businessman
Education: High School
Foreign Language: English
World War I Service: No
EINSATZKOMMANDO: **A**
Position: Liaison Officer to Army Group North
Einsatzkommando Service: July 1941–September 1942
Other Assignment: SD Cologne; SD Reval; Police commander, Dorpat
Waffen-SS Service: Yes (unit unknown)
Highest Award: None listed
Postwar Sentence: No judicial proceedings discovered
Notes: Spent eight months in USA before the war; serious knee operation, 1939
National Archives File: A3343 SSO-238B

Wiebens

First Name: Wilhelm
Date of Birth: 17 March 1906
Place of Birth: Rüstringen
Highest Rank: SS-Obersturmbannführer
SS Number: 16617
Date Entered SS: 31 July 1933
NSDAP Number: 546524
Date Entered NSDAP: 1 May 1931
Marital Status: Married
Religion: Agnostic
Civilian Occupation: Businessman
Education: High School
Foreign Language: No
World War I Service: No
EINSATZKOMMANDO: **9**
Position: Commander
Einsatzkommando Service: February 1942–January 1943
Other Assignment: SD Koblenz; SD Potsdam
Highest Award: War Service Cross 1st Class
Postwar Sentence: 1966, Life
Notes: Served in SA, 1931
No mention of *Einsatzkommando* service in personnel file
National Archives File: A3343 SSO-241B

Wiechert

First Name: Richard
Date of Birth: 19 May 1906
Place of Birth: Angerburg, East Prussia
Highest Rank: SS-Untersturmführer
SS Number: 255287
Date Entered SS: 1 November 1933
NSDAP Number: 4753752
Date Entered NSDAP: 1 May 1937
Marital Status: Married
Religion: Agnostic
Civilian Occupation: Auto mechanic
Education: High School
Foreign Language: No
EINSATZKOMMANDO: **A, Tilsit, EG** in Poland
Position: Not listed
Einsatzkommando Service: 1941–December 1943
Other Assignment: RSHA, Office II C 3 (Budget)
Highest Award: Iron Cross 2nd Class
Postwar Sentence: 1961, 4 years
Postwar Employment: Auto worker
Notes: Eastern People's Medal
No mention of *Einsatzkommando* service in personnel file
National Archives File: A3343 SSO-241B

Wiens

First Name: Heinrich
Date of Birth: 22 March 1906
Place of Birth: Muntau, Russia
Highest Rank: SS-Hauptsturmführer
SS Number: 22984
Date Entered SS: 1 December 1931
NSDAP Number: 663222
Date Entered NSDAP: 1 October 1931
Marital Status: Married
Religion: Agnostic
Civilian Occupation: Unknown
Education: High School
Foreign Language: Russian
EINSATZKOMMANDO: **12**
Position: Not listed
Einsatzkommando Service: 1942–1943
Other Assignment: RSHA; KdS Crimea
Waffen-SS Service: 14th SS Division, 1944-1945
Highest Award: War Service Cross 1st Class
Postwar Sentence: No judicial proceedings discovered
Notes: Lived in Ukraine until 1930; Crimea Shield
Intelligence Officer for 14th SS Division
National Archives File: A3343 SSO-243B

Winkeltau

First Name: Alfred
Date of Birth: 17 December 1916
Place of Birth: Königsberg
Highest Rank: SS-Hauptsturmführer
SS Number: 369616
Date Entered SS: 6 March 1939
NSDAP Number: 7041665
Date Entered NSDAP: 1 November 1938
Marital Status: Married
Religion: Agnostic
Civilian Occupation: Police
Education: High School
Foreign Language: No
World War I Service: No
EINSATZKOMMANDO: **D**
Position: Criminal Police section
Einsatzkommando Service: 22 September 1941 – 14 June 1943
Other Assignment: RSHA; Criminal Police Lodz; Criminal Police Königsberg
Waffen-SS Service: No
Highest Award: War Service Cross 2nd Class
Postwar Sentence: No judicial proceedings discovered
Notes: Served in Hitler Youth, 1933-1938
National Archives File: A3343 SSO-249B

Winkler

First Name: Oskar
Date of Birth: 17 December 1910
Place of Birth: Ischerei
Highest Rank: SS-Hauptsturmführer
SS Number: 196489
Date Entered SS: Not listed
NSDAP Number: 4863426
Date Entered NSDAP: 1 May 1937
Marital Status: Single
Religion: Agnostic
Civilian Occupation: Office clerk
Education: Grade School
Foreign Language: No
World War I Service: No
EINSATZKOMMANDO: **8**
Position: *Einsatzkommando* staff
Einsatzkommando Service: May 1941–October 1941
Other Assignment: SD Bergen
Highest Award: None listed
Postwar Sentence: 1961, 3 years
Notes: Served in Army 64th Artillery Regiment 1935-1936
No mention of *Einsatzkommando* service in personnel file
National Archives File: A3343 SSO-249B

Winkler

First Name: George
Date of Birth: 16 April 1920
Place of Birth: Mainz
Highest Rank: SS-Untersturmführer
SS Number: 323874
Date Entered SS: 1 October 1939
NSDAP Number: 6891074
Date Entered NSDAP: Not listed
Marital Status: Married
Religion: Agnostic
Civilian Occupation: Businessman
Education: High School
Foreign Language: No
World War I Service: No
EINSATZKOMMANDO: **1005**
Position: Not listed
Einsatzkommando Service: 1943-1944
Other Assignment: SD Klagenfurt
Highest Award: War Service Cross 2nd Class
Postwar Sentence: No judicial proceedings discovered
Notes: Served in Hitler Youth, 1933-1939
No mention of *Einsatzkommando* service in personnel file
National Archives File: A3343 SSO-249B

Wirtig

First Name: Hans-Joachim
Date of Birth: 21 April 1912
Place of Birth: Breslau
Highest Rank: SS-Obersturmführer
SS Number: 272374
Date Entered SS: 1 March 1935
NSDAP Number: 4583280
Date Entered NSDAP: 1 May 1937
Marital Status: Married
Religion: Agnostic
Civilian Occupation: Sports Teacher
Education: High School
Foreign Language: No
World War I Service: No
EINSATZKOMMANDO: **A**
Position: Not listed
Einsatzkommando Service: 15 November 1941 – 22 November 1943
Other Assignment: RSHA
Highest Award: None listed
Postwar Sentence: No judicial proceedings discovered
Notes: Served in SA, 1933-1935
No mention of *Einsatzkommando* service in personnel file
National Archives File: A3343 SSO-251B

Witiska

First Name: Dr. Josef
Date of Birth: 5 July 1894
Place of Birth: Iglau, Austria
Highest Rank: SS-Standartenführer
SS Number: 422296
Date Entered SS: 1 March 1938
NSDAP Number: 6289103
Date Entered NSDAP: 1 March 1938
Marital Status: Married
Religion: Agnostic
Civilian Occupation: Lawyer
Education: University
Foreign Language: No
World War I Service: Yes, Iron Cross 1st Class, airman
EINSATZKOMMANDO: **H**
Position: Commander
Einsatzkommando Service: 10 September 1944 to undetermined
Other Assignment: RSHA; SD Graz; SD Salzburg
Waffen-SS Service: No
Highest Award: War Service Cross 1st Class
Postwar Sentence: No judicial proceedings discovered
Notes: Commander, SD Lemberg
National Archives File: A3343 SSO-001C

Wittke

First Name: Fritz
Date of Birth: 14 October 1903
Place of Birth: Unknown
Highest Rank: SS-Obersturmführer
SS Number: 51982
Date Entered SS: Not listed
NSDAP Number: Not a member
Marital Status: Unknown
Religion: Unknown
Civilian Occupation: Police
Education: Unknown
Foreign Language: No
World War I Service: No
EINSATZKOMMANDO: **A**
Position: Supply officer
Einsatzkommando Service: 1941–1944
Other Assignment: Unknown
Waffen-SS Service: No
Highest Award: None listed
Postwar Sentence: No judicial proceedings discovered
Notes: Honorary SS member
National Archives File: A3343 SSO-002C

Wölbing

First Name: Fritz
Date of Birth: 30 October 1906
Place of Birth: Kassel
Highest Rank: SS-Sturmbannführer
SS Number: 383718
Date Entered SS: 27 March 1938
NSDAP Number: 1622154
Date Entered NSDAP: 15 May 1933
Marital Status: Widowed
Religion: Agnostic
Civilian Occupation: Farmer
Education: University
Foreign Language: No
EINSATZKOMMANDO: **C, D**
Position: Ethnic German Liaison Office, liaison officer
Einsatzkommando Service: C, 1942; D, 17 July 1942–1943
Other Assignment: Chief, Office III D, RSHA (SD Domestic, Economy)
SD Triest
Highest Award: Iron Cross 2nd Class
Postwar Sentence: No judicial proceedings discovered
Notes: Served in SA, 1933–1938; wife from Rio de Janeiro
Infantry Assault Badge
National Archives File: A3343 SSO-004C

Wolter

First Name: Willi
Date of Birth: 14 November 1907
Place of Birth: Cleve
Highest Rank: SS-Sturmbannführer
SS Number: 307942
Date Entered SS: 1 September 1936
NSDAP Number: 4616993
Date Entered NSDAP: 1 May 1937
Marital Status: Married
Religion: Agnostic
Civilian Occupation: Lawyer
Education: University of Berlin, Marburg, Königsberg
Foreign Language: English
EINSATZKOMMANDO: **E, 15**
Position: 15 – Commander
Einsatzkommando Service: E, – 1 June 1943; 15, 1 June 1943 – October 1944
Other Assignment: SD Stettin; SD Cologne
Waffen-SS Service: No
Highest Award: War Service Cross 2nd Class
Postwar Sentence: No judicial proceedings discovered
Notes: Served in SA, 1933-1935
Reported missing in action in Rumania, October 1944
National Archives File: A3343 SSO-012C

Woyrsch

First Name: Udo von
Date of Birth: 24 July 1895
Place of Birth: Schwanowitz
Highest Rank: SS-Obergruppenführer
SS Number: 3689
Date Entered SS: 10 June 1930
NSDAP Number: 162349
Date Entered NSDAP: 1 October 1929
Marital Status: Married
Religion: Protestant
Civilian Occupation: Land Owner
Education: High School
World War I Service: Yes, Iron Cross 1st Class, Hussar Regiment 4
EINSATZKOMMANDO: **von Woyrsch**
Position: Commander
Einsatzkommando Service: Polish Campaign
Other Assignment: Higher SS and Police Leader "Elbe", 1940-1944
Personal Staff, RFSS
Highest Award: War Service Cross 1st Class
Postwar Sentence: 10 years, released after 3 years
Notes: Golden Party Badge
Died 14 January 1983 in Swabia
National Archives File: A3343 SSO-014C

Zapp

First Name: Paul
Date of Birth: 18 April 1904
Place of Birth: Hersfeld
Highest Rank: SS-Obersturmbannführer
SS Number: 107180
Date Entered SS: Not listed
NSDAP Number: 4583288
Date Entered NSDAP: 1 May 1937
Marital Status: Married
Religion: Agnostic
Civilian Occupation: Businessman
Education: University
Foreign Language: No
World War I Service: No
EINSATZKOMMANDO: **11a**
Position: Commander
Einsatzkommando Service: June 1941–July 1942
Other Assignment: RSHA; SD Southeast
Highest Award: War Service Cross 1st Class
Postwar Sentence: 1970, Life
Notes: Iron Cross 2nd Class, Crimea Shield, Infantry Assault Badge
Eastern People's Medal
National Archives File: A3343 SSO-018C

Ziemer

First Name: Hubert
Date of Birth: 21 January 1909
Place of Birth: Massold
Highest Rank: SS-Hauptsturmführer
SS Number: 290513
Date Entered SS: Not listed
NSDAP Number: 284544
Date Entered NSDAP: 1 August 1930
Marital Status: Married
Religion: Unknown
Civilian Occupation: Detective Officer
Education: University
Foreign Language: No
EINSATZKOMMANDO: **C**
Position: Not listed
Einsatzkommando Service: Not listed
Other Assignment: Criminal Police Prague
Waffen-SS Service: No
Highest Award: None listed
Postwar Sentence: No judicial proceedings discovered
Notes: Very small personnel file
No mention of *Einsatzkommando* service in personnel file
National Archives File: A3343 SSO-021C

Zietlow

First Name: Fritz
Date of Birth: 24 August 1902
Place of Birth: Schneidemühl
Highest Rank: SS-Hauptsturmführer
SS Number: 6126
Date Entered SS: 1 October 1930
NSDAP Number: 36519
Date Entered NSDAP: 1 March 1926
Marital Status: Unknown
Religion: Unknown
Civilian Occupation: Newspaper editor
Education: University
Foreign Language: No
World War I Service: No
EINSATZKOMMANDO: **H, 1005**
Position: Not listed
Einsatzkommando Service: 1944
Other Assignment: RSHA
Waffen-SS Service: No
Highest Award: None listed
Postwar Sentence: No judicial proceedings discovered
Notes: Short personnel file
National Archives File: A3343 SSO-022C

Zimmermann

First Name: Herbert
Date of Birth: 22 August 1907
Place of Birth: Eisleben
Highest Rank: SS-Obersturmbannführer
SS Number: 118240
Date Entered SS: 8 March 1933
NSDAP Number: 3065321
Date Entered NSDAP: 1 May 1933
Marital Status: Married
Religion: Agnostic
Civilian Occupation: Lawyer
Education: University of Marburg
Foreign Language: No
World War I Service: No
EINSATZKOMMANDO: **B**
Position: Not listed
Einsatzkommando Service: 15 August 1943 to undetermined
Other Assignment: RSHA, Office IV A 1b (Communism); Police Münster
Highest Award: War Service Cross 1st Class
Postwar Sentence: No judicial proceedings discovered
Notes: Commander Security Police Bialystok; visited USA for five months in 1934
Commander Security Police Metz; died 31 December 1965
National Archives File: A3343 SSO-023C

Zöllner

First Name: Albrecht
Date of Birth: 28 January 1914
Place of Birth: Kiel
Highest Rank: SS-Hauptsturmführer
SS Number: 57148
Date Entered SS: 20 December 1931
NSDAP Number: 985347
Date Entered NSDAP: 1 March 1932
Marital Status: Married
Religion: Agnostic
Civilian Occupation: Sales associate
Education: High School
Foreign Language: No
World War I Service: No
EINSATZKOMMANDO: **1 1a**
Position: *Einsatzkommando* staff
Einsatzkommando Service: 1941
Other Assignment: RSHA
Highest Award: None listed
Postwar Sentence: No judicial proceedings discovered
Notes: Golden Hitler Youth Badge
No mention of *Einsatzkommando* service in personnel file
National Archives File: A3343 SSO-025C

Zschunke

First Name: Marcel
Date of Birth: 18 January 1915
Place of Birth: Brussels, Belgium
Highest Rank: SS-Hauptsturmführer
SS Number: 111843
Date Entered SS: Not listed
NSDAP Number: 1329743
Date Entered NSDAP: 1 February 1933
Marital Status: Married
Religion: Agnostic
Civilian Occupation: Unknown
Education: University
Foreign Language: French, English, Italian, Spanish
EINSATZKOMMANDO: **4b**
Position: Not listed
Einsatzkommando Service: 25 November 1941 – 3 August 1942
Other Assignment: RSHA, Office VI B (SD, Foreign, German-Italian Sphere)
Waffen-SS Service: No
Highest Award: War Service Cross 1st Class
Killed in Action: No
Postwar Sentence: No judicial proceedings discovered
Notes: No mention of *Einsatzkommando* service in personnel file
National Archives File: A3343 SSO-025C

3

THE EINSATZKOMMANDO OFFICERS: AN ANALYSIS

Never forget, we are a knightly Order, from which one cannot withdraw, to which one is recruited by blood and within which one remains with body and soul so long as one lives on this earth.[1]

- *Heinrich Himmler*

Now that we have examined the missions and organization of the *Einsatzkommandos*, and have presented key information for each individual officer assigned to these units, we may be able to deduce some overall conclusions concerning these men. In addition, for some categories of information, we can further compare the officers assigned to the *Einsatzkommando* with those nine hundred plus SS officers assigned to service in concentration camps as outlined in a previous work, *The Camp Men: The SS Officers Who Ran the Concentration Camp System*. The analysis of the *Einsatzgruppen* officers is actually a sub-analysis of the SD as a whole, since so many of these officers were from this powerful organization.

AGE

The officers who controlled the *Einsatzkommandos* were relatively young, more than sixty-eight percent were born between 1900 and 1910. This age bracket further meant that most could remember the trauma of World War I, although again, most would have been too young to have served in that conflict. The oldest officer in our study was born in 1882, while the youngest was born in 1921. While no detailed age analysis was performed on the SS officers who served in the concentration camps, it is clear that many more of these camp officers were born before 1900 – as well over one hundred later camp officers were decorated for valor in World War I. In short, the *Einsatzkommando* officers were a younger lot than their concentration camp brethren.

BIRTHPLACE

In examining the birthplace for each officer assigned to the *Einsatzkommandos*, the geographical distribution appears to follow what we might expect between those from urban and rural settings. The following chart shows the most frequently found places of birth for the *Einsatzkommando* officers.

Table 3
EINSATZKOMMANDO OFFICERS
MOST FREQUENT PLACE OF BIRTH

Berlin	24
Magdeburg	7
Breslau	7
Leipzig	7
Kiel	6
Hamburg	6
Munich	6
Frankfurt	5

From these numbers it is obvious that the vast majority of SS officers who served in the *Einsatzkommandos* came from smaller cities, towns and villages, not the most populated cities; as the population from these larger cities in Germany accounts for only about eighteen percent of the total number of serving officers. The same cities accounted for one-sixth of the total number of concentration camp officers as well.

Many *Einsatzkommando* men were not born in Germany proper. Fifteen hailed from Austria, one from Belgium, twenty-four from Russia and two from Switzerland. One was even born to a German mother in St. Louis, Missouri. Several were from the Sudetenland and served in the Czech Army before Germany reoccupied this territory in 1938. Several sources state that Reinhard Heydrich specifically was looking for officers who came from Eastern European German enclaves for assignment to the *Einsatzkommando* (as they would have unique knowledge of the area of operations), but that assertion does not appear to be the case when we examine birthplace.[2] Only six percent of the officers came from this type of background.

From small farm-towns to middle and large cities the SS *Einsatzkommando* officers came from all parts of the Fatherland. Though diverse in their origins, their education, former occupations, the Nazi regime and even a small element of chance steered them to the units organized to carry out mass murder.

EDUCATION

The officers who prosecuted Germany's racial war in the east in the ranks of the *Einsatzkommandos* were predominantly college men. A full forty-three percent of these officers attended the prestigious university system in the nation – a system that admitted only those who passed a special college admission test, the *Abitur*. Berlin, Freiburg, Jena, Frankfurt, Kiel, Munich – nearly every university in Germany had graduates who served in the *Einsatzkommandos*. George C. Browder, in his work *Hitler's Enforcers: The Gestapo and the SS Security Service in the Nazi Revolution* shows through samples of SD personnel – and the officers of the *Einsatzkommandos* were predominantly from the SD – that 43.9 percent of all SD officers in 1936 had attended or graduated from a university. The following table shows the number of *Einsatzkommando* officers who attended or graduated from these prestigious institutes of higher learning:

Table 4
EINSATZKOMMANDO OFFICERS
UNIVERSITY ATTENDANCE

INSTITUTE	***NUMBER OF OFFICERS WHO ATTENDED***
University of Bamberg	1
University of Berlin	17
University of Bonn	4
University of Breslau	3
University of Cologne	3
University of Dresden	1
University of Erlangen	6
University of Frankfurt/Main	3
University of Freiburg	5
University of Giessen	5
University of Göttingen	14
University of Graz	3
University of Heidelberg	5
University of Innsbruck	1
University of Jena	8
University of Kiel	6
University of Königsberg	6
University of Leipzig	9
University of Marburg	4
University of Münster	5
University of Munich	15
University of Prague	1
University of Rostock	2
University of Tübingen	10
University of Vienna	1
University of Würzburg	2

FOREIGN LANGUAGE PROFICIENCY

With such a large percentage of officers finishing high school and attending these prestigious universities, it follows that quite a few *Einsatzkommando* officers would have a degree of proficiency in foreign languages. In fact, several post-war Holocaust history books state that fluency in a language native to the areas of operation for the *Einsatzgruppen* (e.g., Russian, Latvian, Estonian, Lithuanian, Ukrainian) was a major determinant in officer selection for these positions. However, in examining the personnel records for our officer population, we find that only seventeen had documented proficiency in Russian, seventeen in Latvian, four in Polish, none in Lithuanian and one in Ukrainian. Additionally, fifty-six are found to have had training in French, sixty-one in English and sixteen in other western European languages which would have had very little utility when operating in the territory of the Soviet Union.[1] If other officers could speak one of the eastern languages, and this is certainly possible, this proficiency is not reflected in their personnel files.

OCCUPATION

If the medical profession can be said to have provided more concentration camp officers than any other – twenty-nine percent – then certainly the *Einsatzkommandos* were the domain of the lawyer and the policeman. A full twenty-five percent of all officers assigned to these units were lawyers or some type of legal assistants. Even greater was the role of police officials – as we might expect considering that the *Einsatzkommando* drew on personnel from the ORPO and Kripo. These law enforcement personnel accounted for twenty-seven percent of the *Einsatzkommando* officers. Other professions included: architect, baker, barber, bartender, bookseller, businessman, chemist, clergy, dental technician, economist, electrician, engineer, farmer, locksmith, mechanic, opera singer, school teacher and truck driver.

WORLD WAR I SERVICE

As previously mentioned, many of the officers in this study were born too late to have served in World War I. However, forty-eight did fight in the conflict, of whom some fifty-three percent were decorated for valor or were wounded in action in front-line service. During World War I the basic decorations for front-line bravery were the Iron Cross 1st Class and 2nd Class. The Iron Cross 2nd Class indicated a single act of bravery in combat, while the Iron Cross 1st Class was awarded for an additional act or acts of valor. It was only possible for an individual to win each of the classes once. Additionally, to measure wounds received in combat, Kaiser Wilhelm II instituted the Wound Badge on March 3, 1918. Different grades were awarded based on the cumulative number of incidents in which wounds were received. The wound badge in black designated one or two wounds, the badge in white three to four wounds, and the badge in yellow-gold five or more wounds.[3]

In examining the *Einsatzkommando* officers we find that twelve received the Iron Cross 2nd Class for service in World War I while at least seven received the Iron Cross 1st Class. Additionally, eight were wounded in action during this conflict; some seriously enough to preclude further front-line service.

AWARDS AND DECORATIONS

At the outbreak of World War II, the German Armed Forces re-instituted the Iron Cross 1st Class and 2nd Class. Hitler stated that the Iron Cross 2nd Class would reward a single act of bravery in combat beyond the normal requirements of duty. It could be awarded to all members of the Armed Forces or to civilians serving with the military. The Iron Cross 1st Class, also re-instituted on September 1, 1939, was usually awarded for an additional three to five significant acts of valor.[4] Recommendations for both awards went from company to battalion to regiment, with the approving authority resting with the division commander. For non-divisional units assigned to a corps, the corps commander approved receipt of the award. Although the intent was to let an appropriate time pass between the award of the 2nd Class and the 1st Class, this could be compressed to one or two days in special circumstances. For soldiers who had already been awarded the Iron Cross in World War I, the actual World War II version of the decoration was not presented. Instead, they received a clasp denoting the achievement of winning the decoration again in this latest conflict.

On September 1, 1939 Hitler also instituted a new decoration, the *Ritterkreuz* (Knight's Cross of the Iron Cross) for continuous acts of exceptional bravery or, in the cases of higher ranks, for successful execution of battle or for formulating outstanding battle plans.[5] Recommendation for the Knight's Cross required the endorsement of the chain of command through army commander with the final decision resting with Hitler.[6] Prerequisites included previous award of both classes of the Iron Cross. Enlisted personnel as well as officers were eligible for this award. In the course of the war some 7,300 Knight's Crosses were awarded.[7]

Two former *Einsatzkommando* officers received the Knight's Cross of the Iron Cross. *SS-Gruppenführer* Bruno Streckenbach was awarded the decoration August 27, 1944 as the commander of the 19th Volunteer Division of the *Waffen-SS* (Latvian No. 2). The division was involved in heavy fighting against the Red Army in the Baltic area at the time. *SS-Obersturmbannführer* Friedrich Suhr won the award December 11, 1944 as the commander of a battle group of SD troops fighting partisans near Toulouse, France.

On June 3, 1940 Hitler instituted the next higher grade of the Knight's Cross, the Knight's Cross of the Iron Cross with Oak Leaves (*Ritterkreuz mit Eichenlaub*). This award recognized previous winners of the Knight's Cross for continued significant bravery and initiative. Enlisted personnel, officers and foreign military personnel were eligible to receive the Oak Leaves, and by war's end 910 had been awarded.[8] Awards of the Oak Leaves were spread among all of Germany's Armed Forces. Seventy-seven winners of this award were from the

Waffen-SS. One former SS *Einsatzkommando* officer received the Knight's Cross with Oak Leaves: *SS-Gruppenführer* Bruno Streckenbach received the award on January 21, 1945 as commander of the 19th SS Division.

One year later Hitler again introduced another higher grade of award – the Knight's Cross of the Iron Cross with Oak Leaves and Swords (*Ritterkreuz mit Eichenlaub und Schwertern*). This grade recognized previous recipients of the Oak Leaves who accomplished additional feats of military achievement. Although German military personnel of all ranks were theoretically eligible to receive this award, only 159 officers actually did.[9] No former *Einsatzkommando* officer was awarded this decoration.

In total, two SS officers who served in the *Einsatzkommandos* received one of the grades of the Knight's Cross – far less than one percent of the total of Knight's Crosses to the *Waffen-SS* officers as an aggregate. This compares to twenty concentration camp officers who went on to win one of the grades of the Knight's Cross.

On September 28, 1941, Hitler created the War Order of the German Cross in Gold (*Kriegsorden des Deutschen Kreuzes in Gold*) to recognize a level of bravery or service above that required for an Iron Cross 1st Class but below that for the Knight's Cross. An estimated thirty thousand crosses were awarded during the next three and one-half years.[10] Two former *Einsatzkommando* officers received the award: *SS-Standartenführer* Dr. Rudolf Lange won the cross on February 6, 1945 as the commander of the SD in Posen, as did then *SS-Standartenführer* Bruno Streckenbach, commander of the SS Cavalry Division on December 15, 1943. On the other hand, seventeen former concentration camp officers received the German Cross in Gold. Again, considering these low figures, we can conclude that former *Einsatzkommando* officers did not figure prominently in this award.

Hitler also instituted several honors that were given for bravery or service not in a direct connection with combat.[11] Two of these were the War Service Cross 2nd Class and 1st Class (*Kriegsverdienstkreuz*). Both awards were presented in prodigious quantities. Approximately 7,600,000 War Service Cross 2nd Class were awarded while 600,000 War Service Cross 1st Class were presented. Division level commanders could authorize both awards.[12] The War Order of the German Cross in Silver (*Kriegsorden des Deutschen Kreuzes in Silber*) was a companion piece to the aforementioned German Cross in Gold and was presented for non-combat achievement more significant than that affiliated with the War Service Cross. One former *Einsatzkommando* officer received the German Cross in Silver – *SS-Oberführer* Dr. Friedrich Panzinger – as compared to five former concentration camp officers.

The following chart shows the overall distribution of awards for the *Einsatzkommando* officers for whom this information is recorded:[13]

Table 5
EINSATZKOMMANDO OFFICERS
HIGHEST DECORATION RECEIVED

DECORATION	***NUMBER***
Knight's Cross with Oak Leaves and Swords, Diamonds	0
Knight's Cross with Oak Leaves and Swords	0
Knight's Cross with Oak Leaves	1
Knight's Cross	2
German Cross in Gold	1
German Cross in Silver	1
Iron Cross 1st Class (includes Bar)	24
War Service Cross 1st Class	88
Iron Cross 2nd Class (includes Bar)	48
War Service Cross 2nd Class	101

Given these numbers, we can conclude that the German leadership felt that duty at an *Einsatzkommando* comprised both bravery and service, and unlike assignment to a concentration camp, was directly related to combat. Approximately thirty of the SS officers studied, who received the Iron Cross 2nd or 1st Class, did so during their time of service in an *Einsatzkommando*. But not all received a combat award. More *Einsatzkommando* officers received the War Service Cross 2nd Class as their highest decoration.[14]

Germany also instituted a series of war badges to denote service in a particular type of combat. Since several of these awards were received by some *Einsatzkommando* officers, it is appropriate to discuss these decorations here. The Infantry Assault Badge (*Infanterie-Sturmabzeichen*), instituted in 1939, was presented to single out the highly hazardous combat achievement of officers and men of the infantry and mountain infantry. Criteria for the Infantry Assault Badge specified that the soldier take part in at least three infantry assaults, armed reconnaissance, hand-to-hand combat or participate in the restoration of the main line of defense on three different days. The award could be authorized by the regimental commander.[15] Nineteen *Einsatzkommando* officers received the Infantry Assault Badge.

A second award sometimes presented to officers in the *Einsatzkommandos* was the Anti-Partisan War Badge (*Bandenkampfabzeichen*). This award was intended to recognize service by officers and enlisted personnel engaged in combating guerrillas or partisans behind the lines on the eastern front. Personnel accumulated anti-partisan fighting days to qualify for the award – during every day an individual participated in an operation against partisans, he received a day of credit. Twenty days of credit earned the recipient the award in bronze, fifty total days of credit resulted in the award in silver and one hundred fifty days of anti-partisan operations earned the officer or enlisted man the award in gold.[16] Six officers from the *Einsatzkommando* were awarded the Anti-Partisan War Badge.

One final award presented to selected *Einsatzkommando* officers was the Decoration for Bravery and Merit of the "Eastern People" (*Tapferkeits-und Verdienst- Auszeichnung für Angehörige der Ostvölker*). This award was initiated in July 1942 to recognize bravery and service for those deserving Russian, Latvian, Lithuanian, Ukrainian and other Soviet Republic volunteers who assisted the German war effort. The award had two classes, each with several sub-groups concerning whether the award was for bravery or service. After October 1942, German soldiers serving with these Eastern People units were eligible for the award in the 1st or 2nd Class in silver, providing the recipient already held the Iron Cross 1st or 2nd Class.[17] It appears that twenty-four *Einsatzkommando* officers received one of the grades of this award.

The following is a sample recommendation for an award to an officer who had been in the *Einsatzkommandos*, *SS-Oberführer* Dr. Humbert Achamer-Pifrader, former commander of *Einsatzgruppe A*:[18]

> *SS-Oberführer* Dr. Pifrader is the leader of Office IV B in the RSHA. During the afternoon hours of July 20, he got the order to carry through with the arrest of the former Colonel Graf von Stauffenberg at the Bendlerstrasse. After he arrived, Pifrader was taken in custody [by the plotters] after some delay; only surrendering at the point of a machine pistol. During the several hours of custody, *SS-Oberführer* Pifrader displayed an extraordinary, fearless and alert attitude.
>
> When the counterattack began at the Bendlerstrasse, Pifrader immediately assisted in this action. During the resolution of revolt, Pifrader was highly active, especially in the successful questioning of significant members of the traitorous clique.
>
> Earlier, as the commander of the Sipo and the SD in the Ostland, *SS-Oberführer* Pifrader meritoriously excelled in the fight against bandits (receiving the Iron Cross 2nd Class). His contributions in connection with the movement during the difficult days in Austria, his outstanding readiness in every development since the taking over of power, his successful activity within the executive circles of the State Police and, last but not least, his fanatic National-Socialistic attitude, paired with an unheard-of activism, justify the recommendation that he be awarded the German Cross in Silver.

Despite this strong endorsement, Pifrader did not receive the award. One former *Einsatzkommando* officer who received the German Cross in Gold had this recommendation:[19]

> As commander of the Sicherheitspolzei and the SD in Toulouse, *SS-Obersturmbannführer* Friedrich Suhr has conducted the fight against the French Resistance Movement – both national and communist – in an outstanding energetic manner and always led at the front of his commando. Due to this, he contributed very significantly to the destruction of the terrorist movement and to bringing peace to the area. On several occasions of heavy fire fighting, thanks to the leadership of Suhr, there were only small losses among his troop, while the casualties and prisoners of the enemy were very high.
>
> When the region Toulouse was evacuated and the colonel in charge from the army proved to be ineffective, Suhr made the personal decision to lead a group of 21 units which at the start of the withdrawal were in danger of falling apart due to the confusion of their officers. Because of his personality, Suhr organized the units, put them under his command and forged together as a battle group. Leaders and crew of his own commando were distributed to the various units, so that in this way his influence on the battle group consisting of 800 people, among them also many women, was always assured. After a seven-day march (August 19 to August 25, 1944), which had to take place under mostly uninterrupted battles against strong, well armed bandits, Suhr reached the town of Valence. From there, Suhr led his own commando to Vittel via Lyon and in this new area of activity he again resumed his work in the security police until September 8, 1944.
>
> Suhr's strength and personal will to fight – he always made his own decisions in front of his battle group – the freeing of the roads from Bagnols to Baix, as well as occupation of the village of Baix (25 km south of Valence) against most severe enemy resistance is to his credit.
>
> Here Suhr made his own decision on August 22, 1944 to cross over the Rhone and, under the severest technical difficulties, had a ferry built. Under constant air attacks and after the bloody repulse of a bandit attack on the western shore of the Rhone, Suhr led the crossing of his battle group over the river in two days. He secured the ferry long enough so that ensuing other battle groups of the Wehrmacht could reach Baix and could take over the ferry in usable condition.

> It was solely due to the decisive action of Suhr that not only his own battle group, but also the battle groups of the Wehrmacht which followed them could be saved from the heaviest losses and imprisonment and, with that, the Wehrmacht units could be made available as defensive forces in ensuing gathering areas.
>
> *SS-Obersturmbannführer* Suhr, during these days of heavy battles during the withdrawal, was a real example of personal courage, decisiveness and compassionate care for the officers and enlisted men under him.
>
> Therefore, it is my opinion that *SS-Obersturmbannführer* Suhr is particularly worthy of being awarded the German Cross in Gold.

SS-Standartenführer Dr. Rudolf Lange, who had served as the commander of *Einsatzkommando* 2, also received this award. The following is his award recommendation from *SS-Obergruppenführer* Ernst Kaltenbrunner:[20]

> Already during his service as the Commander of Security Police in Riga, *SS-Standartenführer* Dr. Lange has proven to be valuable. For his successful leadership of the forces under him during battles with bandits and for his personal courageous behavior he received the Iron Cross 1st and 2nd Class from the commander of the Army Group North.
>
> In his current position as Commander of Security Police in Posen, while at the same time acting SS and Police Commander Wartheland, *SS-Standartenführer* Dr. Lange has actively worked for the fulfillment of the security police tasks to which he was appointed and for capturing numerous saboteurs and deserters, as well as by organizing shattered army units in an outstanding measure, he has contributed to the strengthening of the effectiveness of the army units positioned here.
>
> More importantly, he has excelled through his diligent and courageous action in battle against the Bolshevik troops encircling his position. Thanks to his valor and courage, the offices of the security police and of the SD in Posen could be recaptured from the enemy. During the course of the fight in the town in front of the offices, seven enemy tanks were destroyed. Lange himself was wounded during this battle.
>
> Based on the courage while facing the enemy and for his merits in gathering together defensive forces against enemy encirclement and the destruction of resistance groups within the fortification Posen, Dr. Lange is worthy of the award for which he is nominated.

SS SERVICE

Early service in the SS seems to have been a valued commodity to Heinrich Himmler and is well represented in *Einsatzkommando* officers. By the end of 1929, one thousand men had joined the SS. One year later membership had risen to 2,700; by the close of 1931 there were almost 15,000 men serving in the organization. On January 30, 1933, the day Hitler assumed the chancellorship of Germany, 52,000 men had joined. And only a year after that membership had risen to 200,000.[21] Many of these original SS members consisted of former *Freikorps* men, out of work intellectuals and lower-middle class Nazi Party men. Later SS members were unofficially known as "March Violets" and viewed with suspicion by the veteran SS.[22]

Himmler established a silver death's head signet ring to be presented to proven SS men, regardless of rank. Initially this ring was to be awarded only to "old fighters", those SS men with a membership number of below 10,000.[23]

Another indicator of the value of a low SS number is found in Nazi legal policy. On October 17, 1939 the Ministerial Council for the Defense of the Reich set up a special judicial system so that there would be a separate punishing authority for SS members. Special SS courts were empowered to handle all military and non-military crimes committed by members of the SS or police. Infractions committed before enlistment could also be looked into. SS and police courts were located at the headquarters of each Higher SS and Police Leader.[24] There was an additional SS and police court attached to the SS Legal Department to deal with offenses of special importance where investigations were particularly difficult. Different officials could convene a court depending on the circumstances of a case. Hitler was the convening authority in the case of death sentences pertaining to all commanders and officers, or in the case of certain serious offenses by senior officials. Himmler was the convening authority on any case he reserved for himself, which included cases against SS members with an SS number below 15,000. Finally, the chief of a main department of the SS (*Hauptamt*) and the HSSPF, within their area of responsibility, were also convening authorities when the above circumstances did not apply.[25]

An additional gauge is found in the annual SS statistics book. The *Statistisches Jahrbuch der Schutzstaffel der NSDAP 1937* indicates that 2,466 SS officers had SS membership numbers under 15,000.[26] Clearly, the SS leadership attached some importance to those who joined the movement in its early, and often difficult, days.

The following table shows a list of the ten lowest SS membership numbers found for the *Einsatzkommando* men and is followed by the distribution of *Einsatzkommando* officers by

SS number. Thirty SS officers with SS numbers lower than 15,000 served, at some point in their careers, in an *Einsatzkommando*.[27]

Table 6
EINSATZKOMMANDO OFFICERS
LOWEST SS NUMBERS

NAME	*SS NUMBER*
Otto Ohlendorf	880
Georg Fuhrmann	1103
Ludwig Teichmann	1789
Lothar Beutel	2422
Anton Weiss-Bollandt	2641
Franz Radif	2675
Horst-Alwin Boehme	2821
Karl Hennicke	3276
Dr. Erich Koerting	3395
Dr. Johann-Georg Meixner	3429

Table 7
EINSATZKOMMANDO OFFICERS
DISTRIBUTION OF SS NUMBERS

SS NUMBER RANGE	*NUMBER OF OFFICERS*
1 - 1,000	1
1,001 - 5,000	14
5,001 - 10,000	9
10,001 - 15,000	6
15,001 - 50,000	36
50,001 - 100,000	49
100,001 +	262

When examining the ten early entrants into the SS, it appears that most advanced reasonably well in their careers. One made *SS-Gruppenführer*, while one attained the rank of *SS-Oberführer*, one was promoted to *SS-Standartenführer* and four advanced to *SS-Obersturmbannführer*.

NAZI PARTY SERVICE

One facet of party affiliation was the Nazi Party's highest decoration for service, "The Decoration of 9 November 1923" (*Ehrenzeichen vom 9. November 1923*), also known as the "Blood Order" (*Blutorden*).[28] Hitler created this decoration in March 1934 to commemorate the failed "Beer Hall Putsch" (attempted overthrow of the Bavarian government) on November 9, 1923 in Munich. Eligibility was initially limited to persons who had participated in the events of November 9th and who were known as "Old Comrades." In 1938, eligibility was expanded to include persons who had rendered outstanding service to the party in the 1920s and had received a Weimar court death sentence and who had subsequently served at least one year in jail, or who had been severely wounded or killed in party service.[29]

SS men figured prominently in the award. Again, according to the *Statistisches Jahrbuch der Schutzstaffel der NSDAP 1937*, 141 SS officers were listed as recipients of this award.[30] The following table shows the five *Einsatzkommando* officers who received the Blood Order. It is apparent that Himmler considered Blood Order recipients to be among the most reliable of officers, fully capable of helping to run the *Einsatzkommandos*. This compares with nine concentration camp officers who received the Blood Order.

Table 8
EINSATZKOMMANDO OFFICERS
BLOOD ORDER RECIPIENTS

NAME	*EINSATZKOMMANDO SERVICE*
Dr. Kurt Christmann	EK 10a
Jakob Oswald	EG B
Alois Persterer	EK 10b
Hans-Fritz Sohns	Sonderkommando 1005
Franz Stark	EG A

Another Nazi service award was the Golden Party Badge (*Goldenes Parteiabzeichen*). Hitler created this award in October 1933. To receive this award, an individual must have had uninterrupted service in the Nazi Party since February 27, 1925 and held a Nazi Party membership number from 1 to 100,000. As previously mentioned, the earlier an individual joined the party, the lower the party number he would receive – the award was designed to recognize the early service of the first party members who joined before it became fashionable to do so. When both criteria were placed in effect, it was found that 22,282 – not 100,000 – persons actually qualified for the award. These individuals began to receive the Golden Party Badge on

November 9, 1933 – the tenth anniversary of the failed Putsch.[31] Over one thousand SS officers wore the Golden Party Badge.[32] Fifty-five concentration camp officers had NSDAP membership numbers under 100,000. For *Einsatzkommando* officers, this total was nineteen.[33] The following two tables show the distribution of NSDAP numbers and a list of the earliest *Einsatzkommando* officers who joined the Nazi Party; all had NSDAP numbers under 25,000, but not all had Golden Party Badges.

Table 9
EINSATZKOMMANDO OFFICERS
DISTRIBUTION OF NSDAP NUMBERS

NSDAP PARTY NUMBER RANGE	*FREQUENCY*
1 - 1,000	0
1,001 - 5,000	3
5,001 - 100,000	16
100,001 - 500,000	67
500,001 - 8,961,479	260

Table 10
EINSATZKOMMANDO OFFICERS
LOWEST NSDAP NUMBERS

NAME	*NSDAP NUMBER*	*GOLDEN PARTY BADGE*
Adolf Ott	2433	No
Georg Fuhrmann	2508	Yes
Otto Ohlendorf	6531	Yes
Wilhelm Baumgarten	6979	Yes
Walter Mosig	11670	Yes
Hans-Fritz Sohns	10820	Yes
Bernhard Fischer-Schweder	17141	Yes

MARITAL STATUS

Heinrich Himmler encouraged members of the SS to marry. In a set of instructions issued in 1936, Himmler stated "the SS man is expected to marry, preferably between the ages of 25 and 30, and found a family."[34] The SS marriage regulations gave Himmler the right to veto the marriage of an SS man, if the *Reichsführer-SS* thought the bride unsuitable. Those SS personnel already married when the regulation came out did not have their union subject to review.[35]

One might imagine that those officers attracted to *Einsatzkommando* service were socially stunted or at least not family-oriented men, but this was not the case. Three hundred twenty-nine (87%) were married, with one man engaged to be married, while six had been married but were widowers. Those divorced number five while those listed as "single" number only twenty-seven.[36] In comparison, some eighty percent of all concentration camp officers were married.

OFFICER RANK

As a group, the SS officers who served at the *Einsatzkommandos* were relatively senior in rank given the enormous tasks they were expected to accomplish in an independent manner, just opposite that for concentration camp officers. The following table presents the distribution of the highest officer ranks these individuals achieved for both organizations.[37] Furthermore, many of the officers actually served at a much lower rank during their *Einsatzkommando* service and achieved one or more promotions later in their career.

Table 11
EINSATZKOMMANDO & CONCENTRATION CAMP OFFICERS
HIGHEST RANK ACHIEVED

RANK	*EINSATZ KOMMANDO*	*CONCENTRATION CAMP*
SS-Obergruppenführer	2	2
SS-Gruppenführer	6	5
SS-Brigadeführer	11	7
SS-Oberführer	10	16
SS-Standartenführer	21	32
SS-Obersturmbannführer	59	63
SS-Sturmbannführer	76	176
SS-Hauptsturmführer	89	286
SS-Obersturmführer	66	226
SS-Untersturmführer	40	89

This tells only part of the story, however, as our sample size for the concentration camp officers is almost four times greater than for the *Einsatzkommandos*. Forty-nine percent of all *Einsatzkommando* officers were field grade or general grade officers (*SS-Sturmbannführer* and higher.) In comparison, only thirty-one percent of concentration camp officers achieved this status. The increased requirements for independent thinking and action necessitated much more in the fluid situation of the *Einsatzkommandos* and brought subsequent reward of higher rank, as compared to concentration camp officers who operated under the same set of conditions day after day.

RELIGION

Yisrael Gutmann, in his *Anatomy of the Auschwitz Death Camp*, explains that SS authorities insisted that all SS personnel renounce their membership in religious organizations. He maintains that while such a step was not required, the SS maintained such information in personnel files; those that did indeed abandon their previous religious beliefs were designated "*gottgläubig*", a euphemism for atheism.[38]

"Agnostic" and not "atheist" would be a more accurate term for *gottgläubig*. Within those officers identified as having served in the *Einsatzkommandos*, thirty listed Protestant as their religious faith, eight listed Catholic and three hundred thirteen designated "gottgläubig" or agnostic.[39] This category probably more accurately reflects what the SS personnel clerks reported under the religion category – we cannot be certain as to what the officers actually believed themselves. In comparison, in 1938 the religious affiliations for members of the SS *Totenkopf* troops were reported as: 2,211 Protestants, 632 Catholics and 6,329 Agnostics.[40]

George Browder also examined religion in his study *Hitler's Enforcers: The Gestapo and SS Security Service in the Nazi Revolution*. His data indicates that 8.2 percent of the SD had withdrawn from the church and become agnostic in 1934, 18.1 percent had done so by 1935, 44.1 percent had withdrawn by 1937, 50.6 percent left by 1938 and 90.1 percent had withdrawn by 1945.[41] This is supported by our finding of 82.3 percent of agnostics in our *Einsatzkommando* sample.

WAFFEN-SS SERVICE

Unlike the officers who served in the concentration camps of whom almost forty-four percent served in the armed SS, the officers of the *Einsatzkommandos* rarely served in the *Waffen-SS*; in fact, only thirty (8 percent) did. Hitler originally envisioned the *Waffen-SS* as an elite, militarized, politically reliable police force. The Führer maintained that this elite had to serve at the front in order to maintain its prestige. Most of the *Einsatzkommando* officers went to other SD positions in the Reich and did not follow their concentration camp brethren to the front. Three *Einsatzkommando* officers are known to have served in the 1st SS Division "Leibstandarte Adolf Hitler," three in the 4th SS Division "Polizei", two in the 9th SS Division "Hohenstaufen" and one each in the 2nd, 3rd, 8th, 12th, 14th, 16th, 18th, 19th, 20th, 29th, 36th and 38th SS Divisions. Twenty-three officers served in an *Einsatzkommando* and then transferred to the *Waffen-SS*. Seven officers served in the *Waffen-SS* and later joined an *Einsatzkommando*.The following table shows those *Einsatzkommando* officers who served in *Waffen-SS* formations:[42]

Table 12
EINSATZKOMMANDO OFFICERS
SERVICE IN *WAFFEN-SS*

NAME	*UNIT*	*DATE*
Wolfgang Birkner	"Leibstandarte Adolf Hitler" Regiment	1934-1936
Hans-Joachim Boehme	4th SS Division "Polizei"	1945
Reinhold-Max Bruennert	1st SS Division "Leibstandarte Adolf Hitler"	1940
Dr. Friedrich Buchardt	XIIth SS Corps	1944
Dr. Erich Ehrlinger	1st SS Division "Leibstandarte Adolf Hitler"	1940
Bernhard Fischer-Schweder	12th SS Division "Hitler Jugend"	1945
Hans Graalfs	502nd SS Heavy Tank Battalion	1944
Dr. Herbert Grohmann	30th SS Division	1944-1945
Erich Hartmann	2nd SS Infantry Brigade	1941-1942
Ernst Hayde	IIIrd SS Corps	1943
Lothar Heimbach	3rd SS Division "Totenkopf"	1945
Werner Hersmann	36th SS Division "Dirlewanger"	1944
	38th SS Division "Niebelungen"	1945

Kurt Junker	SS Infantry Regiment "Der Führer"	1940
Andreas von Koskull	IInd SS Flak Detachment	1943
Dr. Erhard Kroeger	9th SS Division "Hohenstaufen"	1943
Dr. Peter Kroeger	9th SS Division "Hohenstaufen"	1943-1944
Georg Egon Loleit	29th SS Division	1944-1945
Helmut Looss	16th SS Division "Reichsführer-SS"	1944-1945
Walter Potzelt	1st SS Division "Leibstandarte Adolf Hitler"	1941
Werner Schlaetel	4th SS Division "Polizei"	1942-1944
Erwin Schmiel	"Leibstandarte Adolf Hitler" Regiment	1933-1937
Dr. Eberhard Schöngarth	4th SS Division "Polizei"	1943-1944
Dr. Franz Six	2nd SS Division "Das Reich"	1941
Friedrich Störtz	20th SS Division	1944
Dr. Eduard Strauch	IIIrd SS Corps	1944
Bruno Streckenbach	8th SS Division "Florian Geyer"	1943-1944
	19th SS Division	1944-1945
Alfred Tempfer	18th SS Division "Horst Wessel"	
Heinrich Wiens	14th SS Division	1944-1945

OPERATION ZEPPELIN

This is an appropriate point to mention a special combat unit within which a documented twelve *Einsatzkommando* officers served. Code named *Operation Zeppelin*, this SD-led mission under control of Dr. Heinz Graefe had the purpose of forming large units to conduct special operations of counterintelligence and sabotage behind Soviet lines. From March to June 1942, selected SS leaders to include these twelve *Einsatzkommando* officers – toured prisoner of war camps in German occupied Soviet territory in an attempt to recruit appropriate Russian agents. SS personnel in the mission were temporarily attached to the RSHA, Office VI C during this period. While the Germans did recruit several battalions worth of potential agents, they did not employ any large units behind Russian lines. We do not know if the *Einsatzkommando* officers who served in *Operation Zeppelin* ever went behind Soviet lines themselves. Considering what they knew about the large-scale killing operations, sending these men into such an undertaking would have been extremely risky, but we cannot rule it out.[43]

Table 13
EINSATZKOMMANDO OFFICERS
OPERATION ZEPPELIN

OFFICER	***EINSATZGRUPPE***
Dr. Heinz Graefe (commander)	1/V
Joachim Hamann	EK 3, SK 4b
Dr. Hermann Hubig	EG A, SK 1b
Waldemar Klingelhöfer	Vorkommando Moscow
Otto Kraus	EG A, EK 2
Hermann Lumm	EK 5
Hanns Matysiak	EG A
Rudolf Oebsger-Roeder	EG A
Edwin Sakuth	Tilsit
Dr. Wilhelm Schroer	EG D
Heinrich Tunnat	EK 9
Heinz Unglaube	EG C

EINSATZKOMMANDO SERVICE

As mentioned in the introduction, I do not believe that this investigation has uncovered one hundred percent of all the SS officers who served in the various *Einsatzkommandos*. But we do know of 380. The following is a distribution by *Einsatzkommando* of those officers who have been identified as serving with the various units on the eastern front only.

Table 14
EINSATZKOMMANDO OFFICERS
EINSATZKOMMANDO DISTRIBUTION

Einsatzgruppe A, Headquarters	**65**
Sonderkommando 1a	5
Sonderkommando 1b	13
Einsatzkommando 2	26
Einsatzkommando 3	5
Einsatzkommando Tilsit	11
Einsatzgruppe A, Total	***125***

Einsatzgruppe B, Headquarters 41
Sonderkommando 7a 14
Sonderkommando 7b 5
Einsatzkommando 8 14
Einsatzkommando 9 7
Vorkommando Moscow 5
***Einsatzgruppe B, Total* 86**

Einsatzgruppe C, Headquarters 41
Sonderkommando 4a 12
Sonderkommando 4b 11
Einsatzkommando 5 3
Einsatzkommando 6 8
***Einsatzgruppe C, Total* 75**

Einsatzgruppe D, Headquarters 42
Sonderkommando 10a 5
Sonderkommando 10b 5
Einsatzkommando 11a 5
Einsatzkommando 11b 3
Einsatzkommando 12 6
Sonderkommando Astrachan 0
***Einsatzgruppe D, Total* 66**

Einsatzgruppe z.b.V. 14

COMBAT FATALITIES

As earlier reported some SS *Einsatzkommando* officers went on to serve in front-line *Waffen-SS* units, while others took part in anti-partisan operations behind the lines. For some SS officers, these assignments proved fatal. Of the total number of *Einsatzkommando* officers identified in this work, it appears that ten, or some 2.6 percent – were later killed in action, missing in action and presumed dead, or died of wounds.[44] This compares to eight percent of all concentration camp officers who were later killed in action.

The most famous death involving a former *Einsatzkommando* officer was that of *SS-Brigadeführer* Walter Stahlecker. Stahlecker died of wounds inflicted by Soviet partisans in an ambush outside his headquarters at Krasnovardeisk on March 26, 1942.[45] At the time, he was leading an SD group, which included a company of Latvian security troops, in an operation against a partisan-held village.[46] Several others died as well. The following is a summary of those former *Einsatzkommando* officers believed to have been killed in combat:

Table 15
EINSATZKOMMANDO OFFICERS
KILLED IN ACTION

NAME	*EINSATZ-KOMMANDO SERVICE*	*DATE KILLED*
Dr. Humbert Achamer-Pifrader	EG A	25 April 1945
Dr. Walther Bierkamp	EG D	16 April 1945
Franz Grünzfelder	EG A, SK 1b	19 June 1942
Willi Huesch	EG C	26 Dec. 1942
Herbert Lange	EK 2	20 April 1945
Dr. Rudolf Lange	EG 2, EK 2	February 1945
Julius Plath	EG C	29 July 1943
Dr. Walter Stahlecker	EG A	23 March 1942
Alfred Tempfer	SK 7a	22 Sept. 1944
Dr. Rudolf Tröger	EK 16	18 June 1940

Seven officers who are believed to have been killed in action had previously served as *Einsatzkommando* commanders. One was killed in 1940. None of these officers were killed in action in 1941, four in 1942, one in 1943, one in 1944 and four in 1945. Five of those killed in action fell during their service with the *Einsatzkommandos*.

GENERAL OFFICERS

Nineteen SS officers who served in the *Einsatzkommandos* went on to achieve general officer rank. Himmler elevated two men to the grade of *SS-Obergruppenführer*, six officers to *SS-Gruppenführer* and eleven men to *SS-Brigadeführer*. These were small numbers when one considers that as of November 1944 there were ninety-two *SS-Obergruppenführer*, ninety-five *SS-Gruppenführer* and two-hundred seventy *SS-Brigadeführer* in service.[47] The following table lists these nineteen:

Table 16
EINSATZKOMMANDO OFFICERS
GENERAL OFFICERS

NAME	*GRADE*	*SS NUMBER*
Rudolf Querner	SS-Obergruppenführer	308240
Udo von Woyrsch	SS-Obergruppenführer	3689
Otto Hellwig	SS-Gruppenführer	272289
August von Meyszner	SS-Gruppenführer	263406
Arthur Nebe	SS-Gruppenführer	280152
Otto Ohlendorf	SS-Gruppenführer	880

Bruno Streckenbach	SS-Gruppenführer	14713
Dr. Max Thomas	SS-Gruppenführer	141341
Lothar Beutel	SS-Brigadeführer	2422
Dr. Walther Bierkamp	SS-Brigadeführer	310172
Dr. Karl Brunner	SS-Brigadeführer	107161
Ernst Damzog	SS-Brigadeführer	36157
Heinz Jost	SS-Brigadeführer	36263
Erich Naumann	SS-Brigadeführer	107496
Dr. Otto Rasch	SS-Brigadeführer	107100
Dr. Eberhard Schöngarth	SS-Brigadeführer	67174
Erwin Schulz	SS-Brigadeführer	107484
Dr. Franz Six	SS-Brigadeführer	107480
Dr. Walter Stahlecker	SS-Brigadeführer	73041

It is apparent that promotion to general officer was not based solely, or even to a great degree, on early membership in the SS – only four of these officers had SS numbers under 15,000.

POST-WAR JUSTICE AND PUNISHMENT

After the original International Trial of War Criminals at Nürnberg, the American Military Tribunal at this city held twelve further trials. These judicial proceedings covered a wide variety of transgressions from the "doctors' case" to the "IG-Farben case" to the SS Economic Administrative Office. The Trials of War Criminals before the International Military Tribunal, *United States of America vs. Otto Ohlendorf, et al.*, Case No. 9, was popularly called "The *Einsatzgruppen* Case." The proceedings lasted eight months, beginning on July 3, 1947 when indictments were filed against twenty-three defendants. Three were ultimately hanged.

French military tribunals handled various cases; in total, these French proceedings convicted 2,107 persons and sentenced 104 to death. One defendant condemned and executed was former *Einsatzkommando* officer Dr. Erich Isselhorst. Belgium convicted seventy-five persons of whom ten received death sentences. Poland convicted 5,358 German nationals, although we do not know the exact breakdown of sentences or which defendants had served in the *Einsatzkommandos*.[48]

Germany tried several thousand individuals for Nazi-crimes beginning in 1958. None of the defendants were sentenced to death, while seventy-nine appear to have received a sentence of life imprisonment.[49] Over fifty *Einsatzkommando* officers received prison sentences in the German judicial system. Many of the sentences of Life Imprisonment were later reduced. Some death sentences were also commuted. Most never faced judicial proceedings of any sort after the war. It appears from this study that seven *Einsatzkommando* officers actually were put to death as shown in the following table:

Table 17
EINSATZKOMMANDO OFFICERS
SENTENCED TO DEATH AND EXECUTED

NAME	*DATE EXECUTED*
Paul Blobel	7 June 1951
Dr. Wilhelm Fuchs	Unknown
Dr. Erich Isselhorst	23 February 1948
August von Meyszner	24 January 1947
Erich Naumann	7 June 1951
Otto Ohlendorf	7 June 1951
Dr. Eberhard Schöngarth	15 May 1946

Seventy-one other *Einsatzkommando* officers appear to have received lesser sentences ranging from less than five years incarceration to life imprisonment. This may not be a complete list, as the *Zentrale Stelle der Landesjustizverwaltungen*, the German institution charged with maintaining a record of Nazi crimes and corresponding legal proceedings, was less than interested in cooperating with this project.[50] For those millions of victims, post-war justice, or the apparent lack thereof, may seem somewhat out of proportion.

Notes:

[1] It is always possible that additional officers had a degree of proficiency in a language, but had no test results that would have warranted inclusion into his file of a particular language.

[2] The most prominent historian making this assertion was Gerald Reitlinger in *The SS: Alibi of a Nation 1922-1945*. (London: Arms and Armour Press, 1981), p.181..

[3] John R. Angolia, *For Führer and Fatherland; Military Awards of the Third Reich (Volume 1-2)*. (San Jose CA: R. James Bender, 1976), Vol 1, pp. 256, 337 and 343.

[4] Ibid.

[5] Ibid. pp. 356-357.

[6] Martin van Creveld, *Fighting Power*. (London: Arms and Armour Press, 1983), p.126.

[7] John R. Angolia, *On The Field of Honor, A History of the Knight's Cross Bearers (Volume 1-2)*. (San Jose, CA: R. James Bender, 1980), Vol 1, pp. 14-22.

[8] Ibid., pp. 108 and 125.

[9] Angolia, *For Führer, Vol 1*, pp. 366-367.

[10] Ibid., pp. 330-331.

[11] In reviewing the award of the War Service Cross in other services, we find that it was given to medical personnel, mechanics, transportation troops and other logistical staff.

[12] Ibid., pp. 300-302.

[13] While not recorded in many of the files, I believe that many more officers actually received awards and decorations.

[14] Award of the War Service Cross was frequently done on September 1, April 20 and January 30, the anniversaries of the beginning of the war, Hitler's birthday and the Nazi seizure of power, respectively.

[15] Ibid., pp. 80-81.

[16] Ibid., pp. 106-107.

[17] Ibid., pp. 408-410.

[18] Personalakt Dr. Humbert Achamer-Pifrader, Washington, D.C: National Archives Microfilm Publication A3343, Records of SS Officers from the Berlin Document Center, Roll SSO-002.

[19] Personalakt Friedrich Suhr, Washington, D.C: National Archives Microfilm Publication A3343, Records of SS Officers from the Berlin Document Center, Roll SSO-170B.

[20] Personalakt Dr. Rudolf Lange, Washington, D.C: National Archives Microfilm Publication A3343, Records of SS Officers from the Berlin Document Center, Roll SSO-241A.

[21] Segev, *Soldiers of Evil*, p.54.

[22] Höhne, *The Order of the Death's Head*, pp.134-135.

[23] This was gradually expanded to include more senior SS commanders regardless of membership number.

[24] *HSSPF – Höhere SS und Polizeiführer*, Higher SS and Police Leader, Himmler's regional commander in an area. Directly responsible to Himmler for the implementation of all measures related to the security of the state and the treatment of dangerous elements within their realm.

[25] Helmut Krausnick & Hans Buchheim, Martin Broszat and Hans-Adolf Jacobsen, *Anatomy of the SS State*. (New York: Walker and Company, 1968), pp. 250-253.

[26] *Statistisches Jahrbuch der Schutzstaffel der NSDAP 1937*. (Berlin, 1938).

[27] SS numbers are unknown for three officers in the study. Other than a small number who were honorary SS officers, the officers must each have had a number.

[28] The Blood Order had many different unofficial names to include: *Blutorden vom 9. November 1923*, *Ehrenzeichen am Band vom 9. November 1923*, *Erinnerungszeichen für aktive Kämpfer der nationalen Erhebung 1923* and *Ehrenzeichen der NSDAP vom 9. November 1923*.

[29] French MacLean, "The Unknown Generals – German Corps Commanders in World War II." (Masters Thesis, United States Army Command and General Staff College, 1938.)

[30] *Statistisches Jahrbuch der Schutzstaffel der NSDAP 1937*. (Berlin, 1938.)

[31] John Angloia, *For Führer and Fatherland: Political & Civil Awards of the Third Reich*. (San Jose, CA: R. James Bender Publishing, 1978), p. 178.

[32] *Statistisches Jahrbuch der Schutzstaffel der NSDAP 1937*. (Berlin, 1938.)

[33] 34 SS officers in the sample appear to either not have been members of the NSDAP; or if they were, it is not annotated in their files.

[34] Höhne, *The Order of the Death's Head*, p. 156.

[35] Koehl, *The Black Corps*, p.51.

[36] Marital status is unknown for 12 of the officers.

[37] At least through February 1945. The personnel files do not appear to have been adequately updated after this period.

[38] Gutman and Berenbaum, eds., *Anatomy of the Auschwitz Death Camp*, p.298.

[39] While most information concerning religious affiliation came from the officer's SS personnel file, some conversions back to religious faith appear to have occurred in many men sentenced to death after the war.

[40] *Statistisches Jahrbuch der Schutzstaffel der NSDAP 1938*. (Berlin, 1939.)

[41] George C. Browder, *Hitler's Enforcers: The Gestapo and the Security Service in the Nazi Revolution*. (New York: Oxford University Press, 1996), p. 264.

[42] Two officers are known to have served in the *Waffen-SS*, but exact units for them are unknown.

[43] Andrew Mollo, *Uniforms of the SS: Collected Edition, Volumes 1 to 6*. (London: Windrow & Greene, 1997), pp. 369-370.

[44] Killed in Action (KIA) refers to an individual who is killed outright in combat or who dies shortly thereafter on the battlefield. Missing in Action (MIA) is generally categorized when a body is not recovered. An individual classified as Died of Wounds (DOW) is one who expires after reaching medical attention.

[45] Reitlinger, *The House Built on Sand*, p. 233.

[46] Andrew Ezergailis, *The Holocaust in Latvia, 1941-1944*. (Riga, Latvia: The Historical Institute of Latvia, 1996), p. 147.

[47] *Dienstaltersliste der Schutzstaffel der N.S.D.A.P., Stand vom 9. November 1944*. (Reprinted by INFORA Establishment, Vaduz, Fürstentum Liechtenstein, 1985.)

[48] Ibid., pp. 29-31.

[49] Ibid., pp.122-123.

[450] Letter to the author, 19 September 1997, from the *Zentrale Stelle der Landesjustizverwaltungen*. German privacy laws undoubtedly entered into their decision-making. For example, in post-war German trials concerning warcrimes, defendants who were acquitted are identified in court proceedings only by the first initial of their last name, a date of birth and a place of birth – never a complete name. Fortunately, the National Archives (as well as the USHMM) has an alphabetical list of all SS officers. It is a long process to go through every SS officer whose last name begins with a certain initial and match that up with a date and place of birth, but it can be done – and was.

4

CONCLUSIONS

Thank God that sow's gone to the butcher.[1]

- Waffen-SS General Sepp Dietrich upon hearing of Heydrich's death, 1942

THE "TYPICAL" EINSATZKOMMANDO OFFICER

While each individual officer possessed unique characteristics, with a sample this size it is possible to develop a profile for those men who served in the *Einsatzkommandos*. A "typical" SS officer from the *Einsatzkommandos* seems to have been relatively young, in his early thirties, and likely to have been born somewhere other than one of Germany's largest cities. If he did come from a large city, it was most probably Berlin. Similar data for all early SD officers show that 45 percent came from cities of over 100,000 inhabitants, while 39 percent hailed from small towns of less than 25,000 citizens.[2] He was overwhelmingly likely to be married and presumably professed to be agnostic, although his actual religious convictions in private may have been closer to the religion in which he grew up. He was likely to be highly educated, graduating from a prestigious university in either Germany or Austria; his pre-SD profession was most prone to have been that of a lawyer. The "typical" *Einsatzkommando* SS officer did not later serve in the *Waffen-SS* unlike his concentration camp associate who likely did. He would have been in the middle of the commissioned rank system, *SS-Hauptsturmführer*, or a field grade officer such as an *SS-Sturmbannführer* or *SS-Obersturmbannführer*. His highest award probably was the War Service Cross 1st Class, although quite a few possessed a grade of the Iron Cross. While some officers appear to have been punished for various disciplinary infractions during the war, many had spotless records and seem to have been model citizens by the standards of any society. The "typical" *Einsatzkommando* officer stood a good chance of surviving the war and almost an equally good chance of avoiding serious judicial proceedings in the post-war years. While many civilian occupations are represented in this population, service related to the legal field seems to figure prominently. Given the actuarial tables for men in the twentieth century, it is most likely that our "typical" officer resumed civilian life in Germany or perhaps Austria after the war – most probably in some career legal position, raised a family, and died in the 1970s or 1980s.

Based on the analysis of data, I would like to propose several larger conclusions – conclusions made possible by looking at the aggregate statistics of this large SS officer sample.

SONDERKOMMANDO 1005 – "THE TASK OF FOOLS"

Historians have widely discussed the German attempt to cover up the extent of the monstrous crimes at the concentration camps and *Einsatzkommando* killing fields in the east. I believe their motivation was two-fold. First, many Nazis probably felt some doubt as to who would ultimately win the war. If the victors turned out to be the allies, those personnel in the *Einsatzkommando* would receive harsh treatment if their crimes were uncovered. More importantly, despite some post-war works to the contrary, I believe the vast majority of the German people would not have approved of the mass killings if they had known the gory details. It is my opion that the bulk of the Wehrmacht officers were honorable men as were a large percentage of Germans on the home front. While they had a general knowledge that Jews, Communists, homosexuals and other persecuted groups, were being resettled out of Germany or incarcerated in concentration camps, the average German did not – in my opinion – comprehend the enormity of what was transpiring behind the barbed-wire or at the front-line. Had they known, I feel there would have been some type of mass unrest or complaint.[3] In fact, it was one such complaint that spurred the formation of *Sonderkommando 1005* in the first place.

The operation's code name originated in a letter from Gestapo chief Heinrich Müller to Deputy Foreign Minister Martin Luther. The letter relayed an anonymous complaint concerning corpses in the Warthegau district. The letter received a file number – in this case 1005 – and it was from this number that subsequent instructions were undertaken. The task commenced in June 1942 when *SS-Standartenführer* Paul Blobel was appointed to head up Operation (*Akten*) 1005.[4] Not all *Einsatzgruppe* commanders were enthused with the project – *SS-Gruppenführer* Dr. Max Thomas of *Einsatzgruppe C* called the mission "the task of fools."[5]

Some have attributed *Sonderkommando 1005* to Reinhard Heydrich just before his death, while others credit the aforementioned Heinrich Müller.[6] In analyzing those officers identified as serving with the project, however, I believe we see the hand of Heinrich Himmler as well. The following table will help with this assertion:

Table 18
SONDERKOMMANDO 1005 OFFICERS
SS AND PARTY MEMBERSHIP

NAME	***SS NUMBER***	***NSDAP NUMBER***
Paul Blobel (Commander)	**29100**	844662
Günther Fuchs	280145	239728
Karl-Arthur Harder	**4271**	173750
Walter Helfsgott	327242	4750512
Max Krahner	**9777**	472617
Hanns-Elmar Legath	280487	None
Franz Radif	**2675**	**51198**
Hermann Rohlfing	280129	5632257
Walter Schallock	**5738**	315477
Dr. Friedrich Seekel	386689	None
Hans-Fritz Sohns	107396	**10820**
Georg Winkler	323874	6891074
Fritz Zietlow	**6126**	**36519**

Of the thirteen men we can positively identify as *Sonderkommando 1005* officers, five have extremely low SS numbers under 10000, with a sixth under 30000. Three men had NSDAP numbers qualifying them for Golden Party Badges. Hans-Fritz Sohns was a Blood Order recipient. The selection of these officers bear the "fingerprints" of Himmler. We have seen how the *Reichsführer-SS* valued early SS membership. This a strong indicator that the *Reichsführer-SS* issued guidance on what was to be done and what type of men would served in the one commando that would ultimately know where "all the bodies were buried."

EINSATZKOMMANDO ACTIONS – COMBAT OR NOT?

During the peak of the struggle between Germany and the Soviet Union, some 250,000 partisans battled against 500,000 men in the security forces of the Reich. Colonel General Alfred Jodl, Chief of Operations in the Wehrmacht High Command, surmised after the war that German casualties caused by partisan action numbered somewhat less than 50,000. Later postwar estimates put German losses in this fight at 15 - 20,000.[7] In return, the Germans exacted a toll certainly in the millions, if we count actual Soviet partisans, active partisan supporters, inactive partisan families and totally oblivious bystanders. The Operational Situation Reports of the *Einsatzgruppen* reflect the wide disparity of victims and reflect the fusion of these many groups:[8]

> Jews, intellectual Jews, Jewish activists, wandering Jews, rebellious Jews, partisans, Gypsies, communist party functionaries, politruks, commissars, NKVD agents, Asiatics, Krimtchaks, guerrillas, Bolsheviks, hostages, prisoners of war, saboteurs, agitators, political agitators, public nuisances, neglected juveniles, unreliable elements, racially inferior elements, inferior elements, hostile elements, asocials, asocial elements, suspicious elements, undesirable elements, criminals, criminal elements, politically suspicious persons, terrorists, delinquents, murderers, snipers, plunderers, spreaders of propaganda, mentally inferior persons, mental patients, spies, informers, instigators, accomplices, forgers, civilians, pests, collective farm leaders, arsonists.

The following statement written by *SS-Brigadeführer* Walter Stahlecker, commander of *Einsatzgruppe A*, during the war illuminates the way in which the anti-partisan effort blended with the Final Solution:[9]

The network of information, thus built up yielded much information for the *Einsatzgruppe A*, thus enabling them to surround more narrowly the quarters of the partisans. In particular, information was obtained concerning the villagers who had given food or provisional shelter to partisans. On the basis of these reports a great many villages were combed out. After a village had been surrounded, all the inhabitants were forcibly shepherded into one square. The persons suspected on account of confidential information and other villagers were interrogated, and thus it was possible in most cases to find the people who had helped the partisans. These were either shot offhand or if further interrogations promised useful information, taken to headquarters. After the interrogation they were shot. In order to obtain a deterring effect, the houses of those who helped the partisans were burned down on several occasions. The population which had congregated was told of the reasons for the punitive measures. At the same time they were threatened that the whole village would be burned down if the partisans were helped once more and if partisans appearing in the village were not reported as quickly as possible. *The tactics, to put terror against terror, succeeded marvelously.*

The original intent of the mission of the *Einsatzgruppen* was murder. It appears that the German system of awards demonstrated that *Einsatzgruppe* action was sometimes directly combat related – and acknowledged as such, not only by the SS, but also by the army as well. The following table helps illustrate the linkage of army and SS from that vantage point:

Table 19
EINSATZKOMMANDO OFFICERS
ARMY-APPROVED AWARDS

Name	*Unit*	*Award*[10]	*Army General*	*Command*
Heinrich Bergmann	EG A	WSC 2nd	GEN Lindemann	Army Group North
" "	EG A	WSC 1st	LTG Loch	Army Group North
Arno Besekow[11]	EK 2	WSC 2nd	GFM von Leeb	Army Group North
Erich Ehrlinger	EG B	IC 1st	LTG Friderici	Rear Area, Army Group South
Leopold Fischer	EK 2	WSC 2nd	GEN Laux	16th Army
Hans Kraus	SK 1b	IC 2nd	LTG von Arnim	XXXIXth Corps
Waldemar Krause	SK 4b	IC 2nd	LTG Gräser	4th Panzer Army
Erich Kubiak	EK 11b	IC 2nd	GEN von Manstein	11th Army
Rudolf Lange	EK 2	IC 2nd	GEN Lindemann	Army Group North
Johann Meixner	EG A	IC 1st	GEN Lindemann	Army Group North
Otto Ohlendorf	EG D	WSC 1st	GFM Keitel	OKW
Rudolf Schwietering	EG 2	WSC 2nd	GEN Laux	16th Army
Ludwig Teichmann	EG E	WSC 2nd	LTG Bader	Army Commander, Serbia
Erwin Weinmann	SK 4a	WSC 2nd	GFM Keitel	OKW
Richard Wiechert	EG A	WSC 2nd	GFM Keitel	OKW

Einsatzkommando officers received Iron Crosses, Infantry Assault Badges and other awards, just like front-line soldiers did. Many of the awards were approved by army leaders. It is clear that, unlike service at a concentration camp, the German leadership categorized service in an *Einsatzgruppe* as at least equivalent to anti-partisan duty, if not outright front-line service in many cases – front-line service in a war of annihilation.

SD OFFICERS AS EINSATZKOMMANDO LEADERS ASSET OR LIABILITY?

There has been an ongoing debate among scholars concerning which German senior leaders planned and executed the Final Solution – a portion of which was carried out by the *Einsatzgruppen*.

It is my opinion that Adolf Hitler saw the issue of the Jews and selected other ethnic groups in the macro sense. The Führer wanted all "undesirables" eliminated. In Hitler's mind, Germany could never truly be capable of world domination until the state was free of both Jewish presence and influence, and until the world at large was devoid of any Jewish capability to stop, or even hinder, German expansion. Most likely Hitler thought through the issue in enough detail to come to the conclusion that "free" meant "dead."

I believe that Heinrich Himmler understood the global vision of his boss. He also realized that Adolf Hitler was a bit fuzzy about some of the details concerning the "how" and "when" of the Final Solution – Hitler for his part probably believed that his chief lieutenants would all see the problem as clearly as he did. Himmler understood the "when." He comprehended that an undertaking that consisted of murdering millions of people – not only in Germany but also in western and eastern Europe – could only be accomplished under the confusion and "fog" of war. Germany was planning a war that would engulf Europe. As the early campaigns, such as Poland, Scandinavia and France, ended in swift victory, there was an ever-increasing probability that Hitler could achieve all his territorial ambitions very soon. So the "when" in Himmler's mind became "now."[12]

What Himmler seems to have had difficulty conceiving was the "how" – just how immense a task this would prove to be – hence his frequent visits to selected sites of the Final Solution, offering suggestions here and there. So he entrusted Reinhard Heydrich with that aspect. Or perhaps Reinhard Heydrich sensed that Himmler did not grasp the magnitude of such an undertaking and therefore Heydrich felt it necessary to exert his own initiative to determine how this would be accomplished. Conceivably he felt that at the successful conclusion of the Final Solution, he could turn to Hitler and say to the effect of all your disciples it was only I who truly understood what you really wanted – I shared your vision as to what must be done.

No one in the Nazi hierarchy could keep up with Reinhard Heydrich's energy, memory and initiative. He possessed an executive-type instinct; he was a problem-solver – even more importantly, he was a problem-anticipator. Heydrich maintained the perspective to operate within some ill-defined limits of authority; he knew where his own authority ended and where Himmler's, as well as Hitler's, began. With this understanding, Heydrich could function in a unique way with respect to his superior. Perhaps equally important, Heydrich was the master of the position paper, the succinct memo and the mesmerizing briefing.[13]

Reinhard Heydrich was an early advocate for the Final Solution. Many historians now believe that by the summer of 1940, Reinhard Heydrich saw that the strategic direction of the war was leading to a European Nazi hegemony. This, in turn, would establish the conditions for a "territorial Final Solution" as he professed in a letter to Joachim von Ribbentrop, the German Foreign Minister, in June 1940. The distinguished military historian Charles Sydnor, Jr. has even recently shown through triangulation, that Heydrich more than likely submitted a written plan for the Final Solution in January 1941 – some five months before the *Einsatzkommandos* would ply their deadly trade.[14]

However, Heydrich made serious miscalculations; some were due to outside influences, some resulted from his own misjudgments. First, it is quite possible that Heydrich was misinformed perhaps by a count of several million as the exact extent of the number of Jews, gypsies, communist functionaries and other "undesirables" the Germans would encounter as they expanded their empire.[15] Second, Heydrich did not have control of the existing, pre-1941 concentration camps. His SD could put individuals into the concentration camps, but they could not control what happened to these victims once they disappeared behind the barbed-wire. Himmler was far too shrewd to have ever given Heydrich and the SD control of the concentration camp system. That remained with men such as Theodor Eicke, Richard Glücks and Oswald Pohl. And in the Byzantine world of the SS, all three men probably disliked, or at least mistrusted, Reinhard Heydrich.

However, the chief of the SD did control the *Einsatzgruppen* and *Einsatzkommandos*. He could staff them with officers he selected from within his domain and whose loyalty could be assured. Himmler reserved the right of final decision concerning the commanders of these units.[16] But it appears that he went along with Heydrich's recommendations. Despite the magnitude of the task, Heydrich could select officers who would make the *Einsatzkommandos* so efficient that they could complete the mission despite the difficulties. **But Reinhard Heydrich picked the wrong men for the job.**

What did Heydrich have to work with? The SD was not as large as many party and military organizations in Germany, but it did field a considerable number of personnel. By January 31, 1938 the SD had some 5,050 regular and honorary members; this total had risen to 7,230 by December 1938.[17] Many SD officers came from the upper middle class, many of whom were intellectuals who had graduated from the university system. Of the early SD officers, 42 percent had grade school education, 41 percent had some form of higher education and 14 percent possessed doctorate degrees. Forty-seven percent of the early SD men had their civilian careers disrupted by the effects of the Great Depression. Fifty-five percent of the early SD had joined the SS first and then the SD.[18] Many were also products of the German Youth Movement *(Hitler Jugend)*. Their membership in the SD gave the organization a legalistic and intellectual atmosphere that was quite foreign to the front-line-soldier socialism of the SS and the lower-middle-class hubris of the early years of National Socialism.[19]

To train these personnel, the SD established a training school at Bernau near Berlin. Specialists from various departments of the RSHA provided instruction in a variety of subjects. SD personnel coming directly from the Security Police received training at the Leaders' School of the Security Police and SD in Berlin. Other schools included the Security Police School at Fürstenberg, the SD Communications School at Schloss Grünberg, as well as the previously mentioned Border Police School at Pretsch, northeast of Leipzig. The goal of all the training was to prepare an SD officer who could efficiently perform in both the Gestapo and Kripo, although this was never completely achieved. To remedy this, officers were frequently assigned to Gestapo and Kripo offices to gain "on the job" experience.[20]

What Heydrich probably thought he needed as competencies in his *Einsatzkommando* leaders were six-fold:

- experience in combat – as the SS in the *Einsatzkommando* could not be certain that the intended victims would not fight back,
- familiarity with Russian (and Baltic) customs, people and terrain,
- proficiency in foreign languages applicable to the area of operations,
- experience in undertakings requiring logistical expertise,
- the ability to improvise in constantly changing conditions,
- cold-blooded ideological ruthlessness.

Since most members of the SD never served in the *Waffen-SS*, and thus would not have served in action in the early campaigns of World War II, Heydrich would have had to look for seasoning in World War I to validate the experience in combat requirement. On the whole, seventeen percent of all *Einsatzkommando* officers served in this conflict – not nearly as many as Heydrich could have pressed into this service from the manpower pool of available officers in the SD.

As stated earlier, many post-war sources state that the *Einsatzkommando* officers were familiar with Russian customs, people, terrain and were proficient in those foreign languages applicable to the potential *Einsatzkommando* areas of operation. But the review of their officer personnel files does not reveal this statement to be correct. Only twenty-four officers were born in Russia, Latvia, Lithuania or Estonia. Personnel records indicate that only seventeen of the officers were fluent in Russian, with twenty-two fluent in a related language such as Latvian or Polish. The following table lists these "Ethnic Germans" who would have been – from Heydrich's standpoint – excellent assets for a mission of this nature:

Table 20
EINSATZKOMMANDO OFFICERS
"ETHNIC GERMANS"

NAME	*BIRTHPLACE*	*UNIT*
Waldemar Amelung	Kopjoni, Russia	EG A
Waldemar Borck	St. Petersburg	EK 7a
Dr. Heinrich Bosse	Riga	EG A
Leo Brauer	Minsk	EG B
Dr. Friedrich Buchardt	Riga	EG B, EK 9
Hans-Eugen Dressler	Moscow	EG A
Werner Girgensohn	Riga	EG B
Wilhelm Grieffenberger	St. Petersburg	EK 9
Ernst Hayde	Riga	EG D
Waldemar Klingelhöfer	Moscow	Vorkommando Moscow
Andreas von Koskull	Talsen, Russia	EG C, EK 6
Hans Kraus	Riga	EK 3, SK 1b
Otto Kraus	Riga	EG A
Dr. Erhard Kroeger	Riga	EK 6
Dr. Peter Kroeger	Riga	EG C
Egon Loleit	Moscow	EG C
Alexander Mariunas	Dewynaney, Russ.	EG B
Waldemar von Radetzky	Moscow	EG A
Waldemar Schiemann	St. Petersburg	EG A
Hans Schneider	Riga	EG B
Nikolaus Tolle	Vladivostok	SK 1b
Heinrich Wiens	Muntau, Ukraine	EK 12

Nor were the other officers well grounded in undertakings requiring logistical expertise. Lawyers and economists were hardly professionals who know much about supply or transportation. Sixty-six had been in business of some type, which may have brought them into the realm of logistics; even these positions, however, did not equip the future officers for the immense problems of supply and transportation in the expanse of the Soviet Union. Running a haberdashery on the Marienplatz in Munich was far different than provisioning a battalion in the steppes of Russia – in the dead of winter.

As to their suitability – let us not impart our own subjective evaluations of men long gone, but rather examine a selection of officer efficiency reports from the personnel files of these men. The following is a report on *SS-Sturmbannführer* Kurt Graaf, commander of *Einsatzkommando 1c*: (all highlighted areas by the author)[21]

> During the time of August 1 to November 28, 1942, *SS-Sturmbannführer* Graaf was under my command in my capacity as the leader of *Einsatzkommando 1*. During that

time, he led *Teilkommando* Krasnogvardeisk, then for some time was active in the staff of the commando handling organizational matters and then led the Jagdkommando 13. With this commando he was ordered to White Russia at the end of November 1942.

It is not possible for me to give a detailed and comprehensive evaluation of the personality of *SS-Sturmbannführer* Graaf because of the short time he spent under my command. In addition, Graaf also did not have an opportunity during that time to distinguish himself in any special way. **The organizational work with which he was tasked for some time and the preparation for a planned new engagement in part were not his forte. I assume that he also was somewhat lacking in planning capacity and to pursue a goal in this work in order to live up to these tasks.** However, Graaf kept good connections with the Wehrmacht and service authorities within the area of the commando and he succeeded in having a good rapport everywhere.

It is hard to judge how much the successes of the *Jagdkommando 13*, in the engagements southeast of Luga, can be traced back to the leader of the commando.

In my opinion, his strength lies purely in the field of communications, where within the framework of the *Einsatzkommando* he was able to produce valuable information on several occasions and he also diligently and successfully worked on the establishment of the communication network within the active area of the unit. Because of his merits in this area, I have also recommended that Graaf be given the War Service Cross 2nd Class.

I have the impression that the personality of Graaf is not yet mature enough and is slightly unbalanced and that he hardly does anything to fight against his own personal weaknesses and to broaden his horizon when confronted with people with superior traits. He did not always succeed in gaining the respect of the people under him, despite the fact that he undoubtedly was spirited and enthusiastic.

A second report, that concerning Eduard Strauch, also paints a dim view of the talents and capacities of one *Einsatzkommando* officer – a senior officer who once commanded not one, but two, *Einsatzkommandos*:[22]

SS-Obersturmbannführer Strauch has been the commander of the Security Police and the SD, White Russia, in Minsk since February of 1942. He is married and the father of two children. He as well as his family are atheists. He is the owner of the Iron Cross Second Class, the War Service Cross 2nd Class with Swords and the Service Award of the NSDAP in Bronze.

His personality is marked most strongly by his refusal to compromise which borders on harshness, especially when defending and convincing others in connection with philosophical questions. His deliberations and conclusions necessary for this are simple and uncomplicated. In all difficult situations he has proven to be a courageous and extremely cold-blooded leader.

His emotional character is not developed particularly strongly. It is hard for him to put himself into other people's shoes and, therefore, he gains little and has difficulty in making correct judgments. This may also be the basis why he distrusted his troops, which again made him susceptible for gossip. His actions are influenced primarily by emotions and often without using common sense.

His reactions are impulsive and explosive. This results in a strong imbalance of his character, injustice in leading others as well as a misunderstanding between fundamental attitude and action. This explains the fact that he often made decisions too quickly and without having thought them through. This side of his character is expressed most severely under the impeding influence of alcohol.

His personal behavior as the leader of the service office in Minsk was not without influence on his men under him, especially due to the alcoholic excesses. *SS-Obersturmbannführer* Strauch must be held responsible for the unhealthy atmosphere within the service office of the Commander of Security Police and the SD, White Russia, in Minsk. However, it must be taken into consideration that the conditions in White Russia in no way resembled those in the three Baltic states. White Russia is not peaceful. Minsk offers nothing. Repeatedly, the members of the service office were nearly exclusively engaged in fighting against bandits. The constant momentum of danger, the unusual way of life and the lack of a sex life must be counted as the reasons for alcoholic excesses.

His professional accomplishments are good. **Organizational abilities are not particularly well developed.**

Due to service-connected considerations, I find it absolutely necessary that SS-Obersturmbannführer Strauch be replaced and recommend that he be transferred to more orderly conditions.

Next is a report on Heinz Richter written after he returned from the East. Richter was an *Einsatzkommando* commander as well. His superior pulls no punches in his assessment of Richter's ability in this role.[23]

SS-Sturmbannführer Heinz Richter successfully passed the first Government Examination for Lawyers in 1930 and the second one in 1934. He was nominated judge in 1938, and superior judge on April 20, 1943. After he had passed the exams, Richter immediately entered the services of the Security Police. During the years 1936 to 1938, Richter was the commander of the Gestapo office at Allenstein; after that he was transferred to the RSHA. After three quarters of a year's service with the Commanding Officer in Smolensk, Richter came to Paris as leader for investigations. **In the East, Richter was a failure as a commander. The chief of the Einsatzgruppe B characterized Richter as the type of person who is not made to be an *Einsatzkommando* leader.** However, at the right place, Richter can be a very valuable asset. Therefore, in November of 1942 Richter was ordered to the staff of the commanding officer in Paris and there he was engaged as legal officer and leader of investigations. The task to construct from the bottom up the sphere of the investigation leader and SS-legal officer was solved by Richter in an exemplary manner. While working on individual cases, he demonstrated conscientiousness and an awareness of responsibility, next to a healthy secure instinct for correct realistic judgment and behavior in each separate case. With his tactics and practice of interrogations, he knows how to proceed cleverly by using psychology. Even though the BdS Paris states in its valuation that Richter is somewhat difficult in his attitude – he does not always seriously consider everything a problem – but does second a promotion of Richter to *SS-Obersturmbannführer* in view of his overall attitude.

Since no reasons for stopping a promotion of Richter to *SS-Obersturmbannführer* exist, the promotion is to be effective as of November 9, 1943, in view of his service grade in the security police and his active service in the movement before Hitler's take-over of power.

In addition to demonstrating poor performance, other *Einsatzkommando* officers received disciplinary sanctions for outrageous conduct. *SS-Standartenführer* Heinz Seetzen was so disciplined in 1944 with the following letter:[24]

SS-Standartenführer Heinz Seetzen:
Reasons for strong reprimand

While engaged as the leader of a Special Commando of the Security Police and the SD during the years 1941 and 1942, you personally and at times through the contacts of members of the Commando have appropriated postage stamps from Russian post offices and deserted houses and kept them for yourself. **With that, you not only have fulfilled the evidence of looting, but also have demonstrated quite a bad example to the men under your command.**

The fact that I have refrained from introducing SS and police judicial proceedings against you is due to the consideration that otherwise you were a good leader for your commando and could be counted on in difficult situations. However, I now expect that in the future you will painstakingly make the effort that your conduct will be such as is demanded from a member of the SS, especially from a leader.

You have the right to file your rebuttal against this complaint within seven days – counted from the day it was handed to you – through legal channels, addressed to the Main Office SS-Tribunal in Munich.

A member of *Sonderkommando 1005* was also involved in a serious incident. The unit, which was charged with erasing all evidence of the mass murders – the bodies – used Jewish labor groups for the task. Each group of workers was dispatched shortly thereafter to ensure no witnesses would be left to tell the tale. At Kovno, the unthinkable happened, a large group of Jews escaped.[25]

During the night of December 25 to December 26, 1943, a total of 64 Jewish workers escaped from Fort 9 at Kauen. With the assistance of the Army and the Police, search procedures were put into place, with the success that a total of 34 escapees have been recaptured so far and rendered harmless. (Author's note: "rendered harmless" equals murdered.)

The escape itself had been prepared by a small group of Jews within the work commando. A Jew who was engaged in internal service at Fort 9 had spare keys made and released the Jews from their cells after the change of the guards. After sawing through an iron plate which was about 5 mm thick, the Jews descended from the fort on a rope and then, by means of a wooden ladder, they escaped over the former fortification wall into the open. After leaving the fort, the escaping Jews split up into three groups. The organizer of the scheme as well as all other Jews who were participating in a primary position where among those Jews who have been recaptured so far. The search for the other escapees is being continued vigorously.

The investigation regarding the question of guilt has shown that *SS-Obersturmführer* Radif and Gendarmerie Sergeant Apelt **have acted carelessly**. They had not sufficiently regulated and controlled the quartering and guarding, despite the fact that a short time prior to this the Commander of the Security Police and of the SD - Ostland had pointed out with urgency to the commanders and unit commandos of his district the particular necessity of sufficient security, even if other tasks had to remain pending for the moment. Both men held responsible were taken into custody.

The characteristics described above are damning from an efficiency standpoint: looting, setting a poor example for subordinates, failure as a commander, imbalance of character, alcohol abuse, personal weakness, not respecting and lacking in planning capability are not the traits that Heydrich would have desired in selecting officers for a task of this magnitude. Perhaps he had another motive.

I believe that Reinhard Heydrich picked SD officers to participate in the *Einsatzgruppen* actions so they would share in the monstrous guilt – thus cementing their loyalties to the organization and to Heydrich himself. He also selected these men so they would gain experience to prepare them for the future missions of the SD. But the Final Solution of the Jewish question, the Final Solution for the intelligentsia and Communist Party functionaries of the Slavs in the east could also be viewed, in effect, as the final major mission of the SD. The successful conclusion of the Final Solution would serve notice that the Thousand Year Reich was immutably entrenched as the dominant power in Europe. After the Final Solution, the SD's, and by definition Heydrich's, place as a controlling element of the Thousand Year Reich would be secure.

But the *Einsatzkommandos*, even though they inflicted terrible damage, were unable to meet the task. Well over one million Jews in the German-overrun territories of the Soviet Union survived as did tens of thousands of Communist functionaries who fled to join the partisan movement.

Nevertheless, the *Einsatzkommandos* were terrible and wrought unspeakable harm on hundreds of thousands of families wherever the shadow of the SD darkened the ground. Brigadier General Telford Taylor, in his prosecution of several of the commander's of the *Einsatzgruppen* and *Einsatzkommandos* after the war, declared:[26]

> The Defendants were all officers in the SS – most of them high ranking – and all of them joined the SS years before the time, during the latter part of the war, when compulsory recruiting for the *Waffen-SS* began. The close association of all the defendants with one of the most horrible crimes of the SS upon which great stress was laid by the International Military Tribunal in rendering the declaration of criminality, needs no further emphasis here.

But if we do not emphasize these past crimes today – if we do forget, or even worse ignore them, then we will have done history a grave disservice. Even worse, we will have done the hundreds of thousands of victims a grave injustice. The *Einsatzgruppen* and *Einsatzkommandos,* and the SS officers who led them, were the most terrible scourge to descend upon Europe since the Black Death. Ignoring the causes of the Bubonic Plague could harm our health; ignoring these mass murderers, these field men, would wound our souls.

Notes:

[1] Heinz Höhne, *The Order of the Death's Head*: Translated by Richard Barry. (New York: Coward-McCann, 1970), p.166.

[2] Lecture by George C. Browder, U.S. Holocaust Memorial Museum, January 27, 1998.

[3] Perhaps the Germans simply did not want to know what was happening as long as things were progressing well for the average man in the street. However, before we condemn them for this attitude, it may be prudent to reflect on how many Americans in our own era really want to know all the details of what goes on in our own jails and prisons, our abortion clinics, our nursing homes, Dr. Jack Kavorkian's office or even the Oval Office. "It's the economy stupid!" was probably said as often in 1939 Germany as it is in 1998 America.

[4] Yitzak Arad, *Belzec, Sobibór, Treblinka: The Operation Reinhard Death Camps*. (Bloomington, IN: Indiana University Press, 1987), p.170.

[5] Shmuel Spector, "Aktion 1005", *Holocaust and Genocide Studies*, Vol.5 No.2. (Oxford, England: Pergamon Press, 1990), p.172.

[6] Yitzak Arad, *Belzec, Sobibór, Treblinka: The Operation Reinhard Death Camps*. (Bloomington, IN: Indiana University Press, 1987), p.170.

[7] Matthew Cooper, *The Nazi War Against Soviet Partisans, 1941-1944*. (New York: Stein & Day Publishers, 1979), pp. xii - xiii.

[8] Ronald Headland, *Messages of Murder*, p. 54.

[9] International Military Tribunal Nürnberg, *Trials of War Criminals before the International Military Tribunal, Volume IV, United States of America vs. Otto Ohlendorf, et al., Case No. 9.*, p.168.

[10] IC 1st = Iron Cross 1st Class. IC 2nd = Iron Cross 2nd Class, WSC 1st = War Service Cross 1st Class, WSC 2nd = War Service Cross 2nd Class

[11] Awarded the War Service Cross 2nd Class on 20 December 1941 along with 43 other members of EG A.

[12] My own conclusions concerning Himmler are more eloquently stated in Richard Breitman's *The Architect of Genocide: Himmler and the Final Solution*. (New York: Alfred A. Knopf, 1991), pp. 246-248.

[13] United States Holocaust Memorial Museum. Center for Advanced Holocaust Studies Presentation, June 9, 1998: *Reinhard Heydrich and the Early Planning for the Final Solution*, by Charles W. Sydnor, Jr., author *Soldiers of Destruction: The SS Death's Head Division, 1933-1945*.

[14] United States Holocaust Memorial Museum. Center for Advanced Holocaust Studies Presentation, June 9, 1998: *Reinhard Heydrich and the Early Planning for the Final Solution*, by Charles W. Sydnor, Jr., author *Soldiers of Destruction: The SS Death's Head Division, 1933-1945*.

[15] Raul Hilberg estimates that 4,000,000 Jews were living in territories later overrun by the German army. They were located in: the Baltic area (260,000), former Polish territory (1,350,000), Bukovina and Bessarabia (30,000), Ukraine (1,533,000), White Russia (375,000), Crimea (50,000) and other areas seized by the Germans (200,000). Source: Raul Hilberg, *The Destruction of the European Jews*. (Revised edition), pp. 1212-1220.

[16] Richard Breitman, *The Architect of Genocide: Himmler and the Final Solution*. (New York: Alfred A. Knopf, 1991), pp. 150-151.

[17] Andrew Mollo, *Uniforms of the SS: Collected Edition, Volumes 1 to 6*. (London: Windrow & Greene, 1997), p. 341.

[18] Lecture by George C. Browder, U.S. Holocaust Memorial Museum, January 27, 1998.

[19] Höhne, *The Order of the Death's Head*, p. 135.

[20] Ibid., p. 346.

[21] Personalakt Kurt Graaf, Washington, D.C: National Archives Microfilm Publication A3343, Records of SS Officers from the Berlin Document Center, Roll SSO-026A.

[22] Personalakt Eduard Strauch, Washington, D.C: National Archives Microfilm Publication A3343, Records of SS Officers from the Berlin Document Center, Roll SSO-165B.

[23] Personalakt Heinz Richter, Washington, D.C: National Archives Microfilm Publication A3343, Records of SS Officers from the Berlin Document Center, Roll SSO-027B.

[24] Personalakt Heinz Seetzen, Washington, D.C: National Archives Microfilm Publication A3343, Records of SS Officers from the Berlin Document Center, Roll SSO-129B.

[25] Personalakt Radif, Washington, D.C: National Archives Microfilm Publication A3343, Records of SS Officers from the Berlin Document Center, Roll SSO-002B.

[26] International Military Tribunal Nürnberg, *Trials of War Criminals before the International Military Tribunal, Volume IV, United States of America vs. Otto Ohlendorf, et al., Case No. 9*. (Washington, DC: U.S. Government Printing Office, 1949.), p. 378.

APPENDICES

APPENDIX 1: SS RANKS

SS-Reichsführer (Reichsführer-SS)	Reichs Leader
SS-Oberstgruppenführer	General
SS-Obergruppenführer	Lieutenant General
SS-Gruppenführer	Major General
SS-Brigadeführer	Brigadier General
SS-Oberführer	Senior Colonel
SS-Standartenführer	Colonel
SS-Obersturmbannführer	Lieutenant Colonel
SS-Sturmbannführer	Major
SS-Hauptsturmführer	Captain
SS-Obersturmführer	First Lieutenant
SS-Untersturmführer	Second Lieutenant
SS-Sturmscharführer	Sergeant Major
SS-Hauptscharführer	Master Sergeant
SS-Oberscharführer	Sergeant First Class
SS-Scharführer	Staff Sergeant
SS-Unterscharführer	Sergeant
SS-Rottenführer	Corporal
SS-Sturmmann	Acting Corporal
SS-Oberschütze	Private First Class
SS-Schütze	Private

APPENDIX 2: SS PERSONNEL GLOSSARY

The following glossary of German terms – many of which are used throughout the personnel files of the SS field officers – and their English translations, are provided to facilitate further research:

Abschied – discharge/resignation

Akten – documents, records, files

Allgemeine SS – the general SS, the overall body of the SS, distinct from the Waffen-SS.

Alte Kämpfer – old fighter, early member of the party or SS

Amt – bureau, office

Anwärter – candidate; **SS-Junker** – SS officer candidate

ärztliche untersuchung – medical examination
Arbeitsverwendungfähig (a.v.) – fit for labor duty only
Arbeitsverwendungsfähig in der Heimat (a.v. Heimat) – fit for labor duty in the zone of interior only
Garnisonsverwendungsfähig Feld (g.v.F.) – fit for garrison duty in the field
Garnisonsverwendungsfähig Heimat (g.v.H.) – fit for garrison duty in the zone of the interior
Kriegsverwendungsfähig (k.v.) – fit for active service (highest medical classification)
Körperliche Eignumg – physical aptitude

Arzt – medical doctor
Apotheker – pharmacist
Sanitätsoffizier – doctor
Sanitätsoffizier des zahnärtlichen Dienstes – dentist
Standortarzt – station surgeon (chief physician)
Zahnarzt – dentist
Veterinär – veterinary

Ausbildung – training; **Lehrgänge** – schools, training courses

Ausstossen – expel, cashier (stronger dismissal than **Abschied**)

Auszeichnung – awards and decorations

Beförderung – promotion; **Letzte Beförderung** – last promotion date

Beruf (erlernt) – civilian trade
Ingenieur (Dipl.-Ing.) – engineer
Kaufmann – salesman
Student – student
Polizei – police official
Bankbeamter – bank clerk
Rechstanwalt / Jurist – lawyer
Landwirt – farmer
Mechaniker / Handwerker / Maschinist – mechanic
Elektriker – electrician
Lehrer – teacher

Beurteilung – efficiency report
durchschnitt – average
sehr gute Ausfüllung – very good performance

Schwachen und Fehler – poor characteristics (followed by a description)

degradiert – demoted, reduced in rank
Abtreibung – abortion
Sexualverbrechen – sex crimes
Veruntreuung – embezzlement
Pflichtvergessen / Fahrlässigkeit – negligence
Ungehorsam – disobedience
Nichtachtung / Missachtung – disrespect
Alkoholiker / trunksucht – alcoholic / alcoholism
Gehorsamsverweigerung – insubordination

Dienstgrad – rank (See Appendix 1)

Dienststellungen – duty positions
Zugführer – platoon leader
Kompanie-Chef – company commander
Abteilungs-Kommandeur (Abt.-Kdr.) – detachment/battalion commander
Regiments-Kommandeur (Rgt.-Kdr.) – regimental commander
Intendant – official in charge of rations, clothing, equipment, pay, etc **Verbindungsoffizier** – liaison officer
Verflegungsoffizier – rations/mess officer
Vernehmungsoffizier – interrogation officer

Ehefrau – wife
verheiratet – married
ledig – single
geschieden – divorced
verwitwet – widowed
kinder – children
Mädchenname der Frau – wife's maiden name

Einheit – unit

Einsatzgruppe – battalion-size mobile extermination group on the eastern front, primarily Security Police and SD officials.

Einsatzkommando – subordinate command of an **einsatzgruppe**, normally company-size.

Eintritt in die Partei – date entered Nazi Party

Eintritt in die SS – date entered SS

Endlösung – final solution, the German euphemism used here to indicate the extermination of the Jewish race.

Freiwilliger – volunteer

Frontkämpfer – combat veteran

Gauleiter – highest ranking Nazi Party official in a district. Germany was composed of forty-two Nazi Party districts.

Geburtstag / Geburtsort – date of birth / place of birth

Geheim – secret

Geheime Staatspolizei (Gestapo) – the secret police dedicated to the preservation of the Nazi regime.

Hauptamt SS Gericht – the SS Legal Department.

Höhrere SS und Polizeiführer (HSSPF) – Higher SS and Police Leader, Himmler's regional commander in an area. Directly responsible to Himmler for the implementation of all measures related to the security of the state and the treatment of dangerous elements within their realm.

im Felde gefallen / vor dem Feind gefallen – killed in action
- **erschiessen –** killed by shooting
- **erschlagen** – killed by blows
- **leichtverwundundet (le.V.)** – slightly wounded
- **schwerverwundet** – seriously wounded
- **vermisst** – missing in action
- **kriegsbeschädigt** – disabled on active duty
- **Unfall** – accident
- **Beschädigung** – injury
- **Blutvergiftung** – blood-poisoning, infection, gangrene
- **krank** – sick, ill

konfession – religion
- **(ev.)** – Protestant
- **(k.)** – Catholic
- **(ggl.** or **gg.)** – Agnostic

Konzentrationslager (KZ, KL) – concentration camp

Kraftfahrwesen – motor transport

Kriminalpolizei (Kripo) – criminal police under the control of the SD.

Nachrichtenabteilung – signal detachment

Ordnungspolizei (Orpo) – order police, consisting of uniformed police forces in the Third Reich. While separate from the Gestapo and Criminal Police, they handled routine police business and sometimes assisted in carrying out mass executions.

Rassisches Gesamtbild – racial makeup

Reichsführer-SS (RFSS) – Reich Leader Heinrich Himmler

Reichssicherheitshauptamt (RSHA) – Reich Main Security Office in Berlin. In 1941 it was organized as follows:

Amt (Office)	Function
I	**Personnel**
II	**Organization and Law**
II A	Organization and Law
II B	Passports
II C	Budget
II D	Technical Matters
III	**SD Domestic**
III A	Legal Practice
III B	Ethnos
III C	Culture
III D	Economy
IV	**Gestapo**
IV A	Enemies
IV B	Sects
IV C	Card Files
IV D	Speheres of Influence

IV E	Counterintelligence
V	**Kripo**
V A	Policy
V B	Crimes
V C	Identification
V D	Criminal Institute
VI	**SD Foreign**
VI A	General
VI B	German-Italian Sphere
VI C	Russo-Japanese Sphere
VI D	West
VI E	Investigations
VI F	Technical Matters
VII	**Ideology**
VII B	Evaluation

Sicherheitsdienst (SD) – the intelligence branch of the SS.

Sicherheitspolizei – Security Police; a fusion of various criminal police forces and state political police separate from the SS, but closely linked to the SD.

Sonderkommando – special commando

SS-Führungshauptamt (SS-FHA) – SS Leadership Main Office, the headquarters of the Waffen-SS; designed to control the organization of field units of the SS and to monitor the training and replacement units of the Waffen-SS. It additionally looked after training schools of the Waffen-SS. The **SS-FHA** was independent of the SS Main Office.

SS-Hauptamt (SS-HA) – SS Main Office, evolved in the mid-1930s and controlled such functions as personnel, administration, medical, physical training, education, communications and so forth.

SS und Polizeiführer (SSPF) – SS and Police Leader, district commander subordinate to an **HSSPF**.

Stammrolle – personnel roster

Sturmabteilung (SA) – Storm Detachment, the early private army of the Nazi party.

Totenkopf – Death's Head, units which guarded concentration camps. Also the 3rd Waffen-SS Division.

Verfügungstruppe – the first Waffen-SS field troops.

Wachbataillon – guard battalion

Waffen-SS – SS field troops

Wirtschaftliche Verhältnisse – personal financial situation

Wirtschafts und Verwaltungshauptamt (WVHA) – Economics and Administration Head Office of the SS charged with the administration of the concentration camps.

Wohnort – current place of residence

APPENDIX 3: SS OFFICER EFFICIENCY REPORTS

Most of the personnel files for those officers who served in the *Einsatzkommandos* do not include efficiency reports for these specific jobs and assignments. Some that do are reproduced in this appendix.

The following is an efficiency report for *SS-Obersturmbannführer* August Meier, the commander of *Einsatzkommando 5* and *Sonderkommando 4b*. It was written by *SS-Obergruppenführer* Friedrich Jeckeln.[1]

> *SS-Obersturmbannführer* Meier was active in my staff as liaison leader of the *Einsatzgruppe C* from about the middle of July to October 1, 1941. I have learned to know and appreciate Meier as an excellent SS leader who was always ready for action and who in connection with the great tasks in the Ukraine was an extremely valuable supporter of mine. Despite the large distances between the positions of the leader of *Einsatzgruppe C* and my staff, Meier understood the importance to always maintain and perfect communications and in this he contributed greatly to the fact that the work could be done harmoniously and in a positive way in every respect. Above that, *SS-Obersturmbannführer* Meier was in command of several cleansing actions which were initiated by me, and through his good organizational talents and his determination he excelled in the problems that confronted him. Among his comrades, Meier always showed his best sides. In the staff, he was respected and liked as an old national socialist and good comrade. I have very much regretted the departure of *SS-Obersturmbannführer* Meier from my staff.

Another officer who seemed to do well as an *Einsatzkommando* leader was Hans-Gerhard Schindhelm. Schindhelm took command of *Einsatzkommando 8* on November 13, 1942 and was awarded the War Service Cross 2nd Class and the Eastern Front Medal. He received the following efficiency rating from *SS-Standartenführer* Erich Ehrlinger describing his performance:[2]

> On November 13, 1942 Schindhelm took over the *Einsatzkommando 8* in the *Einsatzgruppe B*, located at Mogil'ov. The area of the *Einsatzkommando 8* was marked by heavy activity by bandits who maintained their contacts up to the communities within the sphere of the *Einsatzkommando* and who were continuously active in heavy sabotage acts on public installations, railroads and roads. At the same time there was heavy spy activity by the enemy in the area of Army Group Center in preparation of offensive intentions. Recognizing the fact that additional help by other units was necessary, *SS-Sturmbannführer* Schindhelm started in a timely way to build up a criminal police service (*Hilfskriminalpolizei*), which he further expanded during the course of the year 1943 and which at the end was molded into an instrument for spy and sabotage defense that proved itself many times to be very valuable. With his troops, which were spread all over the area of endeavor, he destroyed numerous terrorist and sabotage troops of the enemy. He was also able to continuously supply the leaders of the *Einsatzgruppe B* with confidential reports as well as the Commander of the Army District with valuable information about movements of the bandits. *SS-Sturmbannführer* Schindhelm was a just superior to his men. He always watched out that they were not occupied with security police and non-SD tasks and that they continued their professional education. During the period of his leadership as commander of the *Einsatzkommando 8* he accomplished extremely good work in the sector of security policy and in addition he took on with great interest and energy the professional security tasks. In his personal demeanor and in private contact, Schindhelm was always a good example for his men. His character and philosophical attitude are without criticism.

The following is a recommendation for promotion for Dr. Helmut Glaser who served in an *Einsatzgruppe* in Poland in 1939:[3]

> Before entering the full-time service in the SS in June of 1938, Dr. Glaser was active as middle school teacher in Klagenfurt. Due to his outstanding knowledge, he was ordered to lead the former Detachment II/2 on July 1, 1939. On August 20, 1939, Dr. Glaser was transferred to *Einsatzkommando 4/I*. He participated in the advance into Poland, later he became commander of the Sipo and ordered to the SD in the District Krakow, and in September of 1940 he was tasked with the leadership of the SD-Section at the same office. Effective March 20, 1941, *SS-Hauptsturmführer* Dr. Glaser was ordered back to the SD office and until further notice was tasked with the deputy command of the SD office.
>
> *SS-Hauptsturmführer* Dr. Glaser is being described as an exemplary, straight, sincere character with greatly above-average capabilities. He is extremely dutiful and correct.

> Even though Dr. Glaser has not yet fulfilled the regulations of the promotion guidelines of November 15, 1942 (his most recent promotion was January 30, 1941), in addition to the fact that due to reasons of his service he could not yet serve as a soldier, because due to his leading position in the SD/RFSS he could not be made available to the Wehrmacht, it is recommended that *SS-Hauptsturmführer* Dr. Glaser, due to his above average merits and especially in recognition of his engagement as deputy section leader be granted a waiver and be promoted to *SS-Sturmbannführer* effective April 20, 1943.

Paul Domnick also served in an *Einsatzkommando* in Poland. The following is a report recommending he be given a commission as an *SS-Untersturmführer*:[4]

> Up to his transfer to the Secret State Police on April 1, 1934, Criminal Inspector Domnick was active in the Secret State Police with the Border Police in East Prussia. From May 1, 1935 he has been a member of the NSDAP and was active as block leader. Domnick is reliable as far as politics are concerned.
>
> On May 26, 1942, Criminal Inspector Domnick left the church and calls himself an agnostic.
>
> As far as his character is concerned, there is nothing negative known about Domnick. He has a friendly relationship with his comrades and he is correct and disciplined in his contact with superiors. His attitude is that of a soldier. As far as it is known here, his social circumstances are in order. Domnick is married and the father of two children.
>
> Criminal Inspector Domnick was ordered to an *Einsatzkommando* in September of 1939, and on November 11, 1939 he was transferred to my command. Immediately thereafter he was tasked with the establishment and administration of this prison camp [author's note: Lublin]. It is thanks to his initiative and his untiring effort that the prison has attained its present exemplary condition.
>
> Domnick has participated successfully in the First Special Drivers' camp in Rabka and is capable to be an SS-leader. Therefore, it is requested that Domnick, based on his service position within the framework of rank parity, be promoted to *SS-Untersturmführer* since this is also justified in the interest of service.

SS superiors also believed that *SS-Hauptsturmführer* Hans Kraus, who served in *Sonderkommando 1b*, should be promoted as well:[5]

> The Commander of the Security Police and of the SD Ostland recommends that *SS-Hauptsturmführer* Hans Kraus be promoted to *SS-Sturmbannführer*. Since the start of the Eastern Campaign, *SS-Hauptsturmführer* Kraus has been active in *Einsatzgruppe A* and since July 1941 he belonged to the *Sonderkommando 1b*. At all times, *SS-Hauptsturmführer* Kraus has been involved in missions in the front lines and has taken part in all of the forward march up to Tichwin. Due to his language capabilities, his dexterity and his talent for tasks in the information sector, he has served the commando with great value. Kraus has also proved to be an able leader, who also during the most difficult situations independently led parts of the commando. Kraus especially excelled in the leadership of non-German units in the fight against Bolshevik bandits when he in several instances led missions with great success.
>
> *SS-Hauptsturmführer* Kraus was awarded the Iron Cross Second Class on March 31, 1942, the Infantry Assault badge on August 10, 1942, and on August 20, 1942 he was awarded the Iron Cross First Class. In addition, he is in possession of the Wound Badge in Black. It is requested that *SS-Hauptsturmführer* Kraus be promoted to *SS-Sturmbannführer* effective November 9, 1942, and that the respective message be relayed.

Fritz Braune was also described to be a proficient SD officer. The following report reflects his service as the commander of *Sonderkommando 4d*:[6]

> Braune possesses a good talent for organization, clear power for decisions and a comprehensive knowledge; in SS-related matters he demonstrates an immaculate attitude. From October 1, 1941 until March 21, 1942 Braune was a member of *Einsatzgruppe C* and tasked with the command of *Sonderkommando 4d*. Except for his age, the conditions of the guidelines for promotion dated November 15, 1942 and the release of July 1, 1941 were fulfilled. It is recommended that, due to his good accomplishments demonstrated so far as well as his active work for the NSDAP before the transfer of power, he be promoted effective January 30, 1943.

The following report concerns one of the "Baltic Germans" who appeared to have the qualities that Heydrich would have considered appropriate for service in the *Einsatzkommandos*:[7]

> From June 1941 on, *SS-Obersturmführer* Waldemar Borck has been with the SD in the East. For this activity, he brings along a special capability, since he grew up in Russia, is in command of the language and knows the

Russian situation precisely. The leader of his unit emphasized his unwavering engagement, his personal attitude which is beyond approach, his consistent diligence in his work and his well thought out actions. As far as awards are concerned, he has been awarded the Eastern Front Medal and the War Service Cross 1st Class with Swords.

Borck is a solidly courageous and decent SS-leader, with clear view of the philosophy and he is of clean character. He has earned a privileged promotion to *SS-Hauptsturmführer* due to his extraordinary achievements and is worthy of it also in respect of his age.

George Egon Loleit was another of the "Baltic Germans" who hailed from Moscow. Loleit served in *Einsatzgruppe C*:[8]

Since the start of the Eastern Campaign, *SS-Untersturmführer* Georg Loleit, SS number 357298 of the 109th SS-Standarte in Posen, was a member of the *Einsatzgruppe C* of the Sipo and the SD and belonged to an *Einsatzkommando*. During the time of his engagement in the East, Loleit registered excellent accomplishments and has proven to be an extremely capable and dutiful SS leader. In the fight against partisan groups, as well as in the execution of other special measures of the security police, *SS-Untersturmführer* Loleit, with untiring commitment and without consideration of his life and health, has fulfilled his duty. Recently Loleit was also awarded the War Service Cross 2nd Class with Swords.

It is requested whenever possible that *SS-Untersturmführer* Loleit be promoted to *SS-Obersturmführer* during the next date scheduled for promotion.

Notes:

[1] Personalakt August Meier, Washington, D.C: National Archives Microfilm Publication A3343, Records of SS Officers from the Berlin Document Center, Roll SSO-305A.

[2] Personalakt Hans-Gerhard Schindhelm, Washington, D.C: National Archives Microfilm Publication A3343, Records of SS Officers from the Berlin Document Center, Roll SSO-078B.

[3] Personalakt Helmut Glaser, Washington, D.C: National Archives Microfilm Publication A3343, Records of SS Officers from the Berlin Document Center, Roll SSO-015A.

[4] Personalakt Paul Domnick, Washington, D.C: National Archives Microfilm Publication A3343, Records of SS Officers from the Berlin Document Center, Roll SSO-160.

[5] Personalakt Hans Kraus, Washington, D.C: National Archives Microfilm Publication A3343, Records of SS Officers from the Berlin Document Center, Roll SSO-209A.

[6] Personalakt Fritz Braune, Washington, D.C: National Archives Microfilm Publication A3343, Records of SS Officers from the Berlin Document Center, Roll SSO-102.

[7] Personalakt Waldemar Borck, Washington, D.C: National Archives Microfilm Publication A3343, Records of SS Officers from the Berlin Document Center, Roll SSO-091.

[8] Personalakt Georg Egon Loleit, Washington, D.C: National Archives Microfilm Publication A3343, Records of SS Officers from the Berlin Document Center, Roll SSO-275A.

APPENDIX 4: ORDER POLICE HOME STATION AND COMMANDERS

Police Battalion	*Home Station*	*Commander*
11	Königsberg	Major Lechthaler
13	Königsberg	
22	Stettin	Major Sternagel
32	Berlin	Major von Braunschwieg
45	Aussig	Major Besser
67	Essen	
101	Hamburg	Major Trapp
133	Nürnberg	
251	Stuttgart	
255	Brüx	
256	Vienna	
303	Bremen	Lieutenant Colonel Hannibal
306	Frankfurt	
307	Duisburg	Major Stahr
		Major Binz
309	Cologne	Lieutenant Colonel Weis
		Major Brückner
314	Vienna	Major Severt
		SS-Hauptsturmführer Christ
316	Recklinghausen	Major Behr
320	Berlin	Captain Dall
322	Vienna	Major Nagel

APPENDIX 5: SONDERKOMMANDO DIRLEWANGER OFFICERS

SS-Sonderkommando Dirlewanger, while not considered a true *Einsatzkommando*, never-the-less often conducted similar operations from 1942 to 1944 in the Minsk area. The following is a partial list of known SS officers who served in this unit during the war. The list is not complete.

SS-Untersturmführer Heinrich Amann
SS-Untersturmführer Antonius Ammerlaan
SS-Hauptsturmführer Werner Blessau
SS-Hauptsturmführer Waldemar Bodammer
SS-Obersturmführer Erich Brandt
SS-Standartenführer Erich Buchmann *
SS-Hauptsturmführer Hans Bünger
SS-Oberführer Oskar Dirlewanger **
SS-Haupsturmführer Ewald Ehlers **
SS-Hauptsturmführer Josef Falter
SS-Obersturmführer Otto Gast
SS-Hauptsturmführer Kurt Gramatke
SS-Hauptsturmführer Josef Grohmann
SS-Sturmbannführer Ernst Heidelberg *
SS-Obersturmführer Egyd Ingruber
SS-Hauptsturmführer Josef Karnop
SS-Hauptsturmführer Friedrich Knöringer
SS-Obersturmführer Theodor Krätzer
SS-Untersturmführer Helmut Lewandowski
SS-Obersturmbannführer Franz Magill *
SS-Hauptsturmführer Ludwig Mann
SS-Obersturmführer Franz de Martin***
SS-Obersturmbannführer Andreas Mayer-Mader **
SS-Obersturmführer Fritz Missmahl
SS-Hauptsturmführer Wolfgang Plaul
SS-Untersturmführer Siegfried Polack **
SS-Sturmbannführer Karl Praefke
SS-Hauptsturmführer Wilhelm Reiner
SS-Obersturmführer Hans Schäftlmeier
SS-Brigadeführer Fritz Schmedes *
SS-Hauptsturmführer Hans Schreier
SS-Untersturmführer Max Schreiner **
SS-Hauptsturmführer Jan Schreuder
SS-Untersturmführer Karl Staib
SS-Hauptsturmführer Rudolf Stöweno **
SS-Obersturmführer Adalbert Trattenschegg **
SS-Untersturmführer Fritz Wagner
SS-Obersturmführer Othmar Walchensteiner **
SS-Sturmbannführer Erwin Walser *
SS-Obersturmführer Hans Georg Weber
SS-Untersturmführer Heinrich Wehninck
SS-Sturmbannführer Kurt Weisse *
SS-Untersturmführer Georg Wild **
SS-Obersturmführer Waldemar Wilhelm
SS-Hauptsturmführer Bruno Wille *
SS-Untersturmführer August Zeller **
SS-Untersturmführer Paul Zimmermann

Key
* Killed during or shortly after the war
** Definitely survived the war
*** Assigned on orders, but may not have reported to unit
No annotation indicates fate unknown

APPENDIX 6: HIGHER SS AND POLICE LEADERS – EINSATZGRUPPE AREA OF OPERATIONS

Higher SS and Police Leader North Russia
Höhere SS und Polizeiführer Russland-Nord

June 22, 1941 – October 30, 1941	*SS-Gruppenführer* Hans-Adolf Prützmann
November 1, 1941 – 1 July 1944	*SS*-Gruppenführer Friedrich Jeckeln

Higher SS and Police Leader Central Russia and White Russia
Höhere SS und Polizeiführer Russland-Mitte und Weissruthenien

June 22, 1941 – November 22, 1942	*SS-Obergruppenführer* Eric von dem Bach-Zelewski
November 22, 1942 – March 23, 1943	*SS-Brigadeführer* Georg Henning von Bassewitz-Behr
March 23, 1943 – July 5, 1943	*SS-Gruppenführer* Gerrett Korsemann
July 5, 1943 – August 7, 1944	*SS-Gruppenführer* Kurt Gottberg

Higher SS and Police Leader South Russia
Höhere SS und Polizeiführer Russland-Süd

June 22, 1941 – December 11, 1941	*SS-Gruppenführer* Friedrich Jeckeln
December 11, 1941 – July 1, 1944	*SS-Obergruppenführer* Hans-Adolf Prützmann

Higher SS and Police Leader Black Sea
Höhere SS und Polizeiführer Schwarzes-Meer

October 29, 1943 – December 25, 1943	*SS-Gruppenführer* Ludolf von Alvensleben
December 25, 1943 – September 16, 1944	*SS-Obergruppenführer* Richard Hildebrandt
September 16, 1944 – September 18, 1944	*SS-Obergruppenführer* Artur Phleps

APPENDIX 7: WAFFEN-SS UNITS AND LEADERS – EINSATZGRUPPE AREA OF OPERATIONS

SS-Brigade 1 Reichsführer-SS
1st SS Brigade (mot)
April 24, 1941 – November 1, 1941 *SS-Brigadeführer* Karl Demelhuber
November 1, 1941 – December 21, 1941 *SS-Oberführer* Richard Herrmann
December 21, 1941 – 30 November, 1942 *SS-Brigadeführer* Wilhelm Hartenstein

SS-Brigade 2 Reichsführer-SS
2nd SS Brigade (mot)
April 24, 1941 – July 5, 1941 *SS-Brigadeführer* Karl von Treuenfeld
July 5, 1941 – January 25, 1943 *SS-Standartenführer* Gottfried Klingemann

SS-Totenkopf Kavallerie Regiment 1 / SS-Kavallerie Brigade
1st SS Totenkopf Cavalry Regiment / SS Cavalry Brigade
February 25, 1941 – August 19, 1941 *SS-Standartenführer* Hermann Fegelein
August 19, 1941 – September 1, 1941 *SS-Sturmbannführer* Gustav Lombard
September 1, 1941 – May 1, 1942 *SS-Standartenführer* Hermann Fegelein

SS-Sonderkomanndo Dirlewanger
SS-Special Commando Dirlewanger
August 1, 1940 – February 15, 1945 *SS-Oberführer* Oskar Dirlewanger

SOURCES

Published Sources

Aly, Götz. *Aktion T4*. Berlin: Edition Hentrich, 1989.

Angolia, John. *Cloth Insignia of the SS*. San Jose, CA: R. James Bender Publishing, 1983.

Angolia, John. *For Führer and Fatherland: Military Awards of the Third Reich*. San Jose, CA: R. James Bender Publishing, 1976.

Angolia, John. *For Führer and Fatherland: Political & Civil Awards of the Third Reich*. San Jose, CA: R. James Bender Publishing, 1978.

Arad, Yitzhak. *Belzec, Sobibór, Treblinka: The Operation Reinhard Death Camps*. Bloomington, IN: Indiana Univeristy Press, 1987.

Arad, Yitzhak, Shmuel Krakowski and Shmuel Spector. *The Einsatzgruppen Reports*. New York: Holocaust Library, 1989.

Bartov, Omer. *The Eastern Front, 1941-1945, German Troops and the Barbarization of Warfare*. New York: St. Martin's Press, 1986.

Berenbaum, Michael and Peck, Abraham J., editors. *The Holocaust and History: The Known, the Unknown, the Disputed and the Reexamined*. Bloomington, Indiana: Indiana University Press, 1998.

Breitman, Richard. *The Architect of Genocide*. New York: Alfred A. Knopf, 1991.

Browder, George C. *Hitler's Enforcers: The Gestapo and the Security Service in the Nazi Revolution*. New York: Oxford University Press, 1996.

Büchler, Yehoshua. *"Kommandostab Reichsführer-SS: Himmler's Personal Murder Brigades in 1941"*, *Holocaust and Genocide Studies*, Vol. 1, No. 1, London: Pergamon, 1986.

Burleigh, Michael. *Death and Deliverance*. Cambridge, England: Cambridge university Press, 1994.

Cooper, Matthew. *The German Army 1939-1945*. New York: Stein and Day, 1978.

Cooper, Matthew. *The Nazi War Against Soviet Partisans, 1941-1944*. New York: Stein & Day Publishers, 1979.

Dienstaltersliste der Schutzstaffel der N.S.D.A.P., Stand vom 1. Oktober 1934. Berlin: Personalkanzlei des Reichsführers-SS, 1935.

Dienstaltersliste der Schutzstaffel der N.S.D.A.P., Stand vom 1. Juli 1935. Berlin: Personalkanzlei des Reichsführers-SS, 1935.

Dienstaltersliste der Schutzstaffel der N.S.D.A.P., Stand vom 1. December 1936. Berlin: Personalkanzlei des Reichsführers-SS, 1937.

Dienstaltersliste der Schutzstaffel der N.S.D.A.P., Stand vom 1. December 1937. Berlin: Personalkanzlei des Reichsführers-SS, 1938.

Dienstaltersliste der Schutzstaffel der N.S.D.A.P., Stand vom 1. December 1938. Berlin: Personalkanzlei des Reichsführers-SS, 1939.

Dienstaltersliste der Schutzstaffel der N.S.D.A.P., Stand vom 9. November 1944. Reprinted by INFORA Establishment, Vaduz Fürstentum, Lichtenstein, 1985.

Edelheit, Abraham & Herschel Edelheit. *History of the Holocaust: A Handbook and Dictionary*. Boulder, CO: Westview Press, 1994.

Ezergailis, Andrew. *The Holocaust in Latvia, 1941-1944*. Riga, Latvia: The Historical Institute of Latvia, 1996.

Geyer, Michael. "German Strategy in the Age of Machine Warfare, 1914-1945," in *Makers of Modern Strategy* ed. Peter Peret. Princeton, NJ: Princeton University Press, 1986.

Gilbert, Martin. *Atlas of the Holocaust*. Tel-Aviv: Steimatsky's Agency Limited. 1982.

Goldhagen, Daniel Jonah. *Hitler's Willing Executioners: Ordinary Germans and the Holocaust*. New York: Vintage Books, 1997.

Graber, G.S. *History of the SS*. New York: David McKay, Inc., 1978.

Hartung, Lothar. *Verleihungs-Urkunden des 3 Reiches*. Fürstentum, Liechtenstein: Infora Research Est., 1982.

Headland, Ronald. *Messages of Murder: A Study of the Reports of the Einsatzgruppen of the Security Police and the Security Service, 1941-1943*. Madison, WI: Associated University Press, 1992.

Hilberg, Raul. *The Destruction of the European Jews*. New York: Holmes & Meier, 1985.

Höhne, Heinz. *The Order of the Death's Head*. Translated by Richard Barry. New York: Coward-McCann, 1970.

International Auschwitz Committee. *Nazi Medicine*. New York: Howard Fertig, 1986.

International Military Tribunal Nürnberg. *Trial of the Major War Criminals before the International Military Tribunal*. Volume XX (30 July - 10 August 1946), Nürnberg, Germany: Allied Control Authority for Germany, 1948.

International Military Tribunal Nürnberg. *Trials of War Criminals before the International Military Tribunal, Volume IV, United States of America vs. Otto Ohlendorf, et al., Case No. 9*. Washington, DC: U.S. Government Printing Office, 1949.

Keilig, Wolf. *Die Generale des Heeres*. Friedberg, FRG: Podzun-Pallas-Verlag, 1983.

Koehl, Robert Lewis. *The Black Corps: The Structure and Power Struggles of the Nazi SS*. Madison, WI: The University of Wisconsin Press, 1983.

Klee, Ernst, Willi Dressen and Volker Riess. *The Good Old Days: The Holocaust as Seen by Its Perpetrators and Bystanders*. New York: The Free Press, 1988.

Kogon, Eugen, Hermann Langbein and Adalbert Rückerl. *Nazi Mass Murder: A Documentary History of the Use of Poison Gas*. New Haven, CN: Yale University Press, 1993.

Krausnick, Helmut, Hans Buchheim, Martin Broszat and Hans-Adolf Jacobsen. *Anatomy of the SS State*. New York: Walker and Company, 1968.

Krausnick, Helmut and Hans-Heinrich Wilhelm. *Die Truppe des Weltanschauungs-krieges: Die Einsatzgruppen der Sichersheitpolizei und des SD 1938-1942*. Stuttgart: Deutsche Verlags-Anstalt, 1981.

Lerner, Daniel. *The Nazi Elite*. Stanford, CA: Stanford University Press, 1951.

Littlejohn, David. *Foreign Legions of the Third Reich, Volume 1-4*. San Jose, CA: R. James Bender Publishing, 1979.

Lucas, Richard C. *The Forgotten Holocaust: The Poles Under German Occupation 1939-1944*. Lexington, Kentucky: The University Press of Kentucky, 1986.

MacLean, French. *The Camp Men: The SS Officers Who Ran the Nazi Concentration Camp System*. Atglen, PA: Schiffer Publishing, 1998.

MacLean, French. *The Cruel Hunters: SS-Sonderkommando Dirlewanger, Hitler's Most Notorious Anti-Partisan Unit*. Atglen, PA: Schiffer Publishing, 1998.

Manvell, Roger. *SS and Gestapo*. New York: Ballentine Books, 1969.

Mehner, Kurt. *Die Waffen-SS und Polizei 1939-1945: Führung und Truppe*. Norderstedt, Germany Militair-Verlag Klaus D. Patzwall, 1995.

Meyer, Heiner. *Berlin Document Center: Das Geschäft mit der Vergangenheit*. Frankfurt, FRG: Ullstein, 1988.

Mollo, Andrew. *Uniforms of the SS: Collected Edition, Volumes 1 to 6*. London: Windrow & Greene 1997.

Office of United States Chief of Counsel For Prosecution of Axis Criminality. *Nazi Conspiracy And Aggression, Volume I*. Washington: United States Government Printing Office, 1946.

Office of United States Chief of Counsel For Prosecution of Axis Criminality. *Trials of War Criminals Before The Nuernberg Military Tribunals Under Control Council Law No. 10, Volume I*. Washington: United States Government Printing Office, 1949.

Padfield, Peter. *Himmler: Reichsführer-SS*. New York: Henry Holt and Company, 1990.

Patzwall, Klaus D. *Der Blutorden der NSDAP*. Hamburg, FRG: Verlag Militaria-Archiv Klaus D. Patzwall, 1985.

Preradovich, Nikolaus von. *Die Generale der Waffen-SS*. Berg am See, FRG: Kurt Vowinckel Verlag, 1985.

Reimann, Viktor. *Goebbels*. Translated by Stephen Wendt. Garden City, NY: Doubleday & Company, 1976.

Reitlinger, Gerald. *The Final Solution*. Northvale, NJ: Jason Aronson Inc., 1987.

Reitlinger, Gerald. *The House Built on Sand: The Conflicts of German Policy in Russia*. New York: The Viking Press, 1960.

Reitlinger, Gerald. *The SS: Alibi of a Nation 1922-1945*. London: Arms and Armour Press, 1981.

Rückerl, Adalbert. *The Investigation of Nazi Crimes, 1945-1978: A Documentation*. Translated by Derek Rutter. Hamden, Connecticutt: Archon Books, 1980.

Rüter-Ehlermann, Adelheid and Rüter, C.F., *Justiz und NS-Verbrechen: Sammlung Deutscher Strafurteile wegen Nationalsozialischer Tötungsverbrechen 1945-1966*. Band I-XXII. Amsterdam: University of Amsterdam Press, 1968.

Schneider, Jost. *Their Honor was Loyalty!* San Jose, CA: R. James Bender Publishing, 1977.

Snyder, Louis L. *Encyclopedia of the Third Reich*. New York: McGraw-Hill, 1976.

Spector, Shmuel. "Aktion 1005", *Holocaust and Genocide Studies*, Vol.5 No.2. Oxford, England: Pergamon Press, 1990.

Statistisches Jahrbuch der Schutzstaffel der NSDAP 1937. Berlin, 1938.

Statistisches Jahrbuch der Schutzstaffel der NSDAP 1938. Berlin, 1939.

Stein, George H. *The Waffen SS: Hitler's Elite Guard at War*. Ithaca, NY: Cornell University Press, 1966.

Tessin, Georg. *Verbände und Truppen der deutschen Wehrmacht und Waffen-SS im Zweiten Weltkrieg 1939-1945, Band I - XVI*. Osnabrück, FRG: Biblio Verlag, 1979.

United States Holocaust Memorial Museum. *Historical Atlas of the Holocaust*. New York: Macmillan Publishing USA, 1996.

Wiesenthal, Simon. *The Murderers Among Us*. New York: McGraw-Hill, 1967.

Yerger, Mark. *Allgemeine-SS: The Commands, Units and Leaders of the General SS*. Atglen, PA: Schiffer Publishing, 1997.

Unpublished Sources

National Archives of the United States, Washington D. C. *Microfilm Publication A3343 Series SSO, Records of SS Officers from the Berlin Document Center*, Series SSO - Officer Personnel Records and Series RS - Race and Settlement Office.

Summary sheet from *Ordensgemeinschaft der Ritterkreuzträger*, 1 January 1980.

United States Holocaust Memorial Museum. Center for Advanced Holocaust Studies Presentation, January 27, 1998: *The SD and the Einsatzkommandos*, by George C. Browder, author of *Hitler's Enforcers: The Gestapo and the Security Service in the Nazi Revolution*.

United States Holocaust Memorial Museum. Center for Advanced Holocaust Studies Presentation, April 1998: *Collaboration in the Holocaust: Crimes of the Local Police in Belorussia and Ukraine, 1941-1944*, by Martin Dean, Senior Historian, Metropolitan Police War Crimes Unit, New Scotland Yard, London.

United States Holocaust Memorial Museum. Center for Advanced Holocaust Studies Presentation, June 9, 1998: *Reinhard Heydrich and the Early Planning for the Final Solution*, by Charles W. Sydnor, Jr., author of *Soldiers of Destruction: The SS Death's Head Division, 1933-1945*.

PHOTO SECTION

Dr. Walter Albert (NA)

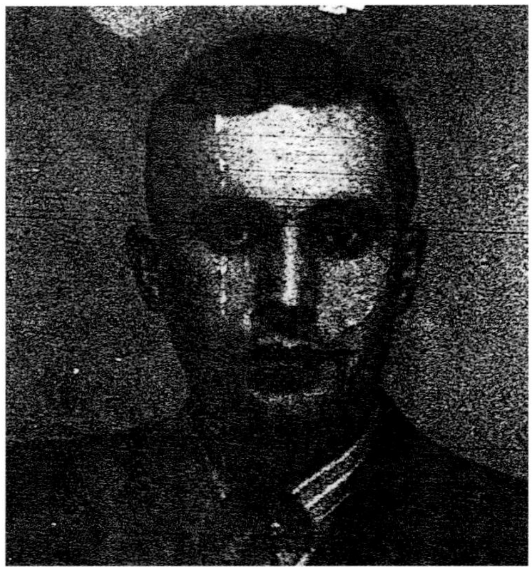

Bernhard Baatz (NA)

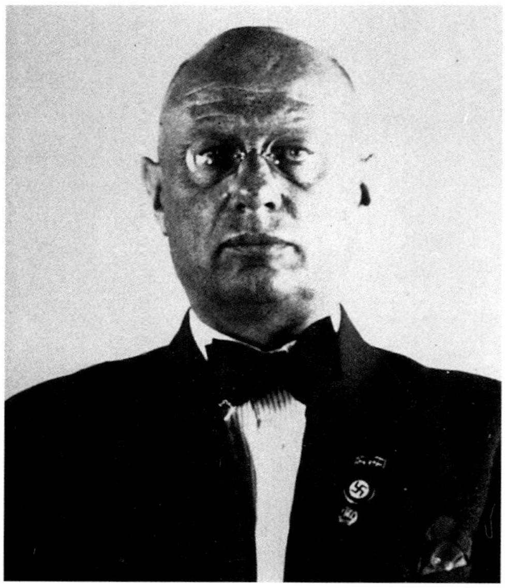

Dr. Horst Barth (BDC)

Dr. Gerhard Bast (NA)

Rudolf Batz (BDC)

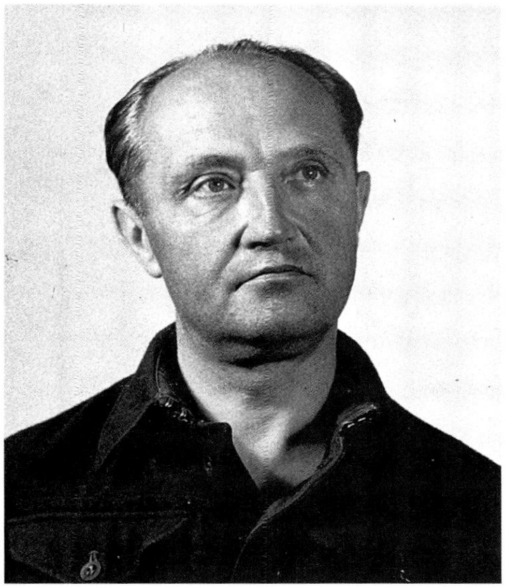

Ernst Biberstein at Nürnberg before trial. (Benjamin Ferencz, courtesy of USHMM)

Dr. Walter Bierkamp (NA)

Helmut Bischoff (NA)

Paul Blobel (USHMM)

Paul Blobel at Nürnberg before trial. (Benjamin Ferencz, courtesy of USHMM)

Dr. Walter Blume (NA)

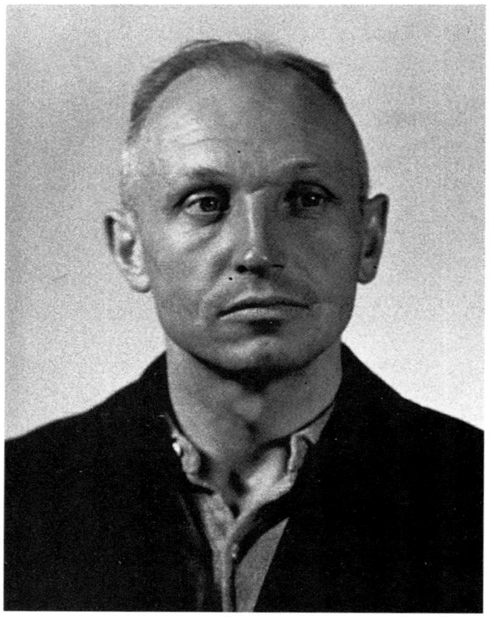

Dr. Walter Blume at Nürnberg before trial. (Benjamin Ferencz, courtesy of USHMM)

Wilhelm Bock (NA)

Wilhelm Bock (NA)

Hans-Joachim Boehme (NA)

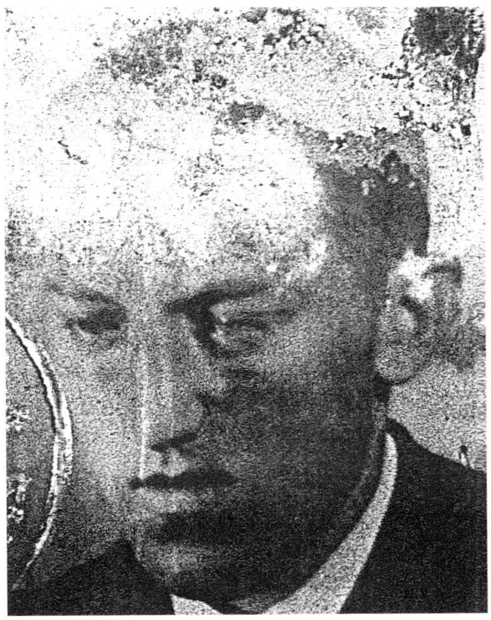

Dr. Heinrich Bolte (NA)

Dr. Otto Bradfisch (NA)

Fritz Braune (NA)

Dr. Werner Braune (NA)

Dr. Werner Braune at Nürnberg before trial. (Benjamin Ferencz, courtesy of USHMM)

Dr. Friedrich Buchardt (NA)

Kurt Burkhardt (BDC)

Dr. Kurt Christmann (NA)

Theodor Christensen (NA)

Ernst Damzog (NA)

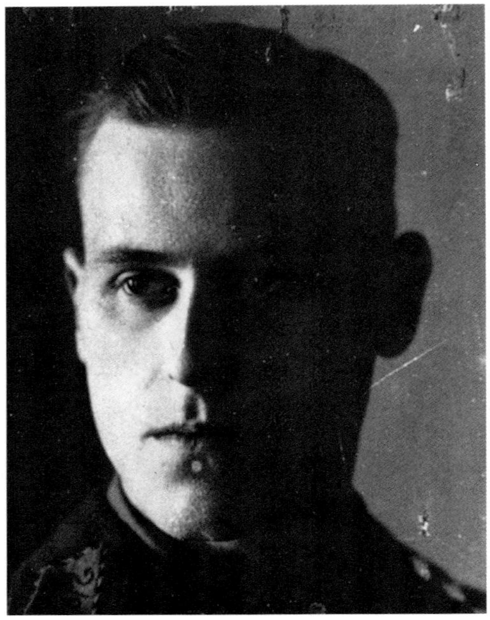

Erich Ehrlinger (BDC)

Dr. Heinrich Fehlis (NA)

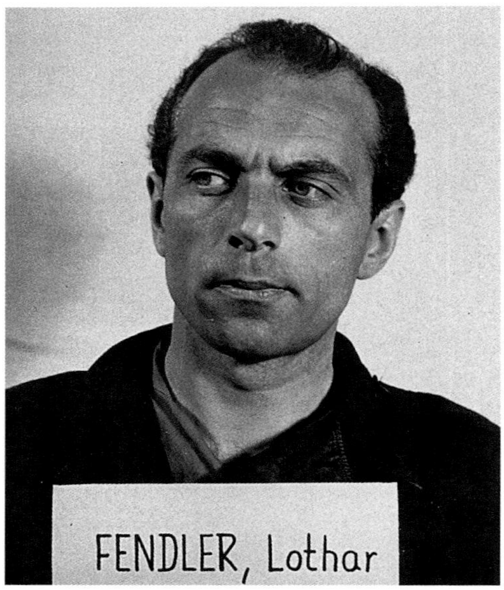

Lothar Fendler at Nürnberg before trial. (Benjamin Ferencz, courtesy of USHMM)

Dr. Alfred Filbert (NA)

Bernhard Fischer-Schweder (USHMM)

Konrad Fischer (NA)

Dr. Wilhelm Fuchs (NA)

Hans Gabel (NA)

Dr. Helmut Glaser (NA)

Josef Gmeiner (NA)

Christoph Gontard (NA)

Kurt Graaf (NA)

Mathias Graf (USHMM)

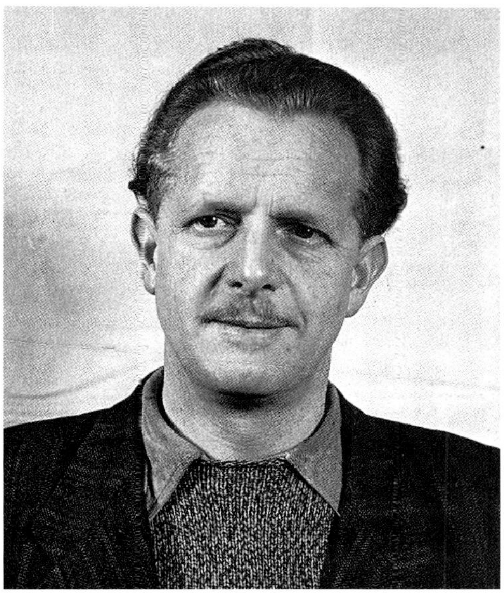

Mathias Graf at Nürnberg before trial. (Benjamin Ferencz, courtesy of USHMM)

Heinz Gräfe (NA)

Wilhelm Greiffenberger (NA)

Dr. Herbert Grohmann (NA)

Dr. Walter Haensch (NA)

Dr. Walter Haensch at Nürnberg before trial. (Benjamin Ferencz, courtesy of USHMM)

Ludwig Hahn (NA)

Joachim Hamman (NA)

Hans Hasse (NA)

Dr. Alfred Hasselberg (NA)

Emil Haussmann at Nürnberg before trial. (Benjamin Ferencz, courtesy of USHMM)

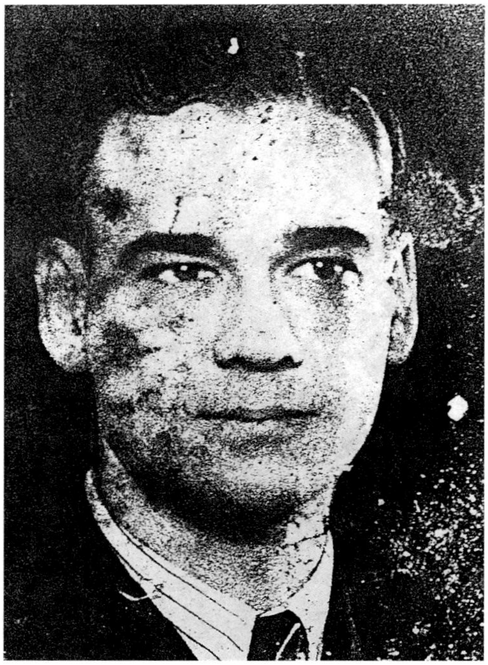

Ernst Hayde (NA)

Heinz Hellenbroich (NA)

Otto Hellwig (NA)

Günther Hermann (NA)

Werner Hersmann (NA)

Eduard Holste (NA)

Hermann Hubig (BDC)

Wolfgang Ilges (NA)

Dr. Erich Isselhorst (NA)

Karl Jaeger (BDC)

Dr. Ernst Jahr (NA)

Eduard Jedamzik (NA)

Dr. Heinz Jost (NA)

Dr. Heinz Jost at Nürnberg before trial. (Benjamin Ferencz, courtesy of USHMM)

Friedrich Kallbach (NA)

Waldemar Klingelhöfer (USHMM)

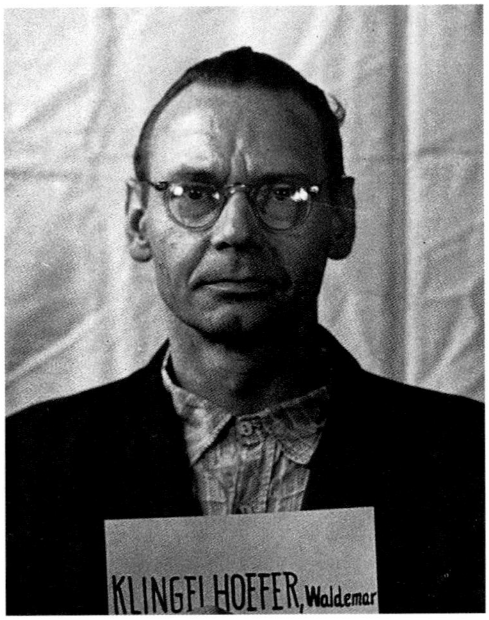

Waldemar Klingelhöfer at Nürnberg before trial. (Benjamin Ferencz, courtesy of USHMM)

Rudolf Korndörfer (NA)

Dr. Erich Körting (NA)

Andreas von Koskull (NA)

Josef Kreuzer (NA)

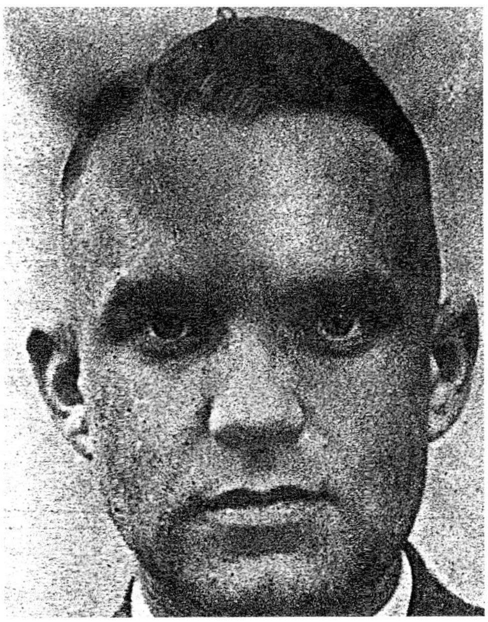

Hans Krieger (NA)

Dr. Gerhard Kroeger (NA)

Dr. Gerhard Kroeger (NA)

Alexander Landgraf (BDC)

Rudolf Lange (NA)

Rudolf Lange (BDC)

August Meier (NA)

Dr. Johann-Georg Meixner (NA)

August von Meyszner (NA)

Robert Mohr (NA)

Walter Mosig (NA)

Bruno Müller (NA)

Wilhelm Nölle (NA)

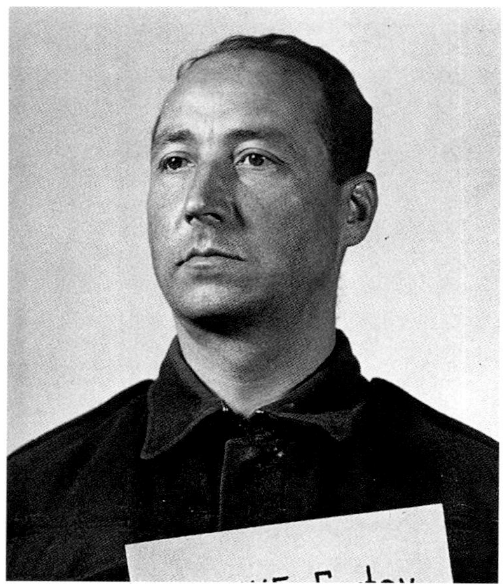

Gustav Nosske at Nürnberg before trial. (Benjamin Ferencz, courtesy of USHMM)

Otto Ohlendorf (BDC)

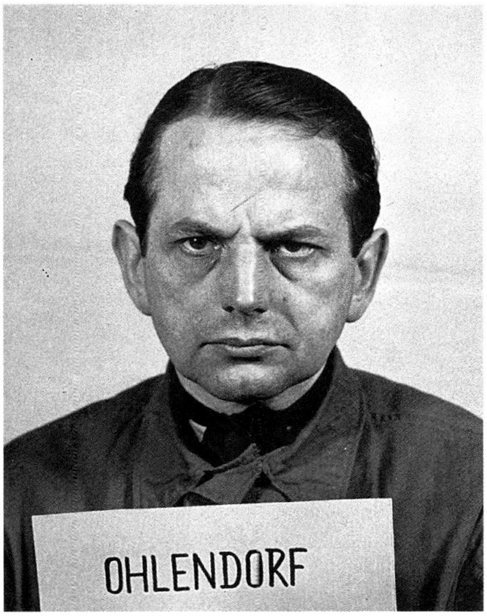

Otto Ohlendorf at Nürnberg before trial. (Benjamin Ferencz, courtesy of USHMM)

Adolf Ott (NA)

Adolf Ott at Nürnberg before trial. (Benjamin Ferencz courtesy of USHMM)

Dr. Friedrich Panzinger (NA)

Dr. Friedrich Panzinger (BDC)

Dr. Manfred Pechau (NA)

Oswald Poche (NA)

Oskar Podlich (NA)

Kurt Pohl (NA)

Walter Potzel (NA)

Rudolf Querner (NA)

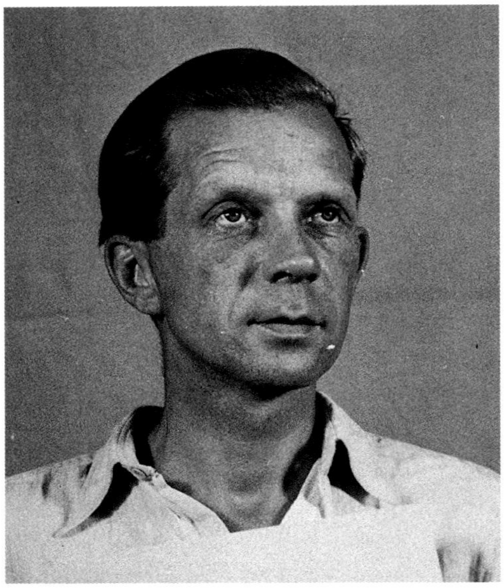

Waldemar von Radetzky at Nürnberg before trial. (Benjamin Ferencz, courtesy of USHMM)

Franz Radif (NA)

Albert Rapp (NA)

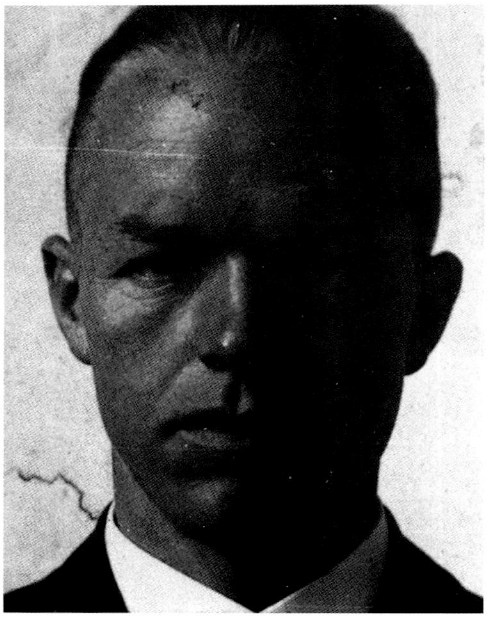

Otto Rasch (BDC)

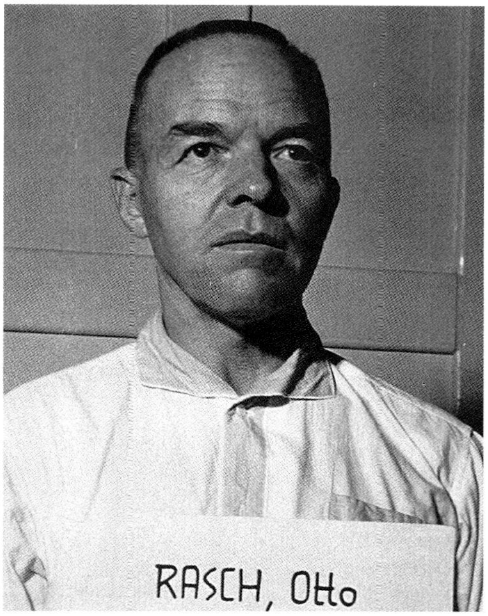

Otto Rasch at Nürnberg before trial. (USHMM)

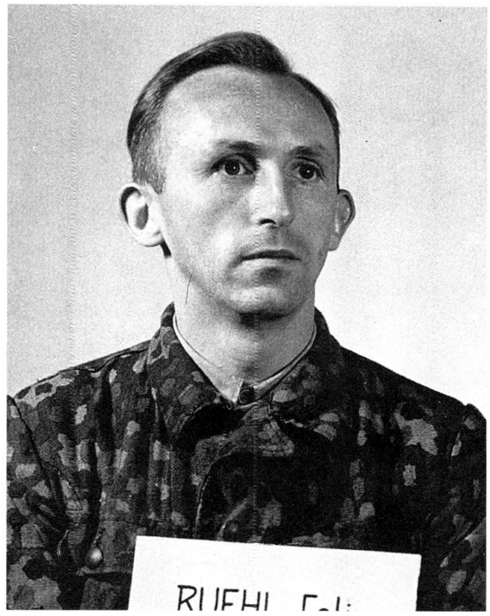

Felix Rüehl at Nürnberg before trial. He appears to be wearing a Waffen-SS camouflage shirt. (Benjamin Ferencz, courtesy of USHMM)

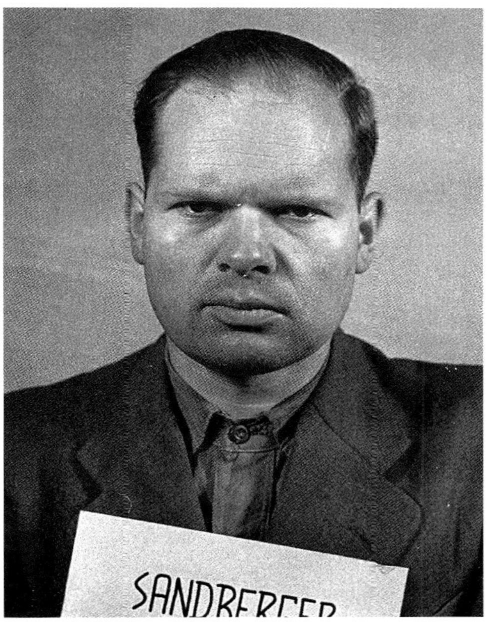

Martin Sandberger at Nürnberg before trial. (Benjamin Ferencz, courtesy of USHMM)

Martin Sandberger (BDC)

Dr. Emanuel Schaeffer (NA)

Oswald Schaefer (NA)

Dr. Wilhelm Scharpwinkel (NA)

Dr. Heinrich Schilling (NA)

Dr. Heinz Schimmeroan (NA)

Hans-Gerhard Schindhelm (NA)

Werner Schlcetel (NA)

Dr. Hellmut Schlierbach (NA)

Hans Schneider (NA)

Dr. Eberhard Schöngarth (NA)

Water Schramm (NA)

Heinz Schubert (USHMM)

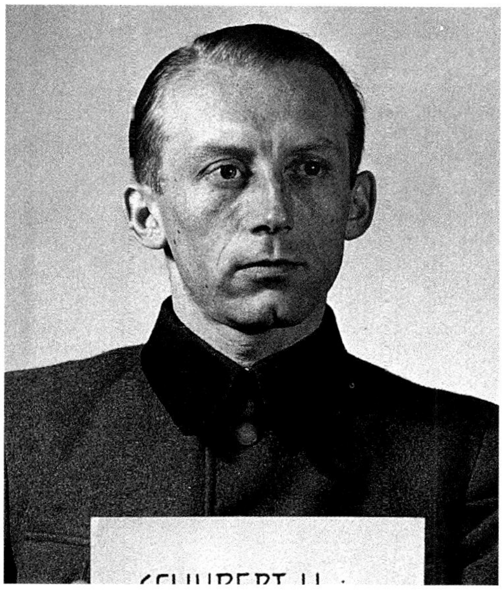

Heinz Schubert at Nürnberg before trial. (Benjamin Ferencz, courtesy of USHMM)

Erwin Schulz at Nürnberg before trial. (Benjamin Ferencz, courtesy of USHMM)

Heinz Seetzen (BDC)

Heinz Seetzen (NA)

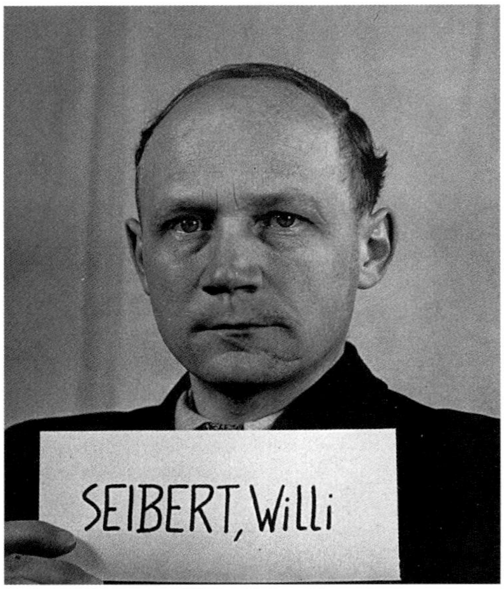

Willy Seibert at Nürnberg before trial. (Benjamin Ferencz, courtesy of USHMM)

Willy Seibert (NA)

Otto Sens (NA)

Dr. Franz Six (NA)

Dr. Franz Six (BDC)

Dr. Franz Six at Nürnberg before trial. (Benjamin Ferencz, courtesy of USHMM)

Franz Sommer (NA)

Hans-Fritz Sohns (NA)

Eugen Steimle (USHMM)

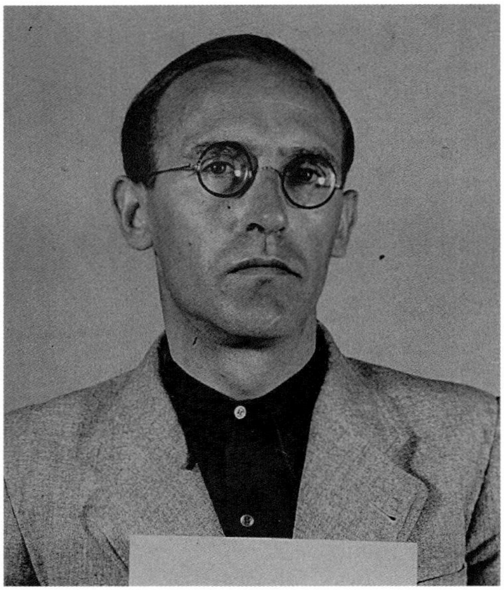

Eugen Steimle at Nürnberg before trial. (Benjamin Ferencz, courtesy of USHMM)

Eduard Strauch (BDC)

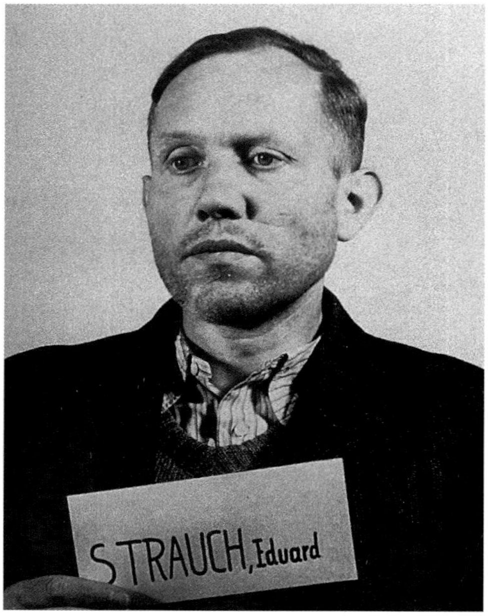

Eduard Strauch at Nürnberg before trial. (Benjamin Ferencz, courtesy of USHMM)

Bruno Streckenbach (BDC)

Ludwig Strube (NA)

Josef Stüber (NA)

Ludwig Teichmann (NA)

Karl Traut (NA)

Dr. Hans Trummler (NA)

Karl Tschiersky (NA)

Karl Tschiersky (BDC)

Hans Weibrecnt (NA)

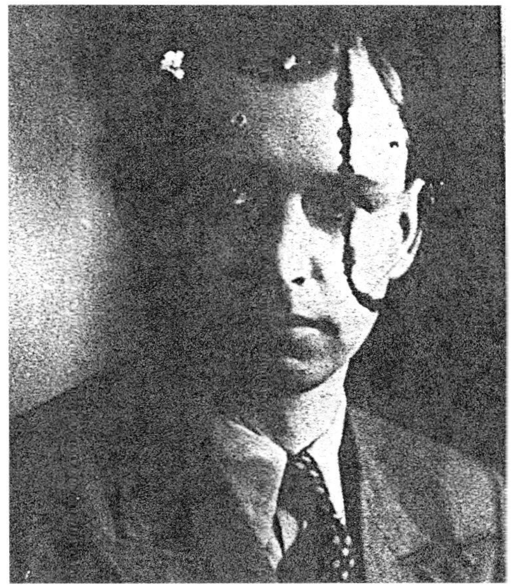

Dr. Erwin Weinmann (NA)

Anton Weiss (NA)

Paul Werner (NA)

Robert Wessel (NA)

Wilhelm Wiebens (NA)

Willi Wolter (NA)

Udo von Woyrsch (NA)

Herbert Zimmermann (NA)

Sonderkommando 4a at work, October 1941. (Hessisches Hauptstaatsarchiv Wiesbaden, courtesy of USHMM)

SD officer of an Einsatzkommando reads an execution order, Poland, September 1939. (Central State Archives of Film, Photo and Phonograph Documents, courtesy of USHMM)

Einsatzgruppe II men guard prisoners shortly before an execution, Poland, September 1939. (Main Commission for the Investigation of Nazi War Crimes in Poland, courtesy of USHMM)

Einsatzgruppe I personnel execute three Poles at Sosnowiec Poland, September 1939. (Main Commission for the Investigation of Nazi War Crimes in Poland, courtesy of USHMM)

Einsatzgruppe I men oversee an execution at Sosnowiec Poland, September 1939. (Main Commission for the Investigation of Nazi War Crimes in Poland, courtesy of USHMM)

SS men lead victims to an execution site, Poland 1939. (Main Commission for the Investigation of Nazi War Crimes in Poland, courtesy of USHMM)

Officers of Einsatzkommando 16 read an execution order prior to a shooting, Poland, September 1939. (Main Commission for the Investigation of Nazi War Crimes in Poland, courtesy of USHMM)

SD personnel of an Einsatzkommando question ethnic Germans in Poland, September 1939. (Jacob Igra, courtesy of USHMM)

SD men of an Einsatzkommando question a Polish priest, September 1939. (Jacob Igra, courtesy of USHMM)

German Police conduct an execution. (Dokumentationsarchiv des Osterreichischen Widerstandes, courtesy of USHMM)

German Police officer shoots a victim at close range. (Lydia Chagoll, courtesy of USHMM)

An Einsatzkommando executes victims. (Dokumentationsarchiv des Osterreichischen Widerstandes, courtesy of USHMM)

Einsatzkommando men watch Jews dig their own graves somewhere in Russia. (State Archives of the Russian Federation, courtesy of USHMM)

Part of the ravine at Babi Yar, the Einsatzkommandos' largest action with 33,771 killed. (Hessisches Hauptstaatsarchiv Wiesbaden, courtesy of USHMM)

Einsatzkommando rounding up suspects, Poland 1939. (Jerzy Ficowski, courtesy of USHMM)

Babi Yar. This is possibly Sonderkommando 1005 exhuming bodies for burning. (Hessisches Hauptstaatsarchiv Wiesbaden, courtesy of USHMM)

German Police in Einsatzgruppe C area shooting Jews. (Archiwum Akt Nowych, courtesy of USHMM)

SS men conduct executions probably in the Crimea in Einsatzgruppe D area. (USHMM)

Einsatzkommando and German Police execute victims. (USHMM)

Jewish men being executed at a small execution trench. Note photographer in background. SS rules prohibited such photography, but some pictures were not confiscated. (State Archives of the Russian Federation, courtesy of USHMM)

Typical Einsatzkommando execution trench. (USHMM)

Einsatzkommendo trial at Nürnberg. Paul Blobel under escort listens to court pass his death sentence. (USHMM)

Poles arrested by members of Einsatzgruppe III walk to a site where they will be executed, September 1939. (Jerzy Tomaszewski, courtesy of USHMM)

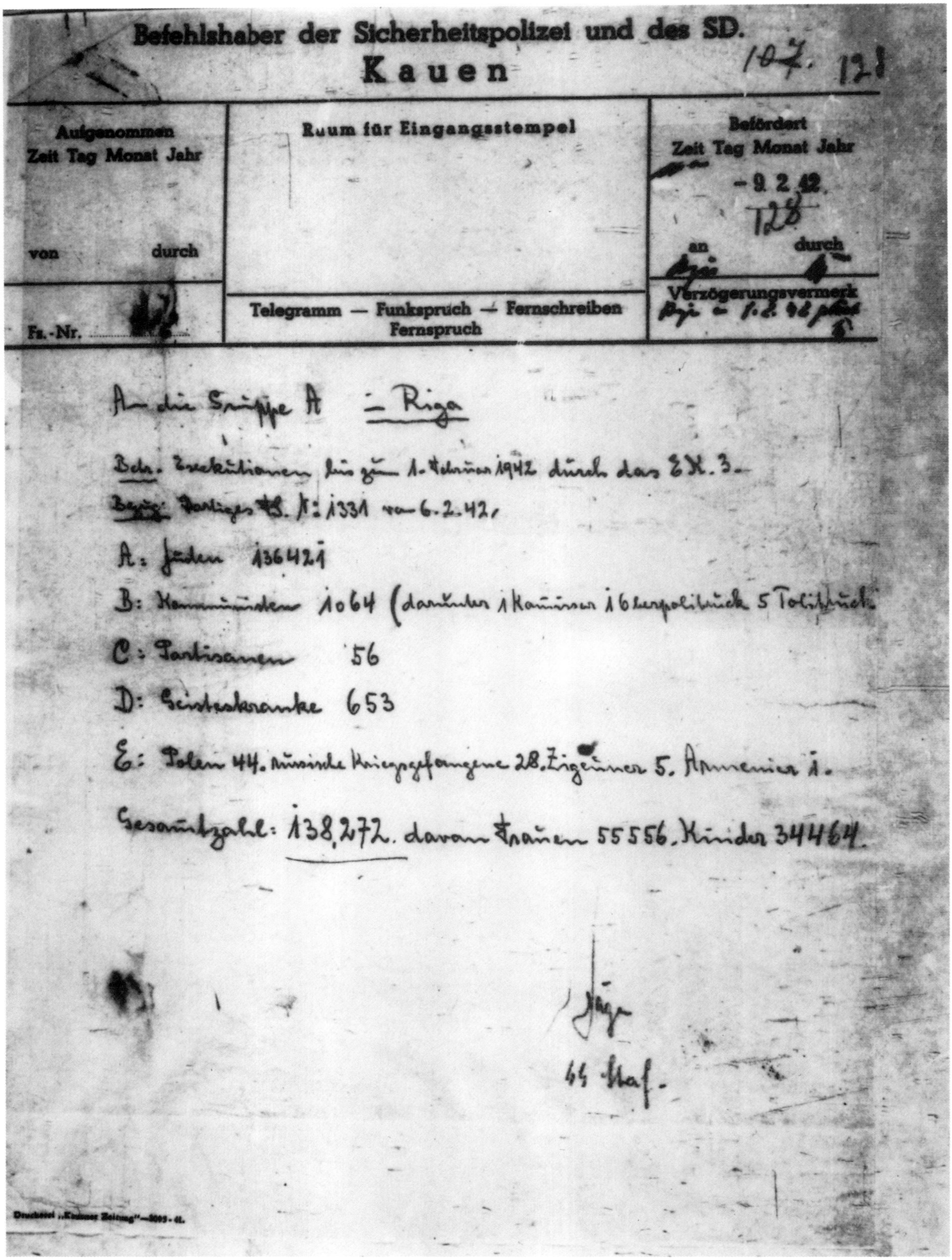

Befehlshaber der Sicherheitspolizei und des SD.
Kauen

107. 128

Aufgenommen
Zeit Tag Monat Jahr

von durch

Fs.-Nr.

Raum für Eingangsstempel

Telegramm — Funkspruch — Fernschreiben
Fernspruch

Befördert
Zeit Tag Monat Jahr
-9.2.42.
128

an durch

Verzögerungsvermerk

An die Gruppe A – Riga

Betr.: Exekutionen bis zum 1. Februar 1942 durch das EK. 3.

Bezug: Dortiges FS. Nr. 1331 vom 6.2.42.

A: Juden 136421

B: Kommunisten 1064 (darunter 1 Kommissar 16 Oberpolitruck 5 Politruck.

C: Partisanen 56

D: Geisteskranke 653

E: Polen 44. russische Kriegsgefangene 28. Zigeuner 5. Armenier 1.

Gesamtzahl: 138.272. davon Frauen 55556. Kinder 34464.

Jäger
SS-Staf.

Cable sent by SS-Standartenführer Karl Jaeger, commander of Einsatzkommando 3. Message states that as of February 6, 1942, a total of 138,272 people were killed in Lithuania. Of this total, 136,421 were classified Jews, 56 were partisans, 653 were mentally feeble, 1,064 were communists, 28 were captured Russian army personnel and 5 were gypsies. Of the total some 34,464 were children.

Widely published photo of a Ukrainian Jew being executed by a member of Einsatzgruppe D near Vinnitsa in 1942. The majority of the onlookers in the background are German army, not SS troops. The soldier third from left wear's a "Swallows' Nest" insignia on each shoulder indicating he is a bugler or bandsman in a regimental band. All military men in this photograph appear to be enlisted personnel. (Library of Congress, courtesy of USHMM)

SS-Obergruppenführer Reinhard Heydrich, perhaps the operational mastermind of the entire Holocaust. Heydrich formed and oversaw Einsatzgruppen operations until he was ambushed in Prague on 29 May 1942. Heydrich died of his wounds a week later and was buried with great pomp in Berlin. (BAK, 69/54/16)

Reichsführer-SS Heinrich Himmler marches in the funeral procession for Reinhard Heydrich, June 1942. Himmler was the leader of all aspects of the SS. As such, he visited the Einsatzkommandos at work on at least one occasion. Himmler committed suicide on 23 May 1945. (BAK, 73/137/15)

Assembled members of 1st platoon of Einsatzgruppe III in Poland, September 1939. Five of the men in the front row with round belt buckles are officers. Those with square buckles are enlisted personnel. (Main Commission for the Investigation of Nazi War Crimes in Poland, courtesy of USHMM)

Einsatzkommando officers in Poland. (Courtesy Andrew Mollo)

SS/SD officers attend Reinhard Heydrich's funeral. Front rank (left to right): Arthur Nebe, Bruno Streckenbach and Heinrich Müller. (Courtesy Andrew Mollo)

Above: SD and police personnel finish their meals. Below: SD officers in discussion, Poland 1939. (Both courtesy Andrew Mollo)

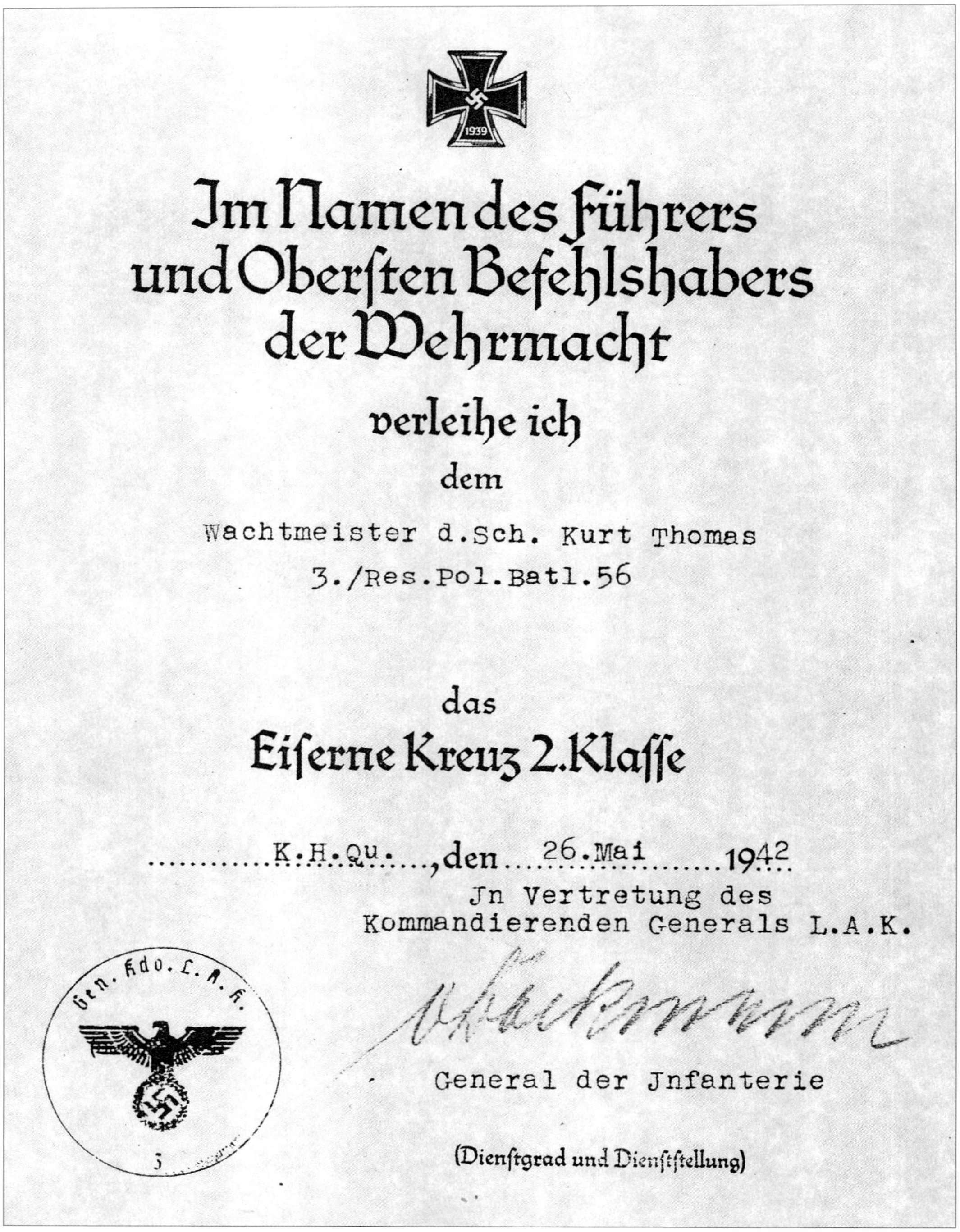

Im Namen des Führers
und Oberſten Befehlshabers
der Wehrmacht

verleihe ich

dem

Wachtmeister d.Sch. Kurt Thomas
3./Res.Pol.Batl.56

das

Eiſerne Kreuz 2.Klaſſe

............K.H.Qu.......,den..........26.Mai..........1942

Jn Vertretung des
Kommandierenden Generals L.A.K.

Gen. Kdo. L. A. K.

General der Jnfanterie

(Dienſtgrad und Dienſtſtellung)

Typical award document for an Iron Cross 2nd Class from the army to a member of a reserve police battalion (in this case the 56th). The document is signed by the commander of the 50th Corps (corps designations were always in Roman numerals.), Lieutenant General Herbert Böckmann. Most award documents did not describe the activity for which the award was presented. However, the documents were frequently accompanied by a Vorschlagslist (nomination list) which did describe the action. Any signing commander, therefore, had ample opportunity to find out what the action was that merited the award. Reserve police battalions frequently assisted the Einsatzkommandos. (Author)

MAPS

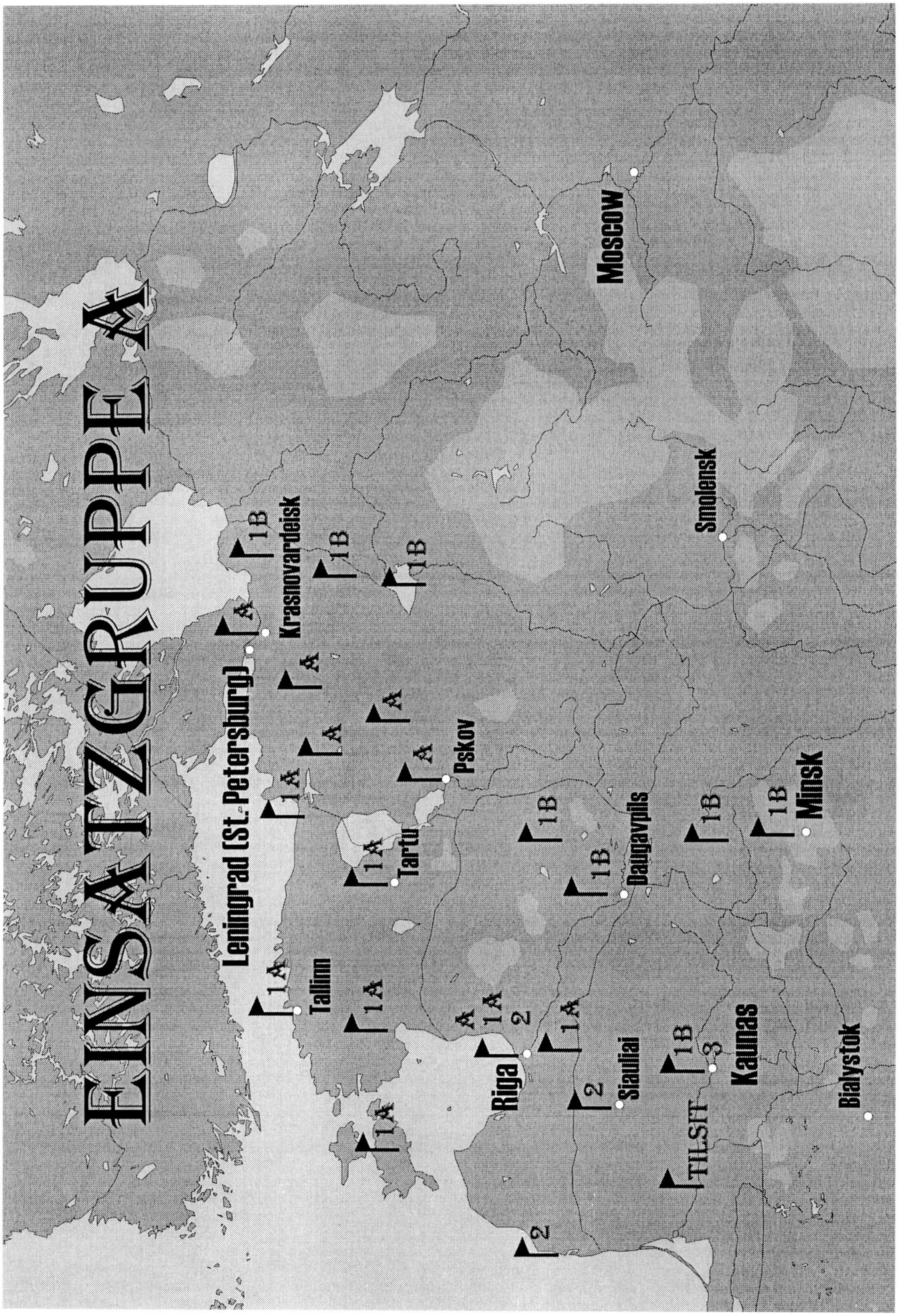
EINSATZGRUPPE A
Leningrad (St. Petersburg)
Krasnovardeisk
Moscow
Smolensk
Pskov
Tallinn
Tartu
Riga
Daugavpils
Siauliai
Kaunas
TILSIT
Minsk
Bialystok

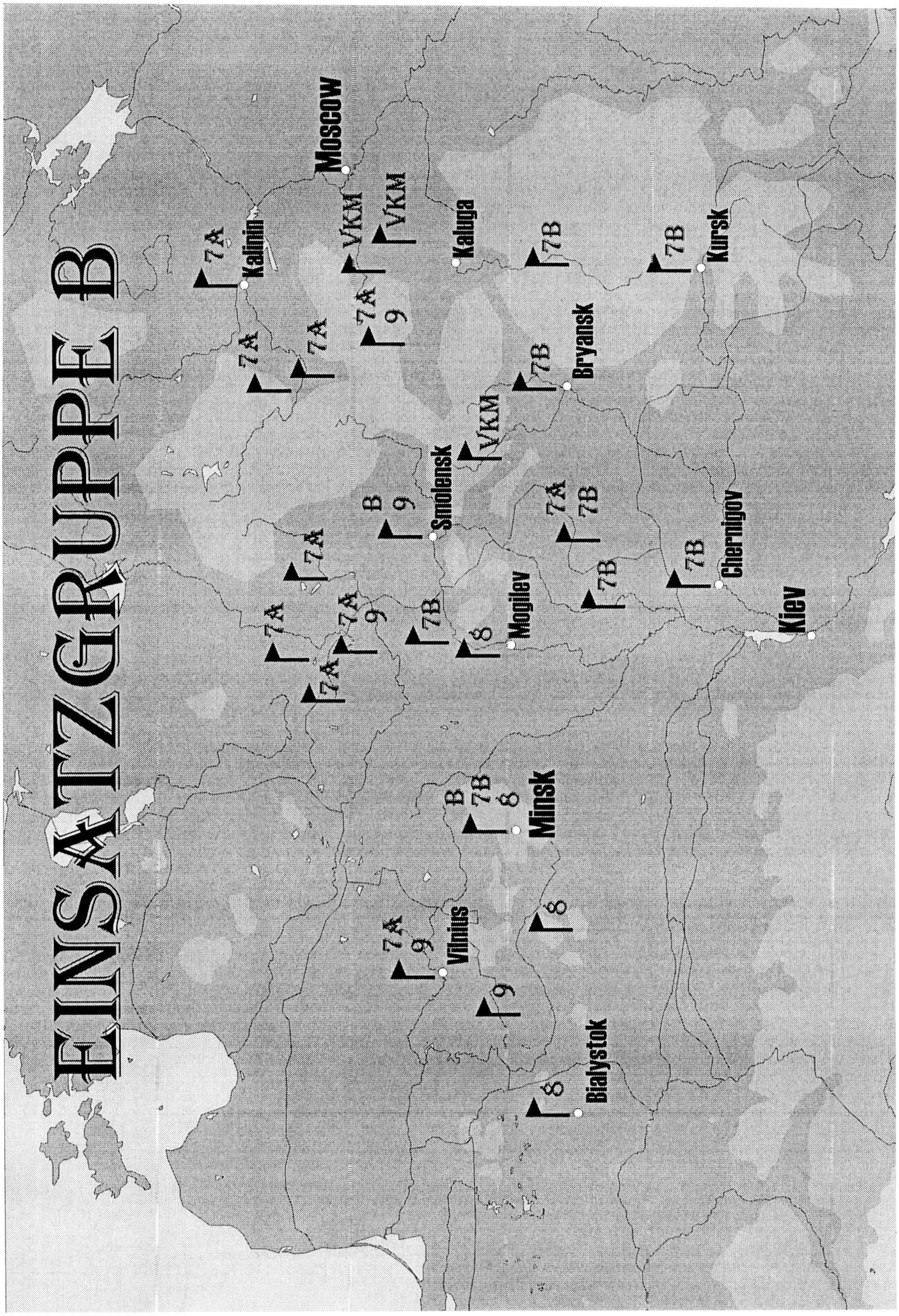
EINSATZGRUPPE B
Moscow
Kalinin
Kaluga
Kursk
Bryansk
Smolensk
Mogilev
Chernigov
Kiev
Minsk
Vilnius
Bialystok
7A
7B
8
9
B
VKM

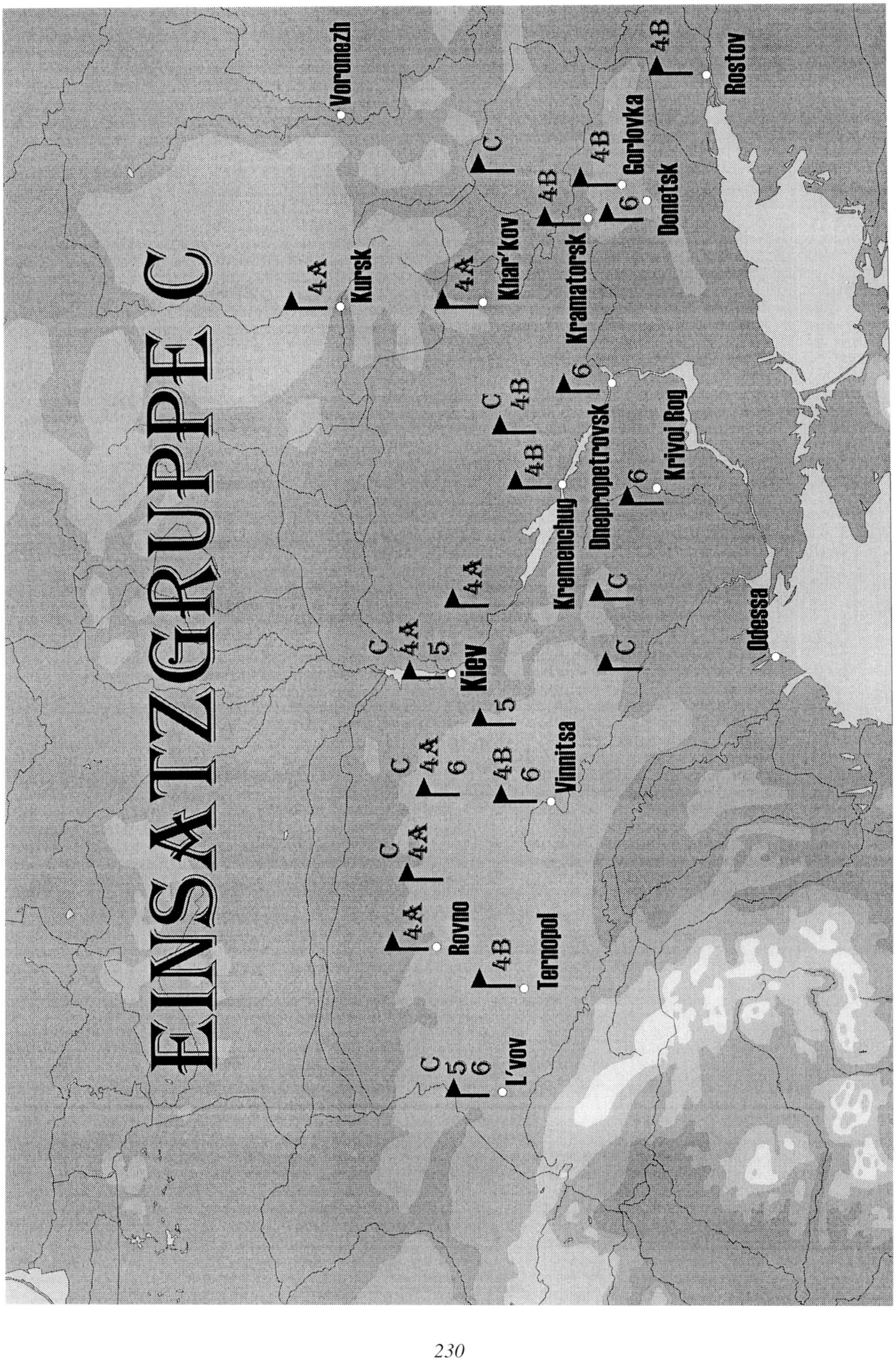
EINSATZGRUPPE C
Voronezh
Kursk
Khar'kov
Kramatorsk
Gorlovka
Donetsk
Rostov
Dnepropetrovsk
Krivoi Rog
Kremenchug
Kiev
Vinnitsa
Rovno
Ternopol
L'vov
Odessa

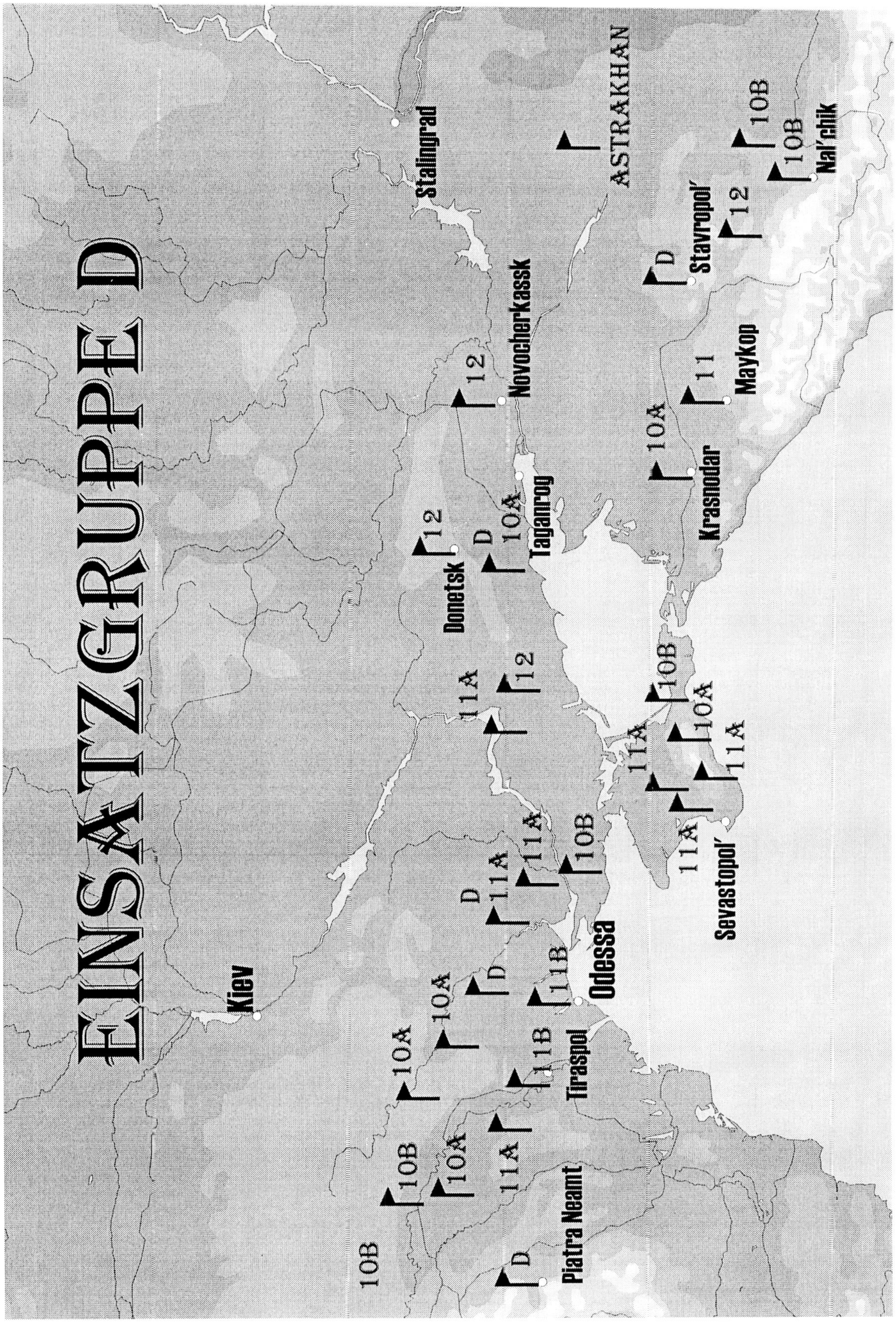
EINSATZGRUPPE D
Kiev
Stalingrad
ASTRAKHAN
Novocherkassk
Taganrog
Donetsk
Odessa
Tiraspol
Piatra Neamt
Sevastopol'
Krasnodar
Maykop
Stavropol'
Nal'chik

Also from the Publisher

Companion volume to "The Field Men."

THE CAMP MEN

The SS Officers Who Ran the Nazi Concentration Camp System

French L. MacLean

Inside these pages you will meet over 960 infamous men – the officers of Nazi Germany's *Totenkopf* (Death's Head). You will encounter the 256 SS officers who worked at Dachau – the SS concentration camp that doubled as a training school for death. You will encounter twelve SS officers who served in Treblinka and the other very secret camps of *Operation Reinhard* – Heinrich Himmler's extermination plan for the Jews of Poland. And, you will confront the 161 SS officers who ran the largest killing center of all time – Auschwitz. These officers of the Death's Head, many of whom later served in the Waffen-SS, were not the bureaucrats who meticulously planned Adolf Hitler's Final Solution from behind a desk in Berlin, or those who quietly scheduled the trains that carried the victims to the camps. Quite the contrary; these men stood on the front-line of the Nazi war to exterminate the Jews. The photographic section of the book, with well over one hundred photographs – a large portion previously unpublished – is the largest collection of photographs of SS camp personnel ever to appear in one work.
Size: 8 1/2" x 11", over 140 b/w photographs, maps
384 pages, hard cover
ISBN: 0-7643-0636-7 $59.95